SYMBOL AND SACRAMENT

A Contemporary Sacramental Theology

MICHAEL G. LAWLER

PAULIST PRESS
New York/Mahwah

Library of Congress Cataloging-in-Publication Data

Lawler, Michael G.
    Symbol and sacrament.

    Bibliography: p.
    Includes index.
    1. Sacraments—Catholic Church.   2. Symbolism.
3. Catholic Church—Doctrines.   I. Title.
BX2200.L33   1987   234'.16   87-7230
ISBN 0-8091-2924-8 (pbk.)

Published by Paulist Press
997 Macarthur Boulevard
Mahwah, New Jersey 07430

Printed and bound in the
United States of America

CONTENTS

For Anya—With Love

INTRODUCTION

Sacramentum propter hominem. Sacraments are for people. This ancient theological principle has guided the many recent efforts which have been undertaken to reform and renew sacramental life in the Christian churches. These efforts have crossed the wide span of the theological spectrum, incorporating insights from Scripture, Christology, ecclesiology, history and liturgiology. They have drawn from the insights and critical reflection of the theological giants of the twentieth century: Rahner, Schillebeeckx, Fransen, Congar, Semmelroth and others. In the last twenty years, the effort of renewal and reform has taken a new turn. It has focused on the data and insights of the human sciences of psychology, sociology and anthropology.

The results from this horizon shift have been momentous, not so much as a need to abandon the past, but as a reaffirmation of the theological intuitions, insights and affirmations discovered in reading the best sacramental theologians. The anthropological turn of sacramental theology has allowed theologians to articulate a harmony between theological claims about the sacraments and what can be sustained and supported from an anthropological investigation of ritual. If the theorem *sacramentum propter hominem* is accurate, this result is not surprising. An investigation of human behavior and existence throws light on sacraments, just as sacraments are disclosive of the human experience and human existence. The great contribution of the 1950's and 1960's was a theological clarification of the *sacramentum.* The contribution of the 1970's and 1980's is a clarification of human experience.

In the last twenty years, an increasing number of texts have attempted to reformulate a sacramental theology which is sensitive to and rooted in the anthropological dimension of ritual. Two parallel interests have also been evident in the literature, an attempt to express the historical changes in the different sacraments and a desire to articulate the theological significance and interrelated nature of the sacraments. The very success of these endeavors created a need for a

1

systematic vision of sacraments which would incorporate the valuable insights from anthropology, history and theology into a consistent and wholistic vision of sacramental life and practice.

The author of the present work breaks new ground by providing us with a much needed synthetic presentation of the Christian sacramental heritage. Dr. Lawler offers us a vision of Christian sacraments rooted in Scripture, sensitive to historical shifts and alterations, alert to debated issues and problems and insightful in its theological interpretation.

The initial chapter of this work unfolds the crucial concept which serves as the key interpretive principle for understanding the Christian sacraments, i.e., the term "prophetic symbol." The second chapter formulates a general vision of sacraments as "prophetic symbols." The author is very persuasive in claiming that symbols are not exercises in frivolity, but rich mediums for getting at what is real. This effort locates the author in the contemporary mainstream of theological reflection. Since the writings of Rahner in the early 1960's, theological reflection on sacraments has commenced with a serious reflection on symbol and symbolic action. Lawler adds a new dimension to this starting point by utilizing anthropological sources and living experience as a basis for appealing to symbolic life and behavior.

Each subsequent chapter is devoted to individual sacraments. This enterprise should not be misconstrued. The author does not segment or break apart sacramental life. Throughout the work, he continually interrelates and correlates one sacramental expression with the others. For example, baptism, confirmation and Eucharist, while treated in different chapters, are theologically interrelated and clearly viewed within the one process of conversion and initiation.

The text follows a consistent method in exploring each of the sacraments. First, it presents significant biblical data. Second, it highlights important historical shifts. Third, it notes contemporary revisions of the sacramental rites and current theological developments. Finally, the author presents his own theological reflection and synthesis. This methodology presents the reader with a clear sense of what is the prophetic symbol expressed in the sacraments and how this sacrament enters into the real experience of people.

This fresh text on the Christian sacraments is not merely an accurate summary and exposition of the theological meaning of the different sacraments. It is also a challenge undertaken with courage and sensitivity. Lawler does not shy away from the many difficult theological and pastoral issues emerging within sacramental life. Rather, he identifies and explores debated issues such as infant baptism, women's ordination, general absolution and the sacramentality of marriage. His courage is refreshing. The author embraces a position on debated issues and sustains this position with clearly articulated theological principles, reasoned insight and pastoral sensitivity.

Creative theological texts are never an end in themselves. They give rise to new questions and insights. Lawler's text provides its reader with a solid understanding of the historical and theological meaning of the sacraments and will equip a wide audience to live and reflect on their experience of God's prophetic symbols with renewed understanding and vigor. The text also suggests that the quest for understanding the sacraments must continue.

Two particular areas demand special attention in the future developments of sacramental theology. First, the living experience of sacramental celebrations must continue to be a fundamental source for theological reflection. People's living experience is the theological link with reality. Second, sacramental theologians must further explore how the human imagination interacts with prophetic symbols and symbolic actions. It is in and through the human imagination that people participate in and understand the symbolic spheres of life.

In times of liturgical reform and renewal, theological reflection is frequently partial, scattered and hesitant. Like good wine, good theology must ferment and age. Lawler's synthetic presentation of the Christian sacraments brings together the varied elements necessary for a solid, insightful and honest sacramental theology. His text lives up to the ancient principle *sacramentum propter hominem*.

George S. Worgul Jr.
Duquesne University

Chapter One
PROPHETIC SYMBOL

PROPHETIC SYMBOL

In the Bible there is an action which, in modern terminology, is called a prophetic symbol. Jeremiah, for instance, buys a potter's earthen flask, dashes it to the ground before the eyes of a startled crowd and proclaims in prophetic words what he is doing. "Thus says the Lord of hosts: so will I break this people and this city, as one breaks a potter's vessel, so that it can never be mended" (19:11). Ezekiel takes a brick, draws a city on it and siegeworks around the city, and then lays siege to the city. This city, he proclaims, is "even Jerusalem" (4:1) and his action is "a sign for the house of Israel" (4:3). On another occasion he takes a sharp sword, shaves his hair with it and divides the hair into three bundles. One bundle he burns, another he scatters to the wind, and the third he carries around Jerusalem and shreds further with his sword. In explanation of his action he proclaims: "This is Jerusalem" (5:5). The prophet Agabus, in the Book of Acts, takes Paul's belt, binds his own hands and feet with it and explains the meaning of his action. "So shall the Jews at Jerusalem bind the man who owns this belt and deliver him into the hands of the Gentiles" (21:11).

Each prophet explains the meaning of his action for the people, which clarifies for us also the meaning of a prophetic symbol. As Jeremiah dashes his pot to the ground and shatters it into pieces, as Ezekiel cuts and burns and scatters and shreds his hair, so God will dash and shatter and burn and shred Jerusalem for its faithlessness. As Agabus binds his hands and his feet, so will the Jews at Jerusalem bind Paul's hands and feet and deliver him into captivity. The prophetic action, which I am calling prophetic symbol, is a human action which proclaims and celebrates in representation the action of God. The meaning and the reality proclaimed in representation by Jeremiah is not the shattering of a cheap pot but God's shattering of Jerusalem. The meaning and the reality proclaimed in representation by Ezekiel

5

is not his haircut nor his drawing of a city on a brick, but again God's shattering of Jerusalem. The meaning and the reality proclaimed by Agabus is not the binding of his hands and feet, but Paul's captivity as under the will of God. The prophetic action is a representative action. That is, it is an action which proclaims and makes real in representation some other action. The prophetic action is a representative symbol.

Prophetic, representative, symbolic action is not limited to those few who were designated as prophets. Israel itself was a prophet and Israel performed prophetic, symbolic actions. In the great *seder* meal, for instance, which was established as the memorial of the exodus (Ex 12:14), the head of the family took, and still takes, unleavened bread and explains that it represents and makes real for those present the affliction suffered by their fathers in Egypt. "This is the bread of affliction our fathers ate in Egypt," he proclaims. It was at such a meal, the New Testament reports,[1] that Jesus "took bread, and when he had given thanks, he broke it and said, 'This is my body which is for you. Do this in remembrance of me' " (1 Cor 11:23–24; cf. Mt 26:26; Mk 14:22; Lk 22:19).

It is difficult not to notice the semantic correspondence between Ezekiel's interpretation of his action, "This is Jerusalem," and the Jewish interpretation of the *seder* action, "This is the bread of affliction our fathers ate in Egypt," and Jesus' interpretation of his action, "This is my body." It is difficult also to avoid Dupont's conclusion: "The bread which he breaks and distributes signifies his body which is going to be handed over; the wine in the cup is the symbol of his blood which he will pour out on the cross for the establishment of the covenant which God wishes to conclude with men."[2] If that is the meaning of Jesus' supper actions and words, and there is growing agreement among exegetes that it is,[3] then it is also the meaning of the eucharistic action and words which derive from them, with one further refinement.

The Hebrew words probably spoken by Jesus at the supper do not mean what we mean today by *body* (a part of a person, that part which is buried after death) and *blood* (another, liquid, part of a person, the part that flows, for instance, when the body is pierced). "*Basar* does not signify a principle or element of a human being, but rather the entire human being in its concrete individuality, with emphasis on its external manifestation. . . . Thus at the supper, Christ's use of the word 'body' signifies his entire self." Similarly, "Jesus' use of the word 'blood' at the supper must be taken in a concrete sense as referring to himself in his totality as a living being."[4] It is not the physical body and blood of Jesus that are proclaimed and made really present in the prophetic, representative, symbolic action of the supper, but Jesus himself in his total personal reality. "This is my body," to a first century Jew, meant "This is me."

The *seder* meal was not the only prophetic, symbolic, representative action in Israel. There were many. One is of particular importance here. It concerns the primordial element of water. In ancient Semitic cosmology, three layers of water encompassed the earth: water below on which the earth floated, the water of the seas and rivers within the earth, and water above the earth which sometimes fell as rain. Always exposed to the arbitrary and unpredictable behavior of these waters, the earth's inhabitants lived an uncertain existence. This precarious condition inspired the creation of a mythological motif which was at the core of Near Eastern religions for a thousand years.

The Babylonian *Enuma Elish* represents the most developed version of this myth. It begins with an account of the birth of younger gods to Tiamat, Sea personified, and Apsu, fresh water personified, and moves quickly to a crisis. Tiamat and Apsu feel threatened by their offspring, and Apsu resolves to destroy them. They, however, learn of his intentions and kill him first, an action which puts them in conflict with Tiamat, now a widow. The younger gods select Marduk as their champion and grant him supreme powers over the universe. Marduk defeats Tiamat and from her corpse fashions the cosmos known to ancient peoples: the heavens and the earth, the sun, the moon and the stars, man and woman. Marduk, now the supreme god of Babylon, creates by overcoming and setting in order the chaotic Tiamat-Sea.

The literature of ancient Israel also evidences the primordial and chaotic water motif. The Priestly creation account of Genesis 1, although a polemic against such ancient, polytheistic mythologies, still betrays clear traces of the tradition which it opposes. It recounts that in the beginning "the earth was without form and void, and darkness was upon the face of *tehom*" (Gen 1:2). *Tehom*, the watery deep, may not be identical with Tiamat-Sea, but it at least recalls that ancient mythical personification of Sea. An even clearer remnant of the primordial battle between god and sea is found in the Book of Job, where it is asserted that "with his power (God) stilled Sea, with his skill he smote Rahab (the mythical sea-monster)" (26:12–13). Yahweh, the great God of Israel, like Marduk, the great God of Babylon, creates by overcoming the chaotic water and setting it in order. Even in the Yahwist creation account of Genesis 2 the power of the primordial water is suggested as Yahweh waits until "a mist went up from the earth and watered the whole face of the earth" (2:6) before he creates.

Neither the writer of the *Enuma Elish* nor the writers of Genesis were remotely concerned with the philosophical idea of creation from nothing. The high god is presented as creating not from nothing but from water. God acts upon water to create life. There are other mythological narratives, the Babylonian *Gilgamesh Epic* and the Israelite account of the great flood, against which the righteous Noah built his ark, which recount how God acts with water to produce death. The same physical water represents in symbolic reality both life and death. Water is a very powerful, if somewhat ambivalent, symbol. It is hardly surprising, then, that it occupied a central place in the liturgical life of Israel. I wish to focus on just one part of that liturgical life, that part called in Hebrew *tebilah* and in English proselyte baptism. Concerning the origins of this rite, Joachim Jeremias observes: "Nearly all scholars who in the last sixty years have concerned themselves with the date of the introduction of proselyte baptism have come to the conclusion that it came into practice in pre-Christian times."[5]

Tebilah is the prophetic, symbolic, representative action which liturgically proclaims and makes real and celebrates the conversion of a Gentile to Israel, the passage from one fixed set of cultural conditions (the state of being a Gentile) to a new fixed set of cultural conditions (the state of being an Israelite). *Tebilah* is the kind of symbolic action characterized by Arnold van Gennep as a *rite de passage*.[6] Such rites of passage are marked by three phases: separation from a previously fixed state, margin or *limen*, aggregation to a new fixed state. It is on the marginal or liminal phase that I wish to focus. The Gentile wishing to become an Israelite must be separated first from his Gentile state. What better way to separate him than to return him, representatively and symbolically, to the primal womb, the water of chaotic nothingness. And so he was immersed in water.

"The subject of passage ritual is, in the liminal period, structurally, if not physically, 'invisible.' . . . A society's secular definitions do not allow for the existence of a not-boy-not-man, which a novice in a male puberty rite is (if he can be said to be anything)."[7] The subject of proselyte baptism, a not-Gentile-not-Jew, is made invisible structurally by being returned to the primordial nothingness, "without form and void, with darkness over the face of *tehom*," as it was in the beginning. And once again Yahweh, as in the beginning, sweeps over the waters and from them brings life. The once-and-former-Gentile is returned to nothingness in symbolic representation and is transformed by Yahweh to newness of life as a now-and-future-Israelite. The three phases of the passage are so distinct that in each phase the subject is named differently. He starts as a Gentile with a personal Gentile name in the separation phase; he is called a proselyte in the liminal phase, with no personal name (a further symbol of his nothingness); and he is called an Israelite with a new personal Israelite name in the aggregation phase.

"New life" is an apt way to describe the outcome of this symbolic action with water. In her study of Bemba girls' puberty rites, Audrey Richards writes that the Bemba speak of "growing a girl" when they refer to initiating her.[8] The import of "growing a girl" is that the transformation achieved in the puberty passage ritual is an *ontological* transformation, not just a progression from one point to another in the social structure. Turner reports, "I have seen Ndembu in Africa drive away grown-up men before a circumcision because they had not been initiated."[9] I have seen the same thing for the same reason among the Kikuyu in Kenya. Indeed, I have been driven off on occasion myself because I was "not a man" (I was then thirty-two). It is not physiology or chronology that "grows" men or women; it is symbolic, ritual action. It is symbolic, representative action also, more specifically the action of Yahweh in the prophetic action, the *opus operatum* as it would come to be called in medieval Christian theology, that grows Israelites in *tebilah*, that effects an ontological change from being a Gentile to being an Israelite. Prophetic, symbolic, representative actions proclaim, effect, and make real what they symbolize.

There is no need for the caveat which Dupont feels obliged to add to his treatment of prophetic symbol. "The idea which we have of symbol or of sign does not correspond to all that a Semite sees there. For him a prophetic action is normally efficacious; it does not only represent what it announces, it effects it also in some way."[10] It is easy to see what he has in mind when he speaks of a sign or a symbol which only represents or only signifies and why he would wish to distinguish such a sign from the Semitic prophetic symbol which not only represents and signifies but also realizes (that is, makes real) what it signifies. He is speaking to what I would call the modern ontological mentality, which distinguishes the real from the merely representative or merely symbolic. However, contemporary symbolic analysis would hold that not only the Semitic, prophetic symbol, but every genuine human symbol, not only signifies and represents another reality, but also realizes in representation the presence of that other reality. This last statement, of course, needs careful elucidation, and to this we now turn.

SYMBOLING: A HUMAN ACTIVITY

All major commentators on symbol agree that men and women are symbolic animals.[11] But beyond that there is a bewildering divergence of opinion about both the process of symbolization and the definition of symbol. In this section I propose to examine various theories of symbol in order to attain a composite theory which will yield an adequate definition.

Alfred North Whitehead sees the origin of symbolism in perception. The *sensation* of one reality leads to the *perception* or taking account of others. For instance, we see a colored shape and we say it is a chair. All we have visually seen or sensed is a colored shape and chair. An artist, for example, might simply stop at the contemplation of a beautiful color and shape. "But those of us who are not artists are very prone, especially if we are tired, to pass straight from the perception of the colored shape to the enjoyment of the chair, in some way of use, or of emotion, or of thought."[12]

The seeing of a colored shape, in Whitehead's terminology, is a symbol. He argues that "the human mind is functioning symbolically when some components of its experience elicit consciousness, beliefs, emotions and usages respecting other components of its experience. The former set of components are the 'symbols', and the latter set constitute the 'meaning' of the symbols."[13] The functioning which allows the transition from the symbol to the meanings is known as symbolic reference.

The active ingredient in interpreting a symbol is this function of symbolic reference, which enables transition from symbol to meaning. That reference, Whitehead argues, is grounded in some community of natures between the symbol and its meaning, though this community of natures does not of itself require symbolic reference. Water, for instance, in natural reality produces both life and death; in symbolic reality, therefore, it is apt to represent symbolically life and death. But the reference from natural to symbolic reality is provided by the human person. "The potter, and not the pot," Whitehead argues, "is responsible for the shape of the pot."[14] Symbolic reference is a process of inference which draws on a theoretical organization learned from past experience of colors and shapes to conclude to the "fact" that one is now "seeing" a chair. Facts, it is important to note, are the end product of a process of perception, which may be represented thus: datum + theory = fact. Facts, as Norwood Russell Hanson asserts, are theory-laden. There is much "more to seeing than meets the eyeball."[15]

Susanne Langer adds to Whitehead's analysis, calling attention to the fact that the symbolic animal (the human being) supplies not only the active ingredient that interprets a symbol, but also the active ingredient that creates a symbol. Meaning comes to men and women through past experience. It derives from impressions, furnished by the senses, both external and internal, but "constantly wrought into symbols"[16] by the creative action of the men and women who sense.

It is the symboling activity of the human subject that makes possible symbolic transformation, that is, the transformation of a mere sensible reality into a more than merely sensible symbol embodying meaning. Such transformation depends ultimately on the human subject, not on some communion of natures between a sensible reality and a meaning which leads, by some ineluctable law, to their union as symbol and meaning. The total process of symbolization from beginning to end, from the first moment of the interpretation of the sensible reality into a symbol to the final moment of the transformation of that symbol, is controlled by the human symbolizer, and not by either the symbol or its meanings. Both symbolic transformation and symbolic reference are learned from the symbolizer's past history, a fact which is easily traced.

A child learns that when she sees a particular colored shape, for instance, she is "seeing" a chair. In the process of socialization she is provided with a conceptual organization which does a great deal more than merely supply her with a name for this colored shape. Once the relationship of colored shape and chair has been internalized, it is not just that she sees a colored shape and calls it a chair. Rather, she "sees" a chair. The colored shape is not simply *called* a chair, but in her theoretical organization *is* a chair. The colored shape enters her world taken for granted, not as colored shape, but as the language-shaped reality, chair. Chair becomes part of the factual world out there, even though in reality it is thus known only as the end product of a complex process of inference from colored shape.

The human animal is in the construction business, the construction of simple sensible realities into symbols, proclaiming and representatively realizing much more crucial, if intangible, realities. The symbolic process is concerned with, specifically, colored shapes and chairs, generally, with symbol and meaning. But the crucial ingredient referring the one to the other is neither shape nor chair, symbol nor meaning, but the symbolizing activity of a human subject. This subject, moreover, never acts in isolation in the symbolic process, but always in concert with a community of like subjects. Subject, symbolic transformation, symbol, symbolic reference and meanings, are all elements in a social world.

At this point the question arises: Why all this symbolic construction? Whitehead provides a comprehensive answer. There are many uses for symbolism, but they may be subsumed under two statements. Symbolism organizes "the miscellaneous crowd into a smoothly running community." It achieves this smoothly running community by making "connected thought possible by expressing it, while at the same time it automatically directs action."[17] Symbols function in three broad areas: the area of human thought, the area of human action, and the area of human interaction.

The most ubiquitous of all symbols in these areas is probably that set of sensible sounds which in symbolic transformation is endowed with meanings and then called language. I mean here not just language in its bare function of communicating meaning, but language clothed with its enormous power to prescribe and control feeling and action and interaction. Just recall the three words, "I love you," to understand the power I am suggesting here. Such power depends, of course, not just on sounds and meanings, but primarily on the way the person has internalized both of these in the process of socialization, and particularly on the emotional history associated with such internalization. In short, the power of language to function in the three areas mentioned above depends not simply on rational aspects of language, but ultimately on personal factors associated with the human subject.

What has been said of the power of language to communicate meaning and to provoke action and interaction can be extended generally to all symbols. Symbols communicate meaning and provoke action and interaction not just to the extent that they are rationally grasped and understood, but more importantly to the extent that a person is involved in them. Symbols require a personal response from an interpreter before they come fully alive. Later I shall specify this further by stating that symbols must be *lived into* to be effective. This important characteristic of symbols enables us to add something to what was said above about society's part in constructing symbols.

Not only individuals use symbols. Societies also use them, to inform their members of, and to direct their action and interaction toward, societies' needs and goals. They use symbols, as Whitehead said, to fashion and organize "the miscellaneous crowd into a smoothly running community." In that smoothly running community there is, as a result of socialization, a symbol-mediated body of socially approved knowledge, which is accepted unquestioningly as the right, good and efficient way of life. It is in no way critical that such socially approved knowledge be demonstrably true according to some all-en-

compassing ontological theory, but simply that it be accepted as true
and as a real component of any situation by a community of people
seeking after truth. Such an approach is akin to Charles Sanders
Peirce's influential theory of truth. "The opinion which is fated to be
ultimately agreed to by all who investigate is what we mean by truth,
and the object represented in this opinion is the real."[18]

Socially approved knowledge is accepted as true, then, not merely
intellectually, but more importantly personally. It is precisely the personal stake that has been invested in such knowledge that makes it
strongly immune to rational argument to the contrary. This fact leads
to a further consideration of the functioning of symbols.

The meaning of any symbol is not grasped with exact scientific
precision. "The meaning is vague but insistent."[19] It is the insistence
of symbolic knowledge, not its conceptual precision, which moves an
individual to the action and reaction associated with the symbol. This
is not to say, however, that a symbol does not yield any rational knowledge. It does. But the dominant paradigm for rational knowledge in
the Western tradition has been Descartes' clear and distinct ideas. The
fact that a symbol does not affect such clear and distinct ideas does not
mean that it effects no ideas whatever. For it does.

Symbolic knowledge yields determinate ideas of the type African,
black, agricultural, etc., as distinct from non-determinate ones of the
type non-African, non-black, non-agricultural. But instead of the clear
and distinct Cartesian ideas beloved of Western science, symbols communicate confused ideas, that is, ideas which are fused together. This
confusion effected by symbols requires that there be continued reflection to bring symbolic knowledge to further precision.

The Kenyan flag, for instance, does not simply inform Kenyans
indeterminately that their country is a non-white, non-industrial nation. Rather it informs them determinately that it is a black, agricultural nation. This determinate knowledge, however, requires further
reflection to fathom what the meanings of black and agricultural actually are as applied to Kenya. On the basis of such determinate, if confused, knowledge, this flag informs Kenyans and moves them to loyal
action and reaction. The most clear-cut result, therefore, of symbols is
eminently pragmatic: the moving of individuals to action and reaction.
It is this power that enables symbols "to organize the miscellaneous
crowd into a smoothly running community."[20]

Whitehead's treatment of symbols situates them where they truly
belong, namely, in the human, social, and personal dimension of existence rather than in either the physical or animal dimension. In the
specifically human world there is found a qualitatively different char-

acteristic which is the mark of distinctively *human* life. Humans have found a way of adapting to their environment that no other animal seems to have found. "Between the receptor system and the effector system, which are to be found in all animal species, we find in man a third link which we may describe as the *symbolic system*. This new acquisition transforms the whole of human life. As compared with the other animals man lives not merely in a broader reality; he lives, so to speak, in a new dimension of reality."[21] That new dimension is the symbolic dimension, created by and for human animals in those processes we have already called symbolic transformation and symbolic reference.

Language, as Whitehead points out, is an important system in our human, symbolic universe. But so too are art, science, myth, and religion. It is within and by means of these symbolic systems that humans experience, understand, know, and judge the truth of the physical, physiological, and human worlds. The human animal has "so enveloped himself in linguistic forms, in artistic images, in mythical symbols or religious rites that he cannot see or know anything except by the interposition of this artificial medium."[22] Men and women do not know reality immediately, but only mediately through the prisms of various symbolic systems.

The symbol-concept is the most universal in Cassirer's work. It covers "the totality of those phenomena in which the sensuous is in any way filled with meaning, in which a sensuous content, while preserving the mode of its existence and facticity, represents a particularization and embodiment, a manifestation and incarnation of meaning."[23] Four elements essential to symbol may be isolated from this definition: (1) a sensible thing or action, which on the physical level is merely a sensible reality, and on the human level is (2) a symbol endowed with meanings; (3) a relation between this sensible reality-symbol and this meaning, which is perceived by (4) a human subject who takes account of these meanings when faced with this symbol.

In general the relation between a sign and its meaning is variously specified in semiotics (that is, the science of signs) as that of the sign "announcing" or "indicating" or "suggesting" its meaning. Cassirer accepts this specification of the relationship for what I shall henceforth call simple signs but not for symbols. And this introduces an important distinction.

The force of the statement that simple signs announce what they signify is this: they do not make present what they signify, but simply announce that it is present. It is precisely this that Cassirer refuses to extend to the case of symbols. For, he argues, "the special symbolic forms are not imitations but *organs* of reality, since it is solely by their agency that anything real becomes an object for intellectual apprehension, and as such is made visible to us."[24]

The relationship of the symbol to its meanings is a relationship which is *sui generis*, and this is clearly enunciated in Cassirer's thought. Simple signs and symbols belong to two different universes of discourse. A simple sign "is a part of the physical world of being: a symbol is a part of the human world of meaning."[25] And there is another, crucial, difference between the two. A simple sign "is related to the thing to which it refers in a fixed and unique way. Any one concrete and individual sign refers to a certain individual thing. . . . A genuine human symbol is characterized not by its uniformity, but by its versatility. It is not rigid or inflexible but mobile."[26] This last characteristic of symbol makes it a much more complex, and also much more powerful, reality than a simple sign.

Paul Ricoeur also argues for the versatility and multivocality of symbols in distinction to the fixity of simple signs, though in different language. He speaks of the double intentionality and the donative nature of the symbol.[27] The reality which constitutes the symbol intends two different meanings. On one level the sensible reality directly intends a literal, natural meaning; on another level symbolic meanings are "donated" in and through the first, literal meaning. Water, on the literal, natural level is both life-giving and cleansing; it donates, therefore, meanings of rebirth and forgiveness of sins when it is used in the symbolic action called baptism. On the natural level a simple meal of bread and wine bespeaks physical nourishment and human sharing and fellowship; on a symbolic level, therefore, it donates these meanings to realize representatively spiritual nourishment and the fellowship of the body of Christ (= Church) in Eucharist. The givenness of the symbolic meanings in the literal constitutes one source of both the power and the mystery of symbols. Ricoeur explains that symbols are opaque, while simple signs are perfectly transparent. "This opacity constitutes the depth of the symbol, which, it will be said, is inexhaustible."[28]

Anthropologist Victor Turner also values the distinction between simple sign and symbol, similarly arguing for the multivocality of symbols in distinction to the univocality of simple signs. He speaks of the many meanings of a symbol as clustering around two poles. One pole, which he names the orectic pole (from *orexis*, the affective and conative aspects of experience), refers to a cluster of physical and physiological meanings. The other pole, which he names the ideological or normative pole, refers to a cluster of "ethical values and principles, religious doctrines, political ideals, family values, the moral components in law, rules of social organization, in short, what most makes for order, continuity and harmony in society."[29] The link between the sensible reality and the meanings clustered around the orectic pole will be closer and more obvious to cursory inspection than that between the symbol and its normative meanings. But both sets of meanings connect to their respective sensible reality and symbol not by some ineluctable law of nature, but only through the thoughts and the feelings and the actions and the reactions of the men and women who live into them.

In a summary statement of this section, then, we can say that men and women live not only in a physical world, but also, and more importantly, in a human world which is a world of meaning. In that human world, they ask not only what a person, action, or thing *is*, but also, and more importantly, what it *means*. The answer to the question of meaning is what specifically constitutes the human world. In this world men and women have so enveloped themselves in linguistic forms, in artistic images, in mythical symbols and religious rituals, that they do not know any reality directly and immediately, but only indirectly through the mediation of one or more of these symbol systems.

The focus of this chapter is on one of those systems, namely, religious ritual, called in theological language *sacrament,* and called in biblical language *prophetic symbol.* Such ritual, in Turner's definition, is "prescribed formal behavior for occasions not given over to technological routine, having reference to beliefs in the mystical beings or powers."[30] The smallest unit of such ritual is the symbol. Ritual, therefore, is complex symbolic action.

SYMBOL: A DEFINITION

The foregoing analysis was intended to lead to an adequate definition of symbol, and we are now at that point. Symboling is a specifically human process in which meanings and realities, intellectual, emotional and personal, are proclaimed, realized and celebrated in representation in a sensible reality within a specific perspective. The sensible reality in which the meanings and realities are proclaimed is thereby transformed into a symbol. In that religious activity called prophetic symbol or sacrament, the sensible reality which proclaims, realizes in representation and celebrates is an action which is transformed into symbolic action. Such symbolic action is known technically as ritual. In what follows, therefore, the term *ritual* will be used as though it were synonomous with the term *symbol.* The only distinction that will be made between them is that ritual is specifically symbolic action.[31]

A symbol and its meanings are related polarly. That is, though they are theoretically distinguishable, they are so correlative that neither is definable except in relation to the other. The polar relationship between a symbol and its meanings is somewhat analogous to the relationship between body and soul. As the soul inheres in the body, so does meaning inhere in the sensible symbol; as the body is the manifestation of the soul, so is the symbol the manifestation of meaning. No more than men and women can deal with souls apart from bodies can they deal with meanings apart from symbols. As there are no bodies without souls, so also there are no symbols without meaning.

Neither symbols nor meanings nor bodies nor souls should be thought of as *things*. Karl Rahner expresses this well in his explanation of the classic medieval doctrine of body and soul. "Body and soul, if the doctrine of *anima-forma corporis* is really understood and taken seriously, are two *meta*-physical principles of one single being, and not two beings, each of which could be met with experimentally."[32] The relationships between body and soul, and between symbol and meanings, are not analogous to the relationships between things that stand side by side in the physical world or between events that follow one another sequentially in the historical world. The relationship between a symbol and the meanings embodied and expressed in it can be understood only by understanding this: a symbol and its meanings coexist for a human interpreter, or neither really exists at all. For all human purposes a symbol *is* the meanings and the realities which it symbolizes in representation.

It is not enough, however, to state that a symbol is the reality it symbolizes. The statement must also be demonstrated as far as is humanly possible. Making love, for example, is a symbol and not a simple sign, for it does not just proclaim the presence of love but also realizes and celebrates that love in representation. So present is the love in the ritual love-making that the ritual, indeed, *is* the love. And because it is the love, the ritual not only makes love present but also incites men and women to appropriate loving action and reaction. These assertions must now be demonstrated.

A man and a woman fall in love. The man loves the woman, but the woman does not yet realize it; that is, for her it has not yet been made real. For her the man's love is still very abstract and remote and, therefore, not at all effective. It remains so until he proclaims it, realizes it and celebrates it in some representative gesture. He writes her a letter, he takes her hand, he kisses her, he says "I love you." In these actions his abstract love is made very concrete, his remote love is proclaimed and celebrated as personally very present, his affective love is made wonderfully effective. In the prescribed formal actions of the ritual of lovemaking the man's love is made real, both for him and the woman, so that both are confronted by it, enriched by it and moved to respond to it. The common phrase which claims that the man and the woman "make love" in such gestures, that is, make it real as concrete, present and effective, would appear to be quite accurate.

In the conventional and obligatory actions, the letter, the holding hands, the kissing, the spoken words, the man's love for the woman is not only indicated but also realized. The actions are not just signs of love. They are also causes of love insofar as they cause it to be present in a context of human action and interaction. They are, that is, rituals of love. And the effect, love realized for both man and woman, is due wholly both to the originating love and to the ritual gestures in which it is representatively realized.

But besides making present what they symbolize, symbols are also multivocal. A symbol "is characterized not by its uniformity but by its versatility. It is not rigid or inflexible but mobile."[33] The single, fixed meaning of a simple sign is communicated clearly and distinctly and predominantly intellectually. The many, fluid meanings of a symbol are communicated confusedly, that is, fused together, not only intellectually but also affectively. A genuine human symbol permeates and grips and stirs the whole human person. It is for this reason that symbols are infinitely richer, both in meanings and in power, than simple signs.

Turner, as we have already seen, speaks of the many meanings of a symbol as clustering around two poles, an orectic pole and an ideological pole. At the orectic pole "are concentrated those *significata* that may be expected to arouse desires and feelings; at the ideological pole one finds an arrangement of norms and values that guide and control persons as members of social groups and categories."[34] Symbols offer not just a set of cognitive meanings for ordering the human world. They offer also, and perhaps more importantly, a set of evocative instruments for arousing and channeling powerful feelings. Whole persons, and not just their intellects, are involved in symbols.

Both sign and symbol communicate meaning, but quite differently. A sign points to some *known* entity: smoke to fire, barber's pole to barber's shop, "$1.79 a pound" to the established economic value of steak. A symbol, on the other hand, points to something relatively *unknown* and therefore mysterious, but postulated as existing:[35] making love to the mysterious reality we call love, cutting and scattering one's hair to the doom of Jerusalem, eating a meal together to those eminently mysterious realities we call God and his Christ. "A sign communicates abstract, objective meaning, whereas a symbol communicates living, subjective meaning. A symbol has a subjective dynamism which exerts a powerful attraction and fascination on the individual . . . we can thus say a sign is dead, but a symbol is alive."[36] As we noted earlier, Paul Ricoeur describes signs as perfectly transparent and symbols as opaque. It is this opacity which constitutes the depth of the symbol, a depth which is inexhaustible.

When a man and a woman have made love, both the rituals and the love that is realized in them are far from transparent. When faced with the rational, objective question, what does it mean that you love me? There is no clear and distinct and objective answer. There is only a confused, living and subjective answer which is verified, that is, made true, in the ongoing living into both the symbols and the love which is mediated in them.

Love is more than holding hands, yet love is made in holding hands. Love is more than kissing, yet love is made in kissing. Love is more than saying "I love you," yet love is made in saying "I love you." Only when the man and the woman live into the symbols do they discover what it means to say that these conventionalized gestures are making love; only then do they understand the symbol; only then do they grasp personally the love that is the symbol. For love is not objectively grasped in itself, but only subjectively as mediated in symbol. As long as the symbol is a living and effective power, both the symbol and the love mediated in it transcend definition. This very transcendence of definition constitutes another source of the symbol's power and fascination over men and women.

Symbol, then, is a way of knowing. But it is not a way of knowing in clear and distinct Cartesian ideas. The meanings mediated in symbols are not objectively defined and detailed. Rather they are subjectively and confusedly grasped, so that the knowledge resulting from them seems vague and opaque. But it is vague and opaque not in the sense that its meaning is obscure or that it is empty of meaning, but rather in the sense that its depth of meaning is unfathomable. The human mind can never get to the bottom of it, can never substitute rational sign for holistic symbol and be done with it. "A true symbol must be *lived into*. That is how its meaning is to be found."[37] To understand symbolically-mediated knowledge a personal as distinct from an objective response is required. The meanings realized in symbols are not grasped in one single glance but only after an ongoing, lived response.

If such a personal approach to knowledge still seems strange to us, it is only because the dominant Western scientific paradigm of knowledge has judged rational, clear and distinct, objective knowledge to be all there is to knowledge. All else is dismissed as "only a symbol," that is, as subjective and unreal. It was Maurice Maeterlinck who conceived of the brain as divided into a Western lobe, the seat of reason and science, and an Eastern lobe, the seat of intuition and symbol. There are increasing signs that his call for a reemphasis on the Eastern lobe is finally being heard and that the Western lobe dominance is diminishing with the growing realization that the human person is more, much more, than pure reason. The message of this chapter is a specific case of that realization, namely that to understand and grasp symbol, prophetic symbol, sacrament, ritual, much more than mere reason is required.

To conclude this section a word needs to be said about meaning and the individual human person. Every person is born naked into the world but no person is born into a naked world. All of us are born into a world replete with symbols and meanings, a world in which ethical values and principles, religious doctrines, political ideals, family values and the rules of social organization are all mapped out for us. To become useful members of that world we must learn its symbols and its meanings, and we must maintain those symbols and those meanings to maintain the world. We learn the necessary symbols and meanings, of course, in the complex process subsumed under the heading of socialization, and as we learn them we learn also who and what we are within the world in which we live. The viability of both the world and the self mediated by meaning depends on the extent to which that self remains in conversation with both the symbols and those other selves who share them publicly with us.

Public symbols and meanings belong primarily to communities and only secondarily to individuals. The first interpreter of a public ritual and symbol is always a community of men and women. For it is always a community that creates and legitimates both symbolic transformation, that is, the transformation of a mere sensible reality into a much more than sensible symbol, and symbolic reference, that is, the connection between this sensible reality-symbol and these much more than sensible realities and meanings. Individuals interpret the symbols and understand their public meanings only to the extent that they stand within the community. This is true for every community, including the religious community. The primary interpreter of the religious ritual and symbol is the religious community. It is from the community that the general consent required for a public symbol derives. The religious individual is at best a secondary interpreter.

But clarification may be needed here. What I have just argued is from the point of view of the *system* of rituals and symbols. If we take another point of view, the point of view of the individual actor within the system, we may have to say something more nuanced. For individuals, socialized into symbol-mediated meanings though we are, remain free. We can still feel in a situation; and we can feel joy even when we are supposed to feel pain, and vice versa. We can still seek ends in a situation and we can seek ends other than the ones we are supposed to seek. We can still understand in a situation; and we can understand that in this particular time we can choose to highlight a particular meaning out of the spectrum of meanings the symbol offers.

In short, the human individual is not a robot. Whatever may be the *public* meanings of a symbol, any individual may create *private* meanings for the same symbol. If such an individual can mobilize social forces from a position of leadership, either jurisdictional or charismatic, then he or she can make such private meanings stick. Thus new meanings would emerge into the public domain, exemplifying and validating the anthropological dictum: people made it and people can remake it. But our earlier assertion still stands. From the point of view of the system of rituals and symbols the primary interpreter of *public* rituals and symbols is always a community. This point will be crucial when we deal with specific religious rituals and their varieties of meanings.

PROPHETIC SYMBOL AS RELIGIOUS SYMBOL

The prophetic symbol is just one kind of symbol; it is a species of the genus symbol. It will have, therefore, all the properties of the genus symbol. I propose now to recapitulate and to underscore those properties as they apply to prophetic symbol.

A first difference between simple sign and symbol should be recalled. A simple sign relates to what it signifies on a one-to-one basis; it refers to a certain individual thing. There is nothing mysterious about a sign; its meaning is clear. A symbol, on the other hand, does not relate to what it signifies on a one-to-one basis, but on a one-for-many basis. "A genuine human symbol is characterized not by its uniformity but by its versatility. It is not rigid or inflexible but mobile."[38] A symbol is charged with many meanings, and once it has caused an interpreter to take account of its many meanings, its work still continues. For there is always more depth of meaning to be uncovered in it, more questions to be asked of it, because the abundance and richness of its meanings are inexhaustible. The human mind can never get to the bottom of a symbol and be done with it. The words "I love you" raise as many questions about meaning as they answer. A symbol, any symbol, is mysterious.

The mysteriousness of symbols in general is well exemplified in the specific case of prophetic symbols. Jeremiah's dashing of his pot to the ground was symbolically transformed in and by a community to proclaim and make personally real in symbolic, representative reality what God, faithful to his solemn covenant, did, does, and continues to do to a faithless city and a faithless people. Ezekiel's cutting, burning, shredding and scattering of his hair was symbolically transformed to proclaim and to realize representatively what God did, does, and will continue faithfully to do to this faithless people. The solemn *seder* meal in literal reality is just a simple family meal. But in symbolic reality it is transformed to proclaim and to make personally real in Israel the presence and action of the faithful God, who led his people from the bondage of Egypt to the milk and honey of the promised land, who continues to do the same for his people today, and who will continue to do the same in the future until all his people are safely in the land of ultimate promise with God himself.

Symbols do lead to the conception of ideas, and of determinate ideas. They lead, however, to the conception not of clear and distinct ideas, but of confused ideas, which require further reflection for further clarification. Symbols communicate at the level of sense and image and feeling and intuition and conception elemental meanings which are grasped, not logically and scientifically, but socially and personally. God, saving presence, saving action, people of God: these are all elemental meanings. They may be grasped only personally, after the manner of symbols; never logically, after the manner of signs. The meanings involved in prophetic symbols are as richly mysterious as the meanings involved in any symbol.

A second difference between simple sign and symbol is this: simple signs announce what they signify; symbols make concretely present what they symbolize. The stop sign at the intersection merely tells the driver that there is an intersection; it does not cause the intersection to be there. Their national flag does not just tell Kenyans that there is a Kenya; it also makes Kenya concretely present for them, with all the sensitive, imaginative, emotional and conceptual meaning associated with it. A prophetic symbol does the same for the presence and action of God among his people as the national flag does for Kenya.

The prophetic symbol of seder, for instance, is a symbol of the presence of God in and with his people. To say that it proclaims and representatively realizes and celebrates that presence is to say, at the least, that it does for the believer what the Kenyan flag does for the Kenyan. God is made really and truly and substantially present in the prophetic representation of the family meal. The theological assertion which states that God himself, at least implicitly, identified himself and his presence with this meal-symbol (cf. Ex 12:14) does no more than strengthen a conclusion reached on grounds which are far from theological. To say, however, that the seder meal is a symbol of God's presence among his people, or even more to say that the Eucharist is a symbol of the presence of Jesus in the Church, has a strange ring in Catholic ears, and so the statement requires further explanation. Such explanation, though, must wait until a later chapter.

A prophetic symbol is not just any symbol; it is a specifically religious symbol. It will have, therefore, the characteristics of a religious symbol, and some consideration must now be given to those.[39] The first one that is usually listed, that it points to realities and meanings beyond itself, is nothing more than a simple definition of the genus "sign," to which religious symbol, and therefore prophetic symbol, belong as a species.

A second characteristic of religious symbols, that they participate in the reality to which they point, is a crucial one for prophetic symbols. For people who believe in and live into them, prophetic symbols proclaim and realize and celebrate in representative reality the saving presence and action of God. The symbol of tebilah symbolizes this presence and action specifically to recreate the Gentile as Israelite. The God of Israel, and the God of Christians too, is always a Creator-God. But in the prophetic symbol of the water-bath, proclaiming and realizing and celebrating death to an old life and God-effected resurrection to a new life, the creative action of God is so effectively proclaimed and realized by being symbolized and represented that for the Gentile participant that creative activity is mysteriously, personally and, above all, interpersonally present. What in natural reality is a rather simple action with water, in prophetic, symbolic reality *is* the creative action of God. Tebilah, therefore, participates in the creative activity of God by proclaiming and realizing and celebrating that activity for believers. To the degree that the symbol effectively concretizes and, therefore, realizes that creative action, it *is* that action for the believer. The symbolic action of tebilah makes creation and is creation just as surely as any ritual of love makes love and is love.

The fact that prophetic symbols participate in the reality which they symbolize illumines an important doctrine in symbolic reality. Men and women are free beings. It is the constant teaching of the Christian churches that their interpersonal relationship with God is also, and must be, a free relationship. Free personal activity on the part of free women and men is essential to their relationship with the gracious God, is essential, as Christians would say, to their reception of grace. The Council of Trent, which many might regard as the most unfree of councils, stated explicitly that justification is received as a gift of God "according to each one's proper disposition and cooperation."[40] It specified this doctrine further in the case of the forgiveness of sins, teaching that "although contrition is sometimes made perfect by love and reconciles God to man before the sacrament (of penance) is received, that reconciliation is not to be attributed to contrition apart from the desire to receive the sacrament which is included in it."[41] Forgiveness of sins and reconciliation with the gracious God is sometimes achieved in an act of perfect love, long before the symbolic ritual of penance-reconciliation, yet they still tend to concrete proclamation, realization and celebration in the ritual. A root reason for this is the characteristic of religious symbols we are here discussing, namely, their participation in the reality to which they point.

The doctrine of the need for at least an implicit desire of baptism or penance-reconciliation for the forgiveness of sins and for reconciliation with God is no more than a theological way of professing what is true for all abstract realities and their concretizing symbols. Creation, re-creation, salvation, justification, contrition, repentance, forgiveness, reconciliation, love, are abstract realities, which the symbolic animal (i.e., the human being) proclaims and makes effectively real in symbols. Abstract reality and symbol, love and ritual of love-making, forgiveness and reconciliation and ritual of forgiveness-reconciliation, re-creation and prophetic symbol of re-creation, as I have said before, either exist together or not effectively at all for human beings. As true love tends to concrete representation and realization in rituals of love, so also the true desire for re-creation to a new life tends to concrete representation and realization in a prophetic symbol of re-creation, for Jews in tebilah, for Christians in baptism. As the ritual of making love *is* love, so also the ritual of re-creation *is* re-creation. Karl Rahner gives voice to this insight when he argues that for men and women "religious moral decisions and attitudes are expressed in such signs, and in fact do not come into existence at all without them."[42]

The general symbolic property I am discussing here, namely, that symbols participate in the reality to which they point, is exactly what medieval theology had in mind when it claimed that sacraments confer the grace they signify *ex opere operato*, always saving the case in which such efficacy is blocked by a totally inadequate *opus operantis*, or contribution of the believing (or more likely non-believing) subject. The prophetic symbol that is seder, and the equally prophetic symbol that is Eucharist, both participate in the saving presence and action of God, indeed each *is* that presence and action for believers, to the degree that the divine presence and action concretely and effectively reaches those believers in those symbols. It is not at all surprising, then, that both Judaism and Christianity urge believers to approach religious symbolic actions as something sacred, not because they are in any sense magic, but only because in and through them the sacred is proclaimed as present and active, is realized as present and active, and is celebrated as present and active by those who live into the symbols with the necessary disposition, namely faith.

Another characteristic of religious symbols and also of prophetic symbols is that they open up dimensions of reality which the human animal cannot reach otherwise. This follows directly from the preceding.

Prophetic symbols realize sacred reality and so participate in that sacred reality, and they do this in a way that could not be done without them. A person, for instance, may believe in general in the presence of God without that belief ever becoming concretely effective. But in the representative, prophetic action of seder, that presence is so proclaimed and celebrated ritually that God is made concretely and effectively present to the person, who is drawn into personal action and interpersonal reaction. Yet, however much prophetic symbols make transcendent reality concretely present for men and women, however many pathways they open up to that transcendent reality, they never allow men and women to master or dominate that reality. The richness and the depth of the reality that lies beyond the sensible continues to lie beyond their understanding. God remains always "that than which nothing greater can be conceived,"[43] even after he has been proclaimed and realized and celebrated in symbolic actions.

Symbols and prophetic symbols make present what they signify and arouse in the person who lives into them an entire range of personal, sensitive, imaginative, intuitive, emotional, conceptual information, action and reaction. A prophetic symbol, unlike a simple sign, is not just a bearer of information but is also a provocation of personal action and reaction that affects the participant's total being. This view has been dealt with earlier in the argument that symbols represent a personal way of knowing, as distinct from a logical one.

The meaning that is embodied in symbols is not defined in clear and distinct and logical concepts. Determinate conceptual knowledge is part of the knowledge resulting from symbolic activity, but the concepts are confused and so the meanings remain opaque and mysterious. Theology reflects upon both the prophetic symbols and the knowledge that is communicated in them in an effort to achieve greater clarity and distinction, but no amount of reflection, analysis or demonstration exhausts the meanings embodied and expressed in sacrament. The meanings remain mysteriously full and rich. The symbol itself is the bedrock in which the meanings are achieved and beneath which it is impossible to go.

To know in prophetic symbol, therefore, as to know through any symbol, is to know personally. The symbolic way of knowing is quite different from the scientific way. The dominant, scientific, Western-lobe mode of knowing takes place in clear and distinct ideas. It is impersonal, detached, so-called objective, seeking, in Roszak's phrase, to "increase what is known, not to deepen the personality of the knower."[44] The symbolic, sacramental, Eastern-lobe mode of knowing is personal, involved, subjective, aiming to increase the knower as much as his conscious knowledge. The symbolic mode of knowing is through seeing, hearing, touching, tasting, smelling, imagining, remembering, associating, emoting, conceiving, judging, deciding, doing, living, experiencing. "A true symbol," and both the prophetic and sacramental symbols are such, "must be *lived into*. That is how its meaning is found."[45]

TWO BASIC QUESTIONS

There are two basic questions men and women can ask about reality. The first is an empirical question: What is that? The second is a *human* question: What is that for us?[46] The first asks about "facts"; the second asks about meanings. The first is a Western-lobe question; the second is an Eastern-lobe one. In the Western tradition since the Enlightenment, the factual question reigns as the so-called objective order, while the meaning question is derogated as the so-called subjective order. Such a hard and fast separation of objective and subjective does not seem to match the real situation.

The simple reality seems to be that both the factual and the meaning questions involve both objective and subjective elements. The factual question is objective to the extent that it asks about what is really out there. But it is also subjective, as I have already shown, to the extent that what is out there is attained only as the result of subjective perception controlled by subjective theory. "At the empirical level of behavior or questioning, we are dealing with perception and therefore with one form of subjectivity."[47] Fact is a composite of objective datum and subjective perception.

If there is a subjective element at the level of empirical questioning, there is undeniably a subjective element at the level of human questioning. But there is equally undeniably an objective element at this level too. If a Cadillac, for instance, means status, position and wealth in the United States, it does so not completely subjectively, but also because of certain empirical characteristics of a Cadillac, because of some community of nature, as Whitehead would say, between human wealth and status and what goes into the making of a Cadillac. The human meanings of a Cadillac are quite different from the human meanings of a plastic tricycle from Woolworth's not entirely subjectively but also objectively, in that much more objective labor exercised on much more valuable materials goes into the making of a Cadillac than of a plastic tricycle. The two basic questions are not entirely separate, but are rather two different ways of humanly interpreting reality. Each has its subjective and its objective side. Both together, in Susanne Langer's pregnant image, provide the warp and the woof of the fabric of meaning.[48] They do so as much in the case of a symbol, a prophetic symbol and a sacrament, as in the case of a Cadillac.

The two questions may be posed, for instance, of the seder meal, or Eucharist. The answer to the empirical question "What is that?" can only be: that is a meal of bread and wine. The only real presence at the natural, sensible, empirical level is the presence of bread and wine, just as the only real presence at that level in a Cadillac is the presence of metal and rubber and leather and polished wood. But at the meaning level, the answer to the human question "what is that for us?" is: for us that is the presence of God and the body of Christ. And that meaning is as objective as the fact that a Cadillac means status, position, and wealth in the United States. Theologically the symbolic meaning is regarded as more objective, more given, for it derives from God's and Jesus' at least implicit identification of themselves with the meal of bread and wine.

Of course, there are subjective statements in the claims of symbolic theology. But so are there in American claims about the meaning of a Cadillac, and indeed in every human claim about meaning. In no case do these subjective elements vitiate the objectivity of the meaning. A stone buried in the ground and dug up again is no more a better symbol of the body of Christ than a plastic tricycle is a better symbol than a Cadillac of position, status and wealth. For the natural meanings associated with meals humans share together donate to the symbolic meal more the meanings of presence, love, friendship, oneness, being and counting for others than does a buried and reclaimed stone. Religious faith does not create, but proclaims, realizes and celebrates, the presence of God in the meanings of the shared meal. That faith is reinforced in its choice of this symbolic ritual by the good news that it was God himself for seder, and later Jesus himself for Eucharist, who identified the recalling of his presence in and through the ritual meal of bread and wine. There is, as I hinted earlier, a certain consternation in some Christian circles when faced with the statement that the Eucharist is a *symbol* of the presence of Jesus. We have seen the care with which Dupont insists on the reality of prophetic symbolic presence for the Semite, as distinct from the Western, ontological mentality, which separates "real" and "symbolic." In this classical dichotomy, whatever else *symbol* may mean, it certainly means *not real.* "It's only a symbol," within this context, means it is not real and so can be ignored when you wish to deal with reality.

Anyone who has followed the view of symbol developed so far in this work will know that I take a very different view. To say *symbol* is not to say *not real*, but rather *fully real*, that is, representatively and concretely and effectively and personally real. Prophetic symbols realize sacred reality precisely by symbolizing it. To say that seder is a symbol of the active presence of the God who saves, or that Eucharist is a symbol of the presence of Jesus for the community called Church, is to say that God and Jesus are proclaimed, realized and celebrated as present in these rituals, really, truly and substantially present, as the familiar theological phrase states it. There are two reasons for this.

The first is anthropological: *all* symbols make present what they symbolize. The second is theological: God and Jesus are reported to have identified their presence with this meal symbol of bread and wine. Seder and Eucharist, and every other prophetic symbol too, are indeed only symbols; but they are only and magnificently symbols, with all the force of real and realizing with which I have invested that word.

Chapter Two
SACRAMENT: A THEOLOGICAL VIEW

This chapter will elaborate the nature of sacrament. It will consider the history of the definition of sacrament in Catholic theology, the nature of sacrament as sign, sign specifically of faith, act of and instituted by Christ. There will be a note of ecumenical significance and an explanatory note on grace in a concluding section on the summary definition of sacrament.

SACRAMENT: HISTORY OF A DEFINITION

It is generally agreed that the Christian Church has sacraments, that is, solemn ritual actions. The number varies from one confession to another, but allowing a spread from the Protestant two to the traditional Roman Catholic seven, or nine as they now are listed, sacraments are acknowledged by all Christians. The term *sacrament*, however, has a long history, and this history must be considered prior to any further discussion. Both Greek and Latin literature contributed to the technical meaning of the word *sacrament*, Greek through the term *mysterion*, Latin through the term *sacramentum*. An understanding of the technical, theological meaning of sacrament begins with an analysis of both these terms.

Still today as in the past Greek theology refers to a sacrament as *mysterion*.[1] Now *mysterion* originally meant something secret, something hidden, something not fully manifest.[2] This sense of *mysterion* is retained in both Old and New Testaments. In the Book of Daniel *mysterion* refers simultaneously to the plan of God for the end times and to some obscure revelation of this plan.[3] In Paul *mysterion* refers to the divine plan to save all men in Christ, a plan determined by God from the beginning and kept secret, but now revealed through the Spirit, through the prophets, through the apostles.[4] The *mysterion* is made known to those of mature faith,[5] or to spiritual persons,[6] not because

29

it is an esoteric knowledge restricted only to the initiated, but because only those who are spiritual, that is, Spirit-filled, accept the knowledge which the Spirit gives.

It should be emphasized that Paul never uses *mysterion* to designate those rituals that are today called sacraments. Even in the classical text of Ephesians 5:32 *mysterion* does not refer to the sacrament of matrimony. It seems, rather, to refer to marriage in terms such as those detailed above, that from the beginning the union of a man and woman in marriage was a secret prophetic symbol of the union of Christ and his Church, a secret which is now made known. But if Paul did not employ the word to designate Christian rituals, the Fathers of the Church certainly did.

It would seem to have been the third century Alexandrians, Clement and Origen, who first began the adaptation of mystery language to the ritual practices of Christians. The word *mysterion* is rarely found in the early Apostolic Fathers in any sense. The second century Apologists use it in multiple senses: to refer to the pagan mystery cults; to describe the birth, death and life of Jesus; to indicate the figures and types of Christ in the Old Testament.[7] But Clement and Origen, borrowing from both Neo-Platonic and Gnostic usage, extend *mysterion* to include Christian ritual practices.

For Clement *mysterion* is a representation of sacred things through perceptible signs. Such, for instance, are the mysteries of the Egyptians.[8] And though he never applies the word *mysterion* to either baptism or Eucharist, he does use related mystery language of them.[9] In Origen *mysterion* is a fundamental, if rather fluid, notion, articulated in such English words as mystery, symbol, sign, image, type, form.[10] He understands a sign to be "when through what is seen something other is indicated." Jonah coming forth from the whale's belly is a sign of Christ's resurrection; the circumcision required of Abraham is a sign of the spiritual circumcision of the heart; the water of baptism is a sign of the death to sin and resurrection to new life of the person in Christ; the bread of Eucharist is a sign of our thanksgiving to God.[11] The rituals of baptism and Eucharist are signs which give men and women insight into the triune mystery of God, Christ and Spirit.

Clement and Origen opened the way for the application of mystery terminology to Christian rituals, and by the fourth and fifth centuries the use of mystery language was fully established.[12] *Mysterion* retained its biblical meanings and acquired new cultural and philosophical ones. One of these deserves special emphasis. It is this. Although *mysterion* referred simultaneously to a secret and to its manifestation, the primary emphasis was always on something secret and mysterious. The revelation of the secret or mystery still left it mystery. We saw in the opening chapter that this point is as important today as it was then for an understanding of symbol. It is equally important for the understanding of sacrament. The sacred realities proclaimed and realized and celebrated in symbols in general and in sacramental symbols in particular are not the kinds of realities and meanings that men and women fully understand, even after revelation. The depth of meaning embodied in symbols is always inexhaustible. The revelation achieved through symbols is always "in a mirror dimly" and "in part" (1 Cor 13:12).

Many things could be, and have been, said about the etymology of the Latin word *sacramentum*.[13] Only one is of major concern to us here: the Latin word *sacramentum* translates the prior Greek *mysterion*.[14] It is, therefore, to be understood in the sense of a secret which is revealed in part.

The word *sacramentum*, of course, was not invented by Church theologians. It was already in common usage, with two meanings. First, it meant the oath of loyalty taken by all soldiers; indeed, it meant oaths in general. Both the oath and the soldier under oath were regarded as consecrated to the gods. Second, in Roman law it meant a deposit of money by way of a pledge made by each party in a civil suit and forfeited to the state by the loser. This money was deposited in the temple and was, therefore, regarded as consecrated to the gods.[16]

The Latin Father Tertullian, who lived in the third century, is the first to use the word *sacramentum* of both baptism and Eucharist. He speaks of baptism as a sacrament analogous to the soldier's oath. As the soldier pledges allegiance to his chief and is thereby consecrated, so in baptism the Christian pledges allegiance to Christ and is thereby consecrated to Christ and to his God.[17] Tertullian looks on Eucharist as a sacrament in a slightly different way, namely, as a perceptible sign of something, better someone, other who sanctifies Christians.[18] This double meaning of *sacramentum* as a sanctifying and as a signifying reality was continued by Cyprian of Carthage.[19] There was thus laid down in the Latin Church the lines of the nature of Christian sacrament that would be developed in a later generation by the great Augustine of Hippo.

It is not possible within the scope of this chapter to offer a detailed account of Augustine's sacramental doctrine. It is doubtful, indeed, if a systematic view of such a doctrine has yet been isolated from the mass of material available.[20] What can be done here with profit is to highlight certain doctrinal elements emerging clearly from the Augustinian corpus, which entered into the subsequent development of the precise and technical definition of sacrament.

Augustine does not clearly distinguish *mysterion* and *sacramentum,* and both have affinities with other words: sign, symbol, figure, allegory and the like. The designation *sacramentum-mysterion* is applied to three classes of reality. First, it is applied to rites of both Old and New Testaments: sabbath, sacrifice, circumcision, ceremonies, temple, feasts, priesthood, anointings, baptism, Eucharist, imposition of hands, religious profession, creeds, the Lord's Prayer. Second, it is applied to symbols or figures: every person, gesture and thing in which allegorical exegesis could find a figure, especially of Christ and the Church. Third, it is applied to the mysteries of the Trinity and the Incarnation.[21]

For Augustine the meanings of *sacramentum-mysterion* range on a broader canvas than those covered by the technical definitions of the twelfth and the thirteenth centuries. But the elements, inchoate in Tertullian and Cyprian, and which would ultimately coalesce into the technical definitions, are already there.[22] Emerging very clearly and explicitly is Augustine's major contribution to sacramental theory: a sacrament is a sacred sign.[23] The relation of this sign and what it signifies is variously explained. They are related as what is seen and what is believed, as what is seen and what is understood, as what is seen and what is. What is signified is also effected, by Christ and the Spirit. Water is the external sacrament of grace; the Spirit effects inner grace. A man baptizes and Christ baptizes, washes and cleanses.[24] It is this efficacy worked by Christ and Spirit that separates a *sacramentum-mysterion* from mere figures and symbols. A sacrament is an *efficacious* sign.

Nowhere does Augustine offer a definition of sacrament in the precise terms of the later manuals and catechisms. But the elements are there. His location of sacrament in the category of sign will come to fruition in the golden age of Scholasticism. And his specification of efficacy as an essential ingredient of sacrament will also become an integral part of the technical definition. That Augustine himself did not include efficacy in his own definition of sacrament explains why he, and subsequent ecclesiastical writers up to the twelfth century, could describe as sacraments such a widely diverse range of realities as those outlined above.

From the death of Augustine until the beginning of the twelfth century, a precise notion of sacrament developed little. This was, if anything, a period of retrogression. For this retrogression one man more than any other was responsible, Isidore of Seville, who lived in the seventh century. In his chief work, a kind of encyclopedia which exerted great influence in the Middle Ages, Isidore defined a sacrament, not in the category of sign, as had Augustine, but in the category of secret and sacred power concealed under visible actions.[25] From this definition evolved the notion of sacrament as a vessel of grace, an understanding which allows all the Christian mysteries to be called sacraments. For four centuries Isidore's definition prevailed over Augustine's. This situation was ended only in the eleventh century when Berengar of Tours revived and appealed to the Augustinian definitions to sustain his theory of Eucharist.

Bergengar's approach to the Eucharist was, briefly, this.[26] A sacrament is a sacred sign. But a sign is not the thing signified; the symbol is not the thing symbolized; the sacrament is not the reality. The Eucharist, therefore, the sacrament of the body of Christ, is not the true body of Christ. In the controversy that such a doctrine provoked, the definitions of Augustine, notwithstanding Berengar's misuse of them, prevailed over Isidore's and opened the way to the final, precise and technical definition of sacrament.

The definitions derived from Augustine, which viewed a sacrament as a sacred sign and as a sign of a sacred thing, were judged to be too broad.[27] Another formula was suggested which, though not explicitly found in Augustine, was in accord with his teaching and enjoyed his authority. A sacrament is the visible form of invisible grace.[28] Abelard attempted to alter this formula to read "the visible sign of invisible grace" in order to keep sacrament in the category of sign, but this suggestion did not receive much support. And the search for a definition went on.

The first precise definition was proposed in the twelfth century by Hugh of St. Victor. Although it is very much a traditional definition, in which a sacrament is seen as a sacred sign, Hugh overcomes the charge that it is too broad by carefully distinguishing sign in the broad sense from sacrament in the strict sense. "What is a sacrament?" he asks. "A sign of a sacred thing," he answers. "Why is a sacrament called a sign of a sacred thing?" he asks. "Because by a visible reality seen externally, another invisible, interior reality is signified," he answers. But "what is the difference between a sign and a sacrament?" he asks. His reply here underscores the notion of a sacrament as *efficacious* sign, the notion that made the technical definition of sacrament finally possible. "While a sign can signify a thing but not confer it, a sacrament not only signifies but also efficaciously confers. A sacrament simultaneously signifies by institution, represents by similitude, and confers by sanctification."[29] The notion of efficacy as being of the essence of the sacramental sign became normative and was part of Peter Lombard's definitive definition: "A sacrament, properly speaking, is a sign of the grace of God and the form of invisible grace in such a way that it is its image and its cause."[30]

In Lombard the search for a definition of sacrament reached its end. A sacrament is a sign, but not all signs are sacraments. Only those signs which confer or cause grace are properly called sacraments. There remained problems to be solved by later theologians: the precise number of sacraments, a problem which still remains unresolved between Roman Catholic and Protestant theologians; the question of marriage, which at the time was held not to confer grace and so could not properly be called a sacrament. But the road from the *mysterion* of the early Church and the Scriptures had reached its end in the technical definition of *sacramentum*. It remained, and still remains, for that road to be made smooth.

SACRAMENT: SIGN

A fundamental assertion in any Christian discussion of sacraments is that sacraments are signs. This assertion, as the previous section showed, originated with Augustine. It has persisted in sacramental theology to the present day, despite some few divergent opinions.

Thomas Aquinas took up the idea of sacrament as sign and explicated it at length. "We speak of sacraments insofar as they indicate a relationship of sign. And in this sense a sacrament belongs in the category of sign."[31] Not every sacred sign, though, is a sacrament, but only that sign "which is a sign of the sacred insofar as it (i.e., the sacred) sanctifies man."[32] A "sacrament is a commemorative sign of what is past, namely, the passion of Christ, namely, grace; it is prognostic of, that is, it announces, future glory."[33] Sacraments are signs: signs of Christ's saving action, signs of grace, signs of glory. They are also, in the finished thought of the later Aquinas, causes of grace; they cause grace instrumentally.[34] Sacraments doubly contain grace, as both signifying and causing grace, as both signs and causes of grace.[35]

The idea that sacraments effect what they signify has been embodied in various aphorisms within, for instance, the Roman Catholic tradition. Sacraments effect what they signify, cause by signifying, are efficacious signs of grace. It should be emphasized, however, that though in popular preaching and piety such aphorisms related the sanctifying of man to the external rite, the theological tradition em-

ployed them to indicate that the sanctification of man is achieved principally by the sacred reality signified by the sacrament, namely, God in
Christ. The principal cause of man's sanctification is this God whose
action is signified in sacraments, not the sign which signifies. The sign
does, indeed, sanctify, but only as God's instrument. Sacraments are
not mechanical grace machines, but personal acts of God in Christ.

Aquinas specified three different causes of man's sanctification:
the passion of Christ, grace, and eternal life. A different trinity of
causes could also be advanced: the saving action of God, the saving
action of Christ, the saving action of the Church. Ultimately, of course,
there is only one cause of man's sanctification and salvation, God. The
man Christ, the Church and the sacraments sanctify and save only as
instrumental causes, only as God uses them to sanctify and to save. It
is, nevertheless, still legitimate to say that the sacred reality which is
signified by the sacraments and which causes grace is threefold: God,
Christ and Church. It is for this reason that sacraments are variously
described as signs and acts of God and of the man Christ and of the
Church. In what follows these three will be linked as one: sacraments
will be treated as signs and actions, in the Church, of God and Christ.

As a conclusion to this section, and in preparation for a subsequent section, the question may now be asked: If only God saves, then
what is the need of sacraments? Why is grace mediated to men and
women in signs, and why must it be so mediated? Aquinas offers three,
mutually reinforcing reasons. The first is that it is a characteristic of
human nature that men and women be led through bodily and sensible reality to non-sensible, intelligible, spiritual reality. The second is
that by sinning men and women subjugated themselves to bodily realities, and so it is apt that the remedies of sin be applied to them through
those same bodily realities. The third reason is that human activity re-
volves so much around bodily things that it is difficult for men and
women to abstract themselves from bodily reality, and so it is again apt
that spiritual realities be proposed to them mediated in the bodily.[36] It
is not God who needs sacraments, and therefore his activity is never to
be thought of as being restricted to such sensible actions. It is men and
women who need sacraments, in virtue of their being human, being
sinners, and being much more facile with sensible and bodily activity
than with intelligible and spiritual.

The reasons Aquinas adduces for the necessity of sacraments are,
naturally, postulated on the basis of Scholastic anthropology, in which
man is perceived as a composite of principles designated as body and
soul. In such an anthropology the approach to spiritual reality through
bodily reality, that is, sacramentality, is evidently most apt. But it is not

necessary to subscribe to this perception to grasp the fittingness of sacraments. Even a contemporary anthropology, which is in no way tied to the body-soul dichotomy, acknowledges what is empirically evident, namely, that men and women enjoy greater facility with the sensible and concrete than with the abstract and spiritual.

The previous chapter dealt with the empirically universal symboling activity of the human animal, which proclaims and realizes abstract, or spiritual, realities and meanings in concrete and sensible forms. The Christian tradition believes that this symboling activity extends into the religious sphere. It further believes that sacraments minister to this need by providing men and women with the opportunity of proclaiming, realizing and celebrating the presence of nonsensible, spiritual reality in sensible, embodied form. Sacraments are necessary in the same way that symbols are necessary; indeed, sacraments are symbolic actions. They are, as we shall see, prophetic symbols.

SACRAMENT: SIGN OF FAITH

When one reads the New Testament, it is impossible not to be impressed by the emphasis on faith as a means of salvation. Jesus complained of the absence of faith frequently and insistently. Paul passionately defended the necessity of faith against the legalism of the Judaizers. Juan Alfaro expresses well what that faith meant and means. It "includes knowledge of a saving event, confidence in the word of God, man's humble submission and personal self-surrender to God, fellowship in life with Christ, and a desire for perfect union with him beyond the grave. Faith is man's comprehensive 'Yes' to God's revealing himself as man's savior in Christ."[37]

The primacy of faith in the total context of salvation was acknowledged and affirmed by the Roman Catholic tradition in the Council of Trent. "We may be said to be justified through faith, in the sense that 'faith is the beginning of man's salvation,' the foundation and source of all justification, 'without which it is impossible to please God' (Heb 11:6) and to be counted as his sons."[38]

The same idea was reiterated in the very important chapter on the sources of justification. There it was stated that the instrumental cause of the sinner's justification is "the sacrament of baptism which is the 'sacrament of faith,' without which no man has ever been justified."[39] The Latin text makes it very clear that the phrase "without which no man has ever been justified" qualifies faith. *Without which* renders the

Latin *sine qua*, a feminine form which can only refer to the feminine word, faith. If it referred to the masculine word baptism, or to the neuter word sacrament, it would have to be *sine quo*.[40] There is not the slightest doubt that the Fathers of Trent wished strongly to affirm the primacy of faith in the question of justification.

Nevertheless, because of the polemical contexts of the time, there was a certain uneasiness in Roman Catholic assertions about faith. Martin Luther had made "faith alone" his banner. The Council, consciously and explicitly, aimed itself at condemning whatever was seen as heretical in his assertion. "The positive Catholic doctrine proposed in the decrees and canons is therefore only the *necessary minimum*, in opposition and contrast to the heretical positions of that time."[41] But Roman Catholic theologians after Trent advanced their positions so exclusively as counterpoint to Luther's "faith alone" that their theology of both sacrament and the role of personal faith in its efficacy suffered detriment. That detriment crystallized in a very restricted notion of *opus operatum*.

In its canons on the sacraments in general, Trent defined two important ideas related to *opus operatum*. It taught, first, that "if anyone says that the sacraments of the new law do not contain the grace they signify or that they do not confer the same grace on him who places no obstacle to it, as if they were merely external signs of the grace and of the justification received through faith . . . let him be anathema."[42] And then it taught, second, that "if anyone says that grace is not conferred *ex opere operato* through the sacraments of the New Law, but that faith alone in the divine promises is sufficient to obtain grace: let him be anathema."[43]

Prior to the Council, nominalistically inclined theologians had argued that the only requirement on the part of a person receiving a sacrament was that he place no obstacle to grace. In practice this meant that he was required only to be free from grave sin, and then the mere positing of the external rite conferred grace. It was just such a mechanical understanding of the *opus operatum* that gave credence to the quasi-magical practices of the fifteenth century Church and to the objections of the Reformers. Since Nominalists constituted a majority at the Council of Trent, it was this nominalist definition which became "*the* exhaustive definition of the *opus operatum* of the efficacy of any sacrament."[44]

The complementary notion of *opus operantis*, the disposition, faith, devotion, love of the person receiving the sacrament, was developed as a completely separate notion. A person could first receive sacramental grace simply by being free from serious sin and having the right intention. Then, *ex opere operantis*, he could receive "other" graces. Such a rigid dichotomy of *opus operatum* and *opus operantis* and of their respective necessities for receiving grace was foreign to the theological thinking of the great Scholastics.

Aquinas uses *ex opere operato* frequently in his early *Commentary on the Sentences*, but never in his final work, the *Summa Theologiae*. This may be taken as an indication of his judgment that the term was not needed to present a genuine Catholic sacramental doctrine. In fact, "the truth that this terminology was intended to bring out was presented satisfactorily, and even in finer detail, in his Christological appreciation of the sacraments."[45]

The Christological character of the sacrament as the work of God in Christ is the fundamental idea underlying Thomas' understanding of *opus operatum*. On this fundamental idea rest other ways of using the phrase. Baptism, for instance, "justifies *ex opere operato:* this is not man's work, but God's." "Baptism does not have its effect because of the merits of the person being baptized, but because of the merits of Christ." Baptism is efficacious "because of the passion of Christ."[46] The notion of *ex opere operato* refers to the efficacy of the sacrament in virtue of the passion of Christ. It is not the external sign which effects grace, at least not as principal cause, but the sacred reality which is signified by the sign, namely, the action of God in Christ.

Thomas also opposes *ex opere operato* to faith alone. Sacraments of the natural law derive their efficacy only from the faith of the man who partakes in them, while sacraments of the new law "confer grace *ex opere operato*."[47] He also distinguishes between the efficacy of a Mass *ex opere operato* and *ex opere operantis*. Essential to the Mass is the body of Christ; accidental to it is whether it is offered by a good priest or a bad one. Accidentally, therefore, "the Mass of a good priest is better because not only does it have efficacy *ex opere operato*, but also *ex opere operantis*."[48]

From these various nuances of the phrase we can distill an understanding of how Aquinas looked upon the notion *ex opere operato*. Nowhere does it imply a contrast between the bestowal of grace and the subjective disposition of the recipient, but rather a contrast between the constitution of the sacrament *qua* external sign and the subjective disposition of the minister or of the recipient. The sacrament is constituted as external sign without any *opus operantis* of either minister or recipient. It is not, however, constituted as *efficacious* sign, that is, as sign which actually mediates grace, without that *opus operantis*.[49] For the great Scholastics *opus operatum* and *opus operantis* were not dichotomized, but were essentially related. The latter was regarded as the "personal aspect in the justifying process of any sacrament, that aspect by which a free and responsible person accepted God's grace conferred by the sanctifying efficacy"[50] of the former.

A sacrament abstractly defined is located within the categories of sign and cause. But a sacrament concretely defined requires a third category, that of subject. There is no concrete possibility of sacramental causality without a human subject in whom grace is caused. There is similarly no concrete possibility of sacramental signification without a subject who acts out a ritual and relates this ritual to some non-sensible reality and meaning. The sign in baptism, for instance, is not just water, but the action of pouring water on a human subject. Nor is it just a case of a subject physically submitting herself or himself to a sacrament, for a sacrament is not just a physical action but also a human one. Men and women are free persons and they are graced and sanctified as such—not against their will, but according to it. If they have no intention of receiving a sacrament, then no external, physical submission to it profits them anything. The sacrament administered by the minister is not received by the subject. The sacrament administered still, indeed, signifies the saving action in the Church of God in Christ, but not as concretely effective for this subject. It is the activity of the subject receiving a sacrament, that is, the *opus operantis*, that makes it a practical sign of faith.[51]

The faith of the Church is required for the very existence of sacraments, for it is the faith of the Church that relates a particular signification with a particular sign. This is what the Church "does" in the sacraments, relates sign and signification. This is what ministers must intend when they administer it. They must intend to do what the Church does, namely, relate this sign and this meaning.[52]

Recipients of a sacrament must do the same thing. They must also intend to relate this sign and this meaning. It is for the perfection of the signification of a sacrament that the personal contribution of the recipient is required. "The subject must signify genuine acceptance of what the Church offers. Otherwise the sacrament is not a *concrete, practical* sign; it is merely a speculative sign of the divine will to save all men."[53] And since sacraments cause by signifying, when they do not signify neither do they cause. The *opus operans* of the recipient is required to make a sacrament fruitful because it is first required to make a sacrament a concrete sign.[54]

Personal faith, therefore, enters into the very essence of sacramentality as the necessary personal complement in the conferring of grace. Men and women are saved as what they are, free persons, not automatically or magically. No person is graced or sanctified or saved unwillingly. Of their very nature grace and salvation, which is its ultimate outcome, require a free acceptance akin to the New Testament composite of faith delineated above. This faith supplies what is necessary to make the sacrament, on the part of the recipient, a fully religious act. It raises the action from the natural, physical level to the human, religious level of ritual and effective sign of saving grace.

A similar conclusion on the necessity of personal faith-involvement in sacraments is imposed by consideration of sacraments in the context of personal encounter. The purpose of concrete sacrament is to bring about such an encounter with a not very concrete God and Christ. Since any genuine interpersonal encounter must involve both parties, the religious intention of the recipient belongs to the essence of any fruitful sacrament, that is, one that is a genuine encounter with God and Christ. "If the sacrament is not thus personally lived with religious intent, the sacramentally-mediated personal encounter with Christ, and therefore with God, cannot take place."[55] Unless the recipient comes to the sacrament with faith and love, unless, as I said in the previous chapter, men and women *live into* the sign, the external sign becomes a lie. For what the sign signifies externally is, in that case, denied internally by the recipient's disposition.

A sacrament which is fully a sacrament is a sign not only of the saving action of Christ and God, but also of the recipient's faith and desire to be saved in the action. A true sacrament requires the simultaneous positing of an external rite or *opus operatum*, which is the sign of Christ's and God's saving action, and an internal faith or *opus operantis*, which transforms that external rite into true human ritual. Only when the external rite and the internal faith are posited together is there free, and therefore fruitful, encounter between men and women and grace and God. The passion of Christ or the saving action of God in Christ, Aquinas insists, "achieves its effect in those to whom it is applied through faith and love and the sacraments of faith."[56]

The Council of Trent defined that sacraments confer the grace they signify on the person who places no obstacle. The Council opted for this minimalistic declaration in order to cover in one single formula the cases of both children and adults, and it applies positively only to the case of children. The Roman tradition, in the Council of Florence, had already carefully specified that, for an adult, "placing no obstacle" meant having a positive, personal intent. The sacraments, it insisted, give grace to those who receive them worthily.[57] This doctrine of the Council of Florence, an ecumenical council as official as the Council of Trent, is much more positive and expansive than Trent's negative and minimalistic doctrine. It is a far cry from any passive, mechanistic view of sacraments which concentrates only on the avoidance of sin.

The doctrine of the Council of Florence demands an active, positive disposition of self-surrendering faith on the part of the recipient of a sacrament. Such a doctrine makes the sacraments true *signs of faith*—signs, that is, not only of the faith of the Church which loyally seeks to proclaim, realize and celebrate in sacramental signs the presence and action of God in Christ, but also of the faith of the recipient who concelebrates that presence with the Church. The Second Vatican Council stamps that position as the truly Catholic position. It teaches that sacraments "not only presuppose faith, but by words and objects they also nourish, strengthen and express it. That is why they are called 'sacraments of faith.' "[58] There can be no doubt about what the Catholic position is: sacraments presuppose faith. A believer comes to sacramental celebrations in and with faith, and with that faith transforms ordinary, simple human actions and words into more than ordinary or simple sacraments. Faith, a man's or a woman's comprehensive "yes" to God, the medieval *opus operantis*, is as essential to any fruitful sacrament as the most carefully executed *opus operatum*.

AN ECUMENICAL NOTE

The role of faith in the sacraments is a problem of crucial ecumenical importance. The central Lutheran tenet of "faith alone" was incorporated in sacramental statements presented to the theologians of the Council of Trent. Two may be singled out. Proposition five read: "Sacraments have never given grace or forgiveness of sins, but only faith. . . . " This proposition is obviously ambiguous. It can be read as "sacraments give only faith," or as "in the sacraments only faith gives grace." Trent read it in the second sense, entirely consonant with another Lutheran proposition presented to the Council: "Sacraments give grace only to those who believe their sins are forgiven."[59]

The Tridentine answer to the question of the necessity of faith in sacramental activity is very nuanced. Those present at the Council wished to acknowledge that there was a sense in which Luther's claim was perfectly orthodox, and so ought not to be condemned. Seripando, Master General of the Conventual Franciscans, was the chief spokesman for this point of view. He argued that Luther's proposition five could be understood in two senses. It could mean, first, that "in the sacraments grace is given only to those who believe their sins are

forgiven, because such is the effect of the sacraments." If it is understood in this sense, then the proposition is orthodox Catholic teaching.
But proposition five can be read in another sense, to mean that in sacraments faith alone is the source of grace, "the sacrament itself ef-
fecting nothing in the matter of grace." In this sense, Seripando
argued, the Lutheran proposition is condemnable, and he was at pains
"to arrange the terms in such a way that the second sense, but not the
first, is condemned."[60]

It is quite clear that Trent, along with Martin Luther and the entire Christian tradition, wished to affirm the absolutely necessary function of personal faith in sacramental efficacy. What they wished to
condemn was not the insistence on the necessity of faith, but the one-
sided insistence on "faith alone" as the source of grace, to the detriment of the sacramental action. It is this affirmation of the role of the
sacrament, and certainly not the negation of the role of faith, that is
contained in the two important canons previously cited. "If anyone
says that the sacraments of the New Law do not contain the grace they
signify or that they do not confer that same grace on him who places
no obstacle to it, as if they were merely external signs of the grace and
of the justification received through faith . . . let him be anathema."
And "if anyone says that grace is not conferred *ex opere operato* through
the sacraments of the New Law, but that faith alone in the divine
promises is sufficient to obtain grace: let him be anathema."[61] In sacraments neither faith alone nor sacrament alone leads to the reception
of grace, but faith *and* sacrament, *opus operantis* which transforms *opus
operatum* into effective sacrament.

According to the Roman Catholic tradition, then, grace is conferred in the sacraments *ex opere operato,* that is, by God in Christ in
and through this concrete ritual. Therein lies one of the major areas
of disagreement between the Roman Church and the Reformation
churches. The Confession of Augsburg proclaims: "They [the Reformation churches] condemn those who teach that sacraments justify *ex
opere operato,* and do not teach that faith is required in their use."[62] Me-
lancthon repeated the same charge in his second Apology for the
Augsburg Confession: "We condemn all those Scholastic doctors who
teach that the sacraments confer grace on the person who places no
obstacle, *ex opere operato* . . . without a good disposition of the heart,
that is, without faith."[63] What is accorded to the efficacy of the sacraments *ex opere operato* is seen by the Reformers as being taken away
from the efficacy of faith and, ultimately, from the unique efficacy of
God.

Though there is some justification for this accusation in popular preaching and piety, it is still a caricature of orthodox Roman Catholic thought. Nowhere did the fathers of the Council of Trent understand *opus operatum* as an external rite which would give grace or justification apart from the subjective disposition of the subject. Rather for them, as for Aquinas, *opus operatum* meant *opus Dei et Christi* (the action of God and of Christ), and *opus operantis* meant the personal contribution of the subject, which was essential for the efficacy of the sacrament. On these two points, Trent's teaching is quite contrary to the teaching the Reformers ascribed to it. The official text, as explained above, makes very clear that the Council was consciously trying to shape a doctrinal synthesis which would hold as important the efficacy of both faith and sacraments in the total process of justification.

In an analysis of remarkable precision and depth, Louis Villette carries much further the Roman Catholic understanding of the inter-relationships of faith and sacrament. He argues that "rooted in the Scriptures and the teaching of the Fathers, systematized in various ways in the Scholastic period, defined if necessary by the Council of Trent, defended and explicated by post-Tridentine theologians,"[64] there are doctrinal constants in the Roman Catholic position vis-à-vis faith and sacrament.

A first theme is the simultaneous and complementary affirmation of both the efficacy of the sacraments instituted by Christ and the ab-solute necessity of personal faith for this efficacy to touch and effect a concrete subject. Up to the Council of Trent Catholic theologians unanimously affirm that the sacraments are efficacious "by" faith, "in" faith, "in proportion to" faith. In reaction to the theories of the Re-formers, Catholic teaching insisted that "faith alone" did not justify, but justified in and through sacraments. This was not, as we have al-ready insisted, to deny the necessity of faith, but only to affirm the ef-ficacy of sacraments. Orthodox Roman Catholic teaching never considered the sacramental conferring of grace to be independent of faith.

A second theme relates to the constitution of the sacraments. This theme attained unanimity already in the baptismal controversies of the early Church, in particular from the time of Augustine. The faith of the Church, not just the faith of the recipient or of the minister, is nec-essary for the constitution of a valid sacrament. A sacrament is not pri-marily a thing, but an act; and an act, not primarily of the recipient or the minister, but of God in Christ in the Church. The sacraments are in representative reality actions of God in Christ, proclaimed, realized and celebrated in the Christian Church in his name. What is required of the minister of a sacrament is at least the intention to do what the

Church does, to do what the Church believes is to be done. And what is required of the men and women who concelebrate those actions as Church and Body of Christ is, at least for the validity of the sacrament, that they intend to proclaim and realize and celebrate the same actions as the Church.

The faith of the communal Church is required for the very existence of sacraments because it is the faith of the Church which, relying on God's word, transforms an ordinary, simple human action into a symbolic action in which God is gracious. It is also by means of the faith of the Church that God uses this ritual to bestow grace. Without the faith of the Church there would be no sacrament, not even a divine seal set upon faith.

The rite is an action, in the Church, of God in Christ, but an action which believing men and women make concretely significative and effective for them by their personal disposition of faith, love, and devotion. The absolute necessity of faith for the sacramental conferring of grace is as much a Roman Catholic as a Protestant teaching. This root agreement should be acknowledged, without, however, ignoring significant differences.

The Protestant traditions, in general, proclaim that sacraments are efficacious through faith. This means that confirmed or sealed faith, not sacraments, effects grace and justification. The Roman Catholic tradition proclaims that sacraments are efficacious through faith. The meaning here is twofold. First, it is proclaimed that the faith of the Church enters into the very constitution of sacrament. Second, it is proclaimed that the personal faith of believers enters into the very constitution of sacrament as concretely significative and effective of grace for them. Thus, contrary to expectation, it would seem that the relationship of faith and sacrament is, minimally, just as vital in the Roman Catholic tradition as in the Reformation traditions.

The particular positions of Luther and Calvin and contemporary Protestant theologians indicate a particular perspective on God and man and their interrelationship, and also on the place of Christ and the Church with respect to grace. This perspective influences judgments on faith and the sacraments. The general Protestant position "ties the sacraments directly to the word of Christ alone, without any mediation on the part of the Church, and sees faith in an entirely individualist context."[65] It would have to be admitted that this position is truer of Calvinism, with its high conception of the transcendence of God with respect to the world, than of orthodox Lutheranism, which seems to have carved out a sort of middle way between total Calvinist transcendence and total Roman Catholic sacramentality.

The Roman Catholic perspective on faith and sacrament rests on its understanding of the essentially sacramental character of the Church. "God has gathered together as one all those who in faith look upon Jesus as the author of salvation and the source of unity and peace, and has established them as the Church, that for each and all she may be the visible sacrament of this saving unity."[66] The Church is the visible sacrament of unity, the Body of Christ, the incarnation in human reality of the presence of Jesus who was, and is, the incarnation in human reality of the presence of God. The Catholic Church perceives the Church as standing in a mediating position between men and women, on the one hand, and Jesus and God, on the other. It perceives the Church as exercising this mediation in symbolic and representative reality, in presence and action and grace and reconciliation and justification and faith. "It is in and by the Church that men come to justifying faith and participate vitally in the sacraments of Christ. It is in and by the Church, in virtue of its faith animated by the Spirit, that personal faith is salutary and sacraments efficacious."[67] This perspective on the mediating role of the Church presupposes, of course, a presence of God in Christ in the Church, a presence which is realized in word, in sacrament, in faith.

The relationship of faith and sacrament in the Catholic tradition presupposes the sacramentality of the total economy of salvation. The saving presence and action of God in Christ is mediated to individuals through that community which is formed and animated by spirit and by faith and which is called Ekklesia-Church. The faith of this Ekklesia is embodied and expressed in sacraments and is shared in by the individual's personal act of faith embodied and expressed and nourished in these same sacraments. As we have already seen, sacraments "not only presuppose faith, but by words and objects they also nourish, strengthen and express it. That is why they are called 'sacraments of faith.' "[68] In these words, the Second Vatican Council puts the Catholic position succinctly and beyond doubt. The faith of the recipient is necessary to transform human words and actions into religious sacraments.

SACRAMENT: ACT OF CHRIST

A statement introduced in the preceding section is basic in any contemporary Roman Catholic exposition of sacraments: "the sacraments are acts of Christ."[69] This statement, as we have seen, is already adumbrated in the insistence of both Augustine and Aquinas that the efficacy of sacraments is Christ-achieved efficacy. Negatively, it eliminates all crude, automatic, magical conceptions of sacraments as effective simply by doing the right action and saying the right words. Positively, it opens up a vast and rich perspective of theological meaning. Sacraments are not things, but religious actions. They are not mechanical grace machines, but sacred actions in which the Church proclaims and makes real and celebrates in representation the saving presence and action of God and his Christ.

In its decree *Dei Verbum,* the Second Vatican Council asserts that God's plan of revelation is realized by "deeds and words having an inner unity."[70] This is a description of the sacramental character of revelation, but it may be viewed also as a description of the sacramental character of the whole economy of salvation. In the Christian phase of this economy three moments may be specified: *incarnation,* in which the eternal God is embodied in the historical man Jesus; *Church,* in which the glorified Jesus is embodied in the community of those who confess that he is the Christ; *sacrament,* in which the Church, the Christ and God are made present and act in ritual actions.

This division of the order of sacramentality seems to be complete, and has been masterfully expounded by Edward Schillebeeckx. The primordial sacrament of God is the man Jesus. From him derive all other sacraments. In his death and resurrection from the dead, grace and salvation are achieved for all. But after his resurrection Jesus is glorified at the right hand of his Father, and if the salvation he accomplished is to be truly "for us," he must somehow be proclaimed, made real and celebrated concretely for us. Such concrete embodiment takes place, the Catholic tradition teaches, in the community of believers called Church, so that this Church may rightly be called the primordial sacrament of the risen Christ and of his saving action. Because the Church is the sacrament of Christ, acts of the church are also called, legitimately, sacraments.[71] The sacramental hierarchy, then, is this. The man Jesus is the sacrament of God. The Church is the sacrament of the risen Jesus and, therefore, also of God. The solemn ritual actions of the Church are sacraments of the presence and the action of Christ and of God. Sacraments, again, are not things. On the one hand, they are the saving presence and action of God and his Christ. On the other hand, for believers they are points of personal encounter with this God and his Christ.

The statement which opened this section needs now to be revised and expanded. Sacraments are actions not only of Christ, but also of God and of the Church. The action of God reaches men and women through a wide range of visible intermediaries. The first of these is the man Jesus of Nazareth whom Christians confess as man-God, and of whom it is said, "He who has seen me has seen the Father" (Jn 14:9). The second is the gathering of believers which is called Church and Body of Christ (cf. 1 Cor 6:12–20; 10:17; 12:12–27; Rom 12:4–5; Eph 1:22–23; 2:14–16; 3:6; 4:4–16; 5:22–30; Col 1:18, 24; 2:19; 3:15). The third are those solemn ritual actions of the Church which are called sacraments. The human animal, as we saw already, is a symbolic animal. The sacramental tradition is no more than the human symbolic tradition extended to the religious sphere.

In contemporary Catholic theology the use of the word sacrament has been extended. It is applied to Christ, who is described as the sacrament of God.[72] It is applied also to the Church, which is described as "a kind of sacrament,"[73] "the sacrament of unity,"[74] "the universal sacrament of salvation."[75] The application of the word to Christ and to the Church and to the individual Christian is an analogical use of the word. Christ, the Church, the Christian and many elements of the Christian life are called sacraments, legitimately, insofar as they are in some way akin to but still quite different from the ritual sacraments, signs and instruments of the grace of God mediated to men and women.

The growing extension of the analogical use of the word sacrament marks a renewed emphasis on the traditional Catholic theme that the grace of God is mediated to men and women in created reality. The Christian doctrines of two or seven sacraments simply focus attention on the general sacramentality of all creation. God always speaks and communicates himself, the Catholic tradition holds, in created "deeds and words."

Prior to the technical definition of the twelfth century, a wide range of created realities was acknowledged as sacramental of relationship to God: circumcision, sabbath, priesthood, figures of Christ in the Old Testament, and a multitude of others. Gradually the idea of the sacramentality of all creation was more narrowly focused in a technical definition, which in turn yielded the idea of the seven sacraments enunciated in the Catholic tradition.[76] The Protestant traditions have affirmed this sacramentality by affirming but two paradigms, baptism and Eucharist. What would seem to be important, however, is not whether Christians profess two or seven sacraments, but whether in whatever they profess they both discern and adequately express the sacramentality of all created reality.[77] And what the Christian tradition discerns and wishes to express in its sacramental doctrine is this. The presence and action of God and his Christ are effectively mediated to believers in symbolic actions called sacraments.

SACRAMENT: INSTITUTED BY CHRIST

Sacraments are ritual actions, in the Church, of God and his Christ. This theological statement includes another, namely, that Christ himself instituted these sacraments. That position is enshrined in the Catholic tradition by the Council of Trent. It teaches that "if anyone says that the sacraments of the New Law were not all instituted by Jesus Christ our Lord . . . let him be anathema." It teaches further that "the Church has always had the power to determine or to change, in the administration of the sacraments, whatever it judges to be more useful to the recipients or to the honor of the sacraments, in keeping with changing circumstances, times or places, always keeping the substance of the sacraments the same."[78] A very common, and commonly known, definition of sacrament is: "an outward sign instituted by Christ to give grace."[79]

These two doctrinal assertions are to be held together. *Because* Christ our Lord established the essential core of sacraments, the Church has no power to tamper with this core. Two crucial questions, however, remain unanswered. What did Christ establish as the essential core of sacraments? And how exactly did he do that? Neither of these questions has been settled dogmatically in any of the Christian churches, and so remains open for theological discussion. Many theoretical answers to these two questions have been proposed over the years. They can be reduced summarily to three.

A first, simple answer, which cannot stand up against the historical evidence, suggests that Christ determined explicitly each and every sacramental ritual. He determined, that is, both the sacramental action and the sacramental words which specify the action. That would mean, for instance, that for baptism he determined that the action would be some form of "immersion" in water and that the words would be some form of "I baptize you . . . etc." A second, more abstract solution, which also cannot stand against the historical evidence, suggests that Christ determined only the basic outline of sacramental ritual and left to the apostolic Church the task of giving this outline more precision. The post-apostolic Church is now bound to these apostolic precisions.

A third, thoroughly sacramental solution suggests that Christ did not determine the sacramental rituals in any explicit way, but did so implicitly in two separate actions. First, by being himself the human embodiment, that is, the sacrament, of God he set a pattern for such sacramental embodiment. Second, that pattern was replicated in his calling of the Church to be his body, that is, his sacrament, in the world. Jesus is the sacrament of God. The Church is the sacrament of Jesus. Formal, solemn actions of the Church, therefore, are actions also of Jesus and of God, implicitly established as such in the twofold establishment of Jesus as the sacrament of God and of the Church as sacrament of Jesus.

Such institution, though implicit, is real institution, "even if it were only later that reflection was directed to its sacramental character that flows from its connection with the nature of the Church. The institution of a sacrament can (it is not necessarily implied that it must always) follow simply from the fact that Christ founded the Church with its sacramental nature."[80] Each time the Church, the sacramental body of Christ, acts formally and solemnly as the Body of Christ its action is sacramental of Christ and of God. In the explicit institution of the Church is the implicit institution of sacramental action. Sacraments are, first, actions of the Church and only because they are actions of the Church are they in sacramental and symbolic reality actions of Christ and of God. Such implicit institution of sacramental actions is also the implicit determination of their meaning, namely, the proclamation, realization and celebration in representation of the presence and action of Christ and of God. It was precisely to embody this presence and action that the Church was called into being.

This book does not require, or permit, a detailed analysis of any of these positions. The questions to which they claim to be the answer have not been dogmatically settled and so remain open for free theological discussion. In this chapter, I have affirmed of sacraments that they are signs, in the Church, of the presence and action of God and his Christ. The solution to the question of institution which seems most in accord with this ecclesial dimension of sacraments, and therefore most persuasive, lies in the direction suggested by solution three. Besides, as I have said, neither of the first two solutions is tenable in the face of the historical evidence. As just one example, and more will appear in subsequent chapters, the emergence of the sacrament we know today as confirmation did not happen until the fourth century, and it was not called confirmation until the Council of Riez in France in 439. The anointing that became confirmation was originally part of a symbol-dense ritual of Christian initiation. The fourth century split it off from that root and made it a separate ritual, not to be faithful to a command of Jesus to "confirm and do it this way" (there is no such command) but for a much more mundane reason, namely, that it wished to reserve that anointing to the local bishop and he could not be simultaneously at all the Easter rituals of initiation in his diocese. Such historical information suggests that the solution to the question of the institution of sacraments by Jesus lies in the direction of solution three.[81]

Contemporary critical biblical scholarship, both Protestant and Catholic, has made it clear that the Gospels are not exact histories of Jesus' life in the way that a modern biography of a famous man is an exact history of his life. Their aim is "not to report all the words and deeds of Jesus in the exact order of their occurrence and in precisely the form and circumstances in which they were spoken and done, as we expect of contemporary biographies."[82] The Gospels do contain historical facts, but in addition to the facts they contain also the early Christian community's interpretation of these facts. Such an understanding of the New Testament makes it difficult to claim that it records actual explicit commands of Jesus to celebrate sacraments, even the two great sacraments of baptism and Eucharist. The New Testament does report such commands and attributes them to Jesus.[83] But whether such commands derive from Jesus or from the early Church's reflection on his words and actions is extremely difficult to say today.

This, however, is not to be interpreted to mean that Jesus does not express his will that there should be sacraments. Even if all the words put in Jesus' mouth by the Gospel writers are not verbatim reports of his speech, they do represent the early Church's understanding of his meaning and of the meaning of his words and actions, and therefore represent the revelation of God in Christ as received by the Church. Christ's institution of baptism and Eucharist is also an implicit institution, implicit in his establishment of a Church. For even if (please note that if) Jesus did not explicitly command on some specific occasion "that baptism should inaugurate membership in the community of his followers, he provided by his own baptism in the Jordan a model for the understanding of Christian discipleship."[84] Similarly, by celebrating a ritual meal with his disciples on the eve of his death, and by eating with them after his resurrection, he provided a ritual way for them to remember and celebrate both his and their new life.

The case of confirmation, though, is quite different from that of baptism and Eucharist, and confirms our thesis of implicit institution. As we have seen, the emergence of the sacrament Catholics know today as confirmation did not take place until the fourth century and for a very accidental, historical, human and mundane reason. The sacrament results from a clear choice of the fourth century Church, and not from any explicit institution by Jesus.

And yet the symbolic actions of confirmation were not chosen entirely at random. The choice followed a traditional Jewish action for ritually symbolizing the gift of God, namely, the laying on of hands, a ritual which Jesus frequently employed. "Christ during his earthly life had laid hands upon various people for various purposes: for blessing children, for healing, for the working of miracles of all kinds. . . . This was an undifferentiated, readily available and obvious rite which could be employed to many ends."[85] The fourth century Church used the same action to proclaim, realize and celebrate in symbolic reality the invisible gift and presence of the Spirit of God to men and women within the sacramental community called Church.

The case of confirmation confirms the general thesis of an implicit institution of sacraments. For if confirmation cannot be shown to have come into existence as a sacrament through an explicit statement of Christ descriptive of the rite, and yet can be shown to have been implicitly instituted by him in the way explained, this solution to the problem of institution becomes a general solution. There is nothing to exclude the same possibility for anointing of the sick, orders and marriage, all cases where an explicit, detailed institution cannot be demonstrated. One case confirms the possibility for all cases.

The metaphysical essence or substance of a sacrament as a sign consists, formally, in its meanings and, materially, in the sensible action in which these meanings are proclaimed, realized and celebrated. The physical essence or substance of a sacrament as a sign consists, formally, in the words spoken and, materially, in the actions performed. The institution of the sacraments by Christ is of their metaphysical essence; the physical essence, that is, the sacramental words and actions, is left to the discretion of the Church.[86] That the Church has always taken seriously its charge of the physical essence is quite clear from the theological history of each sacrament.

SACRAMENT: A SUMMARY DEFINITION

As a result of the foregoing analysis, a contemporary definition of sacrament becomes possible. A sacrament is a prophetic symbol, established by and modeled upon Christ the symbol of God, in and by which the Church, the Body of Christ, proclaims, realizes and celebrates for believers who place no obstacle that presence and action of God, which is rightly called grace. Every element of this definition, with the one exception of grace, has been explained already. A brief comment on each will serve to summarize, and perhaps to clarify further, all that has been said already. An extended note will explain the meaning of grace.

A sacrament is a sign. The category and direction established by

Augustine and carried on by the entire Christian theological tradition is retained. But a sacrament is not a simple sign, and its meanings are not simple meanings. It is, rather, that specialized kind of sign called symbol and, indeed, that very specific kind of symbol called prophetic or religious symbol. A prophetic symbol is an ordinary human action which on one level of reality, the natural-literal level, has an ordinary meaning, but which on another level of reality, the representative-symbolic level, has quite another meaning, indeed set of meanings. Water, for instance, on the natural level means life and death and cleansing. On the level of representative symbol, therefore, immersion in water is wonderfully apt to proclaim and realize and celebrate in representation death and resurrection and cleansing from sin, as it does in baptism. Marriage, for instance, on the natural level, means the union of this man and this woman, and bespeaks their mutual love, mutual caring, mutual service. On the level of representative symbol, therefore, it is wonderfully apt to proclaim and realize and celebrate in representation the union of Christ and his Church, and their mutual love, mutual caring, and mutual service, as it does in the sacrament of Christian marriage. As prophetic symbol, of course, sacrament will have all the properties and characteristics of symbols and religious symbols assigned in Chapter One. Those need not be repeated here.

"A sacrament is a prophetic symbol, established by and modeled upon Christ the symbol of God." This phrase recalls our earlier discussion of institution. By being himself, on the natural level, a man who, on the representative-symbolic level, is believed to be the incarnation, embodiment, symbol of God, and by calling into being a Church which, on the natural level, is but a collection of men and women who, on the representative-symbolic level, are believed to be the incarnation, symbol, Body of Christ, Jesus the Christ set patterns for sacramental realization. In its actions the Church follows these established patterns, and when it acts solemnly and formally as the Body of Christ, its actions are the actions not just of these men and these women, but symbolically also of Christ. Such actions of the Church, therefore, are themselves, eo ipso, sacramental actions. On a natural level, they appear to be ordinary, natural actions: immersion in or with water, anointing with oil, sharing a meal of bread and wine, sharing a marriage. But, on a representative-symbolic level, they are far from ordinary, natural actions. They are symbolic actions, proclaiming and realizing and celebrating in representative reality, respectively, the death-resurrection of Jesus and of believers, the presence of the Spirit of God in believers, the presence of the crucified and risen Christ in his sacramental Body, the loving and indissoluble union between

Christ and his Church. To the extent that these prophetically symbolic actions are patterned upon Christ the symbol of God, we can rightly say that they were established or instituted by him.

Though signs and symbols always signify, they do not always *effectively* signify for any given person. The same is true, therefore, of sacramental-prophetic symbols. A prophetic symbol always proclaims the presence and saving action in the Church of Christ and of God. But that it effectively proclaims and realizes and celebrates that presence for any given man or woman depends upon the man or the woman. This characteristic of symbols is enshrined in the definition in the phrase *believers who place no obstacle*. In the minimalistic meaning of the Council of Trent, placing no obstacle meant being free from grave sin. But in the broader Catholic tradition it means much more. It means, and requires, a positive action of a free person, who believes in, trusts in, surrenders to, accepts, and lives into the personal God mediated in this symbol as grace. Only when such a personal activity, an *opus operantis*, is brought to the symbol does the symbol become an effective symbol for this person, and only then does it effectively proclaim and realize and celebrate the presence and the action in the Church of Christ and of God and of grace. It is the active faith of a believer, who shares the faith of the Church, that transforms ordinary, natural actions into far-from-ordinary prophetic symbols.

The medieval tradition taught that sacraments conferred the grace they signified *ex opere operato*. But the intimately Christological character of this dogmatic assertion has already been demonstrated. A sacrament confers grace, salvation, justification *ex opere operato*, but "this is not man's work, but God's"[87] in Christ. A sacrament effects grace, not because of some magical *opus operatum* or rite, but solely because the *opus operatum* is an *opus Christi et Dei*, an action of Christ and of God. It is God in his Christ who effects grace and justification, not an external ritual, however carefully and validly and licitly executed. Grace is not something dispensed from a sacramental machine. It is, rather, something ultimately and uniquely personal.

The personal character of grace demands an equally personal response, for *personal* bespeaks freedom, responsibility, self-giving, not coercion or automaticity. The essential necessity of this personal *opus operantis* for effective sacramental signification and, therefore, also efficacy is radically asserted in the phrase *believers who place no obstacle*.

As will be demonstrated in the note on grace, grace and salvation always exist for man as *offered*. They exist as not only offered but also *accepted* only when a human person freely and responsibly accepts them. The *opus operantis*, the personal faith, love, trust, living into, expressed in his reception of the sacrament is precisely that element which permits actualization of the sacrament as both practical and efficacious sign. The work of God in his Christ and the work of the believer are together necessary to any fruitful or efficacious sacrament. The declaration of the Council of Florence stands unchanged: sacraments give grace to those who receive them worthily.[88]

A sacrament is a prophetic symbol, in and by which the Church proclaims, realizes and celebrates the presence of *grace*. Now grace is a common theological word, but not necessarily as commonly understood. The English word *grace* derives from the Latin word *gratia* which, in the Vulgate, translates the Greek word *charis*. Grace has acquired many secondary meanings in theological history, but its prime meaning still derives from its scriptural source, where its meaning reduces to three main ideas: "condescending love, conciliatory compassion and fidelity. The basic sense of Christian grace, whatever its later technical or non-Scholastic connotations, should always remind us that God first loved us."[89] John insists that this sums up the secret of grace: "In this is love, not that we loved God, but that he first loved us" (1 Jn 4:10).

In technical theological language, God giving himself in love is called uncreated grace. The effect of this personal love which transforms men and women and their world is called created or sanctifying grace. Grace, therefore, has two traditional theological meanings: first, God giving himself in love,[90] and, second, something other than God, a transformation produced in men and women. These two meanings are, of course, not unrelated, but the exact nature of their relationship has been for centuries a matter for theological dispute.

In the Eastern Catholic tradition the idea of uncreated grace has dominated, created grace remaining a practically unknown concept. Even in the West no clear formulation of created grace was known for eleven hundred years.[91] But the Reformation disputes placed created grace so squarely in the forefront of theological discussion in the West, and post-Reformation Roman Catholic theology made it so much the primary reality of grace, that the use of the word *grace* without addition came to mean created grace, a reality different from God. Uncreated grace, God's gift of himself to men and women, was lost sight of as the source of created grace and, instead, became a consequence or necessary fruit of it. Created grace became the primary reality of grace, and was assumed to yield as one of its fruits the indwelling of God or uncreated grace.

How may this Western view, in which a reality different from God yields the presence of God as its necessary consequence, be harmonized with the view of the Scriptures and the Fathers of the Church, in which created grace appears as the consequence of God's prior self-communication to men? An effort to solve this thorny question has been made in modern theology, and has won wide acceptance.[92] It begins with a consideration of the relationship of the state of grace to the ultimate vision of God which is salvation.

It is common Western teaching that in heavenly glory there is an intimate union between God and the saved. This union is of an interpersonal kind, that is, it is achieved in knowledge and in love. But this creaturely knowledge and love of God are not achieved in the normal way, that is, mediately. Rather, God unites himself immediately to the creature and moves him to know and love God. This union of God and his human creatures in glory is of an ontological nature, that is, it is a union of *beings* before it is a union of conscious knowledge or love. In the vision of God creatures are ontologically assimilated to God before they reflexively know or love God. In fact, it is only *because* they are ontologically united to him that they can know and love him immediately, face to face.

This analysis of the presence of God to creatures in heavenly glory may be applied analogically to the question of how to articulate humanly the presence of God to them in their human lives, that is, to the question of how to talk in human terms about the presence of uncreated grace. For the union between God and men and women in their earthly life is presented in the Scripture and tradition of the Church as the seed and root of their union in heaven. Theologians, therefore, take the theory and concepts relating to the presence of God to his creatures in heavenly glory, their being possessed by and their possession of him, and relate them to the presence of God as uncreated grace in human life.

God, who himself is uncreated grace, creates men and women and their world, and offers himself to them at their creation. It is this offer, which is above and beyond the needs of their human nature, that Karl Rahner characterizes as a supernatural elevation or supernatural existential.[93] In this theory men and women live always and everywhere in an economy of grace; they live in a radically graced world. Creation is but the beginning of grace, the first grace, in which God makes creatures in and with whom he dwells as uncreated grace, and whom he seeks to draw into personal, loving, transforming, and therefore gracious, dialogue with himself. As in the vision of God in heaven, so also in human lives God dwells in his creatures prior to their personally knowing or loving him (Jn 14:23; 1 Jn 2:6, 24, 27–28; 3:6, 24; 4:12–16; 1 Cor 6:19; Rom 5:5; 8:9–16; Gal 4:6; 1 Thess 4:8). The presence of God, of uncreated grace, is not a consequence of the transformation in men and women that is called grace, but rather a cause of it. For that transformation, created grace, exists only when God is actually present and acting to transform.

This, then, raises the question: If men and women live in a fundamentally graced world, what is the specific contribution of Christian sacraments to the living of a life of grace, a life of relationship with God? The answer is not difficult to find, certainly not for anyone who followed and understood the discussion on the functioning of symbols in Chapter One. Boy, for instance, meets girl; boy and girl fall in love; boy loves girl and girl loves boy. There is only one problem: it is not obvious to the boy that the girl loves him; he does not recognize the love for him that is really in her, nor does she recognize the love for her that is in him. And so it remains until they *make love* in some symbolic action of loving. When they do, their mutual love is drawn into mutual and personal realization, and thereafter their relationship is one of ever-growing love to the extent that they continue to make love in the symbols accepted by them. The case of grace and sacrament is almost an exact parallel to the case of love.

Uncreated grace, the loving self-giving of God to all men and women, exists long prior to any sacramental action. Every man and woman created by God is enveloped in grace, for grace "is God himself in his forgiving and divinizing love."[94] Because of this offered uncreated grace, history for every person is a history of possible grace and salvation, quite apart from any sacramental activity. But, as with the boy who does not recognize the girl's love for him, so neither do men and women always recognize the presence of the God who is Grace. To realize the possibility of grace, they need to *make grace,* as he needs to make love, in some symbolic action. Christian sacraments, though they are, of course, not the sole or exclusive ways to make grace, are nevertheless ways to do so. When men and women engage in sacramental action, they proclaim and realize and celebrate in it not only the presence of grace as offered by God, but also the presence of grace as accepted by them. The gracious offer of God and the faithful acceptance of that offer by believers together, in and through the prophetic and symbolic and sacramental action, make grace. The Grace which is made is primarily, and none other than, God himself; only secondarily, and as a consequence of God's presence and action, is it the justifying transformation of men and women that is known as created or sanctifying grace.

If all this is so, it is no longer possible adequately to describe grace in impersonal terms like created quality, accident, *habitus.* Personal terms are required such as God, Father, Christ, Spirit, Love, Lover, Self-communication.[95] This personal characteristic of grace, at least from the human point of view, is included in the definition of sacrament in the phrase *for believers who place no obstacle.* When grace is understood in the context of God's personal offer seeking men's and women's personal response, the mere avoidance of serious sin cannot be considered adequately faithful response, dogmatically recognized as minimal though it be. Men and women are saved only as free, responsible persons. This is as true within the sacramental context as without it. Free, personal acceptance of offered grace is as essential to justification and salvation as the most careful and exact performance of rite. Again, sacraments are not things. They are prophetic symbols in the Church, the Body of Christ, in which the free self-giving of God in Christ is answered with free acceptance by believing men and women.

The foregoing analysis enables us to understand a traditional statement about sacraments, namely, sacrament is a *cause* of grace. Again, the analogy we used earlier will be helpful. Boy meets girl; boy and girl fall in love; but neither yet knows that the other loves him or her; and so it remains until they make love in some symbolic gesture or other. He writes her a letter, he takes her hand, he kisses her, he gives her flowers. In these symbolic gestures he proclaims his love for her, realizes his love, not only for her but also for himself, and celebrates it. And in the symbols she is confronted by his love, enriched by it and moved to respond personally to it. The symbolic actions not only signify love, but they effect love concretely in both the boy and the girl. The effect, love made concrete and practical, is wholly due to the boy and the girl as principal causes and to the symbols of love-making as instrumental causes. As it is with love and the symbols of love, so it is also with grace and the sacramental symbols of grace.

God, uncreated grace, creates men and women and, over and above what is required for their human nature, offers himself to them. Most of his creatures, though, do not recognize this offer of self that is Grace; before they can recognize it in practical concreteness they need to make grace as the boy and the girl need to make love. They do this in symbolic actions called sacraments, which not only proclaim the presence of grace, but also realize it in the concrete and celebrate it. As with love and the symbols of love-making, this effect is due not only to Grace himself as principal cause, but also to the sacramental actions as instrumental causes. The causality of sacraments, then, is quite correctly called symbolic instrumental causality.[96]

If the notion of symbol I am presenting is grasped, there is no problem explaining the causality of sacraments. It is necessary only to recall the specific difference between simple sign and symbol. The former announces that what it signifies is present; the latter proclaims and realizes and celebrates the presence of what it symbolizes. To say symbol, therefore, is already to say cause. And to say sacrament is already to say instrumental cause, for only God and his Christ could ever be the principal cause of his gracious presence. Sacraments cause grace "in the sense that in the Church God's grace is given expression and embodiment and symbolized, and by being so embodied is present."[97]

But there is a theological problem in defining sacrament as a cause of grace, raised by what is known as the valid but fruitless sacrament. The problem may be stated simply. A reality should always verify its definition. If, therefore, a sacrament is defined in terms of causing grace, it should always and everywhere cause grace each time the symbolic action is done. But there are sacraments which, by common theological agreement, do not confer grace, namely, those which are received without the proper disposition. How, then, can a sacrament be defined essentially as a cause of grace?

An initial answer to this question underscores that it is not a good question, for it is rooted in a false presupposition. It assumes a very physical and mechanical notion of both sacrament and grace, as if the sacramental action alone were involved in the conferring of grace, with no personal contribution from those celebrating the action. Such a view is, as I have shown, hopelessly inadequate to deal with genuine human sacrament. Sacrament is defined not merely as a symbol which symbolizes and by symbolizing causes grace, but also as a symbol which confers grace on *believers who place no obstacle to it*. That final qualifying phrase is intended to be an *essential* element in the definition of sacrament, so that if that element is lacking the sacramental symbol does not effect the concrete presence of grace.

The Council of Trent distinguished carefully between what it called containing grace and conferring grace. "Sacraments contain the grace they signify and confer that grace on *those who do not place an obstacle*."[98] Sacraments always contain grace, in the sense that they always symbolize the presence of grace, but they do not always cause grace. They do not cause grace absolutely and indiscriminately and against a person's will. They cause it, that is, they proclaim, realize and celebrate it in representation, only for those who provide the necessary personal climate for it. This climate is described by the Council of Florence as worthy reception, by the Council of Trent as placing no obstacle, and by the classical theological tradition as *opus operantis*. A free, positive, cooperating, personal contribution on the part of believers who celebrate and concelebrate sacraments is an essential requirement for it to cause grace in them.

I have sought to show that a sacrament is a prophetic symbol in the Church. That is, it is an action which, on one level of reality, is a quite ordinary and natural action which, on another level, is a far from ordinary symbol which proclaims and realizes and celebrates in representation what it symbolizes. What transforms ordinary action into prophetic symbol is, in the first place, the faith of the community called Church which, in the second place, is shared by believing members of that community. Without this social and personal faith, this comprehensive yes to God, as we have described it, ordinary action remains just ordinary action: washing with water, anointing with oil, eating bread and drinking wine. It does not become prophetic symbol. And since it does not become prophetic symbol, neither does it proclaim and realize and celebrate that presence and action of God and his Christ which is called, and which causes, Grace.

The sacrament which is a prophetic symbol "is not only the visible manifestation of Christ's redemptive act . . . but [is] also the visible expression of the recipient's desire for grace."[99] Only when the gracing action of God is matched by the accepting faith of a believer is prophetic symbol created and grace caused. In sum and in fine, the definition of sacrament as cause of grace includes not only God's and Christ's and the Church's gracious *opus operatum*, but also the believer's faith-filled *opus operantis*. Sacrament is not a magical imposition of grace, but a free offer of grace which is freely accepted or rejected by a free human being.

SACRAMENT AS COMMUNAL AND PERSONAL

The preceding section hinted at the communal and personal dimension of both faith and sacrament. A more explicit, if brief, treatment of this dimension will conclude this chapter. Symbols, we have seen, function to inform and to provoke to action. They function thus not only for individuals but also for communities. In and through its symbols, a human community proclaims its vision of the human world; it fixes the parameters of that world; it orders the constituent elements within that world; it assigns roles and goals and patterns of believing and acting and reacting in that world. In and through its symbols, a human community proclaims and realizes and celebrates not only what it ultimately believes in, but also what kind of community it wishes to be and what kind of individual it wishes to have as a member. Sacramental, prophetic symbols function that way within the Christian community. They proclaim and realize and celebrate in representation not only the presence and action of God and his Christ, but also the Christian community as a community which believes that the presence is mediated to believers in symbols called sacraments.

The standpoint of this community, therefore, with respect to the presence of God in the world is a standpoint that is thoroughly sacramental. It is a standpoint that is taught to its members and that is mutually reinforced by these members in their ongoing interactions. The Christian world is a world in which God is present, not abstractly but very concretely because very sacramentally. The Christian is a person who relates to God, not abstractly but concretely because sacramentally. Such a world and such a person are fashioned and sustained in the ongoing symbolic interaction which takes place within the Christian community. God and man and woman and their various interactions are elements of the Christian world that are taken for granted. Sacramentality is a bedrock in the Christian tradition.

Several times already in this book I have insisted that symbols are made to be used, and that they are used in a community to inform and to provoke to action and interaction. To repeat Whitehead's phrase: "symbolism makes connected thought possible by expressing it, while at the same time it automatically directs action."[100] Sacraments do that within the Christian community. They inform Christians, in general, of the sacramental nature of their relationship with God and, in particular, of the nature of God and of his Christ, of the nature of the Church, of the nature of the believer, and of what the believer should do about it all. A full development of what sacraments say precisely about God, about Jesus, about Church, about the believer and about the believer's behavior would require a book in itself. I shall sketch that information here only in broad strokes.

Sacraments inform believers that the encounter between God and them in this world is sacramental. They say in actions that both God's offer of gracious presence and the believer's acknowledgement and acceptance of that offer are proclaimed, made real and celebrated in ritual actions. In and from the sacramental practice of their Church, Christians learn that God and his grace are first *concretely* proclaimed, realized and celebrated by them (not, however, first offered to them) in the ritual waters of baptism. They learn that the gift of grace called the Holy Spirit, first proclaimed and realized and celebrated in the waters of baptism, is symbolized again in the anointing in confirmation. They learn that when they have cut themselves off from God and from grace, forgiveness and reconciliation may be proclaimed and realized and celebrated in the ritual of reconciliation. They learn that they celebrate the Body of Christ, both his personal and his sacramental Body, the Church, in the sacred meal of bread and wine. They learn that special moments in their lives are Graced and graced, moments of sickness and death, of marriage, of ordination to ministry. They learn, in short, that the presence of God in the world is proclaimed and realized and celebrated in sacramental symbols, or not concretely at all.

Sacraments also inform believers about God. They portray him insistently as trinitarian, confessing him from the first moment of baptism to the healing moment of anointing as almighty Father, only Son and Holy Spirit. They portray him as an active God: as one who "at the very dawn of creation . . . breathed on the waters, making them the well-spring of all holiness";[101] as the one to "give you a new heart and place a new spirit within you and make you live by statutes" (Ez 36:26–27); as the one who is "the Creator of the universe, maker of man and woman . . . source of all blessing";[102] as "the source of every honor and every office";[103] as the one who "brings healing to the sick through his Son, Jesus Christ."[104] Sacramental symbols inform believers that God is Creator, life-giver, source of every blessing, and invite them to believe and trust and hope and be grateful in a life patterned after the life of Jesus, his Son.

As they provide information about God, sacraments simultaneously provide information about men and women. If God is Creator, men and women appear as his creatures; if God is Father, they appear as his children; if God is the source of all blessings, they are the recipients of his blessings; if God is the giver of the new heart, they stand in need of a new heart; if God is the one who forgives sins, men and women are the sinners who stand in need of forgiveness. This latter piece of information, in particular, is ubiquitous in sacramental activity. Baptism demands an explicit renunciation of sin and of "Satan, father of sin and prince of darkness,"[105] a renunciation which is demanded again in confirmation. The ritual of ordination prays: "From all sin, Lord, deliver us. . . . Be merciful to us sinners."[106] The sick are anointed that they may be freed from sin "and made well again in body, mind and soul."[107] Insistently, the Christian who lives into sacramental symbols learns that he is a sinner.

But if prophetic symbols present man and woman as sinners, simultaneously they offer them hope by presenting Jesus as Savior. He is the one whom God has sent into the world to cast out the power of Satan, to rescue men and women from the spirit of darkness and bring them into the kingdom of light.[108] Confirmation further emphasizes that those who have been freed from sin by dying and rising with

Christ in baptism should reflect in their lives, not the life of sin, but the new life of Christ in the Spirit. And Eucharist, of course, is the great symbolic paradigm of Jesus' self-sacrifice for, and transformation of, the sinful condition. If men and women are informed in sacraments that they are sinners, they are equally informed that there is a Savior, and are invited to believe in him and live according to that belief.

Sacraments, finally, inform about the role of the Church. Those to be baptized are signed with the cross of Christ and, in the name of the Church, are claimed for Christ the Savior. Those who have been baptized are made sharers in the faith of the Church, which confesses the Father, the Son and the Holy Spirit, and rejects Satan and sin. Confirmation in the Church proclaims and celebrates the Spirit, who is first given to the Church; reconciliation reconciles with God by first reconciling, as we shall see, with the Church; the prayer of the Church, made in faith, saves the sick person (Jas 5:13); marriage is celebrated in the Church and is witnessed by the Church in the person of the Church's minister; ministers are ordained to minister in the Church, to proclaim forgiveness in the name of the Church, to celebrate liturgy in the Church, to console the sick in the Church. If the trinitarian God saves men and women in Christ, that gracious salvation, sacraments announce, is proclaimed, realized and celebrated in the symbolic actions of the Church.

What is critical about the information provided to believers by sacraments is that it is absorbed, not logically, but personally, in the way that was claimed earlier for all symbols. The knowledge acquired through sacraments is not scientific knowledge in clear and distinct ideas, but personal knowledge in confused sensation, images, intuitions and ideas. Such personal knowledge is, in Whitehead's judgment, *vague* and, in Ricoeur's, *opaque*. But it is no less informative for being vague and opaque, nor does it provoke any less to action and reaction. On the contrary, precisely because symbolic knowledge is vague and opaque it is powerful, for its vagueness and opaqueness are perceived to bespeak not emptiness, but inexhaustible richness and fullness. Sacramental symbols, as do all symbols, open up depths of reality that cannot be adequately grasped or adequately understood in clear and distinct ideas. Sacraments speak more to the Eastern than to the Western lobe.

Because the knowledge absorbed from sacraments is personal and self-involving, not logical and detached, it is very much value-laden. Of its very nature it provokes the selection of some realities and some forms of actions over others. Symbols are always nomic. They put a definite construction upon the events through which people live, enabling them to orient themselves within the constant flux of their experience. Prophetic symbols do the same. When Christians have successfully internalized the information that God graces them with new life in baptism, with forgiveness and reconciliation in penance-reconciliation, with personal healing in anointing, this information puts reality in order and evaluates it. Following internalization, it makes no sense to ask whether God and Christ are present in sacraments or not. The answer is given prior to the question: of course they are. Unfortunately, the temptation is always there and has not always been resisted in popular preaching and belief, to give a stronger answer, namely, that God is encountered *only* in sacraments. That has never been an orthodox Christian position, not even an orthodox Catholic Christian position, and it has been firmly excluded already in this book.

The explanation of prophetic symbols proposed in this book lets God and believers and their inter-relationship be ultimately important. It lets sacraments be important, but not ultimately; they are important only as symbolic instruments of this relationship within the Christian community. God and believers relate not exclusively in two or nine or even twenty-nine sacraments, but in many prophetic and symbolic ways—not exclusively within the Christian community, but also outside it. Sacraments do not grace and justify and save ultimately; only God does. And God graces and justifies and saves all those men and women, Christian and non-Christian alike, who place no obstacle to his saving action. But for the moment in our human life, faith and symbolically-mediated presence is all there is; only in the end will both faith and sacrament give way to being possessed and possessing. "For now we see in a mirror dimly, but then face to face. Now I see in part; then I shall understand fully, even as I have been fully understood" (1 Cor 13:12).

Chapter Three
BAPTISM: RITUAL OF LIFE AND DEATH

"I baptize you in the name of the Father" (minister pours a first time), "and of the Son" (minister pours water a second time), "and of the Holy Spirit" (minister pours water a third time). It is the sacrament of baptism, and here we begin our delving into the unfathomable depths of what is proclaimed, made real and celebrated in representation in the sacraments.

CHRISTIAN RITUAL

In time a number of Jews heard and believed the unbelievable news that "Christ died for our sins, that he was buried, and that he was raised" (1 Cor 15:3–4). Later they presented the life of Jesus as consistently directed toward this death and resurrection, designated as his *hour*. John defines this hour as a passage: "Jesus knew that his hour had come to pass out of this world to the Father" (13:1). By his death the man from Nazareth is separated from a previously fixed state in which he was named Jesus. In death he is in a liminal state, a state of nothingness, in which he does not have a personal name but is designated simply by what happened to him, the Crucified. But again, as in the beginning, they believed, God breathed life into the nothingness. "God raised him up, having loosed the pangs of death" (Acts 2:24), brought Jesus to a new state of life with him, a state in which he received a new personal name, Christ. His passage is complete.

In the opening chapter of this book I dealt with prophetic symbol in general and with the prophetic water symbol in particular. That water symbol, *tebilah*, to paraphrase Audrey Richard's powerful phrase, grows a Jew.[1] When faced with the question of how to grow to be like Christ, those Jews who became the first Christians reached back into their tradition and retrieved the growing ritual. Jesus had gone down into the chaos of death and from death had been raised by God to newness of life. To grow to be like Christ men and women would have to do the same, go down into death and be raised to a new life. What better way to go down into death—symbolically—than to go down into the primordial water, and from there be raised by God to newness of life? In short, what better way than to be baptized? And so baptized they were.[2]

In the early Syrian church the emphasis of the ritual fell on womb and birth, as in John's "unless one is born of water and the Spirit, he cannot enter the kingdom of God" (3:5). In the early Palestinian church the emphasis fell on tomb and death and resurrection, as in Paul's "were buried, therefore, with him by baptism into death, so that as Christ was raised from the dead by the glory of the Father, [they] too might walk in newness of life" (Rom 6:4). But the tomb and womb, death and life, meanings came together, and the baptismal ritual was explicitly interpreted in both ways. We see this very clearly in the second mystagogical catechesis of Cyril of Jerusalem, who teaches: "Afterwards, you were led to the holy pool of divine baptism, as Christ was borne from the cross to the prepared sepulchre. And each was asked whether he believed in the name of the Father and of the Son and of the Holy Spirit. And you confessed the saving faith and were immersed three times in the water and emerged again. In this way you signified in image and in symbol the three-day burial of Christ. . . . In the very same moment you were both dead and born, and that saving water became *both tomb and mother (womb)* to you."[3]

Cyril's catechesis gives us an insight into how baptism was celebrated. The person to be baptized went down into the baptismal pool, explicitly perceived as a tomb and as a womb, was immersed three times in the name of the Father and of the Son and of the Holy Spirit, and emerged again out of the pool. The going down into the pool evokes meanings of leaving a previous state. The being immersed in the primordial water evokes meanings of being dead to that previous state, of being nothing. The rising out of the water in the name of God evokes meanings of being drawn by God, yet again, as in the beginning, out of nothingness into life.

In this baptismal ritual a Christian is grown, at least inchoately. It is not just a matter of desiring or hoping for or talking about new life. As God transformed Jesus from being dead to being alive with him, so also he transforms the one who is baptized from being not-Christian to being Christian. When they talked about what happened to them as being "a new creation" (2 Cor 5:17), or as being "born of water and the Spirit" (Jn 3:5), they were talking about a transformation in the depths of their beings, not just about a transformation from one point to another in the social order. The transformation can be misunderstood, of course, as it was misunderstood by Nicodemus who interpreted it as returning to the maternal womb. But it is no less real for not being physical. The return to the primordial womb, symbolized by the water, effects a transformation so real that, by general consent in the community of believers, it can be said that it grows a Christian.

The Western Father of the Church, Tertullian (d. ca. 225), declares that it is hardly surprising that baptism gives life, because "water first produced that which had life." He had already explained that in baptism, although a person is dipped in the water without much pomp and emerges apparently little cleaner, he is still transformed by the power of God.[4] The Greek Father, Gregory Nazianzen (d. 390), insists that in baptism God, who created us in the first place, recreates us "with an even more divine creation, loftier than the first," and totally transforming of the first.[5] John Chrysostom also focuses on this theme of old and new creations, and on the power of God which effects both.[6] Gregory of Nyssa (d. 394), yet another Greek Father, insists that though the regeneration achieved in baptism is not a physical regeneration, it is nonetheless real and effected, not by water, but by the power of God "creating and easily producing what he wants, while veiling from us any knowledge of his operation."[7]

Several points are clear. In the early Church baptism was conceived as a new creation, a new birth, effected in and through the ritual water by the Spirit of God, without any merit on the part of man or woman. The various names by which it is known highlight these points. "We call it gift, grace, baptism, anointing, illumination, clothing of incorruption, bath of regeneration, seal. We call it gift because it is given to those who contributed nothing; grace because it is given to debtors; baptism because sin is buried in the waters; anointing, priestly and kingly, because such were those who were anointed; illumination because it is splendor and light; clothing because it veils our shame; bath because it cleanses us; seal because it preserves us."[8] But, for all its wonder, the re-creation and rebirth effected in baptism are not yet definitive. For sin can rise again from the waters, and require, as we shall see, a "second baptism"; the illumination can be dimmed again; shame can appear again through the baptismal clothing; the baptized can be sullied again and can be eroded in his new life—all of which means, quite simply, that the Christian is grown only inchoately in baptism; definitive growth, definitively becoming a Christian, requires a living into that baptism and its demands in one's concrete, historical life.[9]

We have already explained that the many meanings embodied in a symbol cluster around two poles, the orectic and the ideological, and that the bipolar meanings connect and interact through the thoughts, the feelings and the actions of those who live into the symbols. Water is clearly a dominant symbol in the ritual of baptism, indeed *the* dominant symbol from the fourth century onward. At its orectic pole, in the culture in which it evolved as symbol, water was perceived as both life-giving and death-dealing. At its ideological pole, therefore, it readily proclaims, realizes and celebrates thoughts and feelings and actions of life and death. Israelites, first, and then Christians, channeled these thoughts and feelings and actions in the directions that moved them most, Israelites toward the passage of exodus, Christians toward the passage of Jesus from this life to God. But at its orectic pole, as well as meaning life and death, water also means cleansing. And this literal meaning of cleansing gave rise to an ideological meaning of cleansing which became normative in the Christian Church.

In the early centuries of Christianity, the dominant meaning among the many meanings of baptism was that of dying and being raised again like Jesus. Indeed that meaning was so dominant that the baptismal ritual was celebrated only at the Easter season. Already *The Apostolic Tradition* of Hippolytus (ca. 215), which provides a detailed picture of a Roman ritual of initiation,[10] indicates that baptism was celebrated at the Easter vigil. At about the same time, Tertullian explains that "Easter provides a more than solemn day for baptism, a day on which the passion of the Lord, in which we are baptized, was consummated."[11] He allows also that Pentecost, through its connection to resurrection, is also a suitable day. In 447, Pope Leo the Great wrote to the bishops of Sicily condemning their practice of baptizing on the feast of the Epiphany and insisting that baptism at Easter is the apostolic tradition. Easter is the appointed time for baptism, he declares, because "through the image and form of the sacrament (*mysterii*) what is achieved in the members corresponds to what was achieved in the head. For in the baptismal ritual death results from the slaying of sin, the threefold immersion imitates the three days in the tomb, and the rising up from the waters is like the rising [of the Lord] from the tomb." Like Tertullian, though, he allows that Pentecost too may be used as a time for baptism, for it is a kind of completion of Easter.[12]

The time-symbolism of Easter reinforced the proclamation and celebration of death and resurrection. There was no rush to baptize anyone, especially since sacramental rituals were regarded as but parts of the total process of initiating into life in Christ, though the Fathers did exhort their catechumens not to postpone baptism inordinately.[13] But there came a change.

BAPTISM AND ORIGINAL SIN

The literal cleansing meaning of water always donated ideological cleansing meaning to the ritual of baptism. The sins that were believed to be cleansed in the ritual bath, however, were initially personal sins, as Paul makes clear. Writing to the Corinthians he declares: "Neither the immoral, nor idolators, nor adulterers, nor homosexuals, nor thieves, nor the greedy, nor drunkards, nor revilers, nor robbers will inherit the kingdom of God. And such were some of you. But you were washed, you were sanctified, you were justified in the name of the Lord Jesus Christ and in the Spirit of our God" (1 Cor 6:9–11). The author of the Letter to the Ephesians declares more comprehensively that "Christ loved the Church and gave himself up for her, that he might sanctify her, having cleansed her by the washing of water with the word" (5:25–26). And the later author of the Letter to the Hebrews invites them to approach the sanctuary "with our hearts sprinkled clean from an evil conscience and our bodies washed with pure water" (10:22). That cleansing from personal sins continued as a meaning of baptism in the early Church can easily be discerned from the sayings of the Fathers which we have considered.

But in the fifth century, especially under the influence of the powerful Augustine, bishop of Hippo, there emerged a new meaning for the baptismal ritual. Not only does it cleanse from personal sin, but also from that sin of the race that came to be known as original sin, the sin of Adam and Eve, an original parent couple, transmitted by human generation to all their descendants. Every human person, it came to be believed, because descended from Adam and Eve, was born into the world with an inherited stain of sin which required cleansing. From the fifth century onward, baptism was looked upon predominantly as the ritual which cleansed this sin.

It is not my intention to enter here upon a prolonged discussion of original sin. The scope of this book neither demands nor permits such a discussion. But I do wish to make two points, concerning the theologies of original sin and of the ritual of baptism. The first is this: the originally dominant meaning of Christian baptism, namely, celebration of and assimilation into the death and resurrection of Jesus, at a specific time in history, namely, the fifth century, ceded its dominance to a new meaning, namely, cleansing from original sin. The second is this: cleansing from inherited sin makes sound anthropological, and therefore theological, sense—but only in a community of people who perceive themselves as so connected one with the other that the shame of one is the shame of the other. Conversely, it makes no sense, neither anthropological nor theological, in a community of people who perceive themselves as so unconnected and individual that the shame of one leaves the other totally unaffected. I would like to expand on this latter point, however briefly.

Paul has been the great teacher of original sin for Christian thought, specifically in his Letter to the Romans 5:12–21. There he teaches that "sin came into the world through one man and death through sin" (5:12); that "because of one man's trespass death reigned through that one man" (5:17); that "one man's trespass led to condemnation for all men" (5:18); that "by one man's disobedience many were made sinners" (5:19); that "death reigned from Adam to Moses, even over those whose sins were not like the transgression of Adam" (5:14). The name Adam sends us quite naturally to the opening of the Book of Genesis where we read an account of the first sin, the original sin, taken to be a sufficient explanation of the human condition.

But what can it mean that all humans were really and radically implicated in the original sin committed by a distant ancestor, even if the first ancestor, when they were not yet born and made no responsible decision about the action? That is, perhaps, a good, modern, post-Enlightenment question, which presupposes free, individual responsibility as an essential requisite for sin. But can we be sure that Paul, a well-trained, far-from-modern, and very-far-from-post-Enlightenment Jew, shared that presupposition? We should weigh well the possibility that he did not. We should ponder the shrewd words of Jean de Fraine in his classic *Adam et son lignage:* "To understand well the content of the idea under study, it is necessary to cast off the normal philosophic categories and to create in oneself a new mentality, one that is 'semitic' or 'biblical.' "[14] That is sound advice, and but a paraphrase of Pius XI's famous dictum that "we [Christians] are spiritually Semites." We must now try to think like Semites to grasp the points at issue, not only *adam* and original sin, but also Jesus and salvation, and the connection of baptism to both.

Modern biblical exegesis has coined a phrase, *corporate personality,* which is never found in the Bible but sums up concisely the biblical culture's teaching concerning the relationship of an individual and the community to which he belongs. Put briefly, corporate personality means this. On the one hand, that in an ancestor of the tribe are included all the members of the tribe, past, present and future; on the other hand, that in the present members of the tribe are included both the past ancestors and the future descendants. Tribe or community, not individual selves, is the prime source of Semitic personality. The behavior of an ancestor not only prefigures, as in a kind of parable, the situation of his descendants, but also conditions that situation. Such a corporate personality pervades the Old Testament.

Amos, for instance, can address the people of his time thus: "Hear this word that the Lord has spoken against *you*, people of Israel, against the *whole family* which I brought up out of the land of Egypt" (3:1). And Hosea, his eighth century B.C. contemporary, can proclaim: "The Lord has an indictment against Judah, and will punish Jacob according to his way, and requite him according to his deeds. In the womb he took his brother by the heel, and in his manhood he strove with God" (12:2–3). Both prophets identify the present members of Israel with the ancient ancestors who, though long dead, really live on in their descendants. And the key is *really* live on. Corporate personality does not mean just some juridical or literary personification of the tribe in an ancestor. It means real identification. The tribe and the individual, including the individual dead ancestor, are really one, so that what the individual does, even if now he is dead and long gone, is done by the entire tribe, including its present and its future members.

And so to *adam* of Genesis. "When God created *adam* he made him in the likeness of God. Male and female he created them, and he blessed them and he named *them Adam* when they were created" (5:12). It has become common to read the Hebrew word *adam* in English as Adam. That, of course, especially in the superficial teaching to which most Christians are exposed, conveys the impression that it is the name of an individual man. It is not. The Lord God, Yahweh, creates not a male whom he names Adam, but male and female whom together he names *adam*, humankind. The same meaning is obvious in 1:26: "Then God said, 'Let us make *adam* in our image, after our likeness; and let *them* have dominion over the fish of the sea." And in 6:6–7, when Yahweh regrets having made *adam* and decides to wipe him out, it is equally clear that it is a question not of an individual named Adam, but of humankind in general. The *adam* of Genesis is not an individual man's name, but the tribe, the race, collective man, humankind in general.[15]

From within the perspective of corporate personality, *adam* is not just one individual ancestor but the whole tribe of humanity, guilty not just of one individual and horrendous sin but of a succession of sins that extend in a series back to the very beginnings of *adam*. As always in corporate personality, the sin of *adam*, the primordial ancestor or ancestors, not only prefigures but also conditions the situation of his descendants. When communities live into such corporate thinking, when individuals view themselves as radically one with the tribe, it is easy to understand why they might consider themselves sinful long prior to any personal sin. If *adam* is sinful, then so too, of necessity, is each and every one generated from and identified with him. A fifteenth century rabbi, R. Moshe, sums it all up succinctly: "The whole world sinned in the sin which Adam committed, because he was the whole world."[16]

Paul, as we have seen, in Romans 5:12–21, teaches the universal diffusion of sin and death in the human race because of the sin of *adam*. He offers no ancient texts in support of his explanation, seemingly assuming that what he says is well enough known and taken for granted. That would fit well with what I have said about corporate personality in Jewish society. Though it is sometimes suggested by Christian scholars that in Romans 5 we have the first revelation of original sin as understood in the Christian Church,[17] it seems more likely that Paul is leaning on an idea already established in ancient Judaism and quite current in his time.[18]

There is, though, an apparent problem. Paul seems to assume that Adam is an individual person, a numerically first ancestor whose personal characteristics could be delineated. This is hardly surprising, however, since a characteristic of corporate personality is the fluid tension between the individual and the collective, between the ancestor and the race. The problem is not a real problem. Paul, well trained Semite that he is, sees *adam* in the established Jewish way, as corporate personality.

Dubarle judges that Paul has formulated abstractly what Genesis formulated in concrete terms. "If the literary genre of the Eden narrative is taken into account, it will be recognized that the sentence delivered against the first couple is, in the mind of the writer, to attain to all their descendants, that the expulsion from the garden conditions the destiny of their descendants. . . . The author sketches the situation of the race in the sin of the ancestors."[19] Paul accepts this Jewish notion of solidarity. If the ancestor Adam (and "Adam is a name which stands to him for the 'corporate personality' of humankind"[20]) sinned, then all who are solidary with Adam, that is, the entire human race, past, present and future, sinned and are cut off from God. It is, therefore, in very truth that he can say, in Semitic realism, what we have seen him saying: that "sin came into the world through one man and death through sin" (5:12) and "by one man's disobedience many were made sinners" (5:19).

Western that he was, Augustine of Hippo did not live into this Semitic notion of solidarity between race and individual. At his time, and

since his time down to our own, Western Christians were and are
tempted to read the Genesis accounts of the origins of humanity as
scientific history. This history, they believed and believe, tells us of the
origin of the first man and the first woman, whose names we know,
Adam and Eve, and who were graced by God with exceptional gifts
which they lost by a seriously evil original sin. Such were the facts as
they were believed, and Augustine was faced with the task of explaining the relationship between the original sin of Adam and Eve and the
sinful condition of every man and woman born into humanity, a condition which was also known as original sin.[21]

Augustine's explanation derived from another notion of solidarity as articulated within neo-Platonic philosophy. From this point of
view, Adam, the very first man, exemplified in himself all of human
nature. If he sinned, therefore, all human nature, and each and every
individual who shares that nature, sinned. And so he argues: "In
Adam all sinned, since by that power rooted in his nature by which he
could generate them, he and they were all one";[22] "through the evil
will of that one man [Adam] all sinned in him, since all were one in
him, and from him therefore all have original sin."[23] Against the monk
Pelagius, who taught that no human being needs the grace of God
prior to personal sins and that, therefore, a child has no need of baptism, he summarizes after a long discussion of original sin: "Whoever
contends that human nature at whatever age does not need the doctor
who is the second Adam [Christ] because it was not vitiated by the first
Adam . . . is convicted of being an enemy of the grace of God."[24] It is
the solidarity in nature between Adam and the subsequent human race
that imputes the sin of the one also to the other.

It is clear that though the explanations of Paul and Augustine of
why the sin of the ancestor is also the sin of the descendants derive
from differing intellectual and cultural contexts, they both depend for
their intelligibility on the grasp of the solidarity of men and women,
in evil as in good. To grasp their explanations and to be able to live
into them, we would have to live into symbols of human solidarity and
connectedness. That such symbols are not the symbols of the Western
tradition as it is now lived in Europe and the Americas is not *eo ipso* a
compelling argument against the validity of those symbols or of the
doctrine of original sin which is based upon them. That that solidarity,
in which the sin and the shame of the ancestor is the sin and the shame
also of the descendants, makes no sense in a culture where the dominant symbols are not of solidarity but of individualistic separation is no
guarantee that it makes no sense at all.

The modern disciplines of anthropology, psychology and sociology have consistently brought to our attention the indisputable fact that each and every person coming into our world does not come into a naked world, ready to be clothed anew by his or her contributions to it. They demonstrate that our every thought and feeling and action, even those that we judge most intimate and personal and free, is conditioned to some extent by the thoughts and feelings and actions of others who are our ancestors, our parents, our significant others. For Paul and for Augustine *adam* (and/or Adam) sums up that human society which influences us from the first moment of our existence. If that society be sinful, then we are sinful, in the sense that we are in a situation cut off from God and will only further alienate ourselves from him as we learn to sin as the society sinned and sins. If that alienation from God is ever to be bridged so that something other than sin will be learned, then something will have to be done. For that something Paul and Augustine and the entire Christian tradition point us to the ritual waters of regeneration. And this returns us to our treatment of baptism.

In Romans 5:12–21 Paul seeks to explain not only original sin but also salvation from that sin. He does this by setting forth a parallelism between the first Adam, "who was a type of the one who was to come" (5:14), and Jesus, whom he regards as the one who was to come and whom he names elsewhere "the last Adam" (1 Cor 15:45). The paralellism, though, is not exact; for what is effected by the first Adam is remedied by the last Adam, not measure for measure but in superabundance. "The free gift is not like the trespass. For if many died through one man's trespass, much more have the grace of God and the free gift in the grace of the one man Jesus Christ abounded for many" (5:15).

The first Adam bequeaths sin to his descendants, the last Adam, righteousness in abundance. The first Adam bequeaths death, the last Adam life overflowing. The first Adam bequeaths condemnation, the last justification for all humankind. What we have argued for the first Adam holds also for the last Adam, Christ. If in Adam there was corporate personality, so also there is corporate personality in Christ. If those who were in Adam were the body of Adam, so also those who are in Christ are the body of Christ (1 Cor 6:12–20; 10:17; 12:12–27; Rom 12:4–5; Eph 1:22–23; 2:14–16; 3:6; 4:4–16; 5:22–30; Col 1:18, 24; 2:19; 3:15). More than metaphor is intended here; there is also corporate personality—so that in Christ "there is neither Jew nor Greek, there is neither slave nor free, there is neither male nor female, for you are all *one person* (*eis* in Greek = one person, not *en* = one thing, as some translations suggest) in Christ Jesus" (Gal 3:28). Christ, the last Adam, is the ancestor of a new race which redresses and reverses all that was of the first Adam and the first race.

One question remains for this section. Humans become solidary with the first Adam simply by being born and being nurtured in human society. That was what was intended by the traditional Christian doctrine that original sin was transmitted by generation—not just biological generation but also the social generation of socialization. If one is incorporated into the first Adam by generation, one is incorporated into the last Adam by regeneration. If one is incorporated into the first Adam by creation, one is incorporated into the last Adam by re-creation. If in the first Adam one is infected by sin and in a spiritual sense dead, in the second Adam one is cleansed and restored to new life. All of that, regeneration, recreation, cleansing, new life, is achieved in the ritual water. Since Paul, therefore, and following him, the tradition has taught that the corporate solidarity with the first Adam is replaced by corporate solidarity with the last Adam in baptism. "As many of you as were baptized have put on Christ" (Gal 3:27; cf. Rom 6:3–4). John Chrysostom's explicit parallel is clear: "As the womb is to the embryo so the water is to the believer, for in the water he is shaped and formed."[25]

It should be clear now that baptism is a symbol-sacrament, the meanings of which are multiple. Cleansing from original sin has been, since the fifth century, *a* meaning of baptism, but just as clearly it cannot be said to be *the* meaning. That fact is demonstrated historically by another fact, namely, that the Christian Church baptized formally and obligatorily for four centuries without ever thinking of original sin. It is demonstrated theologically by the recent appearance in the Roman Catholic Church of a new Rite of Christian Initiation of Adults which never once makes mention of original sin. Both this new rite and the first four hundred years of baptismal history demonstrate that a meaning, perhaps even *the* dominant meaning, of baptism is that of proclaiming, celebrating and realizing in representation the death and the resurrection of Jesus. There is also another meaning of both water and baptism, which I will deal with in the next chapter, but which I wish to introduce here as a conclusion to this section.

Water is a primal life-source. So too is God. It is not surprising, therefore, that all through the Jewish-Christian Scriptures water serves as symbol for the life-giving *ruah Yahweh*, the breath, the Spirit of God. Isaiah speaks of this Spirit in the image of life-giving water poured out on the desert (44:3). Jeremiah presents God as "the fountain of living waters" (2:13). Joel (3:18) and Zechariah (14:8) present the coming restoration of Israel as a day on which a fountain will come forth from the house of the Lord, a day on which living waters will flow from Jerusalem. Paul connects the life-giving Spirit to the waters of baptism (1 Cor 12:13). John claims that "unless one is born of water and the Spirit he cannot enter the kingdom of God" (3:5), and presents Jesus as promising "rivers of living water" (7:38), explaining that "this he said about the Spirit which those who believed in him were to receive; for the Spirit had not yet been given because Jesus had not yet been glorified" (7:38–39). The same John testifies to both the glorification of Jesus and the giving of the Spirit when Jesus was struck, as Moses struck the rock in the desert, and "there came out blood and water" (19:34).

Water and life, water and Spirit, these are ancient Jewish and Christian meanings. They formed a dominant part of the meanings of early Christian baptism. The death-resurrection of Jesus was perceived as releasing the Spirit of God into the world. The ritual celebration of this death-resurrection, baptism, also released this very same Spirit into the world of believers, the Spirit who had come upon Jesus in his baptism and had designated him Son of God to address God as Abba, Father (Mt 3:16–17; Mk 14:36; Rom 8:15; Gal 4:6). Paul proclaims openly: "You were washed, you were sanctified, you were justified, in the name of the Lord Jesus and in the Spirit of our God" (1 Cor 6:11). He knows of no separate ritual for gifting the Spirit. I shall reserve a treatment of this point until the next chapter.

INFANT BAPTISM

Historical studies indicate that the tradition in the Christian Church since its earliest New Testament beginnings was to baptize infants.[26] There is no evidence that such baptism was understood either as necessary or obligatory, but it was practiced. That it was practiced is, at least, implicit in Augustine's argument about original sin. In his conflict with Pelagius, he argues that if Pelagius acknowledges that "infants are to be baptized for the remission of sins, as is the rule of the universal Church," then he must be forced to acknowledge also that, as infants have no personal sins, they must be guilty of some other sin, which Augustine names original sin.[27] It is that original sin, explained in the solidary way that I explained it, that makes the baptism of infants necessary. There is always the problem that the infant is not capable of the free, personal response required by both. But Augustine has a very nuanced answer to that problem.

Writing to Pope Boniface in 389, in response to a letter that the

Pope had sent him posing some questions about the baptism of infants, Augustine argues as follows: "If the sacraments had no similarity to the things they represent, they would not be sacraments. But they often take their very names from such similarity, as the sacrament of the body of Christ is in some way the body of Christ, and the sacrament of faith is faith. For to believe is nothing more than to have faith. That is why we reply that the infant believes, although he has not any sense of faith. He has faith because this is the sacrament of faith; he is converted to God because this is the sacrament of conversion."[28] His answer is clear and contributed powerfully to the practice of baptizing infants, which became the norm in the Roman Catholic Church: the child *in some way* has faith because baptism is the sacrament of faith, the child *in some way* is converted because baptism is the sacrament of conversion. Questions continued to be asked, however, quite legitimately, about the *some way* in which the child has faith in baptism. But they received no answer that was compelling until the time of another great Doctor of the Church, Thomas Aquinas.

Aquinas postulated that faith is a virtue[29] and that virtue is a habit (*habitus*),[30] an ability to do something, a know-how if you like. The virtue or the habit of faith is the ability or the know-how to make an act of faith. Now sometimes we are tempted to give the same name to both the habit and the act which it makes possible, as in the case of faith both the habit and the act are called by the same name *faith*. This should not blind us, however, to the fact that habit and act are quite distinct. One can have the know-how to drive an automobile without ever actually driving one, and one can have the know-how of faith without ever making an act of faith. Aquinas agrees with Augustine that children are to be baptized, and for the very same reason, namely, that "as in birth they incurred damnation through Adam, so in a second birth they might obtain salvation through Christ."[31] But he advances Augustine's opinion that the child receives faith in baptism in some way to a much more precise point.

The effect of baptism, in children as in adults, is the proclamation and realization of grace and virtues. That he is using *virtue* here in the technical sense of habit or know-how is clear from his further argument against those who object that children cannot receive virtue in baptism because they are incapable of free will. "The cause of their error is that they do not know how to distinguish between habit and act. Seeing children, therefore, to be incapable of *acts* of virtue, they thought they had no *virtues* at all after baptism."[32] In baptism a child receives from the gracious God the virtue or habit or the know-how of faith. For that virtue of faith to be in any way imputed to him for salvation it will have to be translated into acts of faith. In the words of the chapter on symbol, he will have to live into the symbols of faith before they will be imputed to him. In the words of the chapter on sacrament, more is required for the fruitfulness of a sacrament than just some valid rite (*opus operatum*); there is required also some positive disposition on the part of the one receiving the sacrament (*opus operantis*). These points will recur in our discussion of the sacrament of marriage.

The views of both Augustine and Aquinas are, of course, tied to philosophic conceptions of their time. The believing Church and the theologian are free to ask, however, if they are tied forever to such conceptions or if they are free to articulate their faith within the conceptions of their own age. As I have tried to show, the traditional doctrine of original sin and the function of baptism in remedying it in a ritual way made sense for earlier Christians out of their sense of solidarity. It still makes sense for modern Christians imbued with a similar sense of solidarity, though it is no longer necessary to read the Genesis account of the sin of *adam* as the actual history of one couple's sin. In a solidary context, it is meaningful to baptize infants to ritually remedy the sinful effects of the first biological birth in a second birth. But before entering on any further discussion of this meaning of infant baptism, I wish to dwell on an aspect of the teaching of Aquinas that is at variance with the position which came to dominate both Roman Catholic theory and practice with respect to infant baptism. That position came to be known as a *tutiorist* position, or a taking the safest way out.

The constant practice of the Christian Church has been not to baptize the children of non-believers. Aquinas deals with this topic *twice* in his final work, the *Summa Theologiae*, and each time gives the same answer with the same reasoning. That this is contrary to his practice may be an indication of the importance of the topic in his mind. The children of Jews, he argues, and though he does not do it his argument could be extended to other non-Christians, should not be baptized against their parents' wishes.[33] "There are two reasons for this custom. One is on account of the danger to faith. For children baptized before coming to the use of reason, when they come to perfect age, might easily be persuaded by their parents to renounce what they have unknowingly embraced. And this would be detrimental to the faith. The other reason is that it is against natural justice. For a child is by nature in the care of its parents, and it would be contrary to natural justice if a child, before coming to the use of reason, were to be taken away from its parents' custody."[34]

Even what later became a classical tutiorist argument fails to move Aquinas: What if the child dies without baptism? "No one," he replies, "ought to break the order of the natural law, whereby a child is in the custody of its father, in order to rescue it from the danger of everlasting death."[35] The refusal of baptism to the children of non-believers might appear excessive to those in the last few centuries, including our own, who always sought to take the safest way out, but it makes perfect sense from within Aquinas' perspective on God and grace and sacrament. That perspective may be deduced from his treatment of yet another tutiorist position.

If the grace of Christ is more efficacious than the sin of Adam, runs the tutiorist argument, and if the child in its mother's womb is already sullied with the original sin of Adam, then it should be baptized already in its mother's womb to regenerate it. No, responds Aquinas, for a child who has not yet come to a first birth cannot come to a second, ritual one. The child in the womb cannot come under any human influence, including administered sacraments. "[Children] can, however, come under the action of God, in whose sight they live, in such a way that they receive the grace of salvation as a kind of privilege, as happened to those who were sanctified in the womb."[36] That is a monumental judgment, one that should be well-learned by Christians, and one that if well-learned would remove many sacramental misunderstandings and anxieties. Sacraments are for men and women, as are all symbols; they are not for God; they do not exhaust the ways in which God can, and does save. There is a Mystery embodied in the mysteries. But it is a Mystery that escapes them and that "will be gracious to whom I will be gracious, and will show mercy on whom I will show mercy" (Ex 33:19; Rom 9:15). If well-learned, that lesson might make easier decisions about infant baptism.

Traditionally, infant baptism has been justified and practiced on the basis of an argument on the solidarity of *adam*. Such an argument, to repeat, still makes sense. It is still possible to propose a rationale for infant baptism that runs something like this. An infant is born into *adam*, that is, into humanity, and is socialized into that humanity's ways in some particular human community. If *adam* be sinful, and he notoriously is, then the child will learn sinful ways, he will be infected by *adam*'s sins. To counteract such a situation the child will have to be transferred from such a sinful community into the one that consciously lives into and out of the grace of God. Such a grace- or Spirit-filled community, Christians claim, is the Christian Church, and so the child could be transferred into that. The ritual that proclaims and celebrates and realizes that transfer is the sacrament-symbol of baptism.

The dominant meaning of such a rationale is not so much that the sin of *adam* is cleansed, as much as it is that children are introduced

into the believing community that is the Church, where they learn to
live into not just the virtue of faith but also, and more crucially, acts of
faith in the mysterious God who mysteriously raised Jesus of Nazareth
from the dead. Such a rationale celebrates the presence of active faith
in the Church,[37] particularly in that first "domestic church"[38] that is
his family. That rationale presupposes, of course, that the churches,
both domestic and universal, are churches of faith, a presupposition
that is verified not by verbal claims but by acts of faith. That the presupposition is not verified in reality in many segments of the contemporary Catholic Church is a fact that is, sadly, only too well known.

There are many who are baptized and who are, therefore, technically Christian, technically Church, technically believers, but who in
reality are non-Christian, non-Church, non-believers. They are known
today as *baptized non-believers*,[39] that is, those who, though baptized,
have never come to faith. The children of such baptized non-believers
quite naturally learn non-faith and the virtue of faith gifted to them
in baptism never becomes actual faith. This, of course, to paraphrase
Aquinas, is detrimental to faith, and demands, perhaps, a re-evaluation of our practice of infant baptism. That such re-evaluation is already taking place is evidenced by the instruction of the Congregation
for the Doctrine of the Faith that baptism is to be refused to the children of parents who, in the pastor's best judgment, are non-believers,
baptized or not.[40]

It is necessary to recall here what was said in the preceding chapter about the mutual necessity of *opus operatum* and *opus operantis* in sacramental activity. Symbols and sacraments are not things that men and
women have or get, as they might have a car or get a present. Rather
they are *actions* which they do. In Aquinas' pedantic language, "the use
of a sacrament is not merely physical, but in a sense also spiritual."[41]
Men and women are free persons and they are graced and sanctified
according to their will, not against it. A sacrament proclaims and realizes and celebrates in representation God and Christ for the person
participating in it to make interaction between them possible.

Since genuine *human* and *interpersonal* presence and interaction,
as distinct from merely *physical* presence, requires the conscious participation of the interacting parties, such conscious participation of the
one taking part in sacramental activity is required for the essence of
any fruitful sacrament, one, that is, that is a genuine encounter between him and the sacramentally present God. The Council of Florence's doctrine still stands as an authoritative statement of the
Church's position: sacraments give grace (= God) to those who receive
them worthily, that is, with conscious faith. Faith, *opus operantis*, is as

necessary to any fruitful sacrament as the most carefully crafted *opus operatum*. And this returns us to infant baptism.

Sacraments are human actions which need to be lived into for their effectiveness. It is useless to "perform" a sacrament on one who takes no part in the ritual action, who sees nothing, hears nothing, says nothing, does nothing, remembers nothing. Of course, God might save such a one, but not because of a rite or the faith of its minister or of the Church, and still less because of the non-faith of the recipient, but only because of the unmerited graciousness of the God who saves. Now such appears to be the real case with infant baptism. A child who sees nothing, hears nothing, says nothing, does nothing, remembers nothing, is submitted to a water rite. One might argue, as I have indeed argued above, that it is more the faith of the Church, particularly of that domestic church close to the child, his family, godparents and friends, that is celebrated in this ritual and that makes good the lack of any faith on the part of the child. But if that, indeed, is what we are doing, then let us have a ritual that proclaims and celebrates and re-alizes that faith, rather than the faith and the conversion and the personal adherence to the God revealed in Jesus of the child—all of which are clearly not actually real, however real they may be as virtue.

There is no need to rush to baptize a child. The Father of Jesus, under whose graciousness the child falls, can save without it. But there is a need, I believe, for religious ritual on the occasion of the birth of a child, to enable the child's two families, the domestic and Church, to celebrate this gift and to pledge themselves effectively to guide this child to faith in God, the Father of our Lord Jesus Christ. Such a ritual, which is well within the power of the Church to establish and to struc-ture,[42] would have to proclaim and realize and celebrate two things: first, the faith of the child's two families and their joint will to socialize the child into it; second, the already real, if inchoate and precarious, belonging of the child to both these families under God.

It is not difficult to imagine the shape of such a ritual and the prayerful words and actions in which it would be accomplished. In this ritual the ritual actions and words would symbolize what they claim to symbolize, namely the faith of the Church and its pledge to guide this child to faith. On the contrary, the present ritual of infant baptism ap-pears as a very disjointed ritual, claiming to symbolize the faith of the child and his conversion to Christ—neither of which will be actual for many, many years, and if at all only as a result, at least from the human point of view, of a successful socialization in faith carried out by the Church.

But what, then, of the child? Thanks to the socialization he has undergone in his two church families, not just what he has heard in words, but more importantly what he has seen in consistent actions, thanks to the assiduity of the two families in fulfilling their pledge ritualized at his birth, he comes to faith and is converted to God and his Christ in this Church. Now is the time for baptism, not to give faith *in some way*, but to proclaim and celebrate in ritual and so realize and make effective a faith that is already actual. Now the ritual symbol is not disjointed, for it truly symbolizes what it claims to symbolize and is truly a sacrament of faith. Now there is a genuine ritual proclamation and celebration of knowledge of God's saving action in Christ, confidence in the word of God, personal submission and self-surrender to this God, fellowship with Christ in this community called Church, and a pledged desire for union with this God beyond the grave. In short, it really and truly symbolizes a genuine " 'Yes' to God revealing himself as man's savior in Christ."[43]

Such an approach to the question of infant baptism is, I believe, endorsed by the Fathers of the Church, by papal pronouncements, and by the Code of Canon Law, and is emphatically taught in our day by the Second Vatican Council. None of these sources, of course, explicitly deals with the question in the terms in which I have dealt with it. But all that is required is a simple transposition whenever a text reads "no man," "no person," "no one," to "no child."

When the Declaration on Religious Freedom, for example, states: "It is one of the major tenets of Catholic doctrine that man's (read "a child's") response to God in faith must be free. Therefore, no one (read "no child") is to be forced to embrace the Christian faith against his will. . . . The act of faith is of its very nature a free act,"[44] it is not difficult to see what I mean. It states again that "the doctrine of the Church that no one (read "no child") is to be coerced into faith has always stood firm. . . . The person (read "the child") in society is to be kept free from all manner of human coercion."[45] The Decree on the Church's Missionary Activity makes the same point. "When the Holy Spirit opens their hearts non-Christians (read "unbaptized children") may believe and be freely converted to the Lord. . . . The Church strictly forbids forcing anyone (read "any child") to embrace the faith, or alluring or enticing people (read "children") by unworthy techniques."[46] The law of the Church lays down quite emphatically that "no one (read "no child") is to be forced to embrace the Catholic faith against his will."[47] Such an approach represents the unbroken Catholic tradition of the centuries.[48]

There is more to be said about baptism and the whole process of Christian initiation, but I shall defer it until the next chapter when I

deal with confirmation. For the moment, I wish only to echo the judgment of a very traditional interpreter of the Catholic tradition. "The
baptism of infants is not a proper model for the sacramental process.
That the entrance to the kingdom of God takes place unconsciously,
that the subject in question neither perceives nor understands the action of Christ, is a fact so surprising and so unusual from the biblical
point of view that it must be considered absolutely an exception."[49] My
claim is simply this: that the approach I have outlined here, and will
expand further in the next chapter, opens up an acceptable way to take
this exception and to integrate it into the normal sacramental way of
proclaiming, realizing and celebrating in representation personal conversion to and faith in the God and the Father of our Lord Jesus
Christ.

Chapter Four
CONFIRMATION

INTRODUCTION

In 1955 the Roman Catholic liturgical scholar, Josef Andreas Jung-mann, complained that the pastoral preparation of people for the sac-rament of confirmation suffered from the lack of clarity in the theology of confirmation.[1] It was but the latest in a long series of com-plaints about that sacrament.

As far back as 828 Jonas, bishop of Orleans in France, had com-plained that many of his flock were not receiving confirmation until a very advanced age. "There are some [nobles] who defer it for a very long time, a practice which needs to be changed. And among the sim-ple folk there exists such negligence in this matter, partly because of ignorance, partly because they do not care, that some do not receive the consecration of this gift until a very decrepit age."[2] The provincial synod of Lambeth in England in 1281 reported the same situation, and proposed to do something about it by decreeing that "no one be ad-mitted to the sacrament of the body and blood of the Lord, except in danger of death, unless he has been confirmed or has reasonably been prevented from being confirmed."[3] A few years later, in 1287, the Synod of Wurtzburg in Germany made the same complaint and tried to remedy the situation by obliging bishops to visit their parishes and administer confirmation every two years.[4]

Three hundred years later the Council of Trent was still com-plaining. "If ever there was required pastoral diligence in explaining the sacrament of confirmation, now is the time. This fact is easily dem-onstrated, since in the holy church of God this sacrament is totally omitted by many, while there are very few who know how to derive from it the fruit of divine grace which they ought to derive."[5] Jung-mann's judgment, ranged alongside those of innumerable others,[6] is eloquent testimony to the fact that Trent's treatment of confirmation did little to offer a satisfactory theology to underpin the pastoral practice of confirmation.

It was left to theologians of the Anglican Church in England, where the pastoral practice of confirmation has much in common with that in the Roman Catholic Church, to initiate a detailed and highly theological debate about the meaning of confirmation. This debate was sparked by Dom Gregory Dix in a lecture published under the title of *The Theology of Confirmation in Relation to Baptism.*[7] The title has the merit of indicating precisely where the crux of the theological problem lies, namely, in the relationship of baptism and confirmation, specifically with respect to the actualization of the gift of the Spirit.

Dix left no doubt about his position. "The unfortunate thing was that the divorce of the two sacraments in practice led the Western theologians to set up a mistaken theoretical justification of the practice by the transference of the whole content of the major rite into the preliminary (that is, water baptism), and the degradation of the 'baptism of the Spirit' to a mere *augmentum gratiae* (increase of grace)."[8] For Dix, following Tertullian, he claims, "it is not the water but the 'seal' which imparts the Spirit."[9] He was supported in this opinion by L.S. Thornton, who argued that the gift of the Spirit is not received by baptized Christians until they are confirmed by a bishop. Baptized, but as yet unconfirmed, Christians do not have the indwelling Spirit of God.[10]

These opinions have been resolutely, and in my judgment correctly, challenged by G.W. Lampe in his *The Seal of the Spirit.* I share the opinion expressed in his conclusion, though not necessarily the language in which it is articulated. "The convert to faith in Christ receives the indwelling presence of the Holy Spirit by virtue of his participation . . . in the status of sonship to God and freedom of access to the Father which is the gift of God the Son to redeemed humanity. This union with Christ and sharing in his sonship . . . is symbolized and sacramentally effected by baptism which re-enacts the baptism of Jesus in which the Spirit descended upon him, and he was proclaimed Son of the divine Father."[11] These questions of the relationship of baptism and confirmation and of their respective meanings are, of course, questions not only for Anglo-Catholics but also for Roman Catholics. I propose now to confront them.

THE PROBLEM

A critical element in any discussion of the relationship between baptism and confirmation, perhaps even the dividing line, in matters of initiation, between the Church of the first two centuries and the Church of later centuries, is the situation represented in *The Apostolic Tradition* of Hippolytus. As I noted in the previous chapter, this document provides us with a relatively detailed account of a symbol-dense ritual of Christian initiation in Rome at the opening of the third century. The moments of note in the initiation ritual are these: a three year period of catechumenate; exorcism, renunciation of Satan, and an anointing; descent of the catechumens, naked, into the symbolic pool and their immersion by a *presbyteros* in the name of the Father and of the Son and of the Holy Spirit; their anointing by the *presbyteros* and their subsequent introduction into the Church, where they were again anointed, this time by the *episkopos*, and sealed with the sign of the cross; their participation in the Eucharist of the community.

The ritual of initiation described by Hippolytus was a highly complex ritual, revealing the deepest values and aspirations of the people called Christians. There were symbolic things with both orectic and ideological meanings: water, oil, bread, wine, milk and honey. There was symbolic time with the same two-tiered meaning: pre-Easter catechumenate, Easter initiation, post-Easter life in Christ. There was symbolic space: outside the pool, inside the pool, outside the church, inside the church sharing the great banquet meal. But problems would arise for this ritual—not great, speculative problems of theological meaning, but simple, concrete problems of pastoral practice, provoked by structural changes taking place within the young Church. As it spread out from its urban bases into rural areas, an expansion which was already in process before, but was greatly enhanced by, the peace of Constantine, it became more difficult to gather all the candidates for initiation into the bishop's city. The problem this raised was exacerbated when the doctrine of original sin caused the demand for initiation to be more frequent than just once a year at Easter, not only for adults but also for newly born infants. The problem was resolved differently in the East and in the West.

The East delegated the entire initiation ritual to the presbyter, requiring though that the bishop bless the oil for anointing, while the West reserved the imposition of hands, the second anointing and the sealing to the bishop. It was this bishop's part, now cut off from the ritual of initiation, that was to become known as confirmation. It was when this confirmation achieved the status of a separate ritual, fully cut off from baptism, that questions arose about the relationship of the two rituals and about their respective meanings. It was these questions, never satisfactorily resolved, that gave rise in our day to judgments like those of Jungmann already quoted and to theological controversies like those alluded to in the Anglican Church.[12]

BAPTISM, CONFIRMATION AND THE SPIRIT

The theological problem involved in the question of the relationship of baptism and confirmation is quite specific: Does the Holy Spirit indwell a Christian from the ritual moment of baptism or only from the moment of confirmation? Now the traditional *theological* method for finding an answer to such a problem involves a search of the theological sources, which in the Roman Catholic Church are the sacred Scriptures and the living tradition of the Church down through the centuries. For our question, unfortunately, an unbiased search of the sources, that is, a search with no presuppositions about what one ought to find, yields a very complex, not to say very confusing, answer. Put briefly, the sources yield two contradictory opinions; one is that the Holy Spirit indwells Christians from the moment of their baptism, the other that he indwells them only from the moment of their confirmation.

The source of the complexity and confusion lies in the sacred Scripture itself. When the Fathers of the Church in the third and fourth centuries speak of the distinction between baptism, which effects a regeneration, and confirmation, which confers the Spirit of God, and it cannot be denied that they do,[13] it is always in reference to one or other of two texts in the Acts of the Apostles.

The first, and most important, passage is Acts 8:4–19. There we read an account of the preaching of Philip in Samaria, of his baptism of converts there, and of a subsequent visit by Peter and Paul, who came that these converts might receive the Holy Spirit, "for it had not yet fallen on any of them, but they had only been baptized in the name of the Lord Jesus" (v. 16). When Peter and John arrived, they laid hands on the baptized converts "and they received the Holy Spirit" (v. 17). The second passage is Acts 19:1–7. This recounts a visit of Paul to Ephesus, where he finds some dozen disciples who have been baptized in John's baptism but who "have never even heard that there is a Holy Spirit" (v. 2). Paul baptizes them in the name of the Lord Jesus, "and when Paul had laid hands on them, the Holy Spirit came upon them" (v. 6). The later Fathers see in these two texts the testimony to a ritual, namely, the imposition of hands, which is administered after baptism and which confers the Holy Spirit upon baptized Christians.

There is another New Testament event which was consistently put in relation to Christian initiation. It is the baptism of Jesus and the descent upon him, in the form of a dove, of the Spirit of God (Mt 3:13–17). Already in the New Testament itself, Luke twice interprets this descent of the Spirit as an anointing of Jesus. In his Gospel he reports that Jesus applied to himself the words of Isaiah, "The Spirit of the Lord is upon me, because he has anointed me to preach good news to the poor" (4:18). And in his Acts Peter proclaims "how God anointed Jesus of Nazareth with the Holy Spirit and with power" (10:38). Luke presents this baptismal anointing with the Spirit as the beginning of both Jesus' public, prophetic life (3:23) and his struggle with the demon (4:2). The Fathers, given especially their very literal exegesis of Scripture, could not resist connecting Christ's beginnings, marked by his baptism and anointing with the Spirit, with Christians' beginnings, marked by their baptism in water and subsequent anointing.

Joseph Lecuyer would appear to be guilty of the same kind of literalism in his reading of the texts reporting the baptism of Jesus. "A more attentive reading of the Gospel texts should lead to an important finding: it is not during the baptism in the water of Jordan that the Spirit descends upon the Christ, but after he has been baptized (Lk 3:21), when he came out of the water (Mt 3:16; Mk 1:10)." The implication he wishes to insinuate seems to be that there are two quite separate things going on: first the baptism of Jesus, and then the descent of the Spirit. That implication opens the way to the rhetorical question: "How can one not see here an image of confirmation which follows baptism?"[14] How can one not, indeed, especially if one sets out from the established practice of two rituals, first baptism and then confirmation, and accepts that practice as a given. But what if one were to set out from another given, namely, the given of *one* ritual with two symbolic moments in water and oil of anointing? Perhaps then one would perceive a quite different implication. Presuppositions control notoriously both the questions we are able to ask and the answers to them we are able to accept.

Cyprian explicitly links the giving of the Holy Spirit to the Samaritans via the imposition of the hands of Peter and John to "what is done now still among us, that those who are baptized in the Church are presented to the leaders of the Church and by our prayer and the imposition of our hands receive the Holy Spirit and are brought to completion with the Lord's seal."[15] The anonymous writer of the *De Rebaptismate,* also from the second half of the third century, repeats the same assertion that "the Holy Spirit is given to each believer through the imposition of the hands of the bishop."[16] But it is Tertullian, from earlier in the third century, who is advanced as the most eminent proponent of the theory that the gift of the Spirit is conferred only via the imposition of the bishop's hands.

Writing of Christian symbols Tertullian states: "The body is washed that the soul may be cleansed; the body is anointed that the soul may be consecrated; the body is signed that the soul may be strengthened; the flesh is overshadowed by the imposition of hands that the soul too may be enlightened by the Spirit; the body is nourished on the body and blood of Christ that the soul also should be nourished."[17] Writing of baptism he states quite explicitly: "Not that we receive the Holy Spirit in the waters, but that cleansed in the waters we are readied for the Spirit. . . . Then, come out of the waters, we are anointed with a blessed anointing, as they were wont to be anointed into the priesthood. As Aaron was anointed by Moses, whence he is called *christus,* from chrism which is anointing. . . . Then hands are imposed, invoking and inviting in a blessing the Holy Spirit. . . . Then that most holy Spirit descends from the Father upon cleansed and blessed bodies; it rests upon the waters of baptism, as if recognizing its pristine resting place."[18]

It is clear, so the argument runs, that these Fathers and many others who could be cited see two quite distinct rituals, one in water, which cleanses from sin, the other in the imposition of hands, which confers the gift of the Holy Spirit. That judgment about the gift of the Spirit was enshrined as the official Catholic position in a letter of Pope Innocent I to Decentius, bishop of Gubbio, in 416. Basing himself on the action of Peter and John in Acts 8, Innocent declared unequivocally that "not only the custom of the Church, but also the reading of the Acts of the Apostles, demonstrates that the high priesthood belongs only to bishops, either to seal or to give the Holy Spirit."[19] That judgment, of course, controlled the hermeneutic about the conferring of the gift of the Spirit in the Catholic Church down to our day. The gift of the Spirit was believed to be effected ritually in that sacrament which in the fifth century came to be known as confirmation,[20] a fact to which the prayers of the rite of confirmation testify as recently as 1977, as they ask for "the coming of the Holy Spirit," "the gift of the Holy Spirit," "the outpouring of the Holy Spirit."[21] The theological meaning or doctrine that holds that the Holy Spirit is given ritually to Christians, not in the waters of baptism, but in the imposition of a bishop's hands, has long been a secure meaning of the Catholic Church.

But things are not quite as secure as they might appear to a superficial glance. For those very Fathers who make unequivocal statements about the post-baptismal giving of the Spirit make equally unequivocal statements about his being given in baptism. The same

Cyprian who states that the Holy Spirit is given by the imposition of hands states also that "it is through baptism that the Holy Spirit is received, and when one is thus baptized and has received the Spirit, one then comes to drink the chalice of the Lord." That he means water baptism and not the ritual of initiation as described, for instance, by Hippolytus is clarified by his immediate explanation of the water of John 4:13–14 as referring to the "saving baptism of water."[22] Elsewhere, basing himself on the scriptural passage of Eliseus praying over the dead child of the widow, he insists that everyone, even infants, receives the divine gift in equal measure. "One must not say that the same grace, given to those who are baptized, is lesser or greater according to the age of those who receive it. The Holy Spirit is given equally to all, not in proportional measure, but in paternal benevolence and largesse."[23]

Firmilian, quoted by Lecuyer as holding to the position that the Holy Spirit is given after baptism,[24] actually roundly scorns such a position. He argues that if Paul did not lie when he wrote "For as many of you as were baptized into Christ have put on Christ" (Gal 3:27), then surely those who have been baptized have put on Christ. "But if they have put on Christ, they could have received also the Holy Spirit whom Christ has sent. And it is in vain that, when they come to receive the Holy Spirit, we impose hands on them, unless they divide the Spirit from Christ, so that Christ is with heretics but the Spirit is not."[25] Firmilian's position in his letter to Cyprian is clear: if heretics want to receive the Holy Spirit, then they must be rebaptized, not just have hands laid on them.

And what of Tertullian, whose position vis-à-vis the relation of baptism and confirmation is supposed to be so clear? A closer look will show that it is far from clear. The spiritual effects of baptism are listed, for instance, as the remission of sins, freedom from death, regeneration, the coming of the Holy Spirit, sealing and washing.[26] Comparing the Gospel's prodigal son to the baptized Christian, he names the treasure that the baptized prodigal receives as "baptism, the Holy Spirit, eternal hope."[27] It would appear that he judges here that the gift of the Spirit takes place in baptism, a judgment that is ever more clearly enunciated elsewhere. "To whom is truth opened without God? To whom is God known without Christ? To whom is Christ revealed without the Spirit? To whom is the Spirit adapted without the sacrament of faith?"[28]

Even in the *De Baptismo*, which is supposedly the place where Tertullian most clearly states the position that the Spirit is not given in baptism, he develops such a well-delineated analogy between the activity of the Spirit in creation and his activity in baptism that it is hard to avoid the conclusion that the Spirit is, indeed, given to the Christian in baptism. For it is in the water, and in this treatise he equates baptism and immersion in water,[29] that "man, who once had been in the image of God, is returned to God in his image . . . for he receives again the Spirit of God which he had once received from the creative breath, but later lost by sin."[30] It is only after he has stated this, and as if pulling himself up short to guard some established custom, that he makes the statement oft-quoted by those who insist that Tertullian believes the Spirit is given, not in baptism but in some post-baptismal ritual. "That does not mean that we receive the Holy Spirit in the water. But purified in the water by the ministry of an angel, we are prepared for the Holy Spirit."[31] There is inconsistency, not to say confusion, in Tertullian's thought about baptism and the Holy Spirit. That leaves us with the problem of how to isolate his true teaching in this matter.

It seems to me that we have to recognize that Tertullian, Father of the Church though he be, is confused and inconsistent in his explanation of baptism and the gift of the Holy Spirit. It would not be the first, nor the last, time that a great theologian would be confused. Ultimately, of course, the relationship between the Spirit of God and a sacramental action, be that action baptism or confirmation, is a mystery. Humans can contemplate that mystery and to some extent can articulate it, but we can never clarify it to the degree that it becomes non-mystery.

Humans can contemplate that mystery and see reconciliations and resolutions after a period of search rather than at the beginning of the search. And it is precisely at the beginning of the search for the proper relationship between baptism, confirmation and Spirit that Tertullian comes. Refoule expresses it well. "We are here in the presence of theological thought in process. Tertullian seeks, without success, to take account of two traditions, one which attaches the gift of the Spirit to the imposition of hands, the other which makes it one of the effects of baptism. The Holy Spirit would be given, therefore, twice! Tertullian proposes the following determination: to attach to baptism the negative effects (remission of sins), to confirmation the positive effects (illumination, gifts of the Holy Spirit). This unfortunate distinction will be taken up again by many Fathers."[32]

The honest answer to the question whether the Fathers ascribe the gift of the Spirit to baptism or confirmation is that they ascribe it to both. It is at least mistaken, at most dishonest, to claim them for one side or the other. In their beginning efforts to link the revelation, actualization and celebration of the Spirit of God to one or the other, they are caught between both. Given their effort to be faithful to the scriptural evidence, such vacillation is understandable. For that evidence itself, when viewed in isolation from subsequent sacramental development, is equally muddled.

We have already seen the Acts of the Apostles claim that the gift of the Spirit follows from an imposition of hands which follows baptism. But there is also in the very same Acts a clear claim that the Spirit is given in baptism. After Peter's Pentecost speech, the crowd poses the predictable question: "What shall we do?" Peter's reply is limpidly clear. "Repent and be baptized every one of you in the name of Jesus Christ for the forgiveness of your sins; and you shall receive the gift of the Holy Spirit" (2:37–38). Paul, though his theoretical approach to baptism is quite different from Luke's, attests to the same thing. "You were washed, you were sanctified, you were justified in the name of the Lord Jesus Christ and in the Spirit of our God" (1 Cor 6:11); and again, "By one Spirit you were all baptized into one body . . . and all were made to drink of the one Spirit" (2 Cor 12:13). Beasley-Murray does not hesitate. "These Scriptures seem to most exegetes to bear an incontrovertible testimony,"[33] namely, to the conferral of the Spirit of God in baptism.

Theologically, however, we do not really need these explicit proof-texts to convince us that the New Testament links the giving of the Spirit to baptism. For everything that it says about baptism and its effects indicates that the Spirit of God indwells believers from the moment of their baptism. Water, as we saw in the previous chapter, was regarded in ancient Israel as a primal life-source. So too was God. And throughout the Scriptures water serves as symbol for the life-giving *ruah Yahweh*, the wind, the breath, the Spirit of God. Isaiah speaks of this Spirit in the imagery of water poured out "upon the thirsty ground . . . upon your offspring" (44:3). Jeremiah calls the Lord "the fountain of living waters" (2:13). Joel (3:18) and Zechariah (14:8) present the coming great day as a day when a fountain will come forth from the house of the Lord and living waters will flow from Jerusalem. All three Synoptic Gospels report the descent of the Spirit of God upon Jesus at his Jordan baptism, and his immediate designation as beloved Son (Mt 3:17; Mk 1:11; Lk 3:22). Sonship goes hand in hand with possession of the Spirit; and, on the contrary, one cannot be Son of God without the Spirit of God.

But Jesus had another "baptism to be baptized with" (Lk 12:50; cf. Mk 10:38), the baptism of his death. Until that death, with its subsequent resurrection-glorification, "the Spirit had not been given because Jesus was not yet glorified" (Jn 7:39). But when Jesus is struck, as the rock was struck by Moses in the desert, "there came out blood and water (= Spirit)" (Jn 19:34). The death-resurrection-glorification of Jesus releases into the world the Spirit he had received in his baptism, a fact which Luke presents dramatically in his Pentecost narrative as a fulfillment of the prophecy of Joel that "in the last days . . . I shall pour out my Spirit upon all flesh" (Acts 2:17–18).

Now the baptism of Christians proclaims, realizes and celebrates what happened in Jesus as now happening in the baptized. There is death and resurrection (Rom 6:3–4; Col 2:12); there is re-creation (2 Cor 5:17; cf. Gal 6:15); there is a putting on of Christ (Gal 3:27), so that the baptized are in Christ (2 Cor 5:17; cf. Gal. 3:27). But Paul is explicit: "Anyone who does not have the Spirit of Christ does not belong to him" (Rom 8:9). No one can be in Christ without being also in his Spirit. Christians, therefore, in Christ from baptism, are also in his Spirit from baptism; they possess, better are possessed by, the Spirit of God. It is precisely because of this possession that they are "sons of God" (Rom 8:14) and can, therefore, cry out "Abba, Father" (Rom 8:15; Gal 4:6).

If Christian baptism, as it is described in the New Testament, forgives sins (Acts 2:28), cleanses from sins (Acts 22:16), unites with Christ (Gal 3:27), specifically in his death and resurrection (Rom 6:3–4; Col 2:12), gives a share in his sonship (Rom 8:14–15; Gal 4 4:6), is a new creation (2 Cor 5:17) and a regeneration (Jn 3:5; Tit 3:5), it is all because it causes the baptized to be possessed by the Spirit of God. Beasley-Murray sums it up all nicely. "To imagine that one could be in Christ, in the Body, in the Kingdom, participating in the life of the new age, and therefore a new creature, born anew and renewed by the Spirit, and yet not possess the Spirit of Christ, the Spirit of the Body, the Spirit of the Kingdom and the life of the new age is to be guilty of serious misunderstanding of the apostolic teaching. Where Christ is, there is his Spirit. A man is either in Christ or not in Christ; the New Testament does not allow of a compromise position."[34] This judgment is but a modern theological elaboration of Paul's long-standing opinion: "Anyone who does not possess the Spirit of Christ does not belong to him" (Rom 8:9).

The New Testament, then, would appear to teach that, as a rule, baptism in the name of Jesus confers the Spirit of Jesus. Even in Acts 19:2 this would seem to be the implication of Paul's question to the disciples at Ephesus. If they had been baptized, then they *should have* received the Holy Spirit. Why they had not received the Spirit becomes clear when they explain that they had been baptized in John's baptism, not in the name of Jesus. The latter confers the Holy Spirit of God, the former does not. When they are subsequently baptized in Jesus' name and Paul lays hands on them, they receive the Spirit. That this, however, is not the exclusive way to receive the Spirit, and yet is connected with it, appears from Acts 10:44–48, where the Spirit is *first* received, and then baptism, which is not perceived as superfluous, is accorded to the Gentiles. The connection of water baptism and the reception of the Holy Spirit continues throughout the second century,[35] and still is evident in *The Apostolic Tradition.*

The bishop's prayer as he lays hands on the newly baptized in the Latin text of *The Apostolic Tradition* seems clearly to link the gift of the Spirit to the actual water baptism (if such we must call the water-ritual of the initiation ceremony). He prays: "Lord God, who made them worthy to receive the remission of sins through the washing of regeneration of the Holy Spirit, send forth into them your grace that they may serve you according to your will."[36] This prayer, and ritual prayers are always the best hermeneutic of the ritual, seems to link the gift of the Spirit of God to what has already happened in the water rather than to what is about to happen in confirmation (if such we must call the ritual of imposition of hands and anointing in the initiation ceremony).

There is a problem, however, which has to do with the ancient texts of the *Tradition.* The Latin text is not the only extant text. There are others: the *Testament of Our Lord,* and the Sahidic, Arabic and Ethiopic texts of the *Egyptian Church Order.* All of these offer a vastly different prayer at the bishop's imposition of hands. It reads: "Lord God, who made them worthy to receive the remission of sins through the washing of regeneration, make them worthy to be filled with the Holy Spirit. Send forth into them thy grace that they may serve you according to your will." In this prayer the remission of sins is linked to the water, which preceded, and the gift of the Spirit to the imposition of hands, which follows. Dom Gregory Dix advances this reading in support of his theory that baptism forgives sins and confirmation confers the Spirit, without giving any hint that the Latin text has an entirely different reading.[37] In his edition of *The Apostolic Tradition,* he dismisses the Latin text as corrupt at this point, without any explanation.[38]

I do not think, however, that we can dismiss the Latin text quite so cavalierly. For the other texts are not translations of *The Apostolic Tradition,* but adaptations of it. Dix himself admits this with no hesitation, and confesses further that they all rest ultimately on a single manuscript of the *Tradition* and "are therefore ultimately *one* witness to the text of *The Apostolic Tradition,* not four."[39] That leaves us with the *one* witness of the Latin text and the *one* witness of the other texts.

How are we to separate their authenticity? Botte is in no doubt; the Latin version is a faithful witness. "It is even the *only* faithful witness, since the others are all more or less adaptations and not simple translations."[40] Adding to or subtracting from the Latin version on the basis of the others is, therefore, a risky business and never more than mere conjecture. I agree with Botte's preference of the Latin text, which leads to the conclusion that *The Apostolic Tradition* links the gift of the Spirit to water baptism. The Latin prayer recurs, indeed, in much the same form, in both the later Gregorian and Gelasian sacramentaries.[41]

But to return to Hippolytus and to the prayer he reports at the imposition of the bishop's hands, which acknowledges the gift of the Spirit in the water and yet asks for the further grace to do God's will. Does not this prayer offer an early example of the theological approach, which later became so popular, that either assigns to baptism negative effects (remission of sins) and to confirmation positive effects (gift of the Spirit, grace) or presents confirmation as the perfection of baptism?[42] I think not. For the ritual that Hippolytus describes is *one* ritual of initiation, not several rituals in sequence with sequential processes: now this grace is not given, now it is. The Spirit of God and/or grace is proclaimed, realized and celebrated at this time in one complete ritual of initiation. To separate one moment of the ritual from another, though it did later occur both liturgically and doctrinally, would be blatant, anachronistic, dogmatic eisegesis. The solution of our problem lies somehow in the ritual process itself and in the connectedness of its symbols. In the ritual process of initiation, after he imposes hands on them, the bishop anoints the neophytes and prays over them. If we were to uncover the symbolic meaning of this anointing we could go a long way toward solving our problem.

We may take as our starting point a prayer for the Mass in which chrism is consecrated, as it is recorded in the Gregorian Sacramentary. "Confirm this creature, chrism . . . in order that, when the corruption of the first birth shall have been swallowed up, the pure perfume of a life pleasing to you may yield fragrance in each one's temple, after the infusion of the *sanctifying force of anointing*" (my emphasis). The symbolic water symbolizes the swallowing up of the corruption of the first, biological birth by the second, ritual birth in Christ and in his Spirit. The symbolic oil and anointing proclaim further meanings. They reveal to the neophyte, and to the assembled Church, that the new life is to be a holy and a righteous life, guaranteed by the Spirit received in the water, who is not only a Holy Spirit but also a holi- (or sancti-) fying Spirit. The symbolic water and the symbolic oil do not mean chronologically first non-Spirit and then Spirit. Rather do they mean ritually that the life achieved in the water is to be a life of holiness guaranteed by the Spirit of God, who is at once a Spirit of Life and a Spirit of Holiness. As Jesus is signed as *Christos* by the Holy Spirit at his baptism, so too is the believer signed as *christos* by the same Spirit at his baptism. The external anointing administered by the overseer of the local church-body of Christ reveals, realizes and celebrates this internal fact.[43]

This view, though articulated in different language, is not unlike the view of the efficacy of confirmation offered by Thomas Aquinas.[44] Thomas, of course, had in mind not two moments in one ritual process, but two quite distinct sacraments, baptism and confirmation, but still he shares none of the dichotomies in which his predecessors and successors indulged. He does not doubt that confirmation is given, as the very name demonstrates, "to confirm what was previously given,"[45] among which is the Holy Spirit.[46] The general Thomistic view of the relationship between baptism and confirmation, and other sacraments too, is analogous to life in general. There is a moment of origin in life, and for life in Christ this is the moment of baptism. And there are moments of growth, and for life in Christ this is the moment of confirmation and, above all, of Eucharist. Baptism is necessary to live (*esse*), confirmation to live well (*bene esse*).[47]

There is, then, some "perfection" of baptism achieved in confirmation. But this "perfection" has to be very carefully understood. Baptism is complete and perfect in itself; nothing is lacking in it in terms of grace and salvation. If confirmation brings any perfection to it, it is a perfection of super-abundance, a perfection of *bene esse*, not of *esse*.[48] The super-abundance granted in confirmation is compared to the situation of the apostles before and after Pentecost. Before Pentecost, they were possessed by the Spirit, each for his own spiritual life. But at Pentecost the same Spirit possessed them for the preaching of Christ to others.[49] So at baptism the Spirit indwells Christians for their own Spirit-filled lives, and at confirmation the same Spirit possesses them to preach that life to others. Confirmation "et hominem facit ferventem in conscientia et famosum per confessionem."[50]

Aquinas locates the sacramental effectiveness of confirmation, not in the conferral of the Spirit, but in the fortitude to live into a life guaranteed by the previously-given Spirit. Latreille sums it up well, I think, in these words: "The person confirmed is deputed to a spiritual combat, which is distinguished from the spiritual combat of the baptized person as an external combat is distinguished from an internal combat, or as a public testimony is distinguished from a private."[51] Confirmation is the sacrament, not of adult age, for age has little to do with it, but of perfect age, the age, that is, when Christians not only *say* that they are possessed by the Spirit of God, but *live* Spirit-filled lives. This perspective returns all the theological verbiage about baptism and confirmation and Spirit to the simplicity of the gospel. "Not everyone who *says* to me 'Lord, Lord' shall enter the kingdom of heaven, but he who *does* the will of my Father who is in heaven" (Mt 7:21). Not all those who say they have received the Spirit of God in baptism are to be believed, but only those who do Spirit-filled deeds. It is the perfection of such deeds now to be done that confirmation proclaims and celebrates as the perfection of the baptismal life.

THEOLOGICAL REFLECTION

What, then, are we to say about the sacrament of confirmation? What we must say first is clear. If confirmation is a sacrament, and in the Roman Catholic Church it is solemnly taught to be such,[52] then it is a symbolic action which proclaims, realizes and celebrates something other than itself. Pope Paul VI's constitution, *Divinae Consortium Naturae*, introducing and justifying a new ritual of confirmation in the Church, acknowledges as much. At the outset, it quotes the very sacramental words of Tertullian that occupied us earlier: "The body is washed that the soul may be cleansed; the body is anointed that the soul may be consecrated; the body is signed that the soul may be fortified; the flesh is overshadowed by the imposition of hands that the soul too may be enlightened by the Spirit; the body is nourished on the body and blood of Christ that the soul too should be nourished by God."[53] But when we have said that much, what remains to be said is not so clear, including what is proclaimed, realized and celebrated in the ritual. The confusion and ambiguity we discovered in both the New Testament and the Fathers, and of which Jungmann complained in 1955, continues unabated today. A careful analysis of Paul VI's constitution and of the new ritual of confirmation might, however, enable us to come to a clear and consistent picture of what is being symbolized in this ritual.

The new ritual of confirmation was introduced, as were all the new rituals available in the Church today, to satisfy the desire of the Second Vatican Council that sacramental words and actions should be revised to "express more clearly the holy things which they signify," so that believers "should be able to understand them with ease and take part in them fully, actively, and as befits a community."[54] The most important revision in the new ritual of confirmation, without a doubt, is the new sacramental form, that is, the new words to be recited while the anointing with chrism takes place. These new sacramental words, "N., be sealed with the gift of the Holy Spirit," replace those with which many older Roman Catholics will be familiar, namely, "I sign you with the sign of the cross and confirm you with the chrism of salvation. In the name of the Father and of the Son and of the Holy Spirit." This latter formula, customary though it was, was judged to be vague and impoverished in meaning, and not to express clearly what was being symbolized in this sacrament, namely, the gift of the Holy Spirit. So it was replaced with the new formula, which was judged to express that gift clearly.

The use of the adjectives *old* and *new*, however, in this and in many other liturgical cases, is very relative. The so-called old formula is first attested in a twelfth century Roman pontifical,[55] whereas the so-called new formula is attested already in the fourth and fifth century Church.[56] In relation to Church history, which is the old formula and which the new is abundantly clear. It was not because of its age, however, but because it clearly expresses what was being revealed, realized and celebrated in this sacrament, that the new formula was chosen over all other options.

"Be sealed with the gift of the Holy Spirit" leaves no one in doubt about what is being symbolized in this sacrament: it is the gift of the Spirit of God. Paul VI states this explicitly: in the ritual of confirmation "the faithful receive the Holy Spirit as gift."[57] The homily which precedes confirmation,[58] and the bishop's prayer at the imposition of hands, an imposition which Paul decrees not to belong to "the essence of the sacramental rite" but which is, nevertheless, "to be held in high esteem, in that it contributes to the integral perfection of the rite and to a clearer understanding of the sacrament,"[59] state the same thing.[60] This still leaves us, of course, with the same old question. But did not that happen already in baptism? I have already answered that question in the affirmative. There remains now, therefore, the task of clarifying how the Spirit gifted in baptism is gifted, not again but also, in confirmation. It is not too difficult a task.

We know now that in the early Church the sacraments of baptism, confirmation and Eucharist comprised but one ritual of initiation, in which a person was gradually admitted to full membership in both the great Catholic and a local Catholic church. We know also that baptism, confirmation and Eucharist, moments in that one, symbol-dense ritual of initiation, became separated, not for some great, compelling, theological reason, but for the simple, practical reason that the bishop could not be present at every initiation. Vatican II called for the re-

.tual of confirmation to make more lucid "the intimate
lich this sacrament has with the whole of Christian ini-
il VI attests that the aim of the new ritual is to do pre-
This is a first point we must keep in mind. An ultimate
aim of the new ritual of confirmation is to underscore the connection
of this sacrament with the sacraments of baptism and Eucharist, as
comprising with them, as in the beginning, one complete process of
Christian initiation.

The connection of baptism, confirmation and Eucharist is made
quite clear in Paul VI's *Divinae Consortium Naturae*. Basing himself,
much as did Aquinas, on the analogy between natural life and the life
of the Spirit, he asserts that "the faithful are born anew by baptism,
strengthened by the sacrament of confirmation, and finally are sustained by the food of eternal life in the Eucharist. By means of these
sacraments of Christian initiation, they thus receive *in increasing measure* the treasures of divine life and advance toward the *perfection of
charity*."[63]

Confirmation, it is claimed, brings a certain perfection to the life
begun in baptism, and Eucharist brings a further perfection by sustaining it unto eternal life. But, heeding Thomas' warning about *esse*
and *bene esse*, we must tread warily here. Confirmation may perfect
baptism and Eucharist may perfect them both, but we are not obliged
to image that perfection as a sequence from non-Spirit, non-grace, to
Spirit and grace. Rather may we understand it as a sequence from
Spirit and grace to more Spirit and grace, to put materially what I hope
will not be understood too materially. *More* Spirit and grace, of course,
needs careful explanation, with which an analogy, which will recur
again in this book, will help.

In the first chapter I introduced a distinction between mere signs
and symbols. The former are informative signs; they bring something
to our knowledge. The latter are realizing signs; they proclaim, realize
and celebrate what they symbolize. I introduced also the symbols of
making love. A love letter, a kiss, a giving of flowers, sexual intercourse: these actions "make love" in the sense that they proclaim it to
be present; they realize it further (make it *more* in a personal, as distinct
from a quantitative, sense), and celebrate it. It is as just such a realizing
symbol that we can understood the sacrament of confirmation.

The Spirit of God, who is offered as gift to all men and women
from their first moment of life, is proclaimed by, realized for and celebrated by Christians in the ritual of baptism. In the case of those
Christians baptized as infants, however, the indwelling presence of the
Spirit is not personally realized. But as they are slowly nurtured to ac-

tual faith in the Church, that faith draws the objective presence of the indwelling Spirit into personal and interpersonal presence, and rejoices in that presence. There comes a time when believers will wish to proclaim in some solemn way the presence of the Spirit of God within them, both to themselves and to the Church in which they have learned faith. That is the time for confirmation, the solemn ritual in the Christian Church for revealing, realizing and celebrating the presence of the Spirit of God in baptized believers. That ritual makes Spirit just as surely as rituals of love make love.

The Spirit is indeed present in believers from the moment of their baptism, just as love is present within lovers from the moment of their falling in love. But just as love grows and develops out of both the original love and the symbolic actions which proclaim, realize and celebrate it, so too the presence of the Spirit of God grows and develops out of both his original baptismal presence and symbolic actions, including the communal one of confirmation, in which believing Christians proclaim and celebrate his presence. Lovers will tell you how their love becomes more as it deepens with each act of love-making, and will describe each moment of more as a wondrous new gift of love. So also Catholic theology tells us, in the words, for instance, of Paul VI, that the presence of the Spirit in believers becomes personally more in the Spirit-making ritual of confirmation, and describes this perfection of the original baptismal presence as a new gift of the Spirit. Pope Paul aptly teaches that "on the day of Pentecost, the Holy Spirit came down in an extraordinary way on the apostles."[64] It is no exaggeration to describe confirmation as a new Pentecost, because in it the Holy Spirit comes down upon believers, not for the first time, but in a new and humanly truly extraordinary way.

At this point there might arise the question that has been dominant for many these past twenty years. At what age should a person make Spirit? Hopefully this appears now as not a good question, at least in the sense that it is not a question with a definitive and absolute answer. The optimum answer, in my judgment, is also a simple one. Believers should make Spirit in confirmation at the age when they sufficiently believe in and care about the presence of the Spirit of God within them to want to proclaim that presence, to themselves and to others, to realize it further and to celebrate it. That age may vary from person to person. The introduction to the new ritual of confirmation opts for a very carefully worded judgment: "In the Latin church the administration of confirmation is *generally* postponed until *about* the seventh year."[65]

That judgment takes account of two realities: (1) the practice of the Code of Canon Law to presume the use of reason at about age seven; (2) the ancient practice, still current in the Catholic churches in the East, of baptizing, confirming and admitting, even infants, to Eucharist in one continuous ritual of initiation. It does not, though, either obligate to or rule out one or the other. The *general* rule, not the absolute rule, of the Latin Church is that confirmation be deferred until about age seven. But there is offered the option to defer confirmation to an age more mature than seven (and we, quite rightly, are left to discover by some appropriate means what that more mature age might be), for the very general reason "to strengthen the faithful in complete obedience to Christ the Lord and in loyal testimony to him."[66]

But what of the option not to defer confirmation, even for infants, but to celebrate it concurrently with baptism and Eucharist, as in the ancient practice still preserved in the Catholic churches of the East? Obviously in 1987 I am not raising here a practical, pastoral question, for such a question would be answered, I believe, by an affirmation of the status quo. Rather am I raising a speculative, theological question, the answer to which in the long run, though, will determine pastoral practice. I raise it here precisely to uncover the best possible pastoral practice in the still-confused theological situation.

At first glance, the answer to the question of the confirmation of infants is quite straightforward. After all, it was the ancient Catholic practice, and it is still the practice in the Catholic churches of the East. The Roman Catholic Church abandoned this ancient practice, to repeat, not for great, theological reasons, but for purely practical ones. Yet it still continued to baptize infants. Now if the baptism of infants is meaningful, and I argued in the previous chapter that it is, then so too is their confirmation. The reasons I advanced for infant baptism were essentially communal, ecclesial reasons. I believe not only that similar reasons can be offered for infant confirmation but also that they are, in fact, present in germ in the new ritual.

The new ritual of confirmation is through and through a communal ritual. "It is the responsibility of the people of God to prepare the baptized for confirmation," it decrees.[67] The people of God, the Church, is invited to gather to celebrate the confirmation of some of its members, and it is to this people that the word of God as it relates to the Holy Spirit and to confirmation is both proclaimed and explained. It is before the gathered Church that its members to be confirmed confess their Catholic faith, and it is the Church, in the person of its president-bishop, which both accepts this confession of faith and acknowledges it as its own. "This is our faith," it declares. "This is the faith of the Church. We are proud to profess it in Christ Jesus our

Lord."[68] It is, finally, the Church that prays for those to be confirmed that God "will pour out the Holy Spirit to strengthen his sons and daughters with his gifts,"[69] and which admits them to participation in the communal meal after they have been so strengthened. The ritual of confirmation exemplifies abundantly the judgment of Vatican II that "liturgical services are not private functions, but are celebrations of the Church, which is the 'sacrament of unity.' "[70]

But what would be the shape of a ritual of infant baptism–confirmation? Its shape is not difficult to envision. It would be very similar to the present rituals of baptism and confirmation, but reflecting even more clearly the communal dimensions and demands of what is being proclaimed, realized and celebrated, namely, the presence as gift of the Spirit of God, which is creative of new life to be manifested in new Spirit-filled action. Action always follows being and Christian action is no exception; it derives from Christian being. And it is here, once again, as in infant baptism, that there arises a caveat about infant confirmation.

In the preceding chapter I discussed the ambiguity in the Christian doctrine that one of the effects of baptism is faith. Faith, as we saw, may be understood in one of two senses. It may mean the virtue of faith, that is, the power or the know-how to make an act of faith; or it may mean an actual act of faith. The know-how, of course, is a prerequisite for the act, but the act by no means flows automatically from the know-how. Sadly, our times have brought sharply into focus a new, only in the sense of hitherto unacknowledged, phenomenon, that of countless numbers of baptized who have received the virtue of faith in baptism but who have never been moved to an act of faith in the God made known in Jesus. They constitute that anomalous brand of Christian known today as *baptized non-believers*.[71] The Catholic Church needs to examine its conscience carefully with respect to these baptized non-believers, for, in spite of its grandiose claims to be a community of faith, and in spite of its commitment made at their baptisms to lead these baptized to actual faith, it has failed to do so. Its failure means that for them baptism has been fruitless.

Christian doctrine teaches that baptism effects not only the gift of faith, but also the gift of the Spirit of God who makes faith possible. There is an analogous ambiguity here too. That the Spirit of God is revealed, realized and celebrated in Western infant baptism and in Eastern infant baptism–confirmation is beyond Christian doubting. But that the Spirit has been proclaimed and celebrated in the lives of baptized non-believers is very much open to doubt. The presence of the Spirit of God, at least as far as human insight can discern, would appear to have been fruitless in their case—and that, not because the rituals of baptism and confirmation were ineffective, but because the Christian community was ineffective in nurturing so many of its members into faith and into making Spirit.

And so a second thought about infant confirmation. As with infant baptism, it will be humanly effective only in cases where the confirmed infant is nurtured to faith in and celebration of the Spirit who indwells him, whether that nurturing be done by a family-domestic church or by some local church community. But if, as I argued, there is no need to rush to baptize infants, neither is there need to rush to confirm them. There is time enough to baptize–confirm when the child has been converted to the God who is Father and Son and Spirit, believes in that God, and wishes to proclaim, realize and celebrate his presence in the solemn ritual of Christian initiation. The effect of this waited for ritual would be, not to give the know-how of faith, not to give without realization the Holy Spirit, but to proclaim, actualize and celebrate the already established presence of both. There is already in place in the Roman Catholic Church a ritual for such a sequence: the Rite of Christian Initiation of Adults. This is a step by step ritual from initial conversion through intense catechesis to solemn celebration of the ritual of Christian initiation, in which those seeking to be initiated into the Christian Church "hear the preaching of the mystery of Christ, the Holy Spirit opens their hearts, and they freely and knowingly seek the living God and enter the path of faith and conversion."[72] The culmination of the process, the solemn initiation, takes place at Easter time, and everything I said in the previous chapter about baptism as a symbolizing of the death-resurrection of Jesus should be recalled here. "The whole initiation has a paschal character, since the initiation of Christians is the first sacramental sharing in the death and rising of Christ."[73]

The role of the local church in the process is carefully highlighted, and it is instructed to "help the candidates and catechumens throughout their whole period of initiation, during the pre-catechumenate, the catechumenate and the period of post-baptismal catechesis."[74] The help required from the Church is not specified, but it is clear that it is a help to faith, first provoking it in the pre-catechumenate, then nurturing it in the catechumenate, and finally sustaining it in the long haul of post-initiation Christian life and action. The whole ritual shows a careful and correct ordering from conversion to Christ, to faith in Christ, to initiation into Christ. Nor is there any rush to initiate. "The period of time suitable for the catechumenate depends on the grace of God," but it is to be for "an extended period."[75]

This rite of initiation is presently restricted to adults. But there is no theological reason why it should not be extended to the case of infants. If there is no rush to initiate adults, there need certainly be no rush to initiate infants. A faithful community can afford to wait: through a pre-catechumenate in which its children, perhaps already ritually enrolled as those who may one day seek initiation, and therefore already the subjects of its special nurture, experience, are provoked by, and eventually come to accept its faith; through a catechumenate in which it will assiduously nurture that faith in them and proclaim and explain to them the good news of the God made known in Christ; to a time of initiation in which their children, now believers, will not be given unconsciously faith and the Holy Spirit, but will freely and knowingly and personally proclaim, realize and celebrate with them faith in the Spirit of God who has been given to them.

Such a period of waiting would, again, depend "on the grace of God," but would be for "an extended time." To repeat, age has little to do with Christian conversion, faith and initiation.[76] But the wait would be worth it for a community of faith. For at the end of it baptism and confirmation would not be disjointed rituals, claiming to give faith and the Holy Spirit, but in reality producing only non-faith and unrealized Spirit. Rather would they be proclamation and realization and celebration of faith and Spirit, and comprehensively personal ritual response to the God who is revealed, realized and celebrated in Jesus, now confessed as the Christ.

Chapter Five
PENANCE-RECONCILIATION

PREAMBLE

"If anyone has committed a fault let him admit it. If not, let him be silent. From your silence, venerable brothers, I will be able to conclude that you are without fault. In a gathering like this each question is put three times. If, after a question is put three times, anyone deliberately avoids confessing his faults, he becomes guilty of a premeditated lie. But, venerable brothers, our Lord has declared that a lie is a stumbling block in the way of one's fundamental duty. That is why a monk who is aware of having committed a fault and who wishes to be purified must confess his guilt. In this way he will have a peaceful soul."[1]

This is, as the reader has already guessed, an ancient monastic invitation to confession of sins and penance. But it is not, as the reader may also have guessed, a *Christian* invitation; it is a *Buddhist* one. The fundamental duty referred to is the Buddhist *dharma;* a lie is a block to *dharma.* There follows in the Buddhist penitential lists of faults, some of which are "grave and inexpiable," others "grave and expiable," each accompanied by lists of suitable penances. It is very similar to lists of sins and penances in Christian penitentials. Those elements which in the Christian tradition are named sin and its effects, along with the desire for their removal, are apparently deep-seated in universal religious meaning systems. It is not surprising that such meanings and such needs are formalized in ritual behaviors which proclaim, realize and celebrate in representation repentance, forgiveness of sins and reconciliation.

The Christian Gospels portray repentance, forgiveness and reconciliation at the very heart of the preaching of Jesus. He is presented as entering upon his work with the invitation to "repent and believe the Gospel" (Mk 1:15), and as concluding it with the command that "in his name repentance and the forgiveness of sins is to be proclaimed to all nations" (Lk 24:47). That forgiveness is not just a private matter between God and the sinner. It comes somehow through the mediation of the Church, the gathering of those who have believed and have been baptized in the name of Jesus (cf. Mt 18:15). The connection between forgiveness and reconciliation on the one hand and the Church on the other is a very important element in the ritualizing of repentance, forgiveness and reconciliation in the Christian scheme of things. We shall have to consider it in some historical detail.

FORGIVENESS AND RECONCILIATION IN THE LIFE OF THE CHURCH

A central part of the kerygma of the New Testament is that God raised Jesus from the dead (1 Cor 15:3–4; Rom 8:34; Gal 1:1; Eph 1:20; Acts 2:24) and made him head of a gathering of those who are called to believe the good news of his resurrection. This gathering of the called is named in Greek *Ekklesia* and in English *Church*. Members of this Church are said to be "in Christ" (passim). They are said to be the "body of Christ" (1 Cor 6:12–20; 10:17; 12:12–27; Rom 12:4–5; Eph 1:22–23; 2:14–16; 3:6; 4:4–16; 5:22–30; Col 1:18–24; 2:19; 3:15), a body into which they are grown in the ritual waters of baptism, which is imaged, therefore, sometimes as rebirth (Jn 3:5) and sometimes as new creation (2 Cor 5:17; Gal 6:15). Anthropologically, and therefore theologically, more than metaphor is intended here. As we saw in the chapter on baptism, the ritual water is so powerful that it realizes what it symbolizes, in this case the body of Christ. So effective is the water in growing the body of Christ that after baptism "there is neither Jew nor Greek, there is neither slave nor free, there is neither male nor female, for you are all one *person* (the Greek is *heis* = one person, not *hen* = one thing, as some translations might suggest) in Christ Jesus" (Gal 3:28). The result is that what appears at the literal level to be nothing more than a group of men and women is, in symbolic reality, the Church, the body of Christ, the proclamation, realization and celebration of Christ in the human world.

For this Christian Church the mystery of salvation is essentially a mystery of reconciliation which, therefore, occupies a place in the forefront of its cultic life. The Church, body of Christ though it be, is a Church of sinners. Paul, though he demanded a complete change in lifestyle from those in Christ (Rom 6:12; 1 Cor 5:7), never doubted that sin remains a powerful factor even in Christian lives, and constantly warned against it. The lists of sins he reports (1 Cor 6:9–10; Gal 5:19; Col 3:5; Eph 5:3–6) are "manifestly conditioned by actual moral failings of believers."[2] The Ekklesia was always one simultaneously holy and yet in need of purification.[3] Yet it shares Christ's attitude to sin, to sinners, to repentance, to reconciliation. He is reported as proclaiming: "I came not to call the righteous but sinners" (Mk 2:17). And as he does, so does his Ekklesia-body. It sees itself as having the duty of calling to repentance from sin, in imitation of him whom it claims to reveal, realize and celebrate. In cases of gross sin the call to repentance takes a gross form.

Paul reports the classical case in his First Letter to the Corinthians. It is the case of the incestuous man, "living with his father's wife" (5:1). The Church should have expelled such a one from membership, but had not done so. Paul does so, instructing the Corinthians "to deliver this man to Satan for the destruction of the flesh, that his spirit may be saved in the day of the Lord Jesus" (5:5). Delivery to Satan, as the context clearly implies, and as Tertullian explains explicitly later,[4] is excommunication or expulsion from the community. Its purpose is clearly stated: "the destruction of the flesh, that his spirit may be saved." The First Letter to Timothy employs the same formula in excommunicating Hymenaeus and Alexander "that they may learn not to blaspheme" (1:20). Excommunication is not intended to be punitive or vindictive. It is primarily admonition and exhortation, "for the salvation of the spirit," "that they may learn not to blaspheme."

The excommunication of the sinner in no ways implies his final condemnation. He does not become an untouchable. As early as his Second Letter to the Thessalonians Paul gives instructions that one who has been excommunicated from the Church is not to be looked upon "as an enemy" but warned "as a brother" (3:15). And in his Second Letter to the Corinthians he explains how the repentant sinner is to be dealt with. He is to be forgiven and, in later language, to be reconciled. When "punishment by the majority is enough," that is, when it achieves its purpose of calling the sinner to repentance, the Church "should turn to forgive and confront him" (2 Cor 2:5–11). I do not wish here to enter into the discussion of whether the man to be reconciled here is the incestuous man of 1 Corinthians 5:1–5 or not. I accept the modern judgment that he is not.[5] Whether he is or not, of course, is supremely irrelevant, for in either case the text still offers important evidence of ecclesial forgiveness and reconciliation in early New Testament times. It is for this purpose that it is advanced here: to show repentance and forgiveness and reconciliation at the early core of the Church's self-understanding in imitation of him who is its head.

The preceding has been about normative meanings and values. It does not give information about concrete, formal behavior in which such meanings and values are ritualized. That information becomes available only later, with Tertullian. The writings of the immediate post-apostolic age, while giving no great insight into the ritual practice, do, however, perpetuate the meanings seen in the apostolic Church.

The homily known under the title of the Second Letter of Clement openly applies Jeremiah's image of the den of robbers (Jer 7:11; cf. Mt 21:12) to the Church which does not do the Lord's will.[6] It repeats for second century believers the traditional call to repent and sin no more,[7] and to do penance by prayer and fasting and almsgiving. "Almsgiving," it declares, "is a good thing, even as repentance for sin. Fasting is better than prayer, but almsgiving better than both."[8] Confession of sins is also important, as the instructions in the *Didache* make clear. "In the church confess your sins and go not to prayer with an evil conscience";[9] "on the Lord's day gather yourselves together and break bread and give thanks, first confessing your sins, that your sacrifice may be pure."[10]

The outlines of a root meaning and value system are constantly to the fore: sin, repentance, confession. There follows ecclesial forgiveness and reconciliation, and we shall consider that. But first a caveat against anachronism. The *Didache* has sometimes been put forward as evidence of detailed sacramental confession in the early Church. But the view that it represents rather general confession of sin is the more common one, and I share it. "Nothing indicates that there is question here of detailed confession carried out privately by each one who felt guilty. All the members of the community, all together, acknowledge that they are sinners. . . . The recitation of our *confiteor*, either at the beginning of Mass or before Communion, would be what would best correspond to what is described here."[11]

After sin and repentance and confession there follows ecclesial forgiveness. As expulsion from the Church as remedial punishment belongs to the Church, so also does reception back into it as salutary forgiveness. Polycarp urges presbyters to be "compassionate, merciful toward all men," and points out that "if we entreat the Lord that he would forgive us, we ought also to forgive."[12] Given the universal view of the Church as the body of Christ, forgiveness by and reaggregation into it was looked upon as also forgiveness by and reaggregation into Christ and, ultimately, God. Ignatius has no doubt: "As many as shall repent and enter into the unity of the Church, these also shall be of God."[13] And Clement confirms his view: "You that laid the foundation of sedition, submit yourselves to the presbyters and receive chastisement unto repentance. . . . For it is better for you to be found little in the flock of Christ and to have your name on God's roll than to be held in exceeding honor and yet to be cast out from hope of him."[14]

The first clear evidence of prescribed concrete and formal behavior in relation to Christian repentance, forgiveness and reconciliation is provided, as already noted, by Tertullian in his Catholic days. It shows in an already fixed form all the elements attested since the apostolic age. Penance is necessary for the forgiveness of sins.[15] But it is not just an interior attitude; it demands also an external act, which is expressed by the Greek word *exomologesis,* "by which we confess our sins to the Lord."[16] *Exomologesis* intends a rather complex reality, including confession of sins before the Church and before God. Again, confession is to be understood not in the sense of a detailed enumeration of sins, but rather in the sense of a series of actions which cannot but call attention to the sinfulness of the penitent: prostration in sackcloth and ashes, neglect of cleanliness, fasting, groaning, tears, beseeching on bended knee the assistance of the presbyters and of all believers.[17]

These acts, which are in no way optional, take place in a formalized context. The *exomologesis* took place outside the Church.[18] After a period of penance, more or less long but absolutely indispensable, there followed in the normal course of events reconciliation by and with the Church, which Tertullian identifies explicitly with Christ. "The Church is Christ. When, therefore, you reach out at the knees of the brethren, you come in contact with Christ, you beseech Christ. Similarly, when they pour out their tears upon you, Christ lies open, Christ beseeches the Father."[19] When the Church reconciles the sinner, it does so in practice in the person of its local *episkopos*-overseer, as even Montanist Tertullian admits.[20]

Tertullian describes the penitential practice of the Church at the opening of the third century. It is a practice which will continue for four centuries, until the appearance of the so-called Celtic penance. The practice will become ever more formalized as time progresses until it becomes a very fixed ritual in three symbolic acts: enrollment in the order of penitents, doing of penance, forgiveness and reconciliation by the *episkopos* and the Church. But before looking at the symbolic structure of those acts, I wish to note one further root meaning and value in ancient penance.[21] It was a once-only ritual.

Catholic Tertullian gives the definitive formulation. God "has placed in the vestibule a second penance which can open [the closed doors] to those who knock. But once only, since it is already the second time, and never again in the future, because the preceding penance has been in vain."[22] Such a restriction was formulated earlier by Hermas. He poses a question to the spirit which "took" him. "I have heard, sir, from certain teachers that there is no other repentance save that which took place when we went down into the water and obtained remission of our former sins." The spirit responds that he has heard well, but enlarges his answer to explain that God has provided the baptized with one further opportunity of repentance, but "once only."[23] The once-only character of the second penance is justified by dealing with it analogously to the first penance, namely, baptism, which is received only once. Ancient penance, indeed, was regarded as a second baptism,[24] since in it the sinful Christian found once again the forgiveness of all his sins. The once-only character will continue as a feature of penance until the appearance of Celtic penance in the seventh century.

Now we return to consider the formalized practice of the second penance. Recall the order of sacramentality elaborated earlier. Jesus is the incarnation, the proclamation and realization of God. To be with Jesus, therefore, is to be with God; to be apart from Jesus is to be apart from God. The Church is the incarnation, the proclamation and realization of Jesus in the historical world. To be with the Church, therefore, is to be with Jesus and, therefore, with God; to be apart from the Church is to be apart from Jesus and from God. The formal actions of the Church are sacraments, symbolic actions which reveal, realize and celebrate Jesus and God.

The story of the relationship between God and humankind is characterized in the sacred Scriptures as a covenant relationship. The story of God's gracious and saving action is presented as his election of a people as his own. The story of this people's refusal of their election is the story of sin. To put briefly and very abstractly what would take great length if put concretely, sin is what more or less damages God's people's relationship with him. It damages also, therefore, their relationship with Jesus and with the Church. The ritual practice of ancient penance begins with this given, that sin has damaged the believer's relationship with the Church, with the Christ and with God, and proceeds from that given to ritualize the healing of relationships on all three levels.

The sinner begins the penance ritual literally outside the Church, to symbolize his sin-induced situation of being normatively more or less outside the Church. To be separated from the Church, remember, is in symbolic reality to be separated also from Jesus and from God.

The sinner begins his re-entry into the Church, and into right relationship with Jesus and with God, by enrolling in the order of penitents.

Caesar, bishop of Arles, invites sinners to enroll as penitents sooner rather than later, since it is better to apply the remedy to the wound when it is fresh rather than to leave it to fester. He acknowledges that the *exomologesis* is a cause of shame, but advises that the brief period of penance and shame is nothing when compared to the suffering of eternal punishment.[25] In this he echoes Tertullian, who also acknowledged the difficulty and shame of the *exomologesis* but encouraged it with the rhetorical question: "Is it better to be damned in secret or publicly forgiven?"[26] Augustine too urged sinners to enroll publicly as penitents and to do public penance to enlist the support of the Church, "that the Ekklesia may pray for you."[27] Enrollment was accomplished by the imposition of the bishop's hands,[28] without any detailed confession of sins, which was officially reproved by Pope Leo the Great.[29] The enrollment was followed by the sprinkling of ashes on the penitent's head and his clothing in a hairshirt, which was to proclaim, as Caesar of Arles explains, that the penitent was "not a lamb but a goat."[30] This hairshirt was the penitential uniform worn while doing penance.

A final symbolic unit in this part of the penance ritual was that the penitent was ritually expelled from the Church, symbolizing his normative distance from it, from Jesus and from God. This did not mean, save in extreme cases of scandalous sin and excommunication, that he could never be present in the Church while carrying out his penance. It meant rather that he could never take full part in the great ritual meal of Eucharist in which the Church proclaimed, realized and celebrated the body of Christ. Cut off from the church, from Jesus and from God by their sins, penitents were cut off from them in symbolic reality, to provoke thoughts and desires and actions directed toward repentance, forgiveness and reconciliation with all three.

The theological meaning of the imposition of the bishop's hands upon the penitent reveals another root meaning of the ritual entrance into penance.[31] The earliest clear reference to such a ritual in the Church is provided by Origen. He understands James 5:14 to apply to penance and the call for the presbyters to pray over the sick man to apply to a sinner diseased by sin, and calls for a rite of imposition of hands. He understands that rite to be the Church's prayer for the penitent.[32] Cyprian knows the same ritual related by Tertullian, *exomologesis*, penance, reconciliation,[33] and emphasizes the imposition of hands in each stage, seemingly understanding it to mean the granting of peace with the Church. That peace is initiated by the imposition at the enrollment as penitent, is expanded by the frequent blessings of the penitents during their period of doing penance, and is brought to fruition by the imposition of the bishop's hands which finally reconciles the penitents to the Church. At each of these stages, the communication of the Church's peace is regarded also as the communication of the Spirit which is given to it. Literal peace with the Church is in symbolic reality also normative peace with the Spirit of God.[34] It is clear that the ritual of imposition of hands by the bishop, "who in this period was the only one to whom the title of *sacerdos* was applied,"[35] was a truly ecclesial ritual, provoking thoughts and desires and actions focusing on solidarity with the Church.

During their period of penance, penitents had a special place in the assembly,[36] probably at the back of church where they could be seen, recognized as penitents, prayed for and supervized in the doing of their penance. Augustine brings one penitent, a soothsayer (*mathematicus*), before the assembled Church to recommend him to their prayers and supervision.[37] There were also blessings for penitents during the assembly. The Council of Laodicea (350) prescribes that these blessings take place after the dismissal of the catechumens;[38] Augustine speaks of them as taking place at the Eucharist.[39] Leo the Great explains that by these blessings penitents "can be cleansed by fasting and the imposition of hands."[40] The Council of Agde (506) decrees that penitents must receive these blessings and reserves them to the *episkopos*.[41]

The final action of ancient penance was that the penitent, on the completion of his penance, was reconciled by the *episkopos* with an imposition of hands. Leo the Great explains the meaning of the action. "The aids of divine mercy have been so arranged that God's pardon cannot be obtained except by the supplication of bishops."[42] For the mediator of God and men, the man Jesus Christ, has passed on this power to those placed over the Church that they may grant the doing of penance to those who confess and, when they have been cleansed by salutary satisfaction, admit them to communion in the sacraments through the door of reconciliation."[43] That admission to Communion, he insists elsewhere, is achieved "only through the remedy of penance and the imposition of the bishop's hands."[44]

Jerome is just as explicit. "The bishop is the seasoning of the whole Church and of the world. He offers his oblation for the layman, imposes hands on him, prays for the return of the Holy Spirit, and reconciles to the altar him who has been handed over to Satan."[45] What I have already emphasized is abundantly clear here: the way to the reception of the peace and the Spirit of God is through peace with the Church, a peace which is proclaimed, realized and celebrated in representation in the ritual imposition of hands. The fullest participation in that peace, however, happens not in the ritual of reconciliation but in the ritual of the Lord's Supper—and it is to that the reconciled penitent is admitted once he has been reconciled.

One final symbolic dimension of the ritual of ancient penance must be noted, namely, the time symbolism. Leo the Great decreed that Lent is the proper time, not only for preparing for baptism, but also for doing penance.[46] Innocent I declared that "the custom of the Roman Church demonstrates that [penitents] are to be reconciled on the Thursday before Easter."[47] Ambrose has left two sermons testifying to the same thing.[48] The symbolism should be clear.

At the opening of the Jesus story, the angelic message announces his mission: "You shall call his name Jesus, for he will save his people from their sins" (Mt 1:21). Paul reports how the mission was accomplished: "He was put to death for our sins and was raised for our justification" (Rom 4:25). He reports also the understanding of the Pauline Church that Christians are "buried with him by baptism unto death, so that as Christ was raised from the dead by the glory of the Father, we too might walk in newness of life" (Rom 6:4). Baptism, the first penance, was linked to the death-resurrection of Jesus by being celebrated, as we saw, at Easter. Penance, the second baptism, was equally linked to that death-resurrection by being finalized at the same sacred time. That time symbolism proclaimed, realized and celebrated the dimension of death to sin and resurrection to new life that was and is essentially connected with ritual penance. And it did this not only for the penitents who were reconciled, but also for the entire Church which was so intimately involved in the whole ritual process.

If Monica Wilson is correct, and I am convinced that she is, and ritual reveals the values of the group, then ancient penance is a perfect ritual. For it reveals the root perspective in which the ancient Christian Church understands itself: a community possessed by and possessing the Spirit of God poured into the world at the resurrection-glorification of Jesus; a community which reveals, realizes and celebrates the presence of that Spirit, first in the ritual of baptism for the forgiveness of sins, second in the ritual of confirmation for the public proclamation of the word, and third in the ritual of penance for at-one-ment in that Spirit with the Church, with Jesus and with God.

It is no exaggeration to claim that ancient penance was administered by the whole Church. The *sacerdos*-bishop who officiated did so, in Jerome's quaint phrase, as "the seasoning of the whole Church and

of the world," not as some unrooted individual with power. It was unfortunately this important ecclesial dimension which was progressively
lost as the ritual of repentance, forgiveness and reconciliation under-
went its well-known shift in the sixth century Church. The details of
that shift are well enough known, and its Celtic origins are equally well-
known.[49] Here, therefore, I propose only to summarize the peculiar-
ities of Celtic penance vis-à-vis ancient penance, so that the nature of
the shift which took place can be highlighted. In distinction to the public character of ancient penance, extreme privacy marked its Celtic
cousin. There was no order of penitents into which a sinner had to be
ritually admitted and within which he did his penance. Nor did the
Celtic practice set aside any particular liturgical time for penance, like
the Easter time of the ancient practice. A Celtic sinner could be reconciled at any time on the completion of the so-called tariff penance
imposed on him. Nor was this reconciliation, as in ancient penance,
restricted to the bishop-priest; it could be accomplished by any
priest.[50] The outcome of reconciliation, as described by Finnian of
Clonard, was the same as in ancient penance: it reconciled and restored the penitent "to the altar."[51] But the Celtic penitent, in one final
and obvious distinction from his Roman brothers and sisters, who
could approach penance only once, could be reconciled as often as he
was penitent and carried out the penance. The impression is frequently given that this latter shift was the major shift in the historical
transition from ancient to Celtic penance. There is a sense, of course,
in which that is true. But from a specifically symbolic point of view and
considering the range and the power of meanings involved in symbols,
I believe that the major shift was rather the shift from a public to a
private character. That suggestion I will now detail.

   Arnold Van Gennep definitively characterized a certain type of
ritual as a *rite de passage*, marked by three phases: separation from a
previously fixed stage, a marginal or liminal state, aggregation to a
new fixed state.[52] It will be instructive to consider ancient penance as
such a *rite de passage*. But first there is required a theological preamble,
the importance of which will appear as we go along.

   Certain Jews in the first century heard and believed the almost
unbelievable, "that Christ died for our sins, that he was buried, and
that he was raised" (cf. 1 Cor 15:3–4). Later, when John came to write
of this Christ, he imaged his life as being ordered toward this death
and resurrection, designated as his *hour*. He defined this hour as a passage out of this world to the Father (13:1). By his death the man from
Nazareth was separated from a previously fixed state in which he was
named Jesus. In death he was in a liminal state, a state of nothingness,

in which he did not have a personal name but was known simply by what happened to him, the Crucified. Then "God raised him up, having loosed the pangs of death" (Acts 2:24), established Jesus in a new fixed state with himself, a state in which he was given a new personal title, the Christ. Jesus' passage was complete.

I have argued elsewhere that baptism, the first penance, is truly a *rite de passage.*[53] It does not seem too strong to suggest that ancient penance, the second baptism, is at least a quasi *rite de passage.* In it sinners begin in a fixed state, the state of being separated from the Church, and are known by what they are, sinners. Enrollment in the order of penitents established them in a liminal state, no longer completely sinners, but not yet full members again in the Church. Again, they are known by what they are, penitents. This liminal state is ritualized in two complex ritual gestures. The first is the imposition of the bishop's hands, symbolizing peace with the Church, followed by the expulsion of the penitent, symbolizing that they are not yet full members of the Church. The second is the attendance of the penitents at the banquet meal (members), and the simultaneous refusal to permit them full participation in the meal (not-full members). This liminal state lasts for the penitents until the completion of their passage, which is ritualized in two gestures negating the previous ones, namely, their reception back into the Church and their admission to full sharing in the banquet. The once-and-former sinners have passed to become, in this case again, the now-and-future full members of the Church. They are named now, again, Christians.

Two points need to be emphasized. The first is that passage implies movement from a *terminus a quo* to a *terminus ad quem.* It is the *passing* which is central here and, therefore, in ritual, the enabling of the passing. In the paradigmatic salvation event, his death-resurrection, Jesus passed from earthly life through death to life with God. Christians share this passage of Jesus in symbolic reality, initially in baptism, by passing from life outside the body of Christ through ritual death in the symbolic water to new life in the body of Christ. They share it again in second baptism, penance, where they again make the same passage. Crucial to both these passages is the enabling of the passing by the Church. In both rituals the entire Church is essentially and publicly involved, provoking and sustaining in the passer thoughts and desires and actions centering on communion with the Church, with Christ and with God. It is precisely this radical involvement of the Church, enabling and provoking the passage, that ultimately constitutes both rituals as *public.*

The second point is this, that passages achieved in both the first and the second penances are explicitly linked to the paschal passage of Jesus by the time of their celebration. As Jesus achieved his passage to life with God through his death and resurrection, so Christians achieve their passages from sinful death to life in the Church, and therefore in Jesus and in God, not only in imitation of his paschal passage but also, and more importantly, participating in its power. The Lenten enrollment as penitent, and the paschal-related reconciliation in and with the Church, placed the connection of the ancient penance ritual to the paschal passage of the Christ squarely in the forefront for both the reconciliation-seeking penitent and the reconciliation-granting Church to see.

Both the public involvement of the Church and the symbolic linkage of the ritual to the death-resurrection of Jesus were destroyed by the victory of Celtic penance over the ancient Roman practice. Celtic penance was, of course, not the sole cause of the demise of ancient penance. That demise was already well under way when Columban arrived in Gaul, as is attested by Abbot Jonas in his Life of St. Columban. "The medicinal practice of penance and the love of mortification were scarcely or little found in these places."[54] When Celtic penance arrived on the continent of Europe, ancient penance was already in decay, because of both the severity of the penances imposed and their lifetime social consequences and the rigidity of the principle which forbade the repetition of penance. What I wish to emphasize here is only that the different Celtic *praxis* led to the obscuring of two crucial *theoretical* dimensions of ancient penance, namely, its essential ecclesial and therefore public character and its essential connection to the death-resurrection of Jesus.

Of these two, the shift from public to private penance was ultimately the most radical, in terms of both *theoria* and *praxis*. For it separated penance from its ritual root in the Church. However much later theory struggled to present the priest in the confessional as the minister of the reconciling Church, the praxis presented him rather in the guise of a delegate of the judging God. And the custom, which became the norm, of absolving and reconciling before the completion of the penance did away with the practice of doing the penance over time, a practice which was necessary to the ritualizing of the *passing*. All of this reduced the ritual to an individual rather than an ecclesial action. So separated from the Church did the ritual of penance, indeed all the sacramental rituals, become that Thomas Aquinas in his major *Summa Theologiae* could pass directly from his treatment of Christ to his treatment of sacraments without any linkage to the Church. This made the greatest theological difference, in my opinion, in the treatment of the minister of the sacraments.

I suggested earlier that it was not too strong to assert that the minister of ancient penance was truly the Church. But Thomas and the long tradition which followed him focused so exclusively on the priest-minister, and particularly on his juridical connections to Christ, that any notion of the Church as minister was simply submerged. Once the ecclesial, public dimension of the ritual was bypassed in both practice and theological theory, and the ritual became a private triad of God, minister and individual penitent, it was but a short step to an even more private dyad of God and penitent alone to the exclusion of anyone else. The practice of private confession continued, of course, for many centuries. But it was, I am convinced, more out of a routinization of Christian life in which confession, especially the once-a-year Easter variety, became a firmly rooted habit, than out of a consciousness of serious sin. When the intensity of Christian life diminished, as it unquestionably diminished in our day, that routinization gave way to the situation that was and is well known. "The sacrament of penance as it currently exists in the sacramental life and discipline of the Church occupies a less important and even a marginal role in the lives of many Catholics."[55] Any confessor can verify the truth of that judgment.

There are signs that the Church's part in sacramental forgiveness and reconciliation is being rediscovered in the contemporary Church. It has been commonplace among Roman Catholic theologians over the past twenty years to stress that by penance we are reconciled not only to God, but also to the Church. Vatican II enshrined that position in its teaching, echoing the ancient words of Ambrose: "It is the Church that is wounded by our sins."[56] The new ritual of reconciliation issued in 1973 insists that "the sin of one harms the others," and penance therefore "entails reconciliation with brothers and sisters who are always harmed by our sins."[57] In ancient penance the Church was unified in prayer. It was this ecclesial prayer, formally and functionally symbolized in the prayer of the *episkopos*, that was the efficacious means of reconciling sinners to the Church, to Jesus and to God. "God's pardon cannot be obtained," to repeat Leo's judgment, "except by the supplication of bishops."

It is not difficult, either theologically or ritually, to understand why the Church must be the active minister, not only in penance but in all the sacramental actions. Jesus, to repeat, is confessed by Christians as the incarnation and realization of God. It is in and through the activity of Jesus, they further confess, that forgiveness of sins and reconciliation with God were achieved and continue to be achieved. But Jesus acts, they believe, in and through the actions of his Church-body. If he is to pray for and achieve forgiveness of sins and reconciliation, it can now be only in and through that body. Schillebeeckx puts it very well. "That which Christ as *Kyrios* is doing invisibly through his glorified body in heaven for all men on earth he does visibly for the same men through his earthly body the Church, which is thus the one who 'is always praying and interceding for us' and is the 'holy Savior.' Even in the sacrament of penance, where we have most lost the communal character of the action, the grace of forgiveness of sins is assured to the penitent because *the Church, together with Christ,* is praying for him."[58]

THE RITE OF PENANCE-RECONCILIATION[59]

The new rite of penance issued by the Congregation for Divine Worship in 1973 is generally regarded as the end-product of a process set in motion by Vatican II's Constitution on the Liturgy, which decreed that "the rite and formulas for the sacrament of penance are to be revised so that they give more luminous expression to both the nature and the effect of this sacrament.[60] I grant that it is such an end-product. But it is a very schizophrenic one, tightly caught in the now-classic contemporary tension between a traditional understanding that has not yet disappeared from either theory or practice, and a new understanding that has not yet rooted in either. I must explain what I mean.

The Constitution on the Liturgy embraced a dynamic model of liturgy which views sacraments as "celebrations of the Church." It decreed that "it is to be stressed that whenever rites, according to their specific nature, make provision for communal celebration involving the presence and active participation of the faithful, this way of celebrating them is to be preferred as far as possible to a celebration that is individual and quasi-private. This rule applies with special force to the celebration of Mass and the administration of the sacraments."[61] The new rite of penance, on the other hand, offers a barely muted version of the individual, private model of the sacrament generated in and embraced by Scholastic theology. It insists that "*individual,* integral confession and absolution remain the only *ordinary* way for the faithful to reconcile themselves with God and with the Church."[62] And though it states that "the whole Church, as a priestly people, acts in different ways in the work of reconciliation entrusted to it by the Lord,"[63] its overall tenor is still derived from the model which sees the ritual of penance as a kind of court in which an individual penitent, suitably contrite and prepared to make satisfaction, seeks judicial absolution from an individual priest.

We can get a little closer to the heart of the tension delineated above by considering another document relating to the sacrament of penance and in which the new rite is rooted. This document is the *Pastoral Norms for General Sacramental Absolution* published by the Congregation for the Doctrine of the Faith in 1972.[64] I make three summary statements about those norms. First, they reaffirm the norms established by the Council of Trent, as of divine law, that integral confession of serious sins, that is, their confession according to their number and species, is required for their sacramental forgiveness.[65] Second, they broaden somewhat the circumstances under which general absolution may be given, but still maintain that such absolution is an exceptional and extraordinary way to celebrate the sacrament. Third, and importantly, they affirm an obligation in penitents who have received general absolution to confess their serious sins privately within a year of having received absolution.

These pastoral norms raise two questions which will enable us to clarify positions. First, is the new rite of reconciliation the absolute end-product of the process initiated by Vatican II, the end beyond which we cannot and will not go? To that question I shall answer no. It is but an intermediary product which must be superseded to give clearer symbolic expression to both the essential nature and the effects of the sacrament. Second, in the ultimately envisaged end-product of the revision of sacramental reconciliation will the obligation to integral private confession of already-forgiven sins be retained? To that question I shall answer yes. It is required, I believe, by the essential nature and effect of this sacrament that such sins be submitted by the individual believer to the scrutiny of the minister of the Church. Both questions and answers, of course, require careful elaboration.

The new rite offers three forms of celebrating reconciliation. There is a rite for reconciliation of individual penitents, a traditional one-on-one interaction between an individual penitent and a minister of the Church. There is a rite for reconciliation of several penitents with individual confession and absolution, ultimately, again, a one-on-one interaction between an individual penitent and a minister, but preceded by a communal service of the word. There is, finally, a rite for reconciliation of several penitents with general confession and absolution, a thoroughly communal rite. In spite of their different names, however, and their differences in ritual actions, the three rites are *structurally* identical. Each opens with an introductory rite: a greeting, a sign of the cross, an admonition. There follows a liturgy of the word, or readings, offered as optional in the first rite, but really integral to symbolizing the nature of this ritual. The liturgy of the word is followed by a liturgy of reconciliation: confession of sins (private or general), prayer of repentance, absolution (private or general). There is then a concluding rite: a blessing, a prayer or song of praise, a dismissal. It is this common structure that highlights the essential meanings embedded in the ritual of reconciliation.

In the economy of salvation in the Jewish-Christian tradition God always has the initiative, for it is he who calls sinners to repentance, forgiveness and reconciliation. He has mercy always on whom he will have mercy, he graces whom he graces.[66] The new rite of reconciliation, in all its forms, seeks to underscore this initiative by giving a priority to the proclamation of the word of God. That is why the reading of the word should never be omitted, not even in the first form where it is optional. It is not the minister, ultimately, who calls the sinner to repentance, to forgiveness, to reconciliation; it is not even the Church. It is God in his Christ who calls. His word, therefore, should be proclaimed to manifest this dimension of the ritual. It is to God's summons, mediated in his word, that sinners respond in the next part of the ritual. They repent, ritualize that repentance in acts of sorrow and confession of sins, and receive from God and Christ through the mediation of the Church and its minister forgiveness and reconciliation. They are again at one, in formally symbolized reality, with the Church, with Christ and with God. They are ready for the high moment of their reconciliation and at-one-ment in the great banquet of the Eucharist.

It is the ritual of the Eucharist that is the culmination of the ritual reconciliation of sinners, just as it was the ritual of the Eucharist that was the culmination of their initiation into the Church, the body of Christ. It is not uncommon for the faithful still today to believe that reconciliation must always precede Communion. But such belief is of a purely extrinsic relationship: penance must chronologically precede Eucharistic Communion. What I am asserting here is a much more intrinsic and essential link between the two. Not only does reconciliation chronologically precede Eucharist, but also it is essentially ordered to it and, indeed, finds its own fulfillment in it.[67]

God's summons to sinners mediated in the Church; sinners' responses encouraged, sustained and blessed in this Church; God's forgiveness and reconciliation again mediated in this Church; the great eucharistic ritual of reconciliation; their essential nature and effects—all these are best ritualized in a *public, communal* ritual. That fact is theologically recognized in the new rite of reconciliation by the inclusion of two communal forms as legitimating ways of celebrating the sacrament. But one of those forms, the rite of general confession and absolution, is vetoed for *ordinary* use and is specified as an *extraordinary* rite. This raises again my first question: Is the new rite of reconciliation an absolute end point in the process set in motion by Vatican II? My answer to that question was no. I must now explain that answer.

The new ritual itself insists, as we saw above, that there is a very communal dimension to sin and forgiveness and reconciliation. Sin always harms our brothers and sisters, and reconciliation is always with our brothers and sisters as historical manifestation of our reconciliation with God. To effectively ritualize the communal aspect of both sin and reconciliation; to effectively reveal that sin is not just a matter between an individual sinner and God (I am not the only sinner, but belong to a community of sinners to whom I have obligations); to effectively underscore the ministry of the believing community, and not just of its designated leaders, to sinners (as I hear God's word I experience it not only as a call to be ministered to, but also as a call to minister to those other sinners who stand side by side with me in this Church and this world)—to make all these communal dimensions symbolically explicit there is required a thoroughly communal ritual. Such a ritual is already provided in the third form of the new rite. There remains only the further, minute step of permitting this form as an *ordinary* way to celebrate the sacrament.[68]

But just to declare the form of general confession and absolution an ordinary way to celebrate the sacrament of reconciliation would not be quite enough. To emphasize ritually the essential nature and effect of this sacrament as a symbolic action in which God in Christ in this Church forgives and reconciles sinners, and so withdraw the sacrament from its exclusively juridical context, the formula of absolution must reflect this nature and this effect. We know from the Gelasian Sacramentary that the solemn reconciliation of penitents on Maundy Thursday in ancient penance was introduced by a long prayer. The form of absolution was contained in that prayer; the form was, that is, deprecative. The deprecative formula continued with unquestioned validity in the East, but was replaced in the West in the thirteenth century by the declarative, judicial formula "I absolve you from your sins . . . " said by the priest. As long as the formula was deprecative, the ritual connection between the forgiving and reconciling action of the Church in its minister and that of God in Christ was clear. But when that formula was replaced with the declarative formula, the ritual connection was obscured, not to say lost entirely, and the priest emerged in the character of a presiding judge, in both ecclesiastical practice and theological theory. The new rite of reconciliation is schizophrenic here also. A consideration of its formula of absolution will demonstrate that.

The new rite prescribes that, at the moment of absolution, the priest is to extend his hands, or at least his right hand, over the head of the penitent. This is the ancient symbolic gesture of the imposition of hands, with its ancient meaning of granting peace with the Church. As his hands are extended he is to pray: "God, the Father of mercies, through the death and resurrection of his Son has reconciled the world to himself and has sent the Holy Spirit among us for the forgiveness of sins. Through the ministry of the Church may God give you pardon and peace. *And* I absolve you from your sins in the name of the Father, and of the Son, and of the Holy Spirit."[69]

The introduction to the new rite decrees that the essential words of absolution in this formula (the Scholastic *form*) are: "I absolve you from your sins in the name of the Father, and of the Son, and of the Holy Spirit." It then proceeds to elucidate the formula further. The formula of absolution, it states, reflects the fact that the reconciliation of the penitent comes from the mercy of the Father; it reflects the connection between the reconciliation of the penitent and the paschal mystery of Christ; it reflects the role of the Holy Spirit in the forgiveness of sins; finally, it reflects the ecclesial aspect of the sacrament because reconciliation with God is asked for and given through the ministry of the Church.[70]

All of this would be quite true, were it not for the *and* which I have emphasized. For that *and* abruptly disconnects what follows it from what precedes it, *and* indicates succession from what precedes, but not dependence on it. The form as it stands does not give entirely luminous expression to the essential nature of this sacrament as the forgiving and reconciling action of the triune God, mediated in the forgiving and reconciling action of the Church and its minister. The little *and,* especially when coupled with the insistence on the priest's words of absolution as the essential form, still presents the priest as a separate judge, rather than as the essentially connected minister of the Church and of God. This form need not, and must not, be the absolute end. It could be brought into line with what it seeks to proclaim, realize and celebrate quite easily.

The replacement of the disconnecting *and* with something like a connecting *therefore,* a word which indicates dependence on what precedes it, would be enough to establish a luminously clear formula. It appears to be a very minor change. But since, as I said before, ritual prayers are the best indication of the essential nature of the ritual, it is a truly major change which would manifest clearly the essential connection in the ritual between the reconciling actions of the minister, of the Church and of God. For those who might worry about the "traditional" nature of the declarative formula, it is as new as the thirteenth century in the Western Church, it has never been used in the Eastern churches, and the universal Church got along quite well without it for thirteen centuries. If the ancient gesture of the imposition of hands, which also disappeared in the thirteenth century, can be restored to its rightful place in the ritual of reconciliation, so too can the deprecative formula of absolution which manifests much more luminously than the declarative formula the essential nature of this sacrament.

This explanation of the answer to the first of my two questions leads me to the second one. What about the integral confession of serious sins required by the Council of Trent and retained by the new rite of reconciliation, even after general confession and absolution? I have no doubt that Trent intended to declare that integral confession was of "divine law."[71] That makes the Tridentine statement an important dogmatic precedent to be understood, but it does not make it an absolute precedent to be followed slavishly. A common hermeneutic principle in the theological tradition is that conciliar statements are to be understood in their historical contexts, a principle acknowledged by no less an authoritative body than the Roman Congregation for the Doctrine of the Faith.[72]

Considering the doctrine of Trent on integral confession within its historical context the illustrious Tridentine scholar, Hubert Jedin, declares unequivocally that "the Council of Trent in no way condemned, in express and explicit words, the thesis that absolution can be given in a general way after a general confession." His reasoning for such a conclusion is lucidly clear, and on a basis universally accepted for reading conciliar statements. "For this thesis was held by none of the Reformers and appears in none of the articles proposed [to the Council] either at Bologna or at Trent. The Council had affirmed several times its intention to *limit itself to the condemnation of errors propagated by the Reformers*."[73] Trent was concerned, not with general confession and absolution, but only with the necessity of confessing serious sins. Its teaching on integral confession, therefore, cannot be used to forbid absolutely general confession and general absolution. There is, in fact, no dogmatic argument from Trent forbidding general confession and absolution as an *ordinary* way to celebrate the sacrament of penance. The Council's purpose was "to defend, against the

Protestants, the custom of integral confession as in conformity with divine law, and not to affirm that it was the *only* possible way of confessing."[74]

What, then, of the obligation to confess privately serious sins, even after they have been ritually forgiven by general absolution? It makes sound *pastoral* sense to me to retain such an obligation. But I hasten to add, and to emphasize as strongly as I can, that such an obligation is not so that sins may be "properly" forgiven by private and integral confession. Sins, the constant tradition of the Catholic Church insists, are truly forgiven at the moment when a sinner is truly sorry for them, and are ritually forgiven in the case under discussion at the moment of general absolution. Why, then, retain the obligation to confess serious sins privately, after they have been forgiven already?

First of all a minimalistic answer, to satisfy those who might fear that general confession and absolution is just too easy. Since ritual is symbolic action, sinners should not merely *say* they are sorry (though that, of course, is a minimal way to do it) but should also *do* some symbolic action to proclaim, realize and celebrate their sorrow, repentance and reconciliation. Such an action might be the subsequent one-on-one confession of serious sins to the Church's designated minister. But, secondly, a better, more theological and pastoral answer. The Church, the incarnation and body of Christ in the world, has a mission to minister to sinners. That ministry is not only to forgive their sins and to reconcile them, but also, and perhaps more importantly, to invite them, as did Christ, to sin no more. To carry out that ministry there is required the guiding, advising, cajoling, directing, sustaining and strengthening of sinners, tasks which can be carried out optimally only in one-to-one situations. The private confessing of serious sins after they have been forgiven in general absolution is to allow that ministry to be done.

The subsequent private confession of previously forgiven sins demands a change of perspective in both penitents and confessors. To be truly effective, such confession needs to be seen, not as a residual and juridical obligation, but rather as a personal and Christian and salutary value. If the sacrament of reconciliation truly ritualizes for any given penitent both God's call to conversion and repentance and the sinner's response to that call, then the subsequent private confession of serious sins will be perceived as a means to an ever-fuller repentance and reconciliation with the Church, with Christ and with God.[75] But if the sacrament does not truly ritualize God's call and the sinner's response, if it is just another, mechanical way out of sin, then, of course, the last situation is no better than the first—but no worse either. In the last, and indeed first, resort sacraments are actions of faith. If that faith be lacking, if the *opus operatum* of God in Christ in the Church is not matched by the *opus operantis* of the penitent, then the sacrament is fruitless, whether it be the rite of private confession and absolution or that of general confession and absolution. As we have seen several times already, and will see again, nothing happens in sacramental action without the cooperation of a believer who wants something to happen.

If something does happen in the sacrament of penance, if the sinner does experience in symbolic reality the forgiveness of sins and reconciliation, then it is a moment for *celebration*. And so the *Ordo Paenitentiae* establishes that "the sacrament of penance is *celebrated*"; that "the reconciliation of penitents may be *celebrated* at any time on any day"; that "the season of Lent is most appropriate for *celebrating* the sacrament of penance."[76] When I asked my nine year old what celebrate meant, she responded immediately that it meant to do something with joy. I am sure more could be said, but I think it would all come back to that. Celebration connotes acts of rejoicing, as at a new spring, a new birth, a new life, a new moment. That is probably why the new rite of reconciliation mentions the celebration of penance in the same breath as the celebration of "the paschal mystery in the Easter triduum with renewed hearts."[77]

And we sinners have much cause for joy, if we but stop to think what is being proclaimed, realized and celebrated in the ritual of reconciliation. God, steadfastly faithful as always in spite of our severe provocations, summons us to repent of our sins; his Christ, whose life was totally dedicated to calling sinners to repentance, calls us again; the Spirit of God, who was poured into our hearts at baptism for the forgiveness of sins and whom we celebrated in confirmation, moves us to repent and be forgiven; the Church, wounded by our sins,[78] offers us forgiveness and reconciliation; and, moved by these loving gestures, we repent, are forgiven and are reconciled. There is cause enough for joy, cause enough for celebration. That celebrations are always better when shared with others is just one more reason for a genuinely communal celebration of penance. These considerations, I believe, provide an answer to a question put to me recently: Has the confessional disappeared from Catholic life? Now the confessional held an honored place, and played an important role, in Catholic life, and I can envision circumstances in which it will still play a role. But one thing can be said without fear of contradiction: the confessional was never a place for celebration.

Finally, lest in our excess of joy we forget to give thanks and praise to the triune God and his Church who called us to repent, forgave us and reconciled us, every celebration of penance ends with the invitation to "give thanks to the Lord, for he is good."[79] It is, indeed, right and fitting to give him thanks and praise, as we pray elsewhere, in the ritual of the Eucharist. That Eucharist is *the* ritual of thanksgiving and praise for the wonderful works which God accomplished in Christ, including the work of reconciling sinners to himself. It is also the ritual in which sinful believers are most intimately reconciled and made at one with the Church and with God. What more natural, then, that thanksgiving and praise for forgiveness and reconciliation achieved in symbolic reality in the sacrament of reconciliation should reach its high point in the sacrament of Eucharist. The ritual of penance, as I have said several times, does not merely precede the ritual of Eucharist in time, but is also essentially ordained to it and finds its culmination in it. As we end our consideration of the sacrament of penance and reconciliation, it is time to consider that Eucharist into which it naturally flows.

Chapter Six
EUCHARIST

THE PASCHAL MEAL

Hippolytus reports that following the bishop's imposition of hands and anointing those being initiated into the Church were admitted to Eucharist. The ritual of initiation, which grows Christians, reached its culmination in the Lord's Supper. We have just seen in the preceding chapter that the ritual of reconciliation also reaches its culmination in the Eucharist. We must now consider this most central of Christian sacraments. Its ritual character and its symbolism, all are agreed, are somehow connected with the last meal Jesus shared with his friends. It is there, then, that we must begin.

Matthew, Mark and Luke present the Last Supper as a celebration of a Jewish paschal meal.[1] John does not. He reports that Jesus' accusers "did not enter the praetorium so that they might not be defiled, but might eat the Passover" (18:28; cf. 19:14, 31), indicating that when Jesus was brought before Pilate the Passover lambs had not yet been eaten. That discrepancy between the Synoptics and John has been the topic of much scholarly discussion. That discussion, however, is not at issue here, since it concerns more the date of Jesus' death than the meaning of Eucharist. What is at issue here is that the primitive Christian tradition reflected on Jesus' Easter doings in a paschal context and reported them in that context (1 Cor 5:7; Jn 1:36; Mk 14:12–16; Lk 22:15). That makes it necessary for us to clarify first the meanings of the Jewish paschal ritual before considering those of the Christian Eucharist.

Roland de Vaux suggests that the Passover ritual originated in the religion of nomadic shepherds, that it was initially the sacrifice of a young animal to ensure the well-being of the flocks, and that it was offered as the tribes set out for their spring pastures. The blood of the sacrificed animal was sprinkled on the family tent poles to ensure also the safety of the tribes.[2] Several symbolisms were at work in this ritual.

The time was symbolic, the time of spring, proclaiming, realizing and celebrating the rebirth of life. The sacrificed animal was a *young* animal, evoking images of a new life poured out to ensure the safety (including the ultimate safety or salvation) of all the tribe. It was this ritual of spring that became the liturgical memorial and celebration of the momentous Israelite event of the exodus.

Exodus 12 presents this ritual as a family feast, the most dominant meaning of which is the strengthening of the family and tribal bond. "All the congregation of Israel . . . shall take every man a lamb according to their fathers' houses" (12:3). If the united family is too small to eat a whole lamb, then neighbors are to unite in the numbers required to eat a lamb. The broad context of the Passover ritual is that of a family meal. The dominant symbols are specified: a lamb, the blood of which is sprinkled on the doorposts and lintel of the house where the meal is eaten (symbolizing the life of all from the death of the lamb), unleavened bread, girded loins, sandaled feet and staff in hand (12:11), all symbolizing the imminence of the exodus journey. The Deuteronomic reform removed both the slaying of the lamb and the eating of the meal from family home to national temple (2 Kgs 23:21; 2 Chr 34:29–35:19), underscoring tribal and national rather than family bonds. But by the time of Jesus the huge volume of pilgrims who came to Jerusalem for the feast precluded the possibility of eating the meal in the temple, and that part of the ritual was restored to the homes of Jerusalem.

Passover was to be "a memorial day" (Ex 12:14). But the structure of the ritual meal indicates that it is meant to be not just a memorial that recalls the fact that God *saved* Israel in past ages, but also one in which there is revealed and realized and celebrated the fact that God *saves* Israel now. It is also, strange though it sounds in ears accustomed to English, a memorial which represents God's great definitive act of salvation in his future great day. It is a memorial, finally, in which not only does Israel remember God, but God remembers Israel and saves it.

As already noted, the prescribed dress for the ritual is the dress of people ready to move: sandals and staff and clothing bound up for the journey. The food evokes the same experience: the bread, unleavened to symbolize the haste of its baking; three wafers of bread to symbolize "*kohen* (priest), *levi* (levite), and *yisrael* (Israelite), together symbolizing the entire Jewish community";[3] the lamb, unbutchered, roasted and eaten in haste; the bitter herbs, to symbolize the bitterness of the Egyptian bondage; the clay-colored puree, to symbolize the mortar from which Israelites built Egyptian cities; the salt water, to symbolize the tears shed in Egypt; and the four joyful cups of wine, to symbolize Israelite celebration of the four wonderful works of God. "*I will bring you out* from under the burden of the Egyptians, and *I will deliver you* from their bondage, and *I will redeem you* with an outstretched hand, and *I will take you* for my people, and I will be your God" (Ex 6:6–7).

There is a fifth, undrunk, cup of wine, the so-called cup of Elijah. This adds an eschatological dimension to the ritual, for it symbolizes a mighty work of God which remains to be accomplished: "*I will bring you into the land* which I swore to Abraham, to Isaac and to Jacob" (Ex 6:8). That land may be in literal reality the land of Canaan. But even more is it in symbolic reality the land of the final promise, God's gathering of his people to himself in final salvation. That time, the great day of the Lord, will be ushered in by the coming again of the great prophet, Elijah. No one knows when that day of the Lord will be, not even the Son of Man, as Jesus will later say in the Gospel (Mt 24:36). But *that* it will be is guaranteed by the faithfulness of God already demonstrated by the fact that he led Israel to the promised land of Canaan.

But more evocative than the ritual symbols, and indeed creative of the meanings of the meal, is the *haggadah*, the prayer of the father of the family, both explaining the meaning(s) of the meal and blessing God for them. The *haggadah* demands that the participants in the meal realize exodus thoughts and desires and actions.

Over the bread the father prays: "This is the bread of poverty which our forefathers ate in the land of Egypt. This year *we* are here; next year may we be in the land of Israel. This year *we* are slaves; next year may we be free men." In response to the prescribed questions of the children, "Why is this night different from all other nights?" he recounts how *we* were Pharaoh's slaves in Egypt, and how the Lord brought *us* forth from there, and how we would still be slaves there had he not brought us out. But that the participants in this meal are not only keeping memory of a past exodus but also involved in symbolic reality in a present exodus of their own is clearest from the prescribed question of, and the answer to, the "wicked child." He asks "What is this service to you?"—to *you*, and not to *me*, thereby removing himself from the community of Israel. He is answered that it is "because of what the Lord did for *me* when I came forth from Egypt"— for *me*, not for *you*, wicked child.[4] The wicked child has excluded himself from the community, and so is not saved now, just as surely as he would not have been saved at the Reed Sea. The way to salvation then was through the waters of the sea; now it is through the celebration of the ritual meal.

It is against this background that we can gain insight into the meanings of Jesus' action at the Last Supper. By setting the supper into a Passover context, the Synoptic authors relate the *haggadah* of Jesus to the moments of the ritual meal. He explained the unleavened bread, not in the traditional words, "This is the bread of poverty which our forefathers ate in the land of Egypt," but in unheard-of words, "This is my body." He explained the cup of wine, in Paul's and Luke's tradition, in the words, "This cup is the new covenant in my blood," and, in Mark's and Matthew's, in the words, "This is my blood of the covenant." By, at least, setting the Last Supper in a paschal context, the evangelists symbolically link it, and therefore also the Eucharist which derives from it, to the paschal meal. By reporting unheard of *haggadah* they report their community's conviction that what Jesus had done was take the ancient ritual, the memorial of the exodus passage and covenant, and establish it as a new ritual, the memorial of his passage from earthly life through death to life with God and of the new covenant established by it. This new ritual grows, indeed, out of the old, but it is a *new* ritual, with significantly new meanings. It is our task now to inquire into its dominant meanings.

THE ECCLESIAL MEAL

The first element of the Eucharistic ritual I want to highlight is its character as community meal. We recall this characteristic of the ancient Passover ritual. That the same tribal or community character was retained in the Christian meal is clear from the tradition reported by Paul in his First Letter to the Corinthians. But to fully grasp that tradition and its implications, we must go behind the meal for a moment and inquire into the self-understanding of the primitive Christian community. The central kerygma of the New Testament is that God raised Jesus of Nazareth from the dead (1 Cor 15:3–4; Rom 8:34; Gal 1:1; Eph 1:20; Acts 2:24), and made him head of a body which is Ekklesia-Church. Members of this Church are said to be "in Christ" (passim). They are said to be the body of Christ (1 Cor 6:12–20: 10:17; 12:12–27; Rom 12:4–5; Eph 1:22–23; 2:14–16; 3:6; 4:4–16; 5:22–30; Col 1:18,24; 2:19; 3:15), a body into which they are grown in baptism, imaged sometimes as rebirth (Jn 3:5) and sometimes as new creation (2 Cor 5:17; Gal 6:15). More than simple metaphor is intended here. The powerful water ritual realizes what it symbolizes: it grows in symbolic reality the body of Christ. But for Paul, as later for Hippolytus, the fullness of the body of Christ is attained not in the ritual of baptism, but in the ritual of the Lord's Supper. "Because there is one bread, we who are many are one body, for we all partake of the one bread" (1 Cor 10:17). The meal, which in literal reality is the coming together of men and women to share bread and wine, in symbolic reality is the coming together of the body of Christ to symbolize, that is, to proclaim, to realize and to celebrate, its essential unity in Christ.

So crucial is the literal coming together to the symbolizing of the body of Christ that when there is no real literal community, neither is there any symbolic community with or in Christ. The ritual is destroyed when there is a divided community, as there is in the Corinthian community, and Paul complains that "when you meet together, it is not the Lord's Supper that you eat" (1 Cor 11:20). He warns that "anyone who eats and drinks without discerning the body [namely, of Christ, the gathered community in its symbolic reality] eats and drinks judgment upon himself" (11:29). A prime and normative meaning of the Christian ritual meal is an ecclesial meaning, namely, that around this table is gathered the body of Christ to proclaim, to realize and to celebrate itself as such. "This Church is my body."

The uncovering of another normative meaning of the Christian meal begins with the realization that the preferred time for its solemn celebration is Sunday. There is a meticulous, scholarly dispute about whether Christians made the transition from sabbath to Sunday in New Testament or post-New Testament times.[5] I do not intend to enter into that dispute here, since it concerns the *when* of Sunday, whereas I am interested here in the *why* of Sunday. But we can accept from that dispute what is agreed by all, namely, that in the middle of the second century Christian writers justify Sunday celebration of the Lord's Supper on the basis of two reasons. The first is that it was on the first day of the week that God created, the second that it was on the same day that God raised Jesus from the dead.[6] The advancement of the resurrection of Jesus as a reason for the Sunday celebration of the Lord's Supper, a reason which "in time became the dominant reason for Sunday observance,"[7] leads us to an understanding of a second normative meaning of the Christian meal.

The core of the early Christian kerygma, the beacon in the light of which the first Christians interpreted all the events of Jesus' life, was the belief that God raised him from the dead. This belief was a central reason for their choice of Sunday as their day of worship. The Gospels record that the resurrection of Jesus took place on a Sunday (Mk 16:2,9; Mt 28:1; Lk 24:1; Jn 20:1, 19). They record also that Jesus appeared to chosen disciples not only on that first Easter Sunday, but also on the following Sunday (Jn 20:26). In the light of contemporary redaction criticism, the evidence of this one text from the fourth Gospel at the end of the first century ought not to be overpressed for historical validity. But even if it does not record an historical happening, that is, even if that appearance did not take place on a Sunday, the text assumes greater, rather than less, significance. For it then indicates the strong Christian belief at the end of the first century that the observance of Sunday was rooted in the resurrection event.

There is also abundant New Testament evidence that the disciples' immediate post-resurrection encounters with their Lord took place, or were placed, in the meal-setting that dominated their immediate pre-resurrection encounter. The kerygmatic summary in Acts 10:40-41 announces that "God raised him on the third day and made him manifest; not to all the people but to us who were chosen by God as witnesses, *who ate and drank with him after he was raised from the dead.*" Acts 1:4 announces in the same vein: "*While eating with them* (or, as Oscar Cullman would have it, 'while taking salt together'[8]), he charged them not to depart from Jerusalem." Luke's Emmaus narrative records that "when he was at table with them, he took the bread, and blessed it, and broke it, and gave it to them" (24:30). He also has Jesus ask, "Have you anything here to eat?" and they give him "a piece of broiled fish, and he took and ate it before them" (24:42–43). There is a parallelism between Jesus' pre-resurrection meal with his disciples, his post-resurrection meals with his disciples, and the Lord's Supper. The latter stands in continuity with the other two, and Sunday, as the day on which God raised Jesus from the dead, becomes the normative time for its solemn celebration. This "Sundayness" of the ritual meal enhances another of its normative meanings, namely, its meaning as a *memorial* meal.

THE MEMORIAL MEAL

Joseph Baciocchi, who is sometimes credited with the opening of new ways to consider the Eucharistic mystery in contemporary theology,[9] says of the biblical notion of memorial that "it is the key to the mystery of the Eucharist."[10] We have already alluded to this biblical notion. We have noted that it is a strange kind of memorial, one that not only remembers what God did in the past, but also remembers that what he did in the past he continues to do now and will continue to do also in the future. It cannot be otherwise theologically. For God's great biblical quality is his *hesed,* his steadfast and faithful love: as he *was* for his people, so he *is* for them, and so always he *will be.* The memorial of God's great exodus action was the Jewish Passover meal; the memorial of his wonderful works in Jesus is the Eucharistic meal. In both these meals, of course, as we have already noted, not only does his people remember God, but he remembers them.

God's wonderful work in Jesus of Nazareth is multiform. God was in this man from the first moment of his human existence, so that the deeds and words of Jesus are the deeds and words of God. This is what Christians mean by incarnation. God ruled this man's life, which is what Christians mean when they say that Jesus was righteous; and he ruled this man's death, which is what they mean when they say that Jesus was "obedient unto death" (Phil 2:8). His righteous life and righteous death led Christians to view Jesus as Isaiah's righteous servant, who was "wounded for our transgressions, bruised for our iniquities" (Is 53:5), and who gave his life as "a ransom for many" (Mk 10:45), "a ransom for all" (1 Tim 2:16). The righteous God, they believed, responded to this righteous life and death by raising Jesus from the dead "for our justification" (Rom 4:25), and by calling into being for himself a new people to believe in this new passover. Called thus to believe, this people is named in Greek *Ekklesia*, those who are called, and in English *Church*.

With this people God enters into a new covenant sealed, as are all covenants, in blood, this time the blood of Jesus. He pours out upon it the Spirit of truth, to guide it "into all the truth" (Jn 16:13), of God, of his Christ, of his Spirit, of his Church, of his covenant. It is all of this, incarnation, resurrection, outpouring of Spirit, redemption, forgiveness of sins, Ekklesia-body of Christ, covenant, that is remembered in the memorial meal. It is all of this that is remembered as the mighty work of God in the past, in the present and in the eternal future. A simple meal among brothers and sisters in Christ, a meal like many others they might share together, is symbolically transformed to be the ritual action which proclaims, realizes and celebrates all that God has done, is doing and will do in Christ. If this emphasis on the Eucharistic celebration as memorial meal sounds like something new in Catholic ears, it is only because the speculative theology of the past thousand years focused so exclusively on the presence of Jesus in bread and wine that it managed to obscure the memorial aspect. But Eucharist as memorial is far from a new-fangled idea. It is an idea as old as the Church. Already in the New Testament, the tradition reports that Jesus transformed the Passover memorial into a memorial of himself with the explicit command: "Do this in memory of me" (1 Cor 11:25; Lk 22:19). Reflecting and reflecting upon the tradition of his time, Paul teaches that the Lord's Supper keeps memory specifically of the death of Jesus. It proclaims "the Lord's death until he comes" (1 Cor 11:26). But he grasped, perhaps better than anyone else ever did, that the Jesus who died was and is the Jesus whom God raised from the dead (cf. 1 Cor 15, passim), and he never mentioned the death of Jesus without also, at least, implying the resurrection. If, therefore, the Lord's Supper proclaims the Lord's death, it equally proclaims his resurrection from the dead and his exaltation to the right hand of the Father. The heavy emphasis, though, in post-Tridentine theology on the Eucharist as sacrifice caused it to be presented, and commonly perceived, almost exclusively as proclamation of the Lord's death. That is an emphasis and a mis-perception that the contemporary Roman Catholic theological tradition seeks to correct.

The Eucharist is a memorial meal. It is an action which remembers, an *anamnesis* as the Greek language of the liturgy would have it. Such it was, quite universally, for the early Fathers of the Church, whose opinions can be represented by a particularly striking statement from John Chrysostom, rightly called the Doctor of the Eucharist. "The best way to keep a blessing is to keep memory of the blessing, and to offer assiduous thanksgiving. And, therefore, those awesome mysteries, which are so saving and which we celebrate, are called thanksgiving (*eucharistia*), because they keep memory (*anamnesis*) of the blessings, show forth the central actions of divine providence and move us to give thanks in everything."[11] Such it was too for all the early liturgies, including the Roman.

The documents of the teaching Church, the *magisterium*, consistently present the Eucharist as a memorial. When he established the feast of Corpus Christi, Urban IV praised the Eucharistic ritual as a wonderful and saving memorial of our redemption.[12] The Council of Trent taught that the Lord Jesus left to his Church a visible memorial, "by which the bloody sacrifice to be offered once on the cross might be represented and its memory kept until the end of time," and that "celebrating the old Passover . . . he instituted a new Passover . . . in memory of his exodus from this world to the Father."[13] Vatican II employed the notion of memorial as a key way to describe the Eucharist. A central text, which sums up much of what I have been saying, is worth quoting and reflecting upon at length. "At the Last Supper, on the night when he was betrayed, our Savior instituted the Eucharistic sacrifice of his body and blood. He did this in order to perpetuate the sacrifice of the cross throughout the centuries until he should come again, and so to entrust to his beloved spouse, the Church, a memorial of his death and resurrection: a sacrament of love, a sign of unity, a bond of charity, a paschal banquet in which Christ is consumed, the mind is filled with grace, and a pledge of future glory is given to us."[14] The importance of memorial terminology as a Catholic way to articulate the meaning of Eucharist can be gauged from the fact that that text is repeated almost word for word in the *Instruction on the Cult of the Eucharistic Mystery* issued by the Congregation of Rites in 1967.[15]

And so a summary question and a summary answer to conclude this section. What does it mean that Eucharist is a sacrament? It means this. The Church, the body of Christ, gathers to celebrate in literal reality a simple meal. But in symbolic reality this is no simple meal. This is a sacred, ritual meal in which the ordinary human actions of blessing and eating and drinking bread and wine take on symbolic meanings. This meal is not just a meal; it is the sacramental or symbolic *memorial* meal of the Church. Nor is this meal just dead memorial, mere commemoration of past events and their effects. Rather is it dynamic and efficacious memorial, that is, one in which the Church remembers, proclaims, realizes and celebrates what God did in Christ, what God does in Christ, and what God will do definitively in Christ. Now all that God did in Christ we have already enumerated. And when the Church and the individual believers who comprise it gather to keep memory of it subjectively, God objectively does now what he did before: he incarnates his Christ again, this time in the symbol of the meal; he saves his people through the death and resurrection of this Christ, forgiving their sins and reconciling them to himself; he pours out his Spirit upon them; he calls them to be Church and body of Christ and to be faithful to their covenant with him; and he pledges to them, again, that they will be his people unto eternal life.

In this sacramental meal, therefore, Jesus continues to be present as incarnated in his Church. He is, of course, always present there, faithful to his promise to be with it "always, to the close of the age" (Mt 28:20). But this meal, in a way that I shall elaborate in a subsequent section, reveals that presence, realizes it in symbolic reality and celebrates it. Confronted by this symbolic, but no less real, presence it is not surprising that the Church would be invited to lift up its heart and give thanks. For it is truly right and fitting that it should offer *Eucharistia*, praise and thanksgiving for so great and multiform a work and for so simple an action to keep memory of it.

EUCHARISTIA

Christians, I have argued, keep memory of Jesus, their Lord, and of the wonders which God has accomplished in and through him: incarnation, resurrection, exaltation, forgiveness of sins, reconciliation, outpoured-Spirit, Ekklesia-body of Christ, covenant, eternal life. It makes an impressive list of wonderful works of God (*mirabilia Dei*). And nothing would be more predictable, of course, nor more laudable, than that grateful believers would wish to give thanks for such *mirabilia*. And give thanks we do, as we keep memory in the ritual meal aptly called Eucharist. I do not wish to challenge such laudable gratitude, but I do wish to enter a warning that the rush to give thanks, noble though it be, might obscure an even more laudable response to *mirabilia*, namely, wonder and praise.

According to Jean Paul Audet, lexicographers are agreed that the primary meaning of the verb *eucharisteo* in both classical and koine Greek is to give thanks.[16] The substantive *eucharistia*, therefore, means thanksgiving. But Audet hastens to point out the proximity of two other verbs and their substantives to *eucharisteo-eucharistia*. They are *eulogeo*(bless)–*eulogia*(blessing) and *exomologiomai*(give praise)–*exomologesis*(praise). All three verbs and substantives belong together; they form a cluster. In this section, it is my intention to call attention briefly to the related meanings involved in this cluster.

The Christian Eucharistic meal, as we have seen, derives from an older Jewish eucharistic meal. That kind of meal was known as *berakah*, of which two forms may be noted. The first and simpler, better more spontaneous, form has two elements: first, a blessing and, then, a brief statement of the motive for which the blessing is given. This motive is always a wonderful work of God which touches the person making *berakah*. The second form offers a much more formalized and lengthier statement of motive and centers upon the wonder of all that God has done for his people as remembered now by that people. Now, as we have also seen, this remembrance of the *mirabilia Dei* represented them as happening not just in some past time, but also in this present for the participants. Realizing that, we may agree with Audet that the psychological state underlying *berekah* is "above all that of admiration and joy, not of gratitude, which remains subordinated, in fact, to the fundamental feeling of admiration, and is therefore secondary."[17] The formal *berakah* concludes with another blessing after the *anamnesis*.

The Gospels do not give us many explicit details of Jesus' *berakah* at the Last Supper. They merely record that he said a "blessing" over the bread,[18] and then give his words over the bread ("This is my body"), his words over the cup ("This is the cup of my blood"), and, only in Luke and Paul, his command to "do this in memory of me." Later theology concentrated on the words over the bread and the cup, creating a very one-sided emphasis on the *ontological* consideration of what this bread *is* ("my body") and what this wine *is* ("my blood"). It did not ask seriously, until recent times, about the meaning of the *action* of giving thanks. My presentation so far in this chapter has concentrated on the ritual action, the meal, which is in memory of the considerable wonders of God in Jesus of Nazareth. As always in the tradition of biblical memorial, this memorial recalls the wonders not only as past, but also as presently taking place for the gathered Church. That is cause enough for admiration for and praise of the God who performs such wonders. And that, in turn, is cause enough for thanksgiving.

No wonder, therefore, the *liturgically* preferred name for the sacred meal (as distinct from the recently *theologically* preferred name of *Mass*) has been *Eucharistia*, along with its now-understood cluster companions, *eulogia* and *exomologesis*. No wonder also that, from the earliest Christian times, the *Eucharistia* was linked liturgically with the day of the most wonderful of God's most wonderful works, the Lord's resurrection, namely, Easter day and Sunday, rather than with, for instance, the day of its institution. The memorial meal is also sacrifice, as I shall show in the next section. This section simply notes, lest it be forgotten, that the sacrifice is a "sacrifice of praise" (*sacrificium laudis*),[19] a sacrifice of blessing, and finally a sacrifice of thanksgiving.[20]

THE SACRIFICIAL MEAL

"*That* the Mass is truly a sacrifice, drawing its sacrificial efficacy wholly from the redemptive sacrifice of Christ, has always been maintained in Catholic theology; but the question of *how* it is a sacrifice is one that is open to further investigations."[21] Already in 1562, the Council of Trent summarized dogmatically the belief of the Catholic Church about the Mass as sacrifice: that in the Mass there is offered to God a true and proper sacrifice; that the Mass is not just a sacrifice of praise and thanksgiving, not just a mere memorial (*nuda commemoratio*) of the sacrifice of the cross; that the Sacrifice of the Mass in no way derogates from the sacrifice of the cross.[22] But it in no way specified in what sense specifically the Mass was to be understood as sacrifice. It in no way decided between the various theological explanations of the schools of the relationship Mass-sacrifice of Jesus.[23] I shall argue here that the Mass Eucharist is, indeed, a sacrifice, and specifically by being a memorial meal. Not a meal *and* a sacrifice, but a sacrificial meal.

Van Der Leeuw has shown effectively that in every religion which

offers sacrifice, the sacrifice is oriented essentially toward communion.[24] Men and women offer something to God, thereby symbolizing,
that is, proclaiming, realizing and celebrating, the offer of themselves.
God offers them a gift in return, symbolizing in the gift the offer of
himself. This mutual offering of gifts and selves establishes both communion and covenant between men and women and God. Sacrifices
were offered in Israel. A gift, a victim if you like, was offered to God
on the altar; what was left of this victim was eaten in a sacred meal, and
was God's gift to his people. In this mutual communion in sacrificial
gifts, there was established in symbolic reality both communion and
covenant between God and Israel. The Jewish tradition saw in this
communion sacrifice the most complete sacrifice, and by the time of
Jesus saw the paschal meal as such a communion-sacrifice.[25] It was this
meal, with its essential sacrificial nuances, that Jesus established as the
memorial of his paschal sacrifice.

After all the highly abstract and speculative disputations of the
past, it seems so simple. The Eucharist is essentially a meal.[26] But it is
no simple meal; rather it is a highly formalized ritual meal, a memorial
of the paschal passover of Jesus from historical life to life at the right
hand of his Father. I have already explained that and all that it implies.
Here I add only that this meal, precisely as memorial of the sacrifice
of Jesus, *is* the sacrifice of Jesus represented in symbolic reality for the
Church to participate in it. This meal, we recall, is not just subjective
remembering of the death-resurrection (= the sacrifice) of the Christ,
but is also the objective, realized, symbolic presence of that sacrifice. It
is that sacrifice here and now commemorated and symbolically represented for the Church, the incarnation and body of Christ, to participate in it.

At one point in the memorial meal elements of the meal are
blessed, that is, God is praised and thanked for this food which we
share. In the New Testament reports this blessing is followed by the
words: this is my body given for you, this is my blood shed for you.
These same words are spoken during the Eucharistic memorial. In
both instances, they express the meaning of the action of the meal:
they indicate the presence of Jesus realized in symbolic reality in this
meal. The Hebrew words probably spoken by Jesus at the Supper do
not mean what we mean today by *body* (a part of a person, that part
which is buried after death) and *blood* (another, liquid, part of a person, which flows, for instance, when the body is cut). "*Basar* does not
signify a principle or element of a human being, but rather the entire
being in its concrete individuality, with emphasis on its external manifestation. . . . Thus, at the Supper, Christ's use of the word 'body' sig-

nifies his entire self." Similarly "Jesus' use of the word 'blood' at the Supper must be taken in a concrete sense as referring to himself in his totality as a living being."[27] It is not merely the physical body and blood of Jesus which are realized in symbolic reality by being remembered, but Jesus himself in his total personal reality.

But a precision must be added. The explanatory words point out that it is not Jesus at just any moment of his existence that is remembered and realized, but Jesus as given-for-you and poured-out-for-you. In short, it is Jesus as sacrificed, Jesus as done to death (gift to God) and raised from the dead by God (gift from God). The eating and drinking of the meal-elements, bread and wine, establishes that communion and covenant between God and the Church that is so sought after in all sacrifice. That the presence of the sacrificed Jesus and the communion between God and the Church is effected in symbolic reality in no way militates against its reality. For, I must continue to insist, symbolic is in no way opposed to real.

J.M.R. Tillard sums up all I have been saying *almost* nicely. "The Church is not content to 'redo' mechanically the actions of Christ; she *enters*, mysteriously but really . . . into the intention of Christ offering himself to his Father. But because his sacrifice (in fact, the historic sacrifice of the death-resurrection event mysteriously re-presented) is already accepted, she receives in return, in the eating of the victim, *communion* in the divine benefits which the Father has conferred on this victim for her. If sacrifice and communion are at this point linked in the very dynamism of the Eucharist, the Eucharistic body of Jesus cannot but be his Spirit-filled body, the body of the Lord."[28]

The Jesus who is remembered, realized and celebrated as present in the ritual meal is the "Spirit-filled" Jesus, the risen Lord, the one who was offered and who offered himself in sacrifice. Jesus is now frozen for eternity as the one who was sacrificed. Whenever he is present, he is present as the one who was sacrificed, the one who was done to righteous death and raised (= accepted) by God. That is enough to make the memorial meal, in which he is made present, the memorial also of his sacrifice. It has been common theological practice to emphasize the separate consecrations of bread ("my body") and wine ("my blood") as the sacramental representation of the separation of the Lord's body and blood, and therefore of his death. But this is not so. If the explanations of *body* and *blood* which I set forth above have been followed, it will be clear that they represent, not death or separation, but the whole person of the Christ. The two consecrations do not symbolize death. If the meal is sacrificial, it is not because it symbolizes death, but because it symbolizes the sacrificed Jesus as present. There are two consecrations only because there are two elements, bread and wine, needed to constitute the meal in literal reality and the symbol of the Lord's presence and sacrifice in symbolic reality.

But to return to what I said of Tillard's view, that it sums up *almost* nicely what I had been saying. Where I part company from him will serve to clarify further the understanding of Eucharist as sacrificial meal. The parting of the ways arises over what Anthony Stephenson once called "the little hyphen."[29] In Tillard's view, and it has been a rather common Roman Catholic view, in the memorial meal the sacrifice of Jesus is "mysteriously re-presented." There is the little hyphen; and it makes a big difference. For *re-present*, and *re-call* which is equally at stake here, means present again and call again. They can give, and have given, the impression that in the Eucharist the once-and-for-all sacrifice of Jesus happens *again*, as if once was not enough. It was this kind of explanation of the sacrificial character of the Eucharist that provoked the protests of the Reformation theologians. It is against this kind of explanation that I wish to raise a caution.

We may begin, as one may frequently begin in Roman Catholic theology, with Thomas Aquinas. There are three of his statements to which I wish to call attention. The first occurs as part of the answer to the question: Is the effect of Christ's priesthood atonement for sin? "As for the sacrifice which is offered daily in the Church, it is not a sacrifice distinct from the one Christ himself offered, but its *commemoration*."[30] The second occurs in answer to the question: Is it right to give this sacrament many names? "This sacrament has a triple meaning. One looks to the past, inasmuch as it is *commemorative* of the Lord's passion, which was a true sacrifice. And according to this it is called a sacrifice."[31] The third occurs as part of the answer to the question: Is Christ immolated in this sacrament? "As the celebration of this sacrament is a *representative image* of the passion of Christ, so the altar is representative of the cross itself, on which Christ was immolated in his proper form."[32] These three will serve as indication of Thomas' view on Eucharist as sacrifice, and the words are instructive. Eucharist is a commemoration and/or representation of the sacrifice of Christ.

Stephenson is absolutely correct. "*Commemoratio* does not mean a re-calling, but a recalling." Nor does *representatio* mean a re-presentation, but a representation. "Alas, the little hyphen does transform the theory; and awe and bad theology compensate ill for lack of understanding."[33] Even if one does not grasp the precise meaning of the Latin words Thomas still leaves no room for doubt, for he asserts explicitly that the Sacrifice of the Mass is not a sacrifice distinct from Christ's sacrifice on Calvary, but its commemoration. It is what I have argued. The memorial meal does not re-call but recalls, does not re-present but symbolically represents, not just Jesus but Jesus specifically as sacrificed. There are not two sacrifices, that of Calvary and that of the Mass, but only one, that of Calvary recalled and represented in the Mass. There are not two sacrificial actions, that of Jesus and that of the Church, but only the one unique and definitive sacrificial action of Jesus, now represented in symbolic reality so that the body of Christ may participate in it. Calvary is not brought to us, again, in our history, for "at the altar a real shedding of his blood is impossible."[34] Rather the Church, in its memorial meal, makes present in symbol and in sacrament both the Lord who was sacrificed and, therefore, also his sacrifice so that it may commune in both.

The mutual unity of memorial meal and sacrifice of Jesus is the clear, contemporary Roman Catholic explanation of the Eucharist. In 1967, the instruction *Eucharisticum Mysterium* taught it unequivocally. "The Mass, or the Lord's Supper, is at one and the same time and inseparably: a sacrifice, in which the sacrifice of the cross is perpetuated; a memorial of the death and resurrection of the Lord who said, "Do this in memory of me" (Lk 22:19); a sacred meal in which the people of God participate in the benefits of the paschal sacrifice through communion in the body and blood of the Lord, [and] renew the covenant established between God and men once and for all in the blood of Christ."[35] The instruction refers back to Vatican II's Constitution on the Liturgy, which teaches equally clearly: "Our Savior at the Last Supper . . . instituted the Eucharistic sacrifice of his body and blood, in which the sacrifice of the cross is perpetuated down the ages until he comes, and left to the Church, his beloved spouse, a memorial of his death and resurrection . . . a paschal meal in which Christ is eaten."[36] One can detect the careful choice of words: the Eucharist *perpetuates* the sacrifice of the cross. Assiduously avoided is *represent*, with the possible mis-reading caused by the little hyphen.

Eucharisticum Mysterium continues on to insist further that "in the Mass, therefore, the sacrifice and the sacred meal pertain so much to the same mystery that they are joined one to the other with the tightest bond. For the Lord is offered in the Sacrifice of the Mass when 'he begins to be sacramentally present as the spiritual food of believers under the signs of bread and wine.' "[37] Here it is citing Paul VI's letter on the Eucharist, *Mysterium Fidei*. The context of the citation is worth giving, as a summary statement of the contemporary Roman Catholic position.

"Both sacrifice and sacrament [and the sacrament is the meal, as immediately is explained] belong to the same mystery and cannot be

separated one from the other. Then the Lord is offered in an unbloody manner in the Sacrifice of the Mass, representing the sacrifice
of the cross and applying its saving power, when through the words of
consecration he begins to be sacramentally present as the spiritual food
of believers under the species of bread and wine (that is, of physical
food)."[38] The point is clear, though the language is carefully re-
strained. The Lord is sacrificed in the Eucharist when he becomes
present in symbolic reality in the symbol or sacrament of the meal
(bread and wine). The Eucharist, that is, is a sacrificial meal. In it believers celebrate a sacred meal, in which they commemorate, sacramentally realize and thereby perpetuate the sacrifice of the cross.

As I pointed out above, sacrifice is oriented essentially toward
communion between God and his people. *Eucharisticum Mysterium* presents the Eucharistic sacrifice as no exception. On the one hand, the
sacrifice of Jesus is rendered present sacramentally by the symbolic
transformation of bread and wine, which are the central elements of
the sacred meal. On the other hand, the sacrifice is represented specifically so that believers might share in its benefits through Communion, that is, by eating the transformed bread as ritual meal. They
participate in the sacrifice by participating in the meal. Full participation in the sacrifice, therefore, requires full participation in the
meal. It requires full sacramental Communion, as *Eucharisticum Mysterium* is at pains to insist. "The action of believers in the Eucharist is
to this end, that . . . through the reception of the Lord's body they may
perfect their communion with God and with one another, to which
participation in the Sacrifice of the Mass ought to lead. . . . Believers
participate most perfectly in the celebration of the Eucharist by sacramental Communion."[39]

One can regret with Tillard the cautious choice of the language.
"Communion is not simply a more perfect (*perfectior*) participation in
the sacrifice, it is the full and perfect participation."[40] But two points
are still clear. The first is that perfect participation in the sacramental
sacrifice requires perfect participation in the sacramental meal; it requires, that is, sacramental Communion in the meal. Such teaching
merely explicates Trent's doctrine, frequently forgotten, or just simply
ignored, that the Eucharist was instituted to be eaten.[41] The second is
that participation in both the meal-sacrifice and its benefits permits of
more or less. The document incorporates, with evident approval, the
opinion of Aquinas. "This sacrifice, as also the very passion of Christ,
though it is offered for all, has effect only in those who are united to
the passion of Christ in faith and charity. . . . Even for them, it is of
more or less value according to their devotion."[42]

This latter point is of supreme importance, not only here, but also in the discussion of the presence of Jesus in the memorial-sacrificial meal. Sacrament is not magic, but requires, as we have seen several times, the free contribution of a free subject. *Opus operatum* must be matched by *opus operantis* for the sacrament to be fruitful. This is true also in the question of the presence of Jesus in Eucharist, to which we must now turn, and in which I shall insist further on Thomas' opinion about more or less.

REAL PRESENCE

We have seen that in the Eucharist what appears on the level of literal reality to be a meal which men and women share together is on the level of symbolic reality a ritual meal, which commemorates and represents Jesus and the self-gift of himself made to and for his people in his death and resurrection. This self-gift is proclaimed and realized for our participatory celebration of it, particularly for that participation which involves eating and drinking the symbolic elements of the meal, bread and wine, in sacramental Communion. For that to happen, of course, he who gave and gives himself in sacrifice must be really present, and the confession of the real presence of Jesus in this meal is the constant tradition of the Catholic Church in a line extending from the New Testament to the present. Both popular piety and theological inquiry have expended a lot of effort on this presence and its reality, and it is on this presence that I wish now to dwell.

It seems to me not only necessary, but also proper, to state at the outset what I think I am about here. I have just stated the faith of the Church, and my own faith as a member of that Church, in the real presence of Jesus the Christ in the memorial meal he established for it. That is one thing. Quite another is the effort to meditate on that presence and to articulate its meaning in all too limited human language. And so, as I state our faith in the mysterious presence of our Lord in the ritual meal, the *mysterium fidei* as it so often has been called, I feel compelled to state also the inadequacy of the human language to remove that mystery or even to express it fully. I wish to appropriate to myself, and invite my readers to do likewise, the wise words of Peter of Capua and Max Thurian.

The former, reflecting at the beginning of the thirteenth century on the various theological efforts to express the *how* of Jesus' presence in Eucharist, delivered the trenchant judgment. "It is not an article of faith to believe that this or that makes the conversion happen, but only to believe that at the proclamation of the words the body of Christ is on the altar."[43] The latter, pursuing the same reflection in the twentieth century, delivers a warning on evacuating the mystery of that presence. "This real and personal presence of Christ in the bread and wine, his body and blood, is a mystery which it will never be possible for the Church to plumb or to explain."[44] With such wise advice taken to heart, we may now inquire into the *how* of the presence of Jesus in the memorial meal.

Between Peter of Capua and Max Thurian, the understanding of the Church concerning how Jesus became present in the Eucharist crystallized in the theory of *transubstantiation*. The discussion of this word may begin reasonably with its use in the Decree on the Eucharist promulgated by the Council of Trent in 1551. "Again, this holy synod declares that through the consecration of the bread and the wine there is effected a conversion of the entire substance of bread into the substance of the body of Christ our Lord, and of the entire substance of wine into the substance of his blood. This conversion is conveniently and properly called transubstantiation by the holy, Catholic Church."[45] In the corresponding canon, there is added the phrase that the *species* of bread and wine remain and that the conversion is very aptly (*aptissime*) called transubstantiation.[46]

The meaning of this touchstone word is made quite clear in Paul VI's *Mysterium Fidei*, which insists on the decisive importance of the Tridentine concept of the substantial conversion of bread and wine into the body and blood of Christ for understanding the presence of Jesus in the Eucharist. The effect of this transubstantiation is a new reality, the reality of Christ, under the visible signs of bread and wine. "When transubstantiation is achieved, the species of bread and wine without a doubt have a new meaning and a new purpose, since they are no longer common bread and common drink, but the sign of a sacred reality and of spiritual food. But they receive a new meaning and a new purpose precisely because they contain a new 'reality,' which we rightly call *ontological*."[47] It is a classical statement of the classical position, dear to, if not well understood by, many Catholics. We must take it into account in our consideration of the presence of Jesus in the memorial meal.

The term *transubstantiation* is indispensable if one wishes to correctly and fully express the faith of the Church in the presence of Jesus in eucharist. That, at least, is the opinion put forward in a recent book on transubstantiation by the French Dominican, Paul Laurent Carle.[48] His book is written explicitly to examine critically two ecumenical statements about Eucharist, the Roman Catholic-Anglican "Agreed Statement on Eucharistic Doctrine,"[49] and an earlier agreement between French Catholic and Protestant theologians.[50] Both documents refrain from the use of the term *transubstantiation*, and Carle judges that such abstention makes it impossible to express fully the Catholic faith in Jesus' presence. I wish to challenge that opinion here.

In his book, as the title indicates, Carle juxtaposes two theological terms, long consecrated in the theological tradition, namely, *consubstantial* and *transubstantiation*. He uses the former in its traditional Christological sense to assert identity of *substance* between the Christ and humankind, that is, to assert essential identity of his human nature with that of the rest of men and women. In the latter term, therefore, Carle argues, substance must mean the same thing, that is, it must assert the essential reality of the human nature of the Christ, and it is this human nature, therefore, which becomes present by the conversion of the substance of the bread and of the wine. In the traditional usage of the Church, *substantia* means the same as *essentia; transubstantiatio*, therefore, means *transessentiatio*, and affirms the *ontological* presence of Christ in the Eucharist as a result of a metaphysical change in bread and wine. This conclusion, Carle judges, is what the Church teaches about the ontological reality of the Eucharistic presence.[51]

Now I have three difficulties with all of this. The first is easily stated: moderns seldom think, speak or act out of a reality called *substance*. The second Carle himself acknowledges and calls a "Copernican revolution." Whereas for the Middle Ages substance bespoke *metaphysical* reality, for moderns it bespeaks *physical* and sensible reality. "When it conceives substance, far from referring it to some noumenon, the contemporary mentality sees no further than the phenomenal skin of reality, that which appears. Substance reduces spontaneously to a cluster of certain observable constants."[52] I shall leave these difficulties for the moment, pending consideration of the third one, which will lead me back to them.

The third difficulty I have with the ontological-essentialist understanding of the presence of Jesus in Eucharist is much more critical than the other two. In its insistence on the objectivity of the presence of Jesus, correct insistence though it be, it tends to project that presence as the presence of an object, a thing, a physical reality. It is not difficult to conclude, as a student once triumphantly told me, that Jesus is as present in the Eucharist as the pews are in the church or the candles on the altar. And it is not such presence that Christians proclaim, realize and celebrate in the Eucharist, for the presence of pews or candles or any other *thing* is not real presence at all. It is presence only in some downward analogical sense. The only real presence is *in-*

terpersonal presence, the presence between two persons actively interacting.

Real presence is to be distinguished carefully from juxtaposition, being *physically* beside another person, in a room perhaps. I have been many times in the same room with others, and so have you, I am sure, and yet completely absent to most of them, and they have been absent to me. Personal presence requires interaction; it requires persons attending to one another, counting for one another, caring for one another. Such presence, to return to Thomas' opinion which led us into this section, admits of more or less. It has effect, to paraphrase him, only in those who are in active interaction; and even for them "it is of more or less value according to their devotion."[53] It is such interpersonal, and not just some physical, presence that Christians confess when we confess the presence of our Lord in Eucharist.

In the memorial meal which is the Eucharist, Jesus is present neither as an object nor as a thing. He is present as the person who gave himself for the salvation of humankind, and he is personally present as personally recalled and represented in the memorial. The sacramental symbol, the meal itself, represented by two of its elements, bread and wine, the parts for the whole, symbolizes neither an abstract, metaphysical essence nor a physical object. It symbolizes rather, that is, it reveals, realizes and celebrates, a person who gave himself for his fellows and, thanks to God's acceptance of his self-giving, continues to make intercession for us (cf. Heb 7:25). This person is personally present to the ecclesial body of Christ, and to each and every one of its members, only if and to the extent that they personally proclaim it by recalling it, personally realize it by representing it and personally accept it by celebrating it in the sacramental meal.

This leads me back to my second objection, namely, that in contemporary mentality *substance* no longer means what the medievals meant by it. Worse, it means something quite contrary. For by taking substance in an essentially physical sense, moderns are tempted to understand transubstantiation in an essentially physical sense, which is not only contradicted by the unmistakable evidence of their senses, but is also the very interpretation that Scholastic theology wished, in the first instance, to exclude by the use of the term. For by the use of the term *transubstantiation* the Scholastics, and the Church, wished to assert, on the one hand, the reality of Christ's presence in the Eucharist and, on the other, the metaphysical nature of the wondrous change which takes place, leaving unchanged the physical properties of bread and wine.

Carlo Colombo expresses this well in a balanced discussion of transubstantiation. "The conversion does not happen in 'experimental' realities. Everything that enters into the realm of experience, whether of common experience (by sight, taste, touch) or scientific experience (conducted with the most refined instruments), *all that* remains unchanged. Not only is the conversion not physically recognizable, but also it does not happen *in realities which are the direct object of experience,* of whatever type it may be. In a word, both the conversion and the realities which are converted are 'transphysical.' "[54] Now if the word, which so precisely expressed and expresses its meanings when correctly understood, is today ambiguous, then of necessity another way to express clearly what needs to be expressed must be sought. It is precisely this search that Catholic theologians have been engaged in since the years following the Second World War.

That search has opened up "a new approach toward the formulation of faith" in the Eucharistic presence of Jesus. That approach has been documented elsewhere,[55] and it is not my intention to repeat the analyses here. My intention is more limited, namely, to set forth a theory which seeks to be faithful to the traditional notion of transubstantiation, while avoiding its contemporary drawbacks. Remembering Thurian, such a theory will seek not to explain the mystery in such wise that it is explained away, but only to explain the presence of Christ in the sacramental meal in a way that enables us to grasp the mystery and reflect upon it humanly.

At this stage of this book the attentive reader will be well aware that I am locating sacrament in the category of sign, specifically in that category of sign called symbol, and even more specifically in the category of that kind of symbol called action-symbol or ritual.[56] "Sacrament," as Aquinas says, "is located in the category of sign."[57] Piet Schoonenberg calls attention to two quite different kinds of action signs. "There are action signs that *bring something to our knowledge,* and so lead to instruction, provoke feelings, or transmit a command (for the last think of traffic signals). But there are also action signs—and here the *action* is of prime importance—where what is shown forth is at the same time communicated or at least offered. The content of this second kind of action sign is always a kind of love or communion: Shaking hands, a kiss etc."[58] Some action signs, that is, are informative signs; others are realizing signs. It is the same distinction, under another name, that I made in Chapter One between simple signs, which merely convey information, and symbols, which proclaim, realize and celebrate what they symbolize.

There are action signs, or rituals, which make present in symbolic reality what they symbolize. In Chapter One I considered some action signs, the rituals of making love. A love letter, a holding of hands, a kiss: these symbols make love, that is, they proclaim it, realize it and celebrate it as present between two people. They do this not only personally, but also objectively in symbolic reality. They make love present personally to the extent that in these symbols one person offers love and another accepts it. They make it present objectively to the extent that love, and lover, once really offered in the symbols, remains really offered whether it is accepted or not. When it is not only offered but also accepted, of course, then it is not only objectively but also personally present, in the sense that both persons live into it, attending to one another, counting for one another, loving one another in these symbols.

The Eucharistic meal, represented by its elements, bread and wine, is such a realizing action symbol. It symbolizes, that is, to repeat, proclaims, realizes and celebrates, the presence of Jesus of Nazareth offering himself for the salvation of all humankind. This presence of both giver and gift in symbolic reality is totally objective, in the sense that in the symbol both are really, truly and substantially, albeit symbolically-sacramentally, present as offered. This presence is as real and objective as the presence of the pews in the church or the candles on the altar—and quite as useless, until it is transformed into personal presence by a Church of, and by individual, believers who acknowledge it and accept it.

Personal presence in symbols is always a presence to faith. But to say that the presence of Jesus in the Eucharistic meal, in the symbols of bread and wine, is a presence to faith is not the same thing as saying that it is a merely subjective presence. It is rather to say, with Aquinas, that his presence has effect only in those who interact with him in the Eucharistic symbols. His presence in the Eucharistic meal has been ineffably real and objective, never merely subjective, since the moment when, identifying himself once and for all with the symbols of this meal, "he took bread, and when he had given thanks he broke it and gave it to them saying, 'This is my body which is given for you. Do this in remembrance of me' " (Lk 20:19). The faith of the Church and of individual believers does not create this presence out of non-presence, but simply draws it from objective presence into personal presence. In this sacred meal, the Church *makes* Jesus, just as really as lovers make love in their pre-established symbols.

This interpretation of the presence of Jesus in Eucharist seems to me to be faithful to the traditional data associated with the theory of transubstantiation, although it refrains from the use of the word. Equally importantly, it seems to be faithful also to the qualities of a

Eucharistic presence that is understood as the presence of a person and not of an object. There is one major, contemporary Church document against which we can measure these claims, Paul VI's *Mysterium Fidei*. At first sight, this appears to reject a symbolic interpretation of the real presence of Jesus in Eucharist such as I have proposed. Schoonenberg characterizes the interpretation of the encyclical thus. It "develops the following thesis: the Eucharist is a symbol, but *it is also* truly the body and blood of Christ; therefore, the Eucharistic change is a trans-signification, but *also* an ontological transubstantiation."[59] This characterization, in my judgment, is accurate[60] and gives insight into the perspective of the encyclical.

Mysterium Fidei grants that there is symbolism in the Eucharist, and to explain its nature adduces two ancient quotations. The first is from the *Didache*. "As for the Eucharist, give thanks . . . that as this bread which is broken was dispersed on the mountains and gathered and made one, so your Church is gathered from the ends of the earth into your kingdom." The second is from Cyprian. "When the Lord calls his body this bread, made by the fusing of many grains, he indicates our people whom he sustains; and when he calls his blood this wine pressed from many grapes and fused into one, likewise he signifies our flock composed of a multitude united together."[61] It is clear from such statements that the encyclical means by *symbol* what I have characterized as a simple or informative sign. For the grains of flour or the pressing of many grapes do not *effect* the unity of the Church, but only *indicate* it.

This conclusion is made even clearer in what follows. "But if Eucharistic symbolism is an apt guide to understanding the proper effect of this sacrament, which is the unity of the mystical body, nevertheless it does not explain or analyze its proper nature. For the constant teaching of the Catholic Church commands us to confess that the Eucharist is the flesh of our Savior Jesus Christ, which suffered for our sins and which the Father in his goodness raised again."[62] Again, symbol is equated only with informative sign, which leads to understanding but does not effect presence. The same perspective is evident in the passage on transubstantiation that I cited orginally. Of course, the encyclical admits, there is a transignation, a change of sign, which informs us of a different reality, but there is *also* a transubstantiation, which *effects* that different reality.[63]

The conclusion appears inescapable. When *Mysterium Fidei* speaks of sign or symbol, it intends a simple or informative sign, which does nothing but convey information. It does not even begin to consider symbol or realizing action sign, which realizes what it symbolizes. And so when it rejects a symbolic approach as an adequate explanation of the presence of Jesus in Eucharist, and insists on the reality of the presence, that is, when it opposes symbol and reality, it is rejecting correctly the simple informative sign. This rejection does not include, because it never began to consider, the approach I have proposed throughout this book, namely, the approach to sacrament as effective, realizing symbol. The rejection of simple informative sign as an orthodox approach to Eucharistic explanation is a perfectly correct rejection of the kind of "symbolism" which excludes real presence and substantial change. It cannot be construed as a rejection also of the kind of symbolism which necessarily includes real presence and substantial change. "In a word, the encyclical leaves room for a broader interpretation of transubstantiation which can be elaborated in various ways."[64] The way I have chosen in this chapter is through the analysis of the realizing symbols of himself and of his sacrifice that Jesus bequeathed to his Church in the memorial meal.

An instructive appendix to this section, particularly to its discussion of the confusion between metaphysical and physical substance, and between personal and physical presence, will be provided by a brief consideration of two apparently new, but in reality very ancient, practices in the Catholic Church. I refer to the practices of receiving Communion in the hands and of the so-called lay minister of Communion. Many Roman Catholics, conditioned by long centuries of hearing that a lay person could not touch the blessed bread become Jesus, were and are horrified to hear that they and lay ministers could now do it. They judge that this "innovation" betrays a distinct lack of respect for Jesus physically held in their unblessed hands.

Now at least one of the sources for that attitude (I do not pretend that it is the sole source) is the acceptance of the theory of transubstantiation in a very physical sense. Such an understanding, as I have already pointed out, contradicts not only the undeniable evidence of our senses, but also the doctrine of the Roman Catholic Church, which insists that transubstantiation names a metaphysical and not a physical change, and that, therefore, the physical realities of the bread, the classical species, always remain. What communicants or ministers touch with their hands are those physical species, not the physical body of Jesus. That they hold, though, the real Jesus in symbolic and sacramental reality, and that therefore our reaching out to and holding of him should be reverent, is the ancient and unbroken tradition of the Catholic Church.

Cyril of Jerusalem, for instance, instructs his newly initiated Christians on both these facts as he instructs them on the proper way to receive Communion in their hands. "Whoever takes Communion does not take bread and wine, but the sacrament of the body and the blood of Christ. When you approach, therefore, do not approach with your hands stretched out or your fingers separated. But with your left hand make a throne for your right, since this one is to receive the king, and in the hollow of your hand receive the body of Christ, and reply 'Amen.' "[65] Four hundred years later John Damascene gives evidence of the same practice as he instructs how Communion is to be received: the hands are to be arranged in the form of a cross to receive the body of the Crucified.[66] These are but two of the many ancient testimonies to the practice of Communion in the hand. It is interesting that the practice was abandoned only in the ninth century, concomitant with the rise of a very physical understanding of the Eucharistic presence of Jesus. The "new" practice authorized in the Catholic Church restores the ancient practice to its rightful place, and emphasizes in a ritual way what I have insisted upon, namely, the metaphysical, symbolic and sacramental, but no less real for that, nature of the transubstantiation involved in the eucharistic mystery of faith.

"THIS IS MY BODY"

The very physically oriented interpretation of the presence of Jesus in the Eucharistic meal was given great impetus in the Church by two historical controversies. The first was in the eleventh century, when Berengar of Tours advanced a "symbolic" interpretation of that presence; the second was in the sixteenth century when certain of the Reformers advanced an equally "symbolic" interpretation. Berengar was forced to swear an oath in which he confessed that "the bread and wine which are placed on the altar . . . are converted into the true and proper and life-giving body and blood of our Lord Jesus Christ . . . *not only in symbol* and the power of the sacrament, but in reality of nature and truth of substance (*in proprietate naturae et veritate substantiae*)."[67] The Council of Trent anathematized the Reformers. "If anyone denies that in the most blessed sacrament there is contained really, truly and substantially (*vere, realiter et substantialiter*) . . . the total Christ, but says he is present in it *only* in symbol or in figure or in power, let him be anathema."[68]

It is clear from a history of the controversies that both Berengar and the Reformers intended the opinion that the presence of Jesus in Eucharist was only symbolic, in the sense that it was in no way real. It is equally clear from a reading of the texts that the magisterium wished to exclude *only* this opinion, and not the opinion which holds that his presence is symbolic and, therefore, real. In the language already used, it wished to exclude the opinion that the sacrament of bread and wine, the ritual meal, was only an informative sign and not a realizing symbol. Post-Reformation Catholic theology, though, concentrated so exclusively and polemically on both symbol as merely informative sign and the reality of Jesus' presence that it submerged, and so obliterated from common understanding, the symbolic and representative character of the Eucharistic meal. Contemporary Catholic biblical exegesis is in accord in interpreting both the action of Jesus at the Last Supper and the Eucharistic action which flows from it in the biblical category of prophetic symbol, which I considered at the outset of this book. This approach underscores again, after a long period of obscurity, the necessarily symbolic nature of both actions.[69]

After all I have said about symbol, there is no need for the caveat which Dupont feels obliged to add. "The idea which we have of symbol or of sign does not correspond to all that a Semite sees there. For him a prophetic action is normally efficacious; it does not only represent what it announces, it effects it also in some way."[70] He has in mind, clearly, the idea of symbol or sign as merely indicative or informative sign, which is, indeed, distinct from the realizing symbol of the Semitic prophetic action. But the idea of realizing symbol which I have advanced throughout this book is identical to, and need not be distinguished from, the prophetic symbol. Dupont is at pains to emphasize the reality of the presence of Jesus in the symbol, something that needs to be emphasized to the ontological mentality that learned to distinguish symbolic and real. I have sought to show throughout, however, that symbolic is in no way opposed to real, but on the contrary bespeaks real in a very profound way. A brief recall of that idea here will indicate the meaning of the words, "This is my body."

We saw in the opening chapters of this book how a reality which has one meaning on one level of reality may acquire quite another meaning on another level of reality. On the level of literal reality water, for instance, means life and cleansing; on the level of symbolic reality those meanings are put together with (syn-ballo = symbol) other, religious, meanings which cluster around cleansing from sin and new life. In the same physical reality, two meanings and two realities, which are not of the same order, are put together so that they are quite inseparable, so that they are not attained by human beings sequentially, but as one. In symbolic reality, the symbol is the reality it represents. And so it is in Eucharist.

In a very ordinary human action, the action of sharing a meal of bread and wine, Christians represent, realize and celebrate the presence among them of Jesus their Lord. They do this, they claim truly, not because they decided to represent Jesus in this meal, but because he identified himself with bread ("my body") and wine ("my blood") and commanded them to continue the representation "in memory of me." The identification, though, of Jesus and bread is not to be thought of on the level of physical reality, no more than the identification of Jerusalem and hair, or the identification of first century bread with the bread of Egyptian affliction, is to be thought of on the level of physical reality. It is on the level of symbolic reality only that there is transformation, transignification and transubstantiation, so that what was bread now *is* in symbolic reality the body of Christ.

But remember, the real presence of Jesus in the symbols of bread and wine is rather a real absence until it is lived into by believers, who accept in faith the words of Jesus identifying himself with these symbols. To symbolize real presence, that is, to proclaim, realize and celebrate it, more is required than just the words of Jesus identifying himself with the sacred meal, powerful *opus operatum* though that be. There is required also the action of believers who accept this *opus operatum;* there is required, that is, faithful *opus operantis.* It is not so much that believers, be they ever so priestly, make Jesus present where he was absent, but rather that in their commemorative meal they proclaim his presence, and actualize it and celebrate it and unite themselves to him as already present. As a man and a woman make love in ritual actions, so also Christians make Jesus in ritual actions, including that of the ritual meal. But neither that love nor that presence of Jesus is made so that it can be definitively plumbed. Both are symbolized as present, but in no way exhaustively possessed. And this leads me to my final comment about the ecclesial meal.

THE ESCHATOLOGICAL MEAL

On the level of literal reality bread and wine are meal elements; on the level of symbolic reality they are symbols of Jesus in the ritual meal of Christians. But there is another meaning for meals on the level of symbolic reality, with which I shall conclude this chapter. Jeremias has shown that the act of eating and drinking is an ancient biblical symbolism representing the vision of God.[71] That symbolism is present, too, in the Christian memorial meal.

Isaiah prophesied that "on this mountain the Lord of hosts will make for all peoples a feast of fat things, a feast of wine on the lees, of fat things full of marrow, of wine on the lees well refined. And he will destroy on this mountain the covering that is cast over all peoples, the veil that is spread over all nations" (25:6–7). It is the promise of the great eschatological meal on the mountain of God when the veil that covers the eyes of the Gentiles will be removed forever and they will see God. From this prophetic origin, the eschatological banquet as a symbol of communion with God is an ever-recurring image. It underpins the wedding feasts of Mark 2:19 and Matthew 22:2, the "Blessed are you that hunger now, for you will be satisfied" of Luke 6:21, and Jesus' announcement in Luke 22:18 that "From now on I shall not drink of the fruit of the vine until the kingdom of God comes." The banquet meal is linked inseparably to the saving rule and vision of God. The banquet meal of Christians continues this linkage.

When God raised Jesus from the dead, he marked him out as "the holy and righteous one" (Acts 3:14), as the one in whom he had ruled, as the one in whom his kingdom had come. When the first Jewish Christians came to celebrate the presence of this righteous one in his ecclesial body, they celebrated it in a meal which not only proclaimed the Lord's death and resurrection, but also pointed forward to his final manifestation in the great day to come. The meal proclaimed "the Lord's death until he comes" (1 Cor 11:26). Because they were convinced he would come soon and remove the veil of mystery, the first Christians celebrated their meal "with glad and generous hearts" (Acts 2:46), and prayed for him to come soon. "*Marana tha;* come, Lord Jesus" (1 Cor 16:22; Rev 22:20).

The prophetic words of the Lord's Prayer, understood in their original form, make it clear that still today Christians pray that the rule of God in Christ, expected for the great day, take place soon. "Our Father, bless your name, do your will on earth as in heaven, establish your kingdom (= rule), and give us today the bread (= banquet) promised for tomorrow."[72] On the level of history, the Lord's Supper is the memorial meal of Christians. On the level of symbolic eschatology, it is the promised banquet that reveals, realizes and celebrates the vision of God in measure enough to sustain the hope of what will be revealed tomorrow. The words of Aquinas, who understood Eucharist so well, still summarize this aspect of it best. The Eucharistic meal is a pledge in history of future glory: *pignus futurae gloriae.* When the Christian comes face to face with the end of his earthly life, this meal will be a central part of the ritual which celebrates and sustains the end. It is to the consideration of that ritual that we must now turn.

Chapter Seven
ANOINTING

Healthy men and women play an active role in their community through their home and their job and their many activities. They feel useful, needed, to some extent even indispensable. Sickness places this active role in jeopardy. The sick are placed in a role of dependence, for which they can make, apparently, no return. They frequently lose courage, become lonely, withdraw into themselves feeling they are no longer useful in society. At such a low point in their lives they need to find meaning, they need to discover a way to be valuable in their community. It is not too difficult to guess that such meaning and value will be found most readily with communal help and support. The Church, the community that confesses that the crucified Jesus is also the risen Christ, offers this help and support in a sacrament of the sick.

A RITUAL OF THE SICK

Any treatment of this sacrament must begin with the evidence from the early Church recorded in the New Testament. Two pieces of evidence are traditionally cited, the apostolic healing ministry (Mk 6:13) and the presbyteral rite of the sick (Jas 5:14-15). Mark reports that the Twelve "cast out many demons and anointed with oil many that were sick and healed them." Now in both the Jewish and the early Christian world oil was used in many contexts. It was used to anoint kings,[1] to anoint priests,[2] to anoint prophets,[3] to anoint objects which would be used in cult,[4] to anoint wounds,[5] for medicinal purposes,[6] and to anoint the dead in preparation for life in another world.[7] Mark, however, calls attention here not to any power in the oil, medicinal or otherwise, but rather to a power in the apostles, a power which they had received from Jesus (6:7), and which is now proclaimed and realized in an anointing with oil. Some Roman Catholic exegetes have claimed to find in this text an express institution of a sacrament of the sick. But the more common view is summarized in Trent's careful judgment that that institution "is insinuated in Mark and commended and promulgated to the faithful by James the apostle and brother of the Lord."[8]

James is the most important New Testament evidence for a ritual of anointing the sick. His promulgation of the ritual appears in a context in which the theme of prayer is applied to three normal life-situations of Christians. Whoever is suffering is instructed to pray. Whoever is cheerful is instructed to sing songs of praise. Whoever is sick is to "call for the elders of the Church and let them pray over him, anointing him with oil in the name of the Lord; and the prayer of faith will save the sick man, and the Lord will raise him up; and if he has committed sins, he will be forgiven" (5:14–15).

It is a minor point, but the life-situations in each case are not introduced as conditional clauses ("if someone is ill") but as independent sentences ("someone among you is ill"). James' saying appears not to introduce anointing of the sick, but to presuppose the prior existence of such a rite. Now *asthenei* does not connote a grave illness, and so this text does not inculcate a ritual of the dying but a ritual of the sick. Some theologians have tried to explain the saving and the raising up of the sick person in a spiritual and eschatological sense, so that they would refer exclusively to some ultimate salvation. That they refer also, and in symbol, to such a meaning may be granted, but the context does not allow that to be the exclusive meaning. "Quite by contrast to the sacrament of extreme unction, the healing aspect stands in the foreground in James 5:15 . . . the words *sozein* (to save) and *egerein* (to raise up) here must have the technical meanings which they would normally have in this connection . . . i.e. 'to heal' and 'to restore to health.' "[9] The elders are called not to a dying person but to a sick person, and there is no cause to interpret save or raise up as referring exclusively to ultimate salvation and resurrection. The outcome of the ecclesial anointing and the prayer of faith is healing that is personal as well as spiritual.

The sick person is to call for the elders (*presbyteroi*) of the Church. I do not wish at this point to enter into the debate concerning the question of whether the *presbyteros* of James' day was equivalent to the *priest* of our day. That I shall do when I consider priesthood. My judgment, though, is that James gives us insight into a Jewish-Christian community which bestowed upon its experienced members official rank as well. Here I wish only to call attention to the institutional character of the rite that is advocated. It is not just elders in age that are recommended, or charismatics with their healing powers. The healing power here is an ecclesial power, ministered by elders who have been given an authority and a ministry in and to the Church.

The elders anoint the sick person with oil and pray over him. The medicinal use of oil, as already noted, was well known in the ancient world. But here the specification that the anointing is "in the name of the Lord" precludes the possibility that we are dealing with a simple medicinal use of oil. Here oil is but the visible sign for the real, invisible healing power, which is both "in the name of the Lord" and "in the prayer of faith." That power extends, of course, not only to spiritual healing, including the forgiveness of sins, but also to total, personal healing, including on occasion physical healing. The sick person is a whole person, and the healing described in the rite is a saving and a raising up of that whole person, not just of either a body part or a soul part. Charles Gusmer expresses it well. "The effects of anointing touch the religious situation of the sick person: the threat to his salvation posed by religious powerlessness and weakness of soul, as well as the temptation and burden to his faith and trust. The sick person shall be raised up from this weakness and saved from the threat that sickness constitutes to his salvation."[10] The Church, through the ministry of its elders, responds to the need of the sick person for present salvation, which then represents in symbol future salvation. To this I shall return.

Further evidence for the early existence of anointing of the sick is derived from a prayer for the blessing of oil of anointing in the Coptic fragment of the *Didache*. "Concerning the word of the oil give thanks thus saying, We thank you, Father, for the oil which you have made known to us through Jesus your Son. Glory is yours forever." This prayer may be as old as James, depending on whether or not the Coptic fragment is accepted as part of the original *Didache* and on the dates of origin assigned to both that and James.[11] The same prayer is repeated, however, almost verbatim in the *Apostolic Constitutions*, in a section which is derived from the *Didache*.[12] *The Apostolic Tradition* of Hippolytus, written about 215, also contains a prayer for the blessing of oil. "O God . . . grant that [this oil] may give strength to all that taste it and health to all that use it."[13]

Since James portrays for us a Jewish-Christian community, it would be predictable that the specific meaning(s) of the anointing with oil would have Jewish roots. It will be useful later, when we ask about the meaning(s) of anointing, to pause here and consider the Jewish meanings. The economic history of the biblical lands shows that oil, grain (bread) and wine were its most important agricultural products—so much so that when Deuteronomy enumerates the blessings of God, it specifically mentions this trio (7:13).

In Jewish mythology, the first sign of the appearance of the new world after the deluge was the *olive leaf* which the dove brought back to Noah (Gen 8:11). Rabbinical teaching insists that this olive leaf came from Eden.[14] Enoch teaches that the tree of life in Eden was an olive tree and that the rivers of paradise flowed with oil and wine (2 Enoch 8:5, Rec. A and B). The Apocalypse of Moses offers a moving account of Adam longing for the "oil of mercy" which flows from this tree of life (9:3). It reports that his wife and son, Eve and Seth, return to paradise to beg God to grant them this oil of mercy, a plea to which the archangel Michael responds. "Do not tire yourself begging and praying for the tree from which flows this oil to anoint your father. It will not be given to you now, but only at the last days. Then all flesh from Adam to that great day will rise, all who are a righteous people. Then all the delights of paradise will be given to them" (13:1–3).

Clearly oil, which was so widespread and vital in the economic life of the people of Israel, took on in their symbolic life the meaning of life from and with God. The Western tradition might wish to call this life *eternal life*. Enhanced with such symbolic meaning, oil is an obvious candidate for use in ritual action at a time when life, personal, physical, and perhaps also spiritual, is threatened. We must always recall James' emphasis, though, that it is not the oil but the prayer of faith in the name of the Lord that heals.

The first unequivocal testimony in the Church to a ritual of anointing such as is described by James is provided in a letter of Pope Innocent I (+417) to Decentius, bishop of Gubbio. Origen had mentioned James but had interpreted him as referring to a ritual of penance, not of anointing the sick. Innocent explains authoritatively that the text of James "is to be received or understood as relating to sick faithful, who can be anointed with the holy oil which is consecrated by the bishop and which may be used by all Christians, not only by priests, when they need anointing." He insists further that the oil "cannot be given to penitents because it is a kind of sacrament, and how can one kind [of sacrament] be judged to be for those to whom the others are denied."[15] This decretal, which became a basic document in the Church for the theological elaboration of anointing of the sick, gives evidence of substantial agreement with the scattered evidence adduced from earlier documents. Anointing of the sick not of the dying, is an established usage in the Church. The blessing of the oil of the sick is a prerogative of the bishop, and endows the oil with a symbolic power that locates it in the category of sacrament.

In his critical study of the history of the anointing of the sick in the Latin Church up to the time of Charlemagne, Antoine Chavasse reaches the somewhat startling, but apparently correct, conclusion that it was precisely the blessing of the oil that was of primary sacramental importance in Rome and elsewhere. The application of the oil in the anointing of the sick was symbolically and sacramentally secondary, merely providing an occasion to use, without any special formula, the already blessed and, *ipso facto*, ritually efficacious oil.[16] While the blessing of the oil was strictly a function of the bishop, its application could be made by presbyters and lay people alike. Caesar, bishop of Arles, exhorts his faithful not to have recourse to pagan practices in times of sickness. For "how much more right and salutary it would be if they hastened to the Church, received the body and blood of Christ, anointed themselves and their kin with the blessed oil and, in accordance with what the apostle James says, receive not only health of body but also remission of their sins."[17] Since, however, Innocent's decretal forbade the sacramental oil to penitents, and since ancient penance was usually postponed, as I explained, until Christians came face to face with death, it is doubtful that much anointing took place.

In contrast to the early period, from the eighth and ninth centuries there is clear and abundant and indisputable evidence for the sacrament of anointing. The earliest commentary available on the Letter of James is that of Bede (+ 735) who, while acknowledging Innocent's decree that not only priests but also any Christian can anoint with oil, states that "now the custom of the Church is that the sick are anointed by priests with the consecrated oil and are healed by the accompanying prayer."[18] The forgiveness of sins, however, Bede judges, is dependent on confession to a priest and cannot be achieved without it.[19] Still well to the forefront in Bede is the idea that anointing is a sacrament of the *sick*. In his commentary on Mark 6:13, which he links to James, he judges that "it is clear that this custom was handed on to the holy church by the apostles themselves, that those who are possessed or sick are anointed with oil consecrated by a pontifical blessing."[20]

A RITUAL OF THE DYING

With the great Carolingian reforms, anointing of the sick began to take on a different character. It was transformed into a sacrament of the dying and its administration was restricted to priests. The General Capitulary of 769–771 decreed that priests should exercise great care "of the sick and of penitents, so that the dying do not pass away without anointing with consecrated oil and without reconciliation and viaticum."[21] The Capitularies Concerning Priests of 810 prescribe that "a priest should take with him from the Lord's Supper two containers, one for chrism, the other for oil for anointing catechumens and the sick, in accordance with the statement of the apostle that when someone is sick he should call in the presbyters of the Church and they should pray over him, anointing him with oil in the name of the Lord."[22] The Burgundian instructions of the Statuta Bonifatii (800–840) prohibit any priest from delivering the oil to any non-priest under pain of being suspended (*honore priventur*), "for it is in the category of sacrament."[23] It was in the same period, as a matter of interest, that synods forbade under serious penalty the sending of Communion to the sick by non-priests.[24] The fact that the consecrated oil and its use in the anointing of the sick is in the category of sacrament could not be more clearly demonstrated: anointing of the sick is located in the same category as Eucharist.

Yet with all the Carolingian emphasis on the obligation of priests to anoint the sick, the sacrament was more in disuse than in use. At the beginning of the ninth century James, bishop of Orleans, repeated the three hundred year old complaint of Caesar of Arles that the sick were consulting sorcerers rather than receiving anointing from the Church.[25] Throughout the Middle Ages bishops and synods continued to insist on the use of anointing,[26] insistence which makes sense only in a situation in which its non-use was more common than its use.

Poschmann advances a convincing argument for such a state of affairs. In distinction to the practice of the early Church, prescriptions in the Middle Ages for the care of the sick always link anointing, penance and communion, as is exemplified in the decree of the General Capitulary cited above. Poschmann theorizes that "the reason for this may well be sought in the introduction into the West of the oriental custom . . . of anointing even ordinary penitents."[27] As anointing gained its place as an element of *penance,* Innocent's prohibition of anointing sick penitents was rendered ineffective. In their case, anointing as an element of the ritual of penance and anointing as an element in the ritual of the sick simply coincided. The common perception of anointing as an element in the penance ritual may, indeed, have been the principal reason for the decline of the anointing of the sick.

I have to emphasize here a point which I passed over in the discussion of ancient penance. The severe demands of ancient penance, remember, did not cease with the reconciliation of the penitent, but continued for the rest of his life. Now the ritual penance of the sick was regarded in every way as equivalent to the classical ancient penance, and in the case of a sick person who recovered the life-long penitential demands became operative. Just as those severe demands contributed in large degree to the decline of ancient penance, so too they contributed to the decline of anointing the sick. And just as penance was deferred until the last possible moment, so too was anointing. Then, quite naturally, the phrase *extreme unction,* which later became the name of this sacrament, but is attested first only in "the tenth or eleventh century" and is in common use only "from the end of the twelfth,"[28] became the way to designate this sacrament.

What began in the Church as a sacrament of the sick became, after a thousand years journey, a sacrament of the dying. That thousand year journey is of theological importance. For it makes true the judgment of a theologian who has spent a great deal of time elaborating the theology of the anointing of the sick. Jean Charles Didier writes that "the expression *extreme unction,* though consecrated by many centuries of use by theology, the ordinary magisterium, the ritual, the Council of Trent, is nevertheless very late, *much too late to be considered traditional:* it does not appear before the twelfth century."[29] In the thirteenth century, therefore, pastoral practice was that anointing of the sick was an extreme unction of the dying, and the great Scholastics of that century theologized on the basis of that unchallenged practice. They viewed extreme unction as a preparation for the passage from this life to the next, and discussed its effect as a preparation for glory. The great Franciscans (Bonaventure and Scotus) saw that effect as the forgiveness of venial sins, the great Dominicans (Albert and Thomas) as the cure of the remains of sin, including guilt if it was present.[30] Thomas teaches also that, secondarily and conditionally, physical healing is sometimes an effect of the sacrament.[31] But, though the Council of Trent leaned heavily on Thomas for its teaching on extreme unction, it refused to canonize any of the Scholastic theories.

Trent's teaching on the sacrament, which in the preliminary text asserted that the sacrament was to be administered "only to those who are in their final struggle and have come to grips with death and are about to go forth to the Lord," was altered in the final text to read that "this anointing is to be used for the sick, but especially for those who are so dangerously ill as to appear at the point of departing this life."[32] The Council also broadened the discussion on the effect of this sacrament to go beyond the remission of sins and its effects and embrace the strengthening of the whole person through the grace of the Holy Spirit.[33]

Despite Trent's attempt, however, to portray the sacrament of anointing as a sacrament of the sick, both post-Tridentine theory and practice continued to portray it and administer it as a sacrament of the dying—until the Second Vatican Council solidly reinforced Trent's view. The preliminary draft of the Constitution on the Liturgy asserted unequivocally that "the sacrament which is commonly called extreme unction henceforth shall be called anointing of the sick; for it is not *per se* a sacrament of the dying but of the sick." The version finally approved by the Council was softened slightly, but still stated that extreme unction is more fittingly called anointing of the sick, and is to be administered "as soon as any one of the faithful begins to be in danger of death from sickness or old age."[34] Paul VI's apostolic constitution of 1972, *Sacram Unctionem Infirmorum,* confirmed anointing definitively as a sacrament of the sick.

There is a point here which appears to be minor, but which is in reality of major importance for pastoral practice. It concerns those who may receive the sacrament of the sick. The official Latin text of the Constitution on the Liturgy states that *extrema unctio* is better called *unctio infirmorum,* and offers some indication of how it understands *infirmorum* by adding that the time to receive this sacrament is when a person begins to be in danger of death "because of infirmity or old age" *(propter infirmitatem vel senium).*[35] Paul VI's constitution repeats the phrase *unctio infirmorum.*[36] Now *infirmorum* is translated into English as sick, but I wish to insert a caveat here.

Latin has very precise words to designate a sick person, *aegrotus (a)* or *aegrotans,* and *infirmus* bespeaks a broader canvas than either of these. The proper subject to receive the *unctio infirmorum,* then, is one who begins to be in danger of death (quite a different condition from the prior one of being on the point of death), from some infirmity, be that infirmity medically classified as sickness or old age or an injury received in an accident. On the other hand, in the meaning of the English *infirm,* blindness is an infirmity; so too is any other chronic physical or psychic handicap. These infirmities, it is clear, do not put those who suffer them in danger of death, any more than the non-infirm are in danger of death. They are not, therefore, the infirmities envisaged as requiring anointing of the infirm. That does not mean, however, that theologians, seeking to elucidate the precise meaning of that anointing, cannot and should not raise the question about the anointing of such infirm. Vatican II's Constitution on the Church declares: "By the sacred anointing of the sick (= *infirmorum*) and the prayer of her priests the whole Church commends those who are ill to the suffering and glorified Lord. . . . She exhorts them moreover to contribute to the welfare of the whole people of God by associating themselves freely with the passion and death of Christ."[37] It is arguable, and I wish to argue it explicitly, that the ministry of the Church, whom we name mother, necessarily extends not only to the periodically infirm but also to the chronically infirm; that they have need of the strengthening envisioned by the sacrament of anointing, precisely to raise them up and insert them explicitly into the mystery of Christ who gives himself that the Church might be built up; that it is, indeed, they who need the benefit of the repeated anointing envisioned and granted by *Sacram Unctionem Infirmorum* each time they undergo a grave crisis of personal meaning, value or faith brought about by their infirmity.

Our historical analysis has shown the journey of this sacrament from sacrament of the sick to sacrament of the dying and back again, from the condition of being on the point of death to that of beginning to be in danger of death. A further, tiny step in the journey is all that is required to embrace all the infirm, even though they do not begin to be in danger of death. James, remember, does not envision danger of death, only sickness. There is nothing I am aware of, not biblical, not theological, not historical, certainly not canonical, to impede such a step.

THEOLOGICAL REFLECTION

We now have sufficient evidence to delineate the ritual meanings of the anointing of the sick. But first recall our basic triadic approach to sacramentality: Jesus, Church, sacrament. The Gospels testify to Jesus' special care for the sick. They present his activity among them as in full agreement with the healing activity of the Old Testament prophets, Elijah and Elisha (2 Kgs 5:1–15), and the proclamations of Isaiah (35:3–6; 61:1–3). They seem to interpret this agreement with and fulfillment of the Old Testament as a restoration (*apokatastasis*) of afflicted creatures as the completion of God's work of creation. Jesus, the Son of God, restores God's creatures to their original whole creation state (*apokatastasis* in Mark 8:25) and, consequently, is proclaimed as one who "has made all things good" (Mk 7:37).[38] These healing-restorations are eschatological, not just in the weak sense that they foretell eschatological salvation, but in the stronger sense that they themselves *are* salvation proleptically received. Just as in the beginning God made all things good (Gen 1), so in the end Jesus, the sacramental man-God, remakes all things good.[39]

The Church, the incarnation of the man-God in the world, continues this healing-restoration ministry. Through that ministry the
sick, who are at a low point in their lives with respect to meaning, to
value, and perhaps to faith, are raised up from their weakness and are
remade personally whole. This human raising up contains echoes of
the ancient tradition of Elijah-Elisha (1 Kgs 17:17; 2 Kgs 4:18–37) and
Isaiah (26:19), and also of Jesus' reply to the messengers from John
the Baptist (Mt 11:5), and is eschatological, again, in the stronger
sense. That is, the human raising up is already personal salvation now,
and also representative symbol of that ultimate salvation guaranteed
in the peace of the Church.

The prayer over the oil in *The Apostolic Tradition*, "O God . . . grant
that [this oil] may give strength to all that taste of it and health to all
that use it," has been interpreted traditionally to mean *bodily* strength
and health. But that is by no means a necessary reading. Strength and
health refer just as naturally to the whole human person, as to his narrowly physical parts. Two separate prayers in the *Liber Sacramentorum*
of Gregory the Great pray for the total raising up of the sick. The first
asks God to "look graciously upon this thy servant, so that when the
need of bodily infirmity is excluded he may be restored to his condition of pristine health through your perfect grace." The second asks
him to "restore [the sick person] to full inner and outer health."[40] Full
human health, and not just either bodily or spiritual health, is asked
for the sick person. The *Gelasian Sacramentary* offers another prayer,
which celebrates the God who dispels *every* weakness and *every* infirmity from human beings. "God of heavenly power, who dispels from human bodies every weakness and every infirmity, be propitious to this
thy servant that with his former health restored he may bless thy
name."[41]

This view of anointing, broadened beyond either purely physical
or purely spiritual health to the raising up of the whole human person,
is the view endorsed by the Council of Trent. It refused, remember,
to take sides in the Scholastic debate over whether anointing forgives
sins or simply clears away the remnants of sins, and extended its effect
to a broader canvas. "The reality and effect of this sacrament is . . . the
grace of the Holy Spirit, whose anointing wipes away sin . . . as well as
the remnants of sin, and comforts and strengthens the soul of the sick
person, by arousing in him great confidence in the divine mercy. Thus
raised up (*sublevatus*) the sick person bears more easily the difficulties
and trials of his illness, resists more easily the temptations of the demon . . . and, where it is expedient for the health of the soul, sometimes receives bodily health."[42]

Trent, of course, functioned out of the classical dualist conception of man as a composite of body and soul, but the phrase "comforts and strengthens the soul of the sick person" is easily compatible with a more modern view of man as a psychosomatic unity, so that it is, as indeed the Council says, not the soul but the sick person that is raised to support the difficulties of his condition. What I suggested at the opening of this chapter is confirmed by Trent. At a low time in their lives, the sick are raised up to a new height of meaning, of value and of faith by the ministry of the Church, symbolically representing the healing ministry of Jesus and of God. It remains for us to elaborate the meaning(s) to which the Church bears witness in the ritual.

Vatican II's Constitution on the Church provides us with a starting point, a statement on anointing that is repeated in Paul VI's constitution. "By the sacred anointing of the sick and the prayer of her priests the whole Church commends the sick to the suffering and glorified Lord, asking that he may lighten their suffering and save them."[43] The sacrament, it teaches, is a concern of the *whole Church*, the Ekklesia, the body of Christ. An ancient Pauline principle is in play here: "if one member suffers, all suffer together" (1 Cor 12:26). When one member of the body looks into the depth of human suffering and despair, the whole body is threatened and reacts to raise up the suffering member. In the ritual of anointing, it gathers to do this. It does so, first of all, on the level of human reality, encouraging and supporting the sick to come to grips with their infirmities and to dominate, rather than be dominated by, them. That, of course, is a great human good in itself, but it is not all there is. For on the level of symbolic reality, that human raising up sacramentally proclaims, realizes and celebrates the definitive raising up promised by and hoped for from God and his Christ.

The norms of Vatican II's Constitution on the Liturgy, which we have already noted, recur here again. "Liturgical services are not private functions, but are celebrations of the Church," and therefore a communal way of "celebrating them is to be preferred, as far as possible, to a celebration that is individual and quasi-private."[44] For the Church to minister as body of Christ, and to effectively symbolize that ministry, more is required ritually than a private anointing of an individual sick person by an individual priest. Church bespeaks community and ecclesial ministry bespeaks communal expression. The new rite of anointing establishes that "the family and friends of the sick have a special share in this ministry of comfort. It is their task to strengthen the sick with words of faith and, by praying with them, to commend them to the Lord who suffered and who was glorified, and to urge the sick to unite themselves willingly with the passion and death of Christ for the good of God's people."[45] Family and friends should be a part of the ritual of anointing, where possible, not only to provide their human support and raising up, but also to represent the support and the raising up offered by the Church, by Jesus and by God.

To see the gathering of family and friends under the leadership of the Church's designated minister as anything other than just a gathering of family and friends requires, of course, a special insight. To see the anointing as anything other than just an anointing with oil requires the same insight. To see the one as a gathering of the Church, the body of Christ in the world, and the other as a sacrament of the healing action of that Church, of Christ and of God, requires that special insight we have already named faith. We recall the Council of Trent's teaching that no one is justified without faith. We recall also its minimalistic teaching that a sacrament confers the grace it signifies on the person who places no obstacle to it, and the more expansive teaching of the equally ecumenical Council of Florence that a sacrament gives grace to those who receive it worthily. We recall also the definition of symboling offered in the second chapter: "a specifically human process in which meanings and realities, intellectual, emotional and personal, are proclaimed, realized and celebrated in representation in a sensible reality *within a specific perspective*."[46]

The phrase I have chosen to emphasize is an essential element in that definition, so that if the specific perspective is ever lacking, the sensible reality remains just that, a sensible reality. It does not become symbol, and does not proclaim or actualize what the symbol seeks to symbolize. The perspective that transforms both a gathering of friends into the body of Christ, and an anointing with oil into the Christian sacrament of the sick, is the faith of the Church shared by the sick person. If, perchance, the faith of the Church is not matched by the sick person, if he is, though baptized, a non-believer, then no symbolic transformation takes place. Anointing is offered as sacrament by the Church, but is accepted by the sick person only as physical anointing. It is not surprising that James insists that "the prayer of faith will save the sick man," or that Paul VI declares that "the anointing of the sick," which includes the prayer of faith, is a sacrament of faith . . . the sick man will be saved by his faith and the faith of the Church."[47] Faith is always required in symbol and in sacrament. The saving action of God is now always mediated, as Aquinas long ago realized, by the faith of the Church.[48]

THE RITE OF ANOINTING

That the saving and raising up effected in the sacrament of anointing is precisely the kind of personal raising up that I have indicated becomes evident from a careful look at the prayer said during the anointing, the Scholastic *form* of the sacrament. "Through this holy anointing, may the Lord in his love and mercy help you with the grace of the Holy Spirit. May the Lord who frees you from sin save you and raise you up (*allevet*)."[49] The prayer contains obvious echoes of James, but there is a subtle precision. Whereas the Latin version of James has *alleviet* for raise up, the prayer in the ritual has *allevet*. Now whatever be the Latin distinction between *allevare* and *alleviare*, and in truth there is little distinction between them, the Roman Ritual now uses the former in respect of persons and the latter in respect of disease or sickness or pain, as in the English *alleviate*.[50] This precision allows us to isolate the general meaning of sacramental anointing. It is the *person* who is to be raised up, not his infirmity that is to be alleviated.

Following up our earlier summary of the Jewish-Christian meaning(s) of oil and anointing, we can now specify a dominant meaning of the sacrament of anointing. It bespeaks life, specifically life as both from and with God—not only present life but also, and more importantly, future and eternal life. The sick are anointed with oil from the symbolic tree of life that stood in the symbolic garden of Eden. The anointing proclaims to them in symbolic reality, at a time when their personal life is at a low point, that life is from God and may be used in the service of God for as long as they have it. It may be used also in the service of the church to which they belong and which mediates to them now the life-giving and life-sustaining action of God. Whether in sickness or in health matters not; life quite simply may be used in the service of God and neighbor. It is revealed to them also in symbolic reality that if, and when, they pass from this life, they do not pass back into the nothingness from which they came, but rather to the new and eternal life with God which they began symbolically in baptism. Michael's solemn promise to Eve and to Seth is fulfilled in symbolic anointing; the sick receive the oil of mercy promised to the righteous ones. As did Jesus, the supremely righteous one, so also the righteous ones who are in Christ since their baptism will pass to the Father.

The intimate link between anointing and baptism is insinuated from the outset of the ritual. A sprinkling of blessed water is accompanied by the prayer: "Let this water call to mind your baptismal sharing in Christ's redeeming passion and death."[51] Here we may be at the very bedrock of the meaning and value the Church holds out to the sick. A central tradition of the New Testament is that "Christ died for our sins, that he was buried and that he was raised" (1 Cor 15:3–4). Those believers who sought to be like Christ reached back into a water ritual which symbolized death-life meanings, and were baptized. The apostle Paul presented this baptism as assimilation to the death and resurrection of Jesus (Rom 6:3–4).[52] The new creation achieved in baptism (2 Cor 5:17; Gal 6:15) is a creation modeled after Christ and, therefore, characterized by a dimension of being for others. In the sacrament of anointing believers are reminded of this for-others dimension of their lives, even when they are sick.

At a low moment of their human and Christian lives the Church clarifies for the sick the in-Christ and for-others dimension of their infirmity, and even of their death. It issues them a ritual invitation, to perceive not just the physical dimensions of their suffering, but also the symbolic, Christian dimension of suffering for others. The sick are told ritually that in their sickness, their weakness, their condition of apparent uselessness, they are strongest and most valuable for "carrying in the body the death of Jesus, so that the life of Jesus may also be manifested" (2 Cor 4:10). They are told that in sickness they are not just people who need to be ministered to, but Christians who can now minister to the Church in a way that was not open to them when they were healthy.

It will take, of course, insightful faith to perceive the symbolic dimensions, on the part of both the sick and the whole ministering Church. But if that faith is present and active, then the prayer of faith will raise up the sick person truly to be a magnificent person for others, a person who sustains others in their anguish at his suffering, and who calls them too, out of their anguish, to be for others. In and through the person of the one who is sick, Christ in his Church once again, and vividly, calls men and women to follow him in his being for others.[53]

And so, finally, for both the sick person and the Church it is of no ultimate consequence whether physical healing results from anointing or not. What is of consequence is a *personal* healing that brings with it not only forgiveness of sin, an effect to which James and the entire Christian tradition testify, but also a *Christian* attitude to sickness and health. The Letter to the Hebrews testifies that it was not simply Jesus' life or death that was redemptive, but rather his attitude toward God in both life and death. "I have come," he proclaims, "to do your will, O God" (10:5–10).

In his life for others Jesus did not shun physical suffering, even death, but accepted them if they had to be. Precisely through this *acceptance*, not merely through the physical suffering or the death, he became a totally new and magnificent human being, raised up definitively to draw all things to himself. Similarly in their lives for others Christians do not shun suffering or death, but accept them if they have to be, and precisely through this acceptance are raised up, though still perhaps physically ill, to be a new and magnificent person showing again the face of a Christ for others to a doubtful Church. This raising up saves the sick person, in the sense already explained, and is also the representative symbol of ultimate salvation hoped for from God. To perceive definitive raising up as represented in the temporal raising up requires, to repeat, faith. But symbols and sacraments, as we have seen several times, always require faith. "The prayer of faith which accompanies the celebration of the sacrament is supported by the profession of faith."[54] If it is not, then the sacramental prayer of faith is but a speaking to the deaf.

VIATICUM

In the case of the sick who are not just in danger of death but are also on the point of death, the new ritual prescribes a further rite in addition to anointing, namely, Viaticum. In fact, for such sick it prescribes a continuous rite, comprised of reconciliation, anointing and Viaticum. That order marks a change from the order of the previous ritual, and is not without symbolic import. The prior sequence was reconciliation, Viaticum and anointing, a sequence which emphasized ritually the dogmatic position that anointing was a sacrament of the dying, a true extreme unction. Now that it is established, again, that it is not a sacrament of the dying, but of the sick, the ritual order is made to manifest that fact. First, there is effected reconciliation and peace with the Church; then, united or reunited with the Church as the case may be, the Church ministers to the sick person in the ritual of anointing; finally it ministers to the dying person in the ritual of Viaticum. It is on this Viaticum that I wish to reflect now, in conclusion to this chapter.

There can be no doubt why Viaticum, the Eucharistic Communion of the dying, is placed as the final sacramental act of the Christian's life. *Eucharisticum Mysterium* makes it abundantly clear. "Communion received as Viaticum is to be regarded as a special sign of participation in the mystery which is celebrated in the Sacrifice of the Mass, namely, the death of the Lord and his passage to his Father. In it, his passage from this life, the believer is strengthened by the body of the Lord and a pledge of resurrection."[55] Viaticum is seen as both representing the passage of the Lord from this life to his Father, a passage achieved in his death *and* resurrection, and offering those dying in Christ a pledge that they too are about to pass to the Father through death *and* resurrection. The value of Viaticum for this passage is, of course, not new in our times. As far back as the first ecumenical Council of Nicaea (325), it was permitted even to those who were excommunicated for having apostasized during persecution. "Concerning those who are departing this life, the ancient and canonical law shall even now be preserved, that whoever is departing this life shall not be deprived of the last and most necessary Viaticum."[56] So necessary was ritual Viaticum thought to be that, in the Church's law, it was permitted even if the dying person had already received Communion that day. It was also the only form of Communion permitted on Good Friday.[57]

The new ritual makes explicit the connection between Viaticum and the Gospel, and indeed the reason for Viaticum, by linking it to the Johannine text, "Whoever eats my flesh and drinks my blood has eternal life, and I shall raise him up on the last day" (6:54). But Paul's instruction to the Corinthians has, at least, equal importance. "As often as you eat this bread and drink this cup, you proclaim the Lord's death until he comes" (1 Cor 11:26). Every Eucharist in the Church, we have already seen, proclaims by recalling, realizing and celebrating not only the Lord's death but also his resurrection. But now, as a Christian in Christ prepares for his death, this final Eucharist takes on the added dimension of recalling for him that Christ's death and resurrection assured that his death, too, will be followed by resurrection. It recalls for him that his passage will be not only into the liminal state of death, but also into the totally new state of eternal life with the Father and his Christ and his Spirit.

Here again the norms of the Constitution on the Liturgy come into play. Since liturgical services are not private functions, but celebrations of the Church, "a communal way of celebrating them is to be preferred, as far as possible, to a celebration that is individual and quasi-private." There is no ritual more a celebration of the Church than the Eucharist, the great banquet in which the body of Christ gathers to keep memory of Christ's death and resurrection. And so the new ritual prescribes that Viaticum should be received during Mass when possible, so that the sick person may receive Communion under both species. It goes on to make precise that "Communion received as Viaticum should be considered a special kind of participation in the mystery of the death of the Lord and his passage to the Father."[58] There are two strands of meaning here.

The first is a communal one. The Church is a community; its memorial meal is a community meal. And so there is nothing more natural than that, when a dying member of the community is to keep memory for, perhaps, the last time, the community should gather to keep memory with him. The second strand of meaning is an eschatological one. The emphasis on Communion under both species reveals an important symbolism, already clarified by *Eucharisticum Mysterium.* "As a sign, Holy Communion has more perfect form when done under both species. For in that form . . . the sign of the Eucharistic banquet more perfectly shines forth, and more clearly expresses both the will according to which the new and eternal covenant is sealed in the blood of Christ and the relationship between the Eucharistic banquet and the eschatological banquet in the kingdom of God."[59]

This is the Church's constant faith and constant proclamation, recalled each time it celebrates Eucharist: that it is people in covenant with God; that its covenant was sealed in its Lord's blood; that it is a covenant which, if faithfully lived into, will lead it to the great banquet which God has prepared for those who love him. In a final ecclesial banquet, the sick person is reminded of these beliefs, and is prepared for his passage. Strengthened in this pledge of future glory, and sacramentally united with the Lord he has confessed, the sick believer is ready, in imitation of that Lord, "to depart out of this world to the Father" (Jn 13:1).

Chapter Eight
MARRIAGE

PREAMBLE

I am an individual human person, a man, married to another human person, a woman, and together we have *experienced* that human union called marriage. Our experience of marriage has been the normal experience of human community, sometimes wonderfully easy and exciting and romantic, sometimes drearily difficult and boring and threatening. But when we were being prepared for marriage, such a total emphasis was placed on its legal and institutional facets (free consent, contractual rights and duties, impediments, indissolubility, fecundity, sins ad infinitum) that we have been forced to ask frequently what all that has to do with our *experience* of marriage. We are also Christians and we have experienced marriage also as Christians, struggling to live into our pledges to one another within the context of our mutual commitment to the God and the Christ in whom we believe. And we have asked, and have been asked, frequently what one commitment has to do with the other. We know, of course, because we have heard it so often, that marriage is a sacrament. But we have been driven to ask what that might mean in this case.

The previous chapters of this work argued that sacraments are symbols which reveal, realize and celebrate meanings beyond themselves. This chapter will argue the same thing for that sensible reality which is as old as humanity itself and which is called marriage. It will argue, namely, that marriage, as Christian sacrament, proclaims, realizes and celebrates meanings beyond the ordinary and inalienable meanings it has in every human society, meanings relating to Church, to Jesus and to God. It is my proposal in this chapter to consider, not the already well trodden ground of the legal and institutional requirements of marriage, but the much less trodden ground of the lived experience, and to show that it is this lived experience that is sacramental. It is this lived experience, marriage in its totality, not just this or that

171

aspect of it, that for Paul is the symbol-sacrament of the union between Christ and his Church. It is marriage in its totality that is also symbolizing sacrament of the steadfast covenant between God and his people, an image of God so distinctively Jewish and Christian. It is also in marriage that Jesus the Christ is again mysteriously incarnated.

AN INTRODUCTORY NOTE ON SEXUALITY

Before beginning the core of my analysis, an introductory word is necessary. The statement with which I began this chapter, that I am a man married to a woman, appears as a truism. For despite varied institutional regulations in various cultures socially sanctioned marriage has been universally a union between a man and a woman. But nevertheless I wish to insist on the male-female nature of marriage in order to insist on the necessarily sexual union involved in it. I hasten, though, to insist that by *sexual union* I do not mean that *genital union* which is commonly known as sexual intercourse or having sex. Sexual union is much more comprehensive than genital union, and if there were a marriage in which, for whatever reason, there was no genital expression, that marriage would still be a sexual union. For man and woman are essentially sexual; there is no escaping it; they are condemned to it. Sexuality bespeaks a man's awareness of himself as male and a woman's awareness of herself as female. It bespeaks a man's awareness of his attraction both to and for a woman, and vice versa. It bespeaks man's and woman's experience of affection and love and of their physical response to that love. That physical response may bespeak genital expression, but it does not do so necessarily, *pace* the modern wisdom so engrossed with having and with counting orgasms.

As a man I have asked myself, and as a teacher I have been asked, frequently: What is the meaning of sexuality? I approach the answer to that question by, first, declaring it to be not a good question. For as posed it assumes that there is an answer just waiting to be uncovered if one but look with sufficient acumen to find it. I believe the reality to be different. And so, secondly, I answer the question about the meaning of sexuality with the judgment that it does not have any meaning apart from the meanings that human beings assign to it. And history shows quite clearly that various societies have assigned various meanings to it.

At a very early stage in human history, when nature and its functioning provided a ready-made basis for human imitation and meaning, human sexuality was perceived as a way to security through fertility and its genital expression as a way to perpetuate the family and the tribe. Such meanings created the long-standing judgment that sexual intercourse was exclusively for the generation of children. I shall call this first period the period of instinctual sexuality. But when humans settled down in city-states and the division of roles became an integral part of human co-existence, another meaning was offered for human sexuality and sexual intercourse. The former was perceived as a way to separate men and women by assigning them different roles, the latter as a way to fulfill those roles. There was created the still-common opinion that one becomes a *man* or a *woman* ultimately by having a child. I shall call this the period of role sexuality.

In the first millennium B.C., when human reason came into its own, there developed another attitude toward sexuality, an attitude I shall designate by the name reasoned sexuality. This perceived sexuality in a supra-personal context, as a way to cooperate with God, and genital activity as a way to cooperate actively, as an action of *procreation*. The Enlightenment in Europe introduced yet another meaning for things human, including sexuality and genitality, and it generated a perception of these latter which I shall call loving, interpersonal sexuality. In this period sexuality was seen as a way to self-communication and self-giving, and sexual intercourse as an interpersonal symbol in which a man and a woman *make love*.[1]

We can now return to the originating question—What is the meaning of human sexuality?—and offer a more precise answer to it. In the initial period, the meaning of sexuality was that it offered a way to security through fertility; the possibility and the actuality of many children, many of whom died early in life, offered security, particularly in one's old age. In the second period, a choice became available; sexuality meant either security or a means of role definition. In the third period that choice became threefold, either security through fertility or role definition or cooperation with God in a sacred venture. In the fourth period that choice became fourfold.

Note that once a meaning has been introduced into history it does not go away. A new meaning does not supplant a prior one, but stands side by side with it as one more option. We could say with truth that, in the case of the meaning of human sexuality and genitality, there has been an historical development from a stage of simplicity (one meaning) to a stage of complexity (several meanings). Who would be so sanguine to declare that the development has now ended, so that no further meaning for human sexuality and genitality will enter the field? None but the perceptively blind, indeed, would be unable to see that in our day further meanings have already entered the field, making even more complex an already complex-enough situation.

Now, however, with all that said, and I shall return to it as I go along, I wish to insist that in the contemporary age we assign too privileged a position in marriage to genitality. That it is important as a way of perpetuating the race or fulfilling one's role of procreating or making love is beyond doubt. But that that is all there is to marriage or to the sacrament of the covenant of God with his people and of Christ with his Church is very doubtful. It is marriage as a man and a woman experience it in its totality that is sacrament, and it is precisely because of that that so much emphasis will be placed upon that total marriage in what follows.

MARRIAGE IN THE BIBLE

As in all other matters, the biblical teaching on marriage should not be seen in isolation. It has a context, that of the Near Eastern cultures with which the people of the Bible had intimate links, specifically the Mesopotamian, Syrian and Canaanite. It is not my intention here to dwell on any one of these cultures and their specific teachings on marriage and sexuality. They were all quite syncretistic and a general overview will be sufficient to give both a sense of the context in all of them and their specific distinctions from what we find in the Jewish Bible. Underlying the themes of sexuality, fertility and marriage in these cultures are the archetypal figures of the god-father and the goddess-mother, together the source of universal life in both the divine and the natural, including the human, spheres. Myths celebrated the marriage, the sexual intercourse and the fertility of this divine pair, thus legitimating and blessing the marriage, the intercourse and the fertility of any earthly pair. Rituals acted out the myths, thus establishing a very real and concrete link between the divine and the earthly worlds, in which men and women share not only in the divine action but also in the efficacy of that action. This is especially true of sexual rituals, which bless sexual intercourse and ensure that the unfailing divine fertility is shared by a man's plants and animals and wives, all important elements in his struggle for survival in those cultures.[2]

With this perspective the biblical view of marriage, genital activity and fertility makes a radical break. It portrays no longer a god-goddess couple, but only God who led Israel out of Egypt and is unique (Dt

6:4). There is no goddess associated with him; he needs none, for he creates by his word alone. This God created man and woman, "male and female he created them and he named *them adam*" (Gen 5:2). This fact alone, God's naming of both male and female as *adam* (= humankind), founds the equality of man and woman, establishes them as "bone of bone and flesh of flesh" (Gen 2:23), and enables them "therefore" to marry and "become one flesh" (v. 24). The later priestly creation account also records the creation of man and woman as *adam* and lays on them the injunction to "be fruitful and multiply and fill the earth" (Gen 1:28).

Equal man and woman, their separate sexualities, their marriage union, their fertility, do not derive from a divine pair whom they are to imitate. Rather they are called into being by the creative action of the sovereign God. Man and woman, *adam*, their sexuality, their genitality, their fertility, all are good because they are the good gifts of God in creation. Later Christian history, as we shall see, will have recurrent doubts about the goodness of genital activity, but the Jewish biblical tradition had none. As gifts from the Creator-God, sexuality, marriage, genitality, fertility were all good, and belonged properly to man and woman, not by some derivation from a divine pair, but as their own. Seen within this context of creation gift they all acquired a deeply *religious* significance in Israel, in distinction to the mythico-magical significance they had in the tribes around it. "What was called into existence by God's creation was sanctified by the fact of creation itself. . . . It was not the sacred rites which surrounded marriage that made it a holy thing. The great rite which sanctified marriage was God's act of creation itself."[3] It was God alone, unaided by any partner, who not only created man and woman, sexuality, genitality and marriage, but also blessed them.

Man and woman together, as we have seen, are named *adam* (Gen 5:2). They are equal in human dignity and complementary to one another; there is no humankind without either one. It is precisely because man and woman are equal, because they are *adam*, because they are "bone of bone and flesh of flesh," that they may marry and "become one flesh" (Gen 2:24). Among the birds of the air and the beasts of the field there "was not found a helper fit" for the man (Gen 2:20), and it is not difficult to imagine man's cry of delight when confronted with woman. Here, finally, after the disappointment of the animals and the birds, was one who was his human equal, one with whom he could truly become one flesh.

That man and woman became one flesh in marriage has been much too exclusively restricted to one aspect of marriage, namely, the genital. It is now well recognized that such an exclusive restriction is not justified. "One personality would translate it better, for 'flesh' in the Jewish idiom means 'real human life.' "[4] In marriage man and woman enter into a full sexual union, not merely a genital one, and in such a union become one person, one life, and so complement each other that they form *adam*. The rabbis go so far as to teach that it is only after marriage and the union of male and female into one whole person that the image of God may be discerned in them. An unmarried man, in their eyes, is not a whole man.[5] And the mythic stories,[6] interested as always in aetiology, the origin of things, proclaim that it was so "in the beginning," and that it was so by God's express design. There could be for a Jew, and for a Christian, no greater foundation for the human and the religious goodness of sexuality, genitality, marriage and fertility. Nor could there be any secular reality better than marriage for pointing to God and his steadfastly loving relationship with Israel. And that was the next step in the development of the sacramentality of marriage.

Central to the Israelite notion of their special relationship with God was the idea of the covenant. Moses reminds the assembled people: "You have declared this day concerning Yahweh that he is your God . . . and Yahweh has declared this day concerning you that you are a people for his own possession" (Dt 26:17–19). The God, Yahweh, is the God of Israel; Israel is the people of God. Yahweh and Israel form a community of life, a community of grace, a community of salvation, a community, one might say, of one flesh. It was only a matter of time until Israel began to image this relationship in marital terms, and it was the prophet Hosea who first did so. He preached about the covenant relationship of Yahweh and Israel within the biographical context of his own marriage to a harlot-wife, Gomer. To understand the images involved in Hosea's preaching, we must understand the times in which he lived and preached.

Hosea preached around the middle of the eighth century B.C., at a time when Israel was well established in Canaan. Many thought, indeed, that it was too well established, for the cult of Yahweh had been influenced by the cult of the Canaanite god, Baal. This cult was situated in the classic mold we saw earlier, that of the god-goddess pair, with Baal the god and earth the goddess. Human sexuality, genitality and fertility were related to these two, a relationship which was acted out in ritual prostitution to which Israelite maidens gave themselves, becoming *harlots*. Hosea was instructed by Yahweh to take such a harlot as a wife, and he married Gomer (1:2–3).

The marriage of Hosea and Gomer, to every superficial appearance, is just like many another marriage. But at a more profound level, it serves as a prophetic symbol, proclaiming, realizing and celebrating the covenant relationship between Yahweh and Israel. The names of Hosea's two younger children reflect the sad state of that relationship: a daughter is named Not Pitied (1:6), and a son Not My People (1:9). As Gomer left Hosea for another lover, so did Israel leave Yahweh for Baal and become Not My People and Not Pitied. But Hosea's remarkable reaction reveals and celebrates the equally remarkable reaction of Yahweh.

Hosea takes Gomer back, indeed he buys her back (3:2); he loves her again *"even as Yahweh loves* the people of Israel, though they turn to other gods" (3:1). This prophetic action proclaims, realizes and celebrates Yahweh's steadfast and unfailing love for Israel. Gomer was "not my woman" and Hosea was "not her man" (2:2), just as Israel was not the bride of Yahweh and Yahweh was not her husband. In both cases, that of the human marriage-symbol and of the divine covenant-symbolized, the one-flesh relationship had been sundered. But Hosea's action both reflects and proclaims Yahweh's steadfastness. An abiding divorce is not possible for Hosea because he recognized that his God is not a God who can abide divorce. As another prophet, Malachi, will report later: "I hate divorce, says the Lord, the God of Israel . . . so take heed to yourselves and do not be faithless" (2:16). Hosea's action proclaims not only his faithfulness to the end, but also Yahweh's. As did Hosea, Yahweh "will have pity on Not Pitied" and will "say to Not My People 'You are my people,' " and they will say "Thou art my God" (2:23), and the covenant marriage will be restored.

What should we make of this marriage between Hosea and Gomer? One basic symbolic meaning is clear: Yahweh is faithful. But there is also a mysterious meaning about marriage. Beyond being just a secular institution, it becomes also a prophetic symbol proclaiming, realizing and celebrating in the secular world, through an institution universally taken for granted in that world, the endless love of God for his people. Lived into in this perspective, lived into in faith as we would say today, marriage proclaims a message for the world and offers the spouses a way to realize in action their vision of God. First articulated by Hosea, this perspective ultimately yields the Christian view of marriage that we find in the New Testament. But first of all it recurs again, as thoroughly established, in the prophets Jeremiah and Ezekiel.

Both Jeremiah and Ezekiel present Yahweh as having two wives, Israel and Judah (Jer 3:6–14), Oholah-Samaria and Oholibah-Jerusalem (Ezek 23:4). Faithless Israel is first "sent away with a decree of divorce" (Jer 3:8), but that does not deter an even more faithless Judah who continued to pollute the land, "committing adultery with stone and tree" (Jer 3:9). Israel and Judah are every bit as much the harlot as Gomer, but Yahweh's faithfulness is every bit as unending as Hosea's. He makes a declaration of undying love: "I have loved you with an everlasting love; therefore, I have continued my faithfulness to you" (Jer 31:3; cf. Ez 16:60–63; Is 54:7–8). Notice again, as in Hosea, that the flow of meaning is not from human marriage to divine covenant, but from covenant to marriage. The belief in and experience of Yahweh's covenant fidelity creates the belief in and the possibility of fidelity in marriage, which then and only then becomes a prophetic symbol of the covenant. Yahweh's covenant fidelity becomes a characteristic to be imitated, a challenge to be accepted, in every human marriage. Malachi, as we have already seen, states the challenge unequivocally: "I hate divorce, says the Lord, the God of Israel. . . . So take heed to yourselves and do not be faithless" (2:16).

The conception of marriage as a prophetic, symbolic image of a mutually faithful covenant relationship is continued in the New Testament, with a new twist. Instead of presenting marriage as the image of the covenant between Yahweh and Israel, the writer of the Letter to the Ephesians presents it as the image of the relationship between the Christ-Messiah and his Church. This presentation is of such central importance to the development of a Christian view of marriage and has, unfortunately, been used to sustain a very diminished Christian view, that we must consider it here in some detail.

The passage in which the author presents his view of marriage,[7] namely, Ephesians 5:21–33, occurs within a larger context, Ephesians 5:21–6:9, which sets forth a list of household duties that exist within the mutual relationships of a family of that time. This list, or *haufstafel* as Dibelius named it,[8] is addressed to wives (5:22), husbands (5:25), children (6:1), fathers (6:4), slaves (6:5) and masters (6:9). What concerns us here, of course, is what is said about the pair, wife-husband. There are two similar lists in the New Testament, one in the Letter to the Colossians, 3:18–4:1, the other in the First Letter of Peter, 2:13–3:7. But the Ephesians' *haufstafel* is the only one to open with the rather strange injunction: "Because you fear Christ subordinate yourselves to one another";[9] or "Give way to one another in obedience to Christ";[10] or, in the weaker version of the Revised Standard Version, "Be subject to one another out of reverence for Christ."[11] This injunction, as most commentators agree, is an essential element of what follows. The author takes over the *haufstafel* form from traditional material, but 5:21 summarizes his critique of it. This critique challenges the absolute authority of any one group over any other, of husbands, for instance, over wives, of fathers over children, of masters over slaves. The author establishes the basic attitude of mutual subordination or giving way of those filled with the Spirit (Eph 5:18), an attitude which covers all he has to say not only to wives, children and slaves, but also to husbands, fathers and masters.[12] Mutual submission is an attitude of all Christians, because their basic attitude is that they "fear Christ." Now this phrase will ring strange in many ears, for fear is not quite how they would describe their relationship with their Lord. It is probably because of this strange ring that the Revised Standard Version rounds off the rough edge of the Greek *phobos* by translating it as *respect*. But *phobos* does not mean respect; it means fear. As in the Old Testament aphorism, the fear of the Lord is the beginning of wisdom (Prv 1:7; 9:10; 15:33; Ps 111:10; Job 28:28).

The apostle Paul is quite comfortable with this Old Testament perspective. Twice in his Second Letter to the Corinthians (5:11 and 7:1) he uses the phrase *fear of God*. In his commentary on Ephesians, Schlier finds the former text more illuminating of Ephesians 5:21,[13] but I am more persuaded to Sampley's opinion that the latter is a better parallel.[14] 2 Corinthians 6:14-18 recalls the initiatives of God in the covenant with Israel and applies these initiatives to Christians, who are invited to respond with holiness "in the fear of God" (7:1). Fear of God is the beginning of wisdom that grasps the mighty acts of God and responds to them with holiness. In 2 Corinthians 6:14-17 that holiness is specified as avoiding marriage with unbelievers. In Ephesians 5:21 wisdom grasps the mighty works of God in Christ and responds to them also with holiness, specified this time as submission to one another. That submission is required of all Christians, even of husbands and wives as they seek holiness together in marriage, and even in spite of the traditional *haufstafel*.

As Christians have all just been admonished to submit themselves to one another, it is no surprise that a wife is to submit herself to her husband, "as to the Lord" (5:22). What may come as a surprise to the ingrained male attitude that sees the husband as supreme lord and master of his wife, and appeals to Ephesians 5:22–23 to ground and sustain that attitude, is the statement about husbands. That statement is not that "the husband is the head of the wife" (which is the usual way it is read and quoted), but rather that "in the same way that the Messiah is the head of the Church is the husband the head of the wife."[15] A husband's headship over his wife is in image of, and totally interpreted and delineated by, Christ's headship over the Church. When a Christian husband understands this, he will understand the grave responsibility he assumes toward the woman given to him in marriage as his wife.

The headship of Christ is unequivocally set forth in Mark 10:45: "The Son of Man came not to be served but to serve, and to give his life." Service and the giving of oneself is the Christ-way of exercising authority, and our author testifies that it was thus that "Christ loved the Church and gave himself up for her" (v. 25). And, therefore, a husband is instructed to be head over his wife by subordinating himself to her, by serving her, by giving himself for her. Authority modeled on the Christ-way of exercising authority does not mean control, giving orders, making unreasonable demands, reducing another person to the status of servant or, worse, slave to one's every whim. It means service. The husband-head, as Markus Barth puts it so beautifully, becomes " 'the first servant' of his wife."[16] It is such a husband-head, and only such a one, that a wife is to fear (v. 33b) as all Christians fear Christ (v. 21b).

The reversal of the *haufstafel* order in v. 33 is interesting and significant. The *haufstafel* enjoined, first, upon wives that they subordinate themselves to their husbands and, second, upon husbands that they love their wives. V. 33 reverses that order, first commanding husbands to love their wives and then warmly wishing that wives might fear their husbands. This fear is not fright of a master. Rather is it loving wisdom which grasps a mighty deed, loving service, and responds to it with love-as-giving-way. Such love cannot be commanded by a tyrant. It is only won by a lover, as the Church's love and subordination to Christ was, and is, won by a Lover who gave and gives himself for her. This is the author's recipe for being one flesh, conquering love and joyous giving way in response. It is a recipe echoed unwittingly by many a modern marriage counselor. That the service of and the giving way to the other is to be mutual is made clear in v. 21. That the love is to be mutual goes without saying, though it is not stated explicitly that the wife is to love her husband. The reasons the author adduces for husbands to love their wives apply to all Christians, even to wives!

Three reasons are offered to husbands for loving their wives. "Husbands should love their wives as (= for they are) their own bodies" (v. 28a); "he who loves his wife loves himself" (v. 28b); "the two shall become one flesh" (v. 31b), a reading which is obscured by the Revised Standard Version's translation, "the two shall become one."

There is evidence in the Jewish tradition for equating a man's wife to his body.[17] But even if there was no such evidence, the sustained comparison throughout Ephesians 5:21–33 between Christ-Church and husband-wife, coupled with the frequent equation in Ephesians of Church and body of Christ (1:22–23; 2:14–16; 3:6; 4:4–16; 5:22–30), clarifies both the meaning of the term and the fact that it is a title of honor and glorification rather than of debasement and diminution. Love is always and essentially creative. The love of Christ brought into existence the Church and made its members "members of his body" (v. 30). In the same way, the love of a husband for his wife (and, of course, her love for him) creates such a unity between them that, in image of Christ and Church, she may be called his body and his love for her, therefore, may be called love for his body. But it is only within the creative love of marriage that, in the Genesis phrase, "the two shall become one flesh." A man did not have this body before marriage, a complement neither had before, which so fulfills each of them that they are no longer just two persons but only one unique married being. For each to love the other, therefore, is for each to love himself or herself.

"Let each one of you love his wife as himself" (v. 33a). Understood within the perspective I have just elaborated, the command makes sense. It makes even more sense when we realize that it is a paraphrase of the great commandment of Leviticus 19:18, repeated by Jesus in Mark 12:31: "You shall love your neighbor as yourself." It does not say in Ephesians 5:33 that a husband should love his neighbor as himself, but that he should so love his wife. Where, then, is the connection between our passage and Leviticus? It is provided through that most beautiful and most sexual of Jewish love songs, the Song of Songs, where in the Septuagint nine separate times the lover addresses his bride as *neighbor* (1:9; 1:15; 2:2,10,13; 4:1,7; 5:2; 6:4). "The context of the occurrence of *plesion* (= neighbor) in Song of Songs confirms that *plesion* is used as a term of endearment for the bride."[18] Other Jewish usage further confirms the interchangeability of wife and neighbor, leaving no doubt that the author of Ephesians had Leviticus 19:18 in mind when instructing a husband to love his wife as himself.

The Torah and Gospel injunction, "You shall love your neighbor as yourself," applies also in marriage. As all Christians are to give way to one another, including husband and wife in marriage, so also they are to love one another as themselves, including husband and wife in marriage. When a man and a woman are joined in love in marriage, to repeat, they cease to be two persons; they become one person, one flesh. For each to love the other is, therefore, for each to love himself or herself. The paraphrase of Leviticus 19:18 says once again what had already been said above in the own-body image and the Genesis 2:24

image of one flesh. What the author says of this latter passage, "This is a great mystery, and I mean in reference to Christ and the Church" (v. 32), will allow us to conclude this analysis of the central New Testament teaching on marriage.

"*This* is a great mystery," namely, as most scholars agree, the Genesis 2:24 text just quoted in v. 31. The mystery involved, as the Anchor Bible translation seeks to show, is that "this [passage] has an eminent secret meaning," and the secret meaning is, in the author's judgment, that it refers to Christ and the Church. All that has gone before about Christ and Church comes to the fore again now: that Christ chooses the Church to be united to him, he as head, she as body; that he loved the Church and gave himself up for her as Savior; that the Church responds to this initiative of Christ in fear and submission. Christ who loves the Church, and the Church who responds in fearful love, thus constitute one flesh, as Genesis 2:24 said they would. The author is well aware that this meaning is not the meaning of the text as it is explained in Judaism, and he states this forthrightly. Just as in the great antitheses of the Sermon on the Mount Jesus pronounces his interpretation of several biblical texts in opposition to established interpretations ("You have heard that it was said to the men of old . . . but *I* say to you": Mt 5:21–22, 27–28), here too our author sets forth clearly that it is his own reading of the text (*I* mean in reference to Christ and the Church": v. 32b).[19]

Genesis 2:24 was an excellent text for the purpose the author had in mind, for it was a central Old Testament text traditionally employed to ordain and legitimate marriage. He acknowledges the meaning of the text that husband and wife become one flesh in marriage; indeed, in v. 33, he returns to and demands that husband and wife live up to this precise meaning. But he chooses to go beyond this meaning and insinuate a typological, superior meaning. Not only does this text refer to the union of husband and wife in marriage, but it refers also to the union of Christ and his Church, which he has insinuated throughout Ephesians 5:1–33. On the literal level Genesis 2:24 refers to human marriage; on a deeper level it refers to the union between Christ and his Church. It is a small step to see human marriage as prophetically representing the union between Christ and his Church. The marriage union proclaims, realizes and celebrates that union which, in turn, provides an ideal model for marriage and for how the spouses should conduct themselves one toward the other.

Ephesians, is not, of course, the only New Testament passage to speak of marriage and of the relationship between husband and wife. In 1 Corinthians 7 Paul does so, portraying marriage less than enthusiastically as a source of divided love in which the love and concern of the spouses for one another siphons off their love and concern for the Lord (vv. 32–35). He presents sexual intercourse with even less enthusiasm, though he allows it between spouses in marriage as a lesser evil than fornication, and carefully asserts each spouse's right to the body of the other (vv. 1–7). The author of 1 Timothy 2:8–15 has something to say about the attitudes of men and women, somewhat disproportionately laying down what is expected of men (v. 8) and women (vv. 9–15). Of supreme interest in this text are the two traditional reasons he advances for the submission of women to men and for the authority of men over women. The first is that Adam was created before Eve, and the other that it was Eve, not Adam, that was deceived by the serpent. The submission of women to men, and by extension of wives to husbands, is legitimated by collected stories of the first human pair. Paul betrays this very same attitude of distrust for women and wives in a very terse and compact statement in 2 Corinthians 11:2–3. For his part, the author of 1 Peter 3:1–6 requires that wives be submissive to their husbands "as Sarah obeyed Abraham" (v. 6). Such arguments on such Old Testament bases were common to many Jewish rabbis, which makes the attitude of the writer to the Ephesians all the more surprising.

The Old Testament passage he chooses to comment on is one which emphasizes the unity in marriage of the first pair, and therefore all subsequent pairs, rather than their distinction. He embellishes it not with Old Testament reference to creation and fall, but with New Testament reference to the Messiah and his love. This leads him to a positive appraisal of marriage in the Lord that was not at all customary in the Jewish and Christian milieu of his time. While he echoes the resounding *no* to any form of sexual immorality (5:3–5), he further offers a more-than-traditional *yes* to marriage and personal, sexual and genital union (5:21–33). For him marriage means the union of two people in one flesh, the formation of a new covenant-pair, which is the gift both of God who created it and the Christ who established it in the love and the peace he has for the Church—so much so that the marriage of a man and a woman becomes the prophetic symbol in the world of the union that exists between the Christ and his Church.

This doctrine does not mythicize marriage as an imitation of the marriage of some divine pair, nor does it idealize it so that historical men and women will not recognize it. Rather, it leaves marriage what it is: a secular, historical reality in which a man and a woman reach out toward each other to become one in love. What is added is this, simple and yet mysteriously complex, that as they reach out to one another they reach out also to their Lord and God, and provide through their marriage a prophetic symbol of the love and fidelity and union that exists between this Lord and his Church. Marriage is neither so secular a reality that the God of grace cannot grace it, nor so mythical a reality that loving human beings cannot live it. Nor is it so base and fragile a union that it cannot be symbol-sacrament of another, more unshakable, union. But I run ahead a bit, and must return to my path.

INDISSOLUBILITY OF CHRISTIAN MARRIAGE

Following our analysis of Ephesians 5:21–33 and of its linkage of the union between a man and a woman in marriage to that between Christ and his Church, I plan to begin here, and complete in a later section, the discussion of a question that is causing much heart-searching in the contemporary Church, the question, namely, of the indissolubility of Christian marriage. I judge it appropriate to introduce the question here for a reason that will become obvious forthwith, and because I believe it is no longer of any value simply to restate the biblical and ecclesiastical law on the matter, for that is already well known. Rather is it now obligatory to search out meanings that may lie behind the law, and the first of these is precisely the nature of *Christian*, as distinct from purely *secular*, marriage as a prophetic symbol of the union between alternatively the covenant God and his people or the redeeming Messiah and his Church.

My analysis has already shown, and I need not repeat it here, that an outstanding characteristic of the covenant God is his *hesed*, his steadfast love and fidelity. Despite every provocation of abandonment, harlotry, adultery, mental cruelty as a modern divorce lawyer might say, he remains faithful to Israel, and in response to and in imitation of this fidelity Hosea remains faithful to the wandering Gomer. The Messiah "gave himself up for [the Church] that he might sanctify her" (Eph 5:25–26), which implies that when he gave himself up for her she was not at all sanctified (cf. Rom 5:6–8), and he promised to be with her always, "to the close of the age" (Mt 28:20; cf. Acts 18:10). The union of God and his people is indissoluble; the union of Christ and his Church is indissoluble; the union of a man and a woman in *Christian* marriage, therefore, is indissoluble, in order to be an effective symbol of both those unions. Note, however, that I have underscored several times that indissolubility is the characteristic of *Christian* marriage, and not just of any and every marriage. I shall reserve the implication of this insistence to a concluding section of this chapter.

There is a second meaning behind the law of the indissolubility of *Christian* marriage, long ago put forward in the Christian Church, and almost equally long ago forgotten by Christians. It has to do with the universal Christian demand for reconciliation, and was first enunciated by the apostle Paul in 1 Corinthians 7:10–11: "To the married I give charge, not I but the Lord, that the wife should not separate from her husband (but if she does, let her remain single or else be *reconciled* to her husband)—and that the husband should not divorce his wife."

This instruction is repeated in *The Shepherd of Hermas*, a book written for the edification of the Christian Church in the first half of the second century. A question is posed: "If one have a wife that is faithful in the Lord and he find her in some adultery, doth then the husband sin if he live with her?" The wife's adultery was a common reason for divorcing her in the early Christian community, and Hermas gives the traditional answer to the question that was posed him. If he does not know of her adultery, the husband does not sin by continuing to live with his wife, but if he does know he shares in her adultery if he does not put her away. A husband, then, can put away his wife because of adultery, but he cannot remarry: "If when he hath put away his wife he marry another, then he likewise committeth adultery." Remaining unmarried after putting away one's wife is to encourage both repentance from the sin and the reconciliation of husband and wife: "For the sake of her repentance, then, the husband ought not to marry; thus the case stands with both husband and wife."[20] The Second Council of Miletus (416), at which Augustine assisted, wanted a civil law passed to require that "neither a man repudiated by his wife nor a woman repudiated by her husband should remarry, but should remain single or be reconciled."[21]

There is, as I have said, a universal Christian demand at play here, the demand for reconciliation. That demand is best seen in the Sermon on the Mount: "If you are offering your gift at the altar, and there remember that your brother has something against you, leave your gift there before the altar and go; first be reconciled to your brother and then come and offer your gift" (Mt 5:23–24). There is a double assertion here: first of the mysterious unity that exists before God between brothers and sisters in Christ, and second of the fact that the rupture of this unity interferes with either's access to God. In the case of such rupture it is required that there be, if not reconciliation, at least a concerted effort toward reconciliation, so that unhampered access to God may be available again for both parties.

This is, of course, a hard saying, but so are many of the sayings laid on those who believe in the God made known in Jesus. He is a God who loves not only his friends, but also his enemies, and the same is demanded of those who would be called children of this God (Mt 5:43–48). Hermas merely explicitates that sometimes, for instance in the case of divorce, brother/enemy can be really sister/wife, and prohibits remarriage in the hope of reconciliation. Once again, this reasoning applies only to *Christian* marriage, only to those who believe in the God made known in Jesus his Christ. And, again, I shall reserve the implications of this to a concluding section of this chapter.

This said, however, one thing remains to be said about the indissolubility of Christian marriage, namely that the Gospel texts which are said to inculcate it have been anything but the subjects of unanimous interpretation. Jesus is reported four times in the New Testament as delivering a judgment on divorce and remarriage, a pair which should never be separated. In one of the great antitheses of the Sermon on the Mount he teaches: "It was also said, 'Whoever divorces his wife, let him give her a certificate of divorce.' But I say to you that everyone who divorces his wife, except on the ground of unchastity (*porneia*), makes her an adulteress; and whoever marries a divorced woman commits adultery" (Mt 5:32). Later in Matthew's Gospel, in a loaded discussion with the Pharisees about the basis on which a man might divorce his wife, Jesus refuses their premises that there is some basis for divorce (and subsequent remarriage) and declares: "I say to you: whoever divorces his wife, except for *porneia*, and marries another, commits adultery" (19:19). Luke 16:18 and Mark 10:11–12 repeat, without the exceptive clause, the condemnation of remarriage after divorce, Mark extending it interestingly to the then unusual case of the wife who divorces her husband.

Paul, of course, antedates all the New Testament writers and he delivers an absolute prohibition of divorce in 1 Corinthians 7:10–17,[22] attributing it to the Lord. "To the unmarried I give charge, not I but the Lord, that the wife should not separate from the husband (but if she does, let her remain single or else be reconciled to her husband)— and that the husband should not divorce his wife." Reading Paul, Mark and Luke it would appear that the New Testament is in agreement: divorce and remarriage are forbidden. But then there are those (in?)famous exceptive clauses in Matthew, which have been the subject of so much analysis, so much polemic, and so little agreement. And because of them we might have to say that apart from the reason of *porneia* divorce and remarriage are contrary to the New Testament.[23]

This book is not the place to reopen the debate on the exceptive clauses, or on the meaning of *porneia* which might be more important.[24] A more complex analysis is required than space permits here, and I am afraid that the confessional positions are so hardened anyway that yet another contribution to the discussion would leave them untouched. For judgments are reached frequently on bases other than the force of the arguments, a fact which is easily demonstrable in the history of the Christian confessions. I will content myself here just by setting forth the varied judgments of these confessions on the Gospel evidence on indissolubility, particularly, as is inevitable, on the Matthean exceptive clauses.

The Latin or Roman Catholic Church in theory has held consistently to the position that the New Testament reports the Lord's prohibition of divorce and remarriage. In practice, however, it has applied this theory only to consummated, sacramental marriages. The Greek or Orthodox Church, on the other hand, while holding firmly in theory to the position that the New Testament reports the Lord's demand for indissoluble marriage, in practice acknowledges that men and women sometimes do not measure up to the Gospel and after divorce allows the remarriage of an *innocent* party (a practice which the Roman Church has never formally condemned). The Protestant churches also allow divorce and remarriage according to their faith-filled reading of the New Testament. As can be seen, there is a wide range of good-faith Christian interpretation in the matter. I shall defer reflection on it until I have dealt explicitly with the question of the sacramentality of marriage. But first we must consider the teachings and the attitudes toward marriage of those early theological writers known as the Fathers of the Church.

THE EARLY CHURCH

The teachings of the Fathers need always to be set in context to be fully grasped. On the one hand, as are all of us, they were creatures of their time, and they reflect their time in their writings. We should not be at all surprised, therefore, when they define marriage as an association between two persons of quite unequal social value, a man who chooses a wife and a woman whose father chooses for her a husband. For such was the definition of the time. But still John Chrysostom advises a husband to deal with a young and shy wife with love and affection, and not just as a chattel.[25] On the other hand, the Fathers had to deal with certain errors which threatened both the value and the future of marriage. The Encratists taught that every baptized Christian is bound to celibacy and continence (in Greek, *egrateia*, hence their name). The more widespread Gnostics pursued their dualist cosmology of one good principle of reality, from which derives the world of spirits, and one evil principle, from which the world of matter derives. Man, they believed, is a spiritual being imprisoned in matter, and to give life to children is simply to cooperate with the evil principle in imprisoning more spirits. Marriage, therefore, which has as an end the generation of children, is evil in itself and is to be condemned as such. The Fathers elaborate a doctrine of marriage which combats these errors.

The early and anonymous *Epistle to Diognetus* portrays the general situation of the early Christians. "Neither in region nor in tongue nor in the social institutions of life do Christians differ from other men. . . . They takes wives as all do, and they procreate children, but they do not abort the fetus."[26] Athenagoras echoes this judgment to the Athenians: "Each of us considers his wife, whom he has taken according to your laws, to be a wife for the procreation of children."[27] Irenaeus directly refutes the Encratists and Gnostics who, he teaches, lay blame on God for creating two sexes for the propagation of humanity.[28]

In the third century two great writers, one from the East and one from the West, provide us with a complete, and in many ways divergent, doctrine of marriage. In the East, Clement of Alexandria continues the fight against the Encratists and Gnostics. Marriage and the procreation of children is in no way sinful. "If marriage according to the law is sinful," he argues, "I do not see how anyone can say he knows God, and say that sin was commanded by God. But if the law is holy, marriage is holy. The apostle, therefore, refers this mystery to Christ and the Church."[29] Those who attack marriage and sexual intercourse and fertility as evil attack the will of God and the mystery of creation, to which even the Virgin and Jesus were subject.[30] Marriage is primarily for the procreation of children.[31] It is "for the sake of the race, the succession of children, and, as far as is in us, the perfection of the world."[32] It brings "some help to creation."[33] Another, and at the time predictable, function of marriage is for the wife to bring help to the husband in the running of his household,[34] particularly in sickness and in old age.[35] Finally, "a pious wife seeks to persuade her husband, if she can, to be a companion to her in those things that lead to salvation."[36]

Already the outlines of what will be the medieval doctrine of marriage are beginning to take shape. Marriage has two ends, the primary end the procreation of children, the secondary one the mutual help of husband and wife. Clement, though, in keeping with his place and time, lays the burden of help upon the wife. Another great Alexan-

drian, Origen, somewhat ambivalently, also lauds marriage, intercourse and fertility as long as they are undertaken with restraint and
"exclusively for posterity,"[37] and he attacks the Encratists for declaring
to the contrary.[38] Unfortunately, his ambivalent attitude toward the
flesh leads him to the opinion that, however good marriage and genitality and fertility may be, especially when a man loves his wife as
Christ loved the Church,[39] genital activity between even a husband and
a wife is always somehow sinful.[40] That is an opinion that will continue
to infect and vitiate Christian thinking about genitality and, therefore,
marriage throughout the history of the Church down to our day.

In the West Tertullian wrote about marriage, in both the early
Catholic and later Montanist periods of his life. In his first book *Ad
Uxorem* (To a Wife) he exhibits the same ambivalence toward the flesh,
marriage and genitality that we have already seen in Origen. He allows
that in the beginning marriage was necessary to populate the earth,
but argues that when the end of the world is near there is no need to
populate the earth. Paul may *permit* marriage as an antidote to concupiscence, but Tertullian is in no doubt: "How much better it is neither to marry nor to burn [with concupiscence]." Marriage cannot
even be said to be good, for "what is *permitted* is not good . . . nor is
anything good simply because it is not evil."[41]

One would be excused for concluding that Tertullian does not
think much of marriage. And yet this same man who is so pessimistic
about marriage in his first *Ad Uxorem* in a second *Ad Uxorem* writes the
most beautiful lines on Christian marriage that one could hope to find.
"How can we suffice to tell the joy of that marriage which the Church
consecrates? . . . What a bond is that of two faithful who are of one
hope, one discipline, one service; both are brothers, both are servants.
There is no separation of spirit and flesh. They are truly two in one
flesh, and where there is one flesh there is also one spirit. They pray
together, they sleep together, they fast together, teaching one another,
exhorting one another, sustaining one another."[42] One might legitimately conclude that between the first and second books Tertullian
had found a wonderful wife. Become Montanist, however, he re-
gressed to his earlier judgments that Paul had simply permitted marriage which is, therefore, though not a sin, nonetheless some sort of a
blot on a perfect Christian life.[43] The latter Montanist part of Tertullian's life was devoted to the pursual of the classic Montanist position
that, though marriage itself was permissible, a second marriage was
thoroughly inadmissible and some kind of debauchery.[44]

It is with Augustine of Hippo, sometimes called the Doctor of
Christian marriage, that we reach the systematic approach to marriage

that was to mold and control the doctrine of the Western Church down to our day.[45] That Augustinian influence was not entirely beneficial, a fact which is widely recognized today. But it was always there. It was to Augustine, for instance, that Pius XI turned in the opening pages of his influential *Casti Connubii* as the wellspring of the truths about marriage to which the Roman Catholic Church adheres. We need, therefore, to look closely at Augustine's teaching on marriage.

The basic statement is firm and clear. Contrary to the teaching of those heretics who would condemn and prohibit it,[46] marriage was created good by God and cannot lose that God-willed goodness.[47] Augustine specifies the good of marriage as threefold: "faith, offspring sacrament. It is expected that in faith neither partner will have genital intercourse with another outside the marriage bond; that offspring will be lovingly accepted, kindly nurtured and religiously educated; that as to *sacramentum* the marriage will not be dissolved and that neither partner, not even for the sake of offspring, will be dismissed to marry another."[48]

In this doctrine of the triple good of marriage, Augustine intends what we would call today the mutual fidelity of the spouses, the procreation and education of the children, and the indissolubility of the marriage. Among these three goods he generally gives priority to procreation, because "from this derives the propagation of the human race in which a loving community is a great good."[49] And yet the good of the sacrament, to some extent, is valued above the good of procreation, as Augustine insists that a marriage cannot be dissolved, "not even for the sake of offspring."[50] Perhaps there is here the seed of a Christian attitude to marriage which moves away from the *social* priority of procreation to the *personal* priority of loving community between the spouses, in the image of the community between Christ and the Church. I shall touch again on that later. For the moment, I shall conclude this summary of Augustine's teaching on marriage by asking about his attitude to genitality, for he transmitted that attitude to the Western Church and it has been responsible for a quite negative view of genitality in Western marriages down to our day.

Augustine's attitude to genitality can be summarized briefly: it is good in itself, BUT . . . Sexual intercourse is good in itself and not evil.[51] As long as it is used for procreation it is sinless, but as soon as spouses forget this good every genital act between them is sinful. "Conjugal genital intercourse for the sake of offspring is not sinful. But intercourse, even with one's spouse, to satisfy concupiscence, is a venial sin."[52] Genital activity, not as an act of concupiscence but as an act of interpersonal love, as a symbolic way of making love, of course, never occurred to Augustine. For no one had ever heard of that meaning in the fifth century. Then, a suspicion and distrust of matter and sexuality were inhaled freely as so much Neo-Platonic dust in the philosophical air. Unfortunately that dust was never quite filtered from the air, and it remained to cloud the ethos of the Western Church, not only about marriage but also about the celibacy and continence required of its clergy.

Others went much further than Augustine. Pope Gregory the Great, perhaps, reached the zenith of this Neo-Platonic revulsion to sexuality and genitality, teaching that every act of genital pleasure, even that between spouses in the act of procreation, was sinful, and forbidding those who had just had pleasurable genital intercourse access to the Church. "The custom of the Romans from antiquity has always been, after genital intercourse with one's spouse, both to cleanse oneself by washing and to reverently abstain from entering the Church for a time. In saying this we do not intend to say that genital intercourse is sinful. But because every lawful genital intercourse between the spouses cannot take place without bodily pleasure, they are to refrain from entering the holy place. For such pleasure cannot be without sin."[53] It is a strong ambivalence toward sexuality and genitality, and it weighed heavily in subsequent history, as I have said, not only on the doctrine and practice of Christian marriage but also, as we shall see in the next chapter, on the doctrine and practice of clerical celibacy and continence.

THE SCHOLASTIC DOCTRINE

Thomas Aquinas took over Augustine's notion of the three *goods* of marriage and transformed them to the *ends* of marriage, a change in terminology dictated by his view of man. Thomas shared with the Greek philosopher, Aristotle, the view that, though man shared the genus of all other animals, he was constituted a species apart from all others by his faculty of reason. This reason enables him to apprehend the ends proper to *human* animals, inscribed in the so-called natural law which reflects the design of the Creator-God. And so, what were for Neo-Platonic Augustine *goods* of marriage become for Aristotelian Aquinas *ends* of marriage, and ends established in a "natural" priority. "Marriage has as its principal end the procreation and education of offspring, an end which belongs to man by reason of his generic nature and which, therefore, is shared with other animals. And so offspring are said to be a good of marriage. But, as the philosopher (Aristotle) says, it has as a secondary end in man alone the sharing in tasks which are necessary in life, and from this point of view husband and wife owe each other faithfulness, which is one of the goods of marriage. There is yet another end in believers, namely, the meaning of Christ and Church, and so a good of marriage is called sacrament. The first end is found in marriage insofar as man is animal, the second insofar as he is man, the third insofar as he is believer."[54]

As is customary in Aquinas, this is a tightly argued and brilliantly sharp delineation of a position, and the terminology *primary end–secondary end* dominated discussions of the ends of marriage in Roman Catholic manuals from then on. But neither the sharpness of the argument nor the undoubted authority of the author should be allowed to obscure a rather peculiar claim, namely, that the primary end of *human* marriage is dictated by man's generically *animal* nature. In the concluding reflection of this chapter I shall discuss three levels of functioning in the human animal, the physical, the psychological and the spiritual, and I shall argue that marriage as both human and sacramental must necessarily be developed on all three levels. I cannot accept as adequate any specification of human sexuality and genitality which links them exclusively only to the physical, the animal, the biological.

Thomas, of course, wishes to insist as always that reason must have control. Not that there is any rational control *in* the genital act. For "animals lack reason. Therefore, in genital intercourse man becomes an animal, for the pleasure of the action and the force of the desire cannot be moderated by reason."[55] But there is reason *before* the act and because there is, genital intercourse between spouses is not sinful. "The excess of passion which destroys virtue (and is, therefore, sinful) is that which not only impedes reason, but destroys it all together. Such is not the case with the intensity of pleasure in genital intercourse, for though a man is not then under control, he has been under the control of reason in advance."[56] Besides, physical nature has been created good by God, so that "it is impossible to say that the act in which offspring are procreated is so completely unlawful that means of virtue cannot be found in it."[57]

There remains some ambivalence toward genital desire, activity and pleasure. They are "occupations with lower affairs which distract the soul and make it unworthy of being joined actually to God, but they are not sinful at all times and in all circumstances. Indeed, within the ends of marriage they are meritorious,[59] and Thomas asserts explicitly that to forego the pleasure and thwart the end would be sinful.[60] This latter opinion leads Messenger to go beyond Aquinas and declare that "both passion and pleasure are natural concomitants of the sex act, and so far from diminishing its moral goodness, if the sex act is willed beforehand according to right reason, the effect of pleasure and passion is simply to heighten and increase the moral goodness of the act, not in any way to diminish it."[61] It is a far cry from Augustine and Gregory, and a move toward the liberation of legitimate sexual intercourse from any notion of sin and its solid implantation as a means and a cause of grace, that is, as a sacrament.

We need to recall here what was said in the opening chapter about the search for a definition of sacrament and about how that definition, emphasizing that sacrament is both sign and cause of grace, opened the way for the inclusion of marriage among the sacraments of the Western Church. The early Scholastics did not doubt that marriage was a sign of grace, but they did doubt that it was a cause of grace. They hesitated therefore to include it among the sacraments. Peter Lombard, for instance, defined sacraments in the categories of sign and cause. "A sacrament, properly speaking, is a sign of the grace of God and the form of invisible grace in such a way that it is its image and its cause. Sacraments are instituted, therefore, not only for signifying grace but also for causing it."[62] He proceeds to list the sacraments of the new law, carefully distinguishing marriage, though, from those that cause grace. "Some offer a remedy for sin and confer helping grace, as baptism; others offer a remedy only, as marriage; others support us with grace and virtue, as Eucharist and orders."[63] Marriage is a sacrament for Lombard, therefore, only in the sense that it is a sign— "a sacred sign of a sacred reality, namely, the union of Christ and the Church."[64]

It was Albert the Great and his most famous pupil, Thomas Aquinas, who firmly established marriage among the sacraments of the Church. In his commentary on Lombard, Albert enumerates various opinions about the sacramentality of marriage, and characterizes as *very probable* the opinion which holds that "it confers grace for doing good, not just any good but specifically that good which a married person should do."[65] In his commentary Aquinas goes further, characterizing as *most probable* the opinion that "marriage, insofar as it is contracted in faith in Christ, confers grace to do those things which are required in marriage."[66] He is even more positive in his *Contra Gentiles*, stating bluntly that "it is to be believed that through this sacrament [marriage] grace is given to the married."[67] By the time he reached his final work, the *Summa Theologiae*, he lists marriage among the seven sacraments without any demur about its grace-conferring qualities. The combined authority of Albert and Thomas ensured a place for marriage among the sacraments of the Church, and by the time of the Reformation their opinion was held universally by Roman Catholic theologians.

THE TEACHING OF THE CHURCH

That Neo-Platonic and Gnostic dualism, which was combated but never definitively overcome by the Fathers of the Church, enjoyed a period of resurgence in the Middle Ages under the banners of the Cathari and Albigenses. It contained, as always, a suspicion, pessimism and downright negativity to sexuality, to genitality, and therefore to marriage, and once again the Church had to defend these good gifts of God. The Second Lateran Council (1139) condemned those who "condemn the bonds of legitimate marriage," and ordered them "to be coerced by external powers,"[68] presumably to accept the goodness and legitimacy of marriage. Such external coercion, of course, would not be approved today, but it does provide evidence of how strongly the Church felt about marriage. Catharism was castigated again in the Council of Verona where, for the first time in a Church document, marriage was listed as a sacrament in the company of baptism, Eucharist and confession.[69] As part of the formula for healing the great schism between East and West, the Council of Lyons (1274) listed marriage among seven sacraments,[70] a listing repeated at the Council of Florence (1439), with the specification that these seven sacraments "both contain grace and confer it on those who receive them worthily."[71]

The concluding section of the Florentine decree deals explicitly with marriage, and is an excellent summary of everything we have said of it up to this point. "The seventh sacrament is marriage, which is a sign of the union between Christ and his Church. . . . A triple good (not *end*) is designated for marriage. The first is offspring accepted and raised to worship God. The second is fidelity, in which each spouse ought to serve the other. The third is the indivisibility of marriage because it signifies the indivisible union of Christ and Church. And, although separation is permissible in the case of fornication (sic), remarriage is not, for the bond of legitimately contracted marriage is perpetual."[72] That marriage is a sacrament; that it contains and confers grace; that it is indissoluble—all these are now established doctrines of the Western Church. When the Council of Trent, then, in response to the Reformation, teaches them, it is merely articulating, not creating, the doctrine and the faith of the Church,[73] and I see no need to go over the ground again. But there is one decision of Trent about marriage that we must pause on, because in its time it was an important and innovative response to a pressing problem, which recurs, albeit in a slightly different form, in our time. I refer to the decree *Tametsi* which invalidated clandestine marriages.

If one wishes to hold that marriage is a sacrament, that it symbolizes the union of Christ and his Church, that it confers grace on those who receive it worthily, that it is indissoluble, a crucial question arises. What makes a marriage? At what precise, if extended, moment in time are two persons sacramentally and indissolubly married? It is a question which vexed Western theologians and canon lawyers for quite some time, for it had two differing answers in the sources of the Western tradition. There was the imperial Roman answer: *consent* between the man and the woman makes marriage. There was the Germanic answer: *sexual intercourse* between the man and the woman makes marriage. Both opinions are found in the Fathers of the Church, and they were hotly debated because the opinion that one accepts will control the answer to the question whether or not Mary and Joseph were truly married.

Augustine, for instance, opted for the Roman solution, and so could accept the union of Mary and Joseph as a true marriage.[74] Jerome, on the contrary, held the Germanic opinion and admitted that Mary and Joseph were not married.[75] The twelfth century Decree of Gratian, which became enormously influential in the Roman Church, combined the two opinions, arguing that both consent and intercourse were required, though differently. Consent initiates a marriage (*matrimonium initiatum*), and intercourse completes it (*matrimonium ratum*). It was this document which opened the way to a compromise theory, which overcame the two competing theories and became the law of the Western Church via the decrees of Pope Alexander III at the end of the twelfth century. Consent makes a marriage, perfect and complete in itself (*matrimonium ratum*), but this marriage is not indissoluble. Genital intercourse makes a consummated marriage (*matrimonium ratum et consummatum*), and it is only this consummated marriage which is indissoluble. The Roman Catholic Church enshrined this compromise opinion in its Code of Canon Law in the twentieth century.[76]

To lovers such intricacies might appear as so much indelicate nit-picking. "We love one another" seems to them a sufficient answer to almost any question. But that it was not just nit-picking, at least at that time, is clear from the history of clandestine marriages. A clandestine marriage is one that is contracted by the simple exchange of consent between a man and a woman, without any witnesses or publicity, and by the end of the Middle Ages such marriages had become the scourge of Europe. They took place between people who could not marry publicly, because their parents would not allow it, or because class distinction forbade it, or because of a multitude of possible reasons. Unfortunately, after a shorter or longer period, many such marriages ended with charge and counter-charge of fornication, prostitution, illegitimacy, etc., none of them at the time, or now for that matter for all our vaunted sophistication, socially "nice" charges.

The Church recognized the validity of such marriages, for consent makes marriage, and regarded them as sacramental and indissoluble when consummated. That sacramental marriages symbolizing the unshakable union between Christ and his Church would cease to be, and that indissoluble marriages would appear to be dissolved, was intolerable for it. To put an end to such individual, social and religious woes the Council of Trent, through its decree *Tametsi*, sought to put an end to clandestine marriages. Although such marriages had, in the past, been recognized by the Church as true and valid marriages (because marriage results from consent), henceforth they would not be. *Tametsi* decreed that a true and valid marriage, one that hopes to be sacramental and indissoluble, must be celebrated in the presence of an appointed priest and of two or three witnesses.[77]

Tametsi transformed marriage from a simple contract, one not restricted by any external legal requirements, to a solemn contract, one in which certain legal formalities had to be met for the contract to be valid. That transformation required a significant change also in the way the sacrament of marriage was celebrated, but that change was a change only in the externals of the celebration, not in the substance of the sacrament. After *Tametsi*, as before, the sacrament of marriage is still constituted by the consent of the man and the woman to marry, not by any external celebration. The change introduced by *Tametsi* was well within the powers of the Church to make, as I explained in Chapter Two.[78] And if that change was within legitimate power, it is still within legitimate power today to make a similar or analogous change in the externalization of consent. I shall return to this point in the final section.

THEOLOGICAL REFLECTION

In a forthright introduction to Dominian's *Christian Marriage*, Father Enda McDonagh employs a very pointed *argumentum ad hominem:* "One might ask how many celibates would regard a theology of celibacy elaborated exclusively by the married as a satisfying and living theology?" It is clear that he thinks the answer to his question is "none," for he had already argued that "there will be no fully satisfying theology of marriage until there are married theologians, until married Christians themselves have the competence and opportunity to explore theologically the meaning of their marriage."[79] The concluding section of this chapter on marriage is the effort of one married theologian to do just that. I do not mean to insinuate, because I do not believe, that celibates have nothing to say about marriage, or that married Christians have nothing to say about celibacy. Each Christian living into his or her new life in Christ in either of these two wholly, and holy, Christian ways has something to say theologically to the other. What the married person, though, can say about marriage, or the celibate about celibacy, derives from their exclusive *experience* of marriage or celibacy, an experience which history shows has a way of impinging upon and shaping theology.

I begin by highlighting two ecclesiastical decisions about marriage. The dispute concerning whether consent or subsequent genital intercourse definitively established a marriage was settled in favor of consent, and *Tametsi* transformed marriage from a simple to a solemn contract. These two decisions handed marriage over to the domain of those expert in consensual contracts and all that is required for their validity and legality, namely, lawyers, specifically canon lawyers in the case of Church marriages. Their professional concerns for legality and validity dominated the doctrinal and moral textbooks on marriage since the Council of Trent, and also, therefore, the doctrinal and moral lectures and sermons. They dominated, too, ecclesiastical pronouncements about marriage. Is it any wonder that when couples, preparing for marriage or already married, read such books and listen to such pronouncements, they come away bemused and asking what that has to do with their experience of love or marriage?

The Code of Canon Law exemplifies the problem nicely. It states: (1) "The consent of the parties, legitimately manifested before persons capable of receiving it, makes marriage"; (2) "Christ the Lord raised the marriage contract between baptized persons to the dignity of sacrament. Therefore, there cannot be a valid marriage contract between baptized persons without it being, by that very fact, a sacrament."[80] There are several problems with these two statements, which yield insight into problems facing *Christian* marriage today.

A first problem is this. To insist exclusively that legitimately manifested consent makes marriage, however true that may be as a precise legal statement of the moment in which two people *become* married, is to run the risk of ignoring and having couples also ignore the importance of their married life together, their *being* married. In classical language, the legal definition lays stress on marriage *in fieri* at the expense of marriage *in actu*. But the sacrament of marriage, the symbolic action which proclaims, realizes and celebrates in the historical world the steadfast covenant of God and his people and of Christ and his Church, cannot be exclusively marriage *in fieri* but must be also, I would dare to say especially, marriage *in actu*.

An old aphorism drawn from marriage counseling gets much closer to both human and sacramental marriage than does the legal code. It takes a catechetical, that is, question and answer, form. Question: When are two people married? Answer: Thirty years later! It is a cute answer, which would wither and die in the cold light of legal examination. For the moment, I am content to insinuate that, in the warm glow of human examination, it comes closer to what couples experience in their marriages, namely, that becoming married, becoming two in one flesh, becoming sacrament of the covenant God and Christ, requires a great deal more than the giving of consent in one legitimated form or other of the two little words, "I do."

A second problem, perhaps even a series of problems, with the Church's present approach to marriage and sacrament is situated in an ambiguity created by two apparently conflicting claims. On the one hand, there is the Code's claim that legitimate consent, in general, makes marriage and, in the specific case of the baptized, makes sacrament. This claim would seem to lead to two conclusions. First, every legitimate consent, howsoever publicly signified, makes valid marriage; second, such valid marriages between baptized persons are sacraments. The first conclusion renders very dubious the long-established ecclesiastical practice of declaring null the marriage of non-baptized persons so that one or other or both, now baptized, may enter into a sacramental marriage. The second conclusion either is called into question by, or itself calls into question, the theory and practice deriving from *Tametsi*, which decrees for baptized persons that any marriage contract not celebrated in the proper canonical form is not valid and, therefore, not sacrament. This introduces an element, extrinsic to the consensual contract itself, and requires it for the validity of both the legal contract and the religious sacrament—a situation which appears to conflict with the Code's claim that legitimately manifested consent makes marriage. One might argue, of course, that the Church as social institution is quite free to establish whatever form of signifying consent it chooses, but that argument fails to come to grips with the fact that a practice introduced historically, as we saw, to safeguard the sacramentality of marriage, *propter bonum sacramenti,* in new circumstances today impinges on the prior right of the human reality of marriage.

I shall return to this point when I deal with the next problem, and for the moment shall content myself by pointing out that all the ambiguity could be resolved by separating the two conflicting claims. Consent, expressed in some adequately public form, makes marriage (at least *in fieri*); consent, expressed in ecclesiastical form to reveal, realize and celebrate participation in the faith of the Church, makes sacrament. Such a strategy would have repercussions for the question of indissolubility, for it is clear from the universal Catholic tradition that it is linked to the *sacrament,* and not just to the human reality, of marriage. Indissolubility is indissolubly *bonum sacramenti.* It is precisely because of this that the Roman Church claims to be able to declare null the marriages of pagans and the civil marriages of baptized persons, so that they can enter into religious, sacramental marriages. I shall defer any further treatment of indissolubility, though, till the final section of this chapter.

There remains one final problem with the present canonical view of marriage. To stress exclusively the identity between the consensual contract and the sacrament of marriage runs the risk of ignoring what is specific to *Christian* marriage. Every marriage in the Western world is constituted by consent. When all that is required of Christian marriage is that baptized persons give the same consent given in all marriages, it is easy for people to get the impression that, after all, Christian marriage is no different from any other marriage, except that it is between Christians. It is easy for both them and the pastors who minister to them to focus so exclusively on the giving of consent that they forget about the married life that follows that giving of consent and is the ongoing concretization of that consent.

Perhaps this impression that Christian marriage is no different from any other marriage is a cause of the present situation in which marriages between Christians are indistinguishable from any other marriages. Perhaps, also, the inability to distinguish specifically Christian marriage is part of the reason why so many of our young folk, insisting truly that they love one another, and not quite so truly that all you need is love, find the religious ritualizing of their already-given consent so trivial and even irrelevant. To declare, indiscriminately, that they are lacking in faith is too sweeping a statement to be true. The problem might be, not so much with their faith, as with the view of marriage that is presented to them, and which does not allow them to suspect that their faith has anything to do with it. But, of course, as we remember from the opening chapters, faith has everything to do with Christian sacraments.[81] It has everything to do also with *Christian* marriage.

We recall here the Council of Trent's teaching that without faith no one is justified. We recall its minimalistic teaching that sacraments confer the grace they signify on the person who places no obstacle to such grace, and the more expansive teaching of the Council of Florence that sacraments give grace to those who receive them worthily. We recall the definition of symbolizing as a "specifically human process in which meanings and realities, intellectual, emotional and personal are proclaimed, realized and celebrated in representation in a sensible reality *within a specific perspective*."[82] That final phrase is an essential element in the definition, so that if the specific perspective is ever lacking the sensible reality remains just that, sensible reality and not symbol. In that case it neither proclaims nor realizes what the symbol symbolizes.

In the case of the sacrament of marriage, the sensible reality is human marriage. The perspective that transforms that human marriage into also the Christian sacrament of marriage is the faith of the Church personally internalized by the marrying couple. If the faith of the Church, which may be presumed to be always present, is not matched by the faith of the couple, which may or may not be present, human marriage is offered by the Church as also sacramental marriage, but is accepted by the couple as merely human marriage. It is the classic case of the valid but fruitless sacrament.[83]

To claim that consent makes marriage is true as a legal statement; there is no marriage, neither simply human nor sacramental, without it. To claim that consensual marriage is a human reality that is symbolically transformed to be sacrament is true as a statement representing the faith of the Church. But to claim that human marriage is transformed to be sacrament by each and every baptized Christian requires a major distinction: by those who share the faith of the Church, yes; by those who do not share the faith of the Church, not at all. No one is justified or graced without faith, not even in sacraments, not even in the sacrament of marriage.

All the sacraments are "sacraments of faith." That is, they "not only presuppose faith, but by words and objects they also nourish, strengthen and express it."[84] What I have just argued is nothing more than the specification of this general sacramental statement to marriage: in marriage only Christian faith makes the difference between universally human reality and *Christian* sacrament. In every symbol, as we have seen, there are two levels of meaning, one literal, the other symbolic. Water, for instance, on the literal level bespeaks life and death, which makes it wonderfully apt to express meanings of death and life on the symbolic level, as it does in baptism. In marriage there are the same two levels of meaning. On the one hand, there is the literal union of this man and this woman; on the other, this union also symbolizes the love of God for his people and of Christ for his Church. In *Christian* marriage there is proclaimed, realized and celebrated not only the love of the spouses for one another, but also the love of God for his people and of Christ and his Church.

In Christian marriage, in fact, the symbolic meaning takes precedence, in the sense that the mutual love of Christ and his Church is the model for the mutual love of husband and wife. And as a husband and wife love one another in marriage, they are not merely this man and this woman loving one another, but they are also the Church— "the domestic church," Vatican II calls them,[85] loving her Spouse and Savior. The key that opens the door to such realized and celebrated meanings is not just the freely given consent of the spouses to one another, but also their faith, their freely given consent, if you will, to Church, to Christ and to God. Consent may make marriage as social institution, but it is faith that makes marriage as Christian sacrament.

Such an approach to marriage as sacrament has serious implications for ecclesiastical practice. For centuries ecclesiastical courts have pronounced judgments on the validity or non-validity of marriages, and today, as is well known, they are delivering more and more judgments of non-validity on the marriages of baptized persons. None of these judgments is based on a defective faith, but rather on a somehow defective consent. Could that practice be changed? Could consent and faith, purely human marriage and sacramental marriage, be separated? Predictably these questions provoke a wide range of answers from theologians and canon lawyers. I do not intend to survey those answers here; it is not difficult to guess that they run the gamut from *absolutely no* to *of course.*[86] What I propose is rather more simple, namely, to offer a *theoretical* answer to the questions, which may help my fellow marrieds, as well as once-marrieds and remarrieds, to come to grips personally with their personal questions.

But we must keep in mind here two separate problems. There is, first, the problem involved in claiming that every marriage between baptized persons is a sacrament. There is, second, the problem in claiming that every marriage between baptized persons which is not celebrated in the canonical form decreed by *Tametsi* is not a sacrament, not a marriage, and therefore effectively concubinage or living in sin. Both problems are, of course, intrinsically connected, and any statement about the one will be *eo ipso* a statement also about the other. We must try to keep this in mind.

A possible counter-claim must be answered at the outset. Canon 1 of the Council of Trent's decree on marriage states emphatically: "If anyone says that *marriage* is not one of the seven sacraments . . . let him be anathema."[87] The much later Code of Canon Law states equally emphatically: "Christ the Lord raised the *marriage contract between baptized persons* to the dignity of sacrament. Therefore, there cannot be a valid *marriage contract between baptized persons* without it being, by that very fact, a sacrament."[88] Notice the different language of the dogmatic and the canonical statements, the former asserting that *marriage* is a sacrament, the latter that the *marriage contract between baptized persons* is a sacrament. The two are vastly different claims.

In a careful analysis of the notions of contract and sacrament at the Council of Trent, Father A. Duval points out that it was not by inadvertence that canon 1 said simply *marriage* and not something like *marriage between baptized persons*, but by deliberate choice. It wished to leave open the debate that the theology of the time could not solve. "Canon 1 of the Council wishes to affirm the existence in the new law of *a* sacrament of marriage—but not that marriage in the new law is always a sacrament."[89] Far from declaring, even implicitly, the inseparability of contract and sacrament, Trent chose deliberately to leave the question open. And the expansion in the Code from marriage to marriage contract between baptized persons may not be considered an explanation, still less an authentic explanation, of Trent's words.

The expansion was made, in fact, by P. Gasparri,[90] a principal formative figure in the codification of the present Canon Law in 1917.[91] But neither his nor the Code's extension of Trent's language binds the Tridentine dogma to an interpretation which it aimed explicitly to avoid, and since there has been no subsequent solemn teaching of the Church on the matter, Trent's position remains the official, dogmatic one. There is *a* sacrament of marriage in the new law, but not every marriage in the new law is a sacrament. It is easier legally, of course, to presume that every such marriage is a sacrament, but legal presumption of the presence of intrinsic requisites does not make a sacrament. Only the real presence of the requisites does that. I shall argue, as I insinuated earlier, that only that marriage approached in Christian faith is Christian sacrament, while that marriage in which there is valid consent but no transforming faith, even if it is between baptized Christians, is a valid marriage and not just concubinage, but is not a valid sacrament.

Another counter-argument has already been disposed of in a previous chapter. The Code's identification of contract and covenant and sacrament in a marriage between Christians derives from a traditional Roman Catholic understanding of the effects of baptism, namely, that it gives the gift of faith and makes one a believer. Now we have already seen that that understanding is a little ambiguous.[92]

Faith may be understood in two quite different senses in the Catholic tradition. It may refer, first, to the virtue of faith, that is, the power or the know-how to make an act of faith; or it may refer, second, to the actual act of faith. The know-how is a necessary pre-requisite for the act, but the act does not follow necessarily and ineluctably from the know-how. I may know how to drive an automobile, but that in itself is no guarantee that I will ever actually drive one. Now, as we have seen, it is the virtue of faith that is gifted in baptism. Before that virtue may be imputed to anyone, it must be activated, freely, deliberately and consciously, into an actual act of faith. It is that actual faith that transforms both the human being into a Christian and human marriage into sacramental, Christian marriage. Sadly, our times have revealed a new, only in the sense of previously unacknowledged, phenomenon, that of countless baptized who have received the virtue of faith in baptism, but who have never made an act of faith in the God made known in Jesus. They constitute an anomalous brand of Christians, those who, though baptized, remain all their lives unbelievers. These *baptized non-believers*[93] ought not to be equated with Christians in Christian law.

Baptism does not give faith nor make believers in any sense other than a very passive one; it gives the know-how to faith and to being a Christian. The Code's assumption, therefore, that Christians are necessarily present from the moment of baptism, and that therefore every valid marriage between baptized persons is, by that very fact, a sacrament, is an assumption which is manifestly false in our day. Of course, it will be very difficult to gauge the faith or non-faith of any given person. But it is, at least, clear that the "Christian faith" of baptized persons today ranges from explicit non-faith to explicit faith in the God made known in Jesus, who is the Christ. It is my contention that the sacramentality of marriage coincides with that range and runs, therefore, from explicit non-sacramentality to explicit sacramentality. The shades between the extremes may be difficult to gauge, but no legal presumption will ever make up for or make good the lack of faith and the consequent lack of sacramentality. Those who marry without Christian faith, be they ever so baptized, whether they marry with or without the prescribed canonical form, marry indeed validly, and therefore do not live simply in concubinage, but do not marry sacramentally.[94]

So what now can we say of marriage? We can say that human marriage is a gift of the Creator-God, who created man and woman different sexes so that, by inalienable right, they could complement one another in marriage and become one complete person. The time has come for Catholic theology to assert the inalienable validity of every human marriage, including the validity of the marriages of baptized persons outside the canonical form. Such was, of course, the practice of the early Christian Church up to the Council of Trent, when the present canonical form was introduced, and continues to be the practice today in situations where a priest may not easily be present.[95] The historical struggle of the Church in eighteenth and nineteenth century Europe to assert, over against emerging states, its rights over the marriages of Christians now has been sufficiently won for it to start taking seriously again its own sacred teaching.

For many centuries the Roman Catholic Church taught, and continues to teach today, that consent makes marriage. The introduction of the present Catholic form by *Tametsi* was aimed at eliminating the social and religious problems generated by the plague of clandestine marriages. Such problems could, of course, still arise today. But they could be avoided by any publicly witnessed ritual; an ecclesiastically witnessed ritual is not indispensable. This would seem to have been honestly and courageously acknowledged by the bishops of France when they instructed their priests to urge baptized non-believers to marry in a non-ecclesiastical civil ceremony.[96] Implicitly acknowledging what I have argued about the connection between Christian faith and Christian sacrament, and recognizing that the marriages of baptized non-believers are not sacramental, they asserted, at least implicitly, that even the baptized do not need Christian sacrament to make human marriage.

This would seem to be also the tenor of the decree of Pope Paul VI establishing that "when Eastern or Latin Catholics enter into marriage with Eastern non-Catholics, in such marriages the canonical form of celebration obliges only for legality; for validity the presence of a sacred minister is enough."[97] It is to be hoped that this decision will be extended to allow new canonical rites, particularly for peoples in the third world in keeping with their own authentic marriage customs. This would be a truly remarkable sign that the Catholic Church is becoming a truly world, as distinct from merely Western, Church.

Such decisions would seem to be well in line with the recent proclamation by Vatican II of the independence of earthly affairs: "Created things and societies themselves enjoy their own laws and values which must be gradually deciphered, put to use and regulated by men."[98] Marriage, as old as humanity itself, and older by far than the Christian Church, is one of those earthly realities which enjoys its own meanings and values apart from the Church. To acknowledge that fact would seem to be in line also with the Church's willingness "to renounce the exercise of certain legitimately acquired rights if it becomes clear that their use raises doubts about the sincerity of her witness or that new conditions of life demand some other arrangements."[99]

It is, of course, my argument that in the case of marriage new conditions have arisen that certainly demand another arrangement. The arrangement I have proposed is one which would be well in line with the ringing words of the Church on religious freedom. "It is one of the major tenets of Catholic doctrine that man's response to God in faith must be free. Therefore no one is to be forced to embrace the Christian faith against his own will. . . . In matters religious every manner of coercion on the part of men should be excluded."[100] It is hard to see how a Church that believes these words could continue to deprive the baptized, believers and non-believers alike, of a right which is inalienably theirs to a human reality created for them by God.

MARRIAGE AS SACRAMENT

In symbol-language, a sacrament is a symbolic action which points beyond itself to meanings which it proclaims, realizes and celebrates; in theological language, it is an action which contains and confers the grace it signifies. The ritual action in the waters of baptism, for instance, reveals, realizes and celebrates the death-resurrection of Jesus and the graces won in it, and confers those graces on those who live into it. What does sacramental marriage reveal and what grace does it confer? To answer this question fully, it is necessary to distinguish two symbolic actions in marriage. There is the action, ritualized in the marriage ceremony, of a man and a woman binding themselves to become one flesh forever. There is also, and much more crucially, the action(s) of living into this binding forever. In ordinary language, both actions are called *marriage*. In theological language, both merit to be called *sacrament*. It is the meaning of this latter statement that I intend to elucidate here.

The Code's statements are now well known to us. "Christ the Lord raised the marriage contract and covenant between baptized persons to the dignity of sacrament." That means that when a man and a woman enter into a contract of marriage, in faith as we have seen, their contract both proclaims and celebrates something else and confers the grace of that something else. In the Jewish and Christian tradition of marriage, there is no doubt what that something else is—it is the mutual covenant entered into by God and his people and by Jesus the Christ and his holy people, the Church.

A couple entering into the contract and covenant of human marriage are saying, "I love you and now solemnly contract to give myself (*myself*, not just *my body*, as the Code says) to you." A Christian couple entering into the covenant of sacramental marriage are saying that, and in and through that much, much more. They are saying also "I love you as God loves his people and as Christ loves his Church." From the first, therefore, this contract is a religious contract. It is graced, that is, God and his Christ are consciously and explicitly to the fore as parties in it, almost as guarantors of it. And this presence of God is not extrinsic to the contract, added on to it from the outside, but rather something intrinsic and essential to it, without which the marriage would not be *Christian* marriage at all. Where God and his Christ are present, there is, of course, grace in abundance.

The mutual love of husband and wife in a Christian marriage is not just any love, but love that is modeled on and sustained by the love of God for his people and of Christ for his Church. It is *hesed*, steadfast love. Such love is not difficult to proclaim; it is difficult only to live into. Once a man and a woman have proclaimed their love for one another in a marriage ceremony, they have then to proclaim it in a married life. Their married life is the ongoing sacrament of marriage which, specifically as *Christian* marriage, reveals, realizes and celebrates in a universally accepted social institution the steadfast love of God for his people and of Christ for his Church. It is an exalted claim to make for Christian marriage, but it is the claim the Church makes when it declares that marriage is a sacrament and that two Christians make when they declare that they are entering into *Christian* marriage. For most married couples, Christian and non-Christian alike, it is a claim that is extraordinarily difficult to live into, because it is extraordinarily difficult for two to become one flesh—and not surprisingly.

I would like to distinguish in the human animal three levels of being and action, which I shall designate as the physical, the psychological and the spiritual. The physical is the level of biology and physiology; it is the level that humans share with others in the genus *animal*. The psychological is the level of sense and imagination and memory and understanding and reason and judgment and emotion; it is the level that is specific to the *human* animal. The spiritual is the level of all that transcends the animal and the merely human, all that reaches within to the depths and without to the beyond of the human; it is the level to which only the *religious* animal, in the broadest meaning of religious,[101] attains.

To become one flesh a man and a woman must become one on all three levels. By this I do not intend the impossible, perhaps not even desirable, ideal that they should agree about everything on all three levels. I intend, rather, that each spouse must understand and come to terms with both his and her own hungers, hopes and dreams on all three levels and also those of the other spouse, and that neither should use their married relationships for any end other than one in which the other is a full partner. All mere selfishness to the exclusion of the other, which is not the same thing as all selfishness, for there is a legitimate self-love,[102] is excluded by a one-flesh relationship. Such one-fleshness is not attained, of course, before, during or immediately after the wedding ceremony. It is learned gradually as husband and wife discover, explore and fulfill their separate and mutual possibilities on all three levels.

The universal, not just the modern, history of marriage demonstrates the difficulty of achieving such harmony. It is constantly threatened by unrestrained selfishness and the desire to control another human being. But it is a harmony which must be achieved if a marriage is ever to become a one-flesh marriage. And until a marriage becomes one flesh it is not fully sacramental of the covenant love of God and the Easter love of his Christ. At best it will remain unconsummated on any but the most superficial of levels and only imperfectly sacramental. It is precisely because of the difficulties involved in becoming one-flesh, and therefore sacramental, that Christian marriage is essentially eschatological. That is, although it is already and inchoately sacrament of the union between God and his people and between Christ and his Church, it is not yet perfect sacrament. This already-but-not-yet dimension of Christian marriage provides it with a comfort and a challenge: a comfort to the extent that Christian spouses can claim, in truth, that their marriage is both modeled on and model of the union between Christ and his Church; a challenge to the extent that they constantly realize, in equal honesty, their falling short of and their need to be more attuned to their model.

The essential ambivalence, leaning toward negativity, which the Christian tradition has shown toward sexuality and genitality demands that I say a special word about their place in one-flesh sacrament. It would be foolish to assume that there is no *theological* problem here;

even our brief conspectus of the history negates such an assumption. It seems to me equally foolish just to say that all the Christian must do about sexuality and genitality is to restrain them and to master them by self-denial. For again history documents that for many Christians, married and unmarried alike, unmitigated acceptance of their God-given gifts of sexuality and genitality is a great deal more difficult than their restraint and control. No, a word must be said, and it must be a word of *reverse discrimination* to balance the rational-Apollonian negativity of the tradition with a Dionysian (I hesitate to say *irrational*) positivity.

Some may judge that Tom Driver has said all there is to say. "Sex is not essentially human. It is not inseparable from the human in us, and it cannot be fully humanized. . . . Christianity should no more idealize sex than it should scorn or fear it."[103] But I feel I must demur. Driver is right if what he means is that neither sexuality nor genitality is *exclusively* human, but he is wrong if he means that they are not *essentially* human. He is right when he says that neither sexuality nor genitality is inseparable from the human but wrong when he says that they cannot be humanized.

Sexuality is essentially human; there has never been a normal human being in biological history who was not sexual. Of course, we humans share it with all animals, but that does not negate its essential humanness. Of course, we humans can use our sexuality only on the physical level of our being, and then it becomes separated from the human and is used only as animals use it. We can do that with any of our animal powers. But sexuality can be humanized—not by preempting it from the physical level (that cannot be done) but by letting it flow through all three levels of the human, the physical, of course, but also the psychological and the spiritual. Indeed sexuality and genitality do not ever need to be humanized, for they are human to begin with. In one-flesh marriage they can, indeed must, take on a distinctively and exclusively human form.

I wish to re-emphasize here that one-flesh marriage requires a husband and a wife to become one on all three levels of being and action which I have specified, for I detect in modern Catholic theology relating to sexuality and genitality a spiritualizing approach, which locates the principal value of human sexuality and genitality exclusively on the spiritual level. The objection to such spiritualizing, as John Giles Milhaven acutely points out, "is not what it puts in there but what it leaves out. Man does do these spiritual, personal things in his sexual life (encounters, communicates, expresses love, etc.), and they do constitute the principal value of human sexuality, but not solely. The bodiliness and sexualness with which he does them changes intrinsically their nature and therefore their value from what they would be in a non-bodied, non-sexual person's life."[104] To transfer human sexuality up to the exclusively spiritual level is just as untrue to human reality as transferring it down to the exclusively animal level.

It is not difficult, however, to understand the mainspring of such a tactic. The elements of sexuality and genitality that lie on the non-spiritual levels, particularly those on the physical level, are precisely the ones that tradition has so conditioned Christians to distrust. But I repeat. To become one flesh, and therefore sacrament of God and his people, of Christ and his Church, a husband and a wife must come to terms with their individual and mutual hungers, hopes and dreams on all three levels of being, including the distrusted physical. Becoming one flesh means not only becoming one spirit, not only one mind, but also one body. Married love is not only *agape*, the love of the spouse for the spouse's sake; not only *philia*, the love of the spouse as a friend; but also *eros*, the love of the spouse for one's own sake. Married love, that leads two to become one flesh, is not entirely selfish love, but it is unquestionably in part selfish love. Now lest that smack of heresy in pious, unreflecting ears, let me put it another way. Married love is loving one's neighbor (= spouse) *as oneself*. Married love, in which each spouse is a full partner, is as much "I love me and you" as it is "I love you." Even better, as Milhaven puts it so beautifully, it is "we love us."[105]

And so to *eros*, that rambunctious, so-called impersonal, so-called subhuman, so-called animal, and definitely selfish and irrational component of human love and human sexuality. The spiritualizers always want it transformed into *agape*. But there is no alchemy to effect such a transformation, and recourse to prayer and frequentation of the sacraments are no substitute for alchemy, as any insightful and honest Christian will tell you. Far better to accept *eros*, to integrate it, and to give it a distinctively human form.

We have learned that Augustine and Gregory judged *eros* negatively, that Aquinas hinted at its essential goodness, that Messenger went beyond them all to assert that the more heightened the passion and pleasure the greater is the moral goodness in *eros*. The latter was a daring move against the Neo-Platonic tide which has swept the Western tradition along. But it is an argument that is sustained by the very tradition against which it moves, for it holds that the more a created reality attains to its natural end, the truer and better and more moral it is. I prefer, however, to put the argument just a little differently and sacramentally.

Sexuality and genitality, sexual passion and genital pleasure, derive their sacramental character, in the first instance, not from any purpose that human beings might assign to them, be it perpetuation of the race, role fulfillment, procreation or making love, but from the simple theological fact that they are from God. They are gifts of God in creation, and they are good gifts. To use them precisely as good gifts of God in the process of becoming one in Christian marriage (and that is the only use I am considering in this chapter) is to use them in a way that points to their origin in God. That is already to use them sacramentally, in a way that is not only human, but also Christian and graceful.

But Messenger is right. The more heightened and the more sharply focused are moral sexual passion and pleasure, the more they achieve their intrinsic nature, the more the gift of God is valued, and the more the Giver is praised. And so in Christian marriage there is no need to fear them, no need to feel guilty for their proper use, no need to avoid them, no need to abstain from Communion in the body of Christ because of them. As I have explained, becoming one flesh includes essentially, though not exclusively, becoming one body. This becoming one body, even in its most violently passionate and pleasurable form, is an element in the symbol-sacrament of marriage, that is, it points beyond itself to the union of God and his people and confers the various graces of that union on the bodily united spouses. That this bodily union is not all there is in becoming one flesh should be clear from everything I have said. I am merely underscoring now that erotic union is an essential part of the one-flesh process.

In response to Driver's view that sex cannot be fully humanized, I am stating again that it does not need to be humanized because it is already fully human, precisely as gifted to *adam* by the Creator-God. That human sexual passion can never be fully humanly mastered I grant, because such mastery attains only to the rational, and passion and pleasure have in them much that is irrational. But one way to respond humanly to the irrational is to accept it playfully and joyfully. Man and woman, husband and wife, do not become fully human by ignoring eros, or by negotiating their way carefully around it, above it or beyond it. They become human only by accepting it and integrating it into the rest of their human, and Christian, lives. Nor can they become one flesh until each has become fully human, each one in herself and himself.

Marriage is a dual process of becoming one, the spouses becoming individually one in themselves and mutually one with one another. Their marriage, as lived-into covenant to love and to serve one another, can be sacrament of the covenants between God and his people and between Christ and his Church only to the extent that it is in reality, not just in ideal, a life in which two have become in very deed one flesh. I do not feel any necessity to call any further attention to the life-long nature of both that task and that sacrament.

What, then, can we say in summary about marriage? We can say that *human* marriage is a God-gifted, life-long community to ensure the most appropriate conditions for life, the life of the spouses with one another as couple and with any children as family.[106] *Christian* marriage is that very same human marriage perceived and lived into in faith as symbol-sacrament of the steadfast and graceful community formed by God and his people and by Christ and his Church.

It is the traditional opinion of the Western Church that the contracting marriage partners *minister* this sacrament to one another. But I believe that judgment needs to be more nuanced. It is the identification of contract and sacrament that makes inescapable the conclusion that the contractants are themselves the sole ministers of the contract-sacrament. But acceptance of the ecclesiastical claim that the validity of the contract-sacrament depends on proper canonical form, which includes the presence of a designated minister, makes it possible, I believe, to argue that that minister has a ministerial role other than that of simple witness.

In human marriage a man and a woman are binding themselves to one another. In Christian marriage they are doing that—and more. They are binding themselves to live and to love not only as spouses but also as *Christian* spouses, proclaiming, realizing and celebrating in their married life the love of the covenant God and of his Christ. They bind themselves, moreover, in and before the Church, which accepts and verifies and guarantees their mutual contract, and commissions them to go forth in its name and live what they have proclaimed. This commissioning is done in its name by its designated representative, who is present therefore not just to witness a contract but also to commission fidelity to it in the name of the Church, of the Christ and of God. It is hardly abusing the language to allow that the Church minister is, at least, a *co-minister* of the sacrament. The traditional theological language misses this point, and so risks dealing with the contract-sacrament as an exclusively individual, rather than as also an ecclesial, action. Without going as far as the Eastern position, which sees the priest as the sole minister of the sacrament of marriage, it seems that he could be allowed, without detriment to the role of the contractants, a role as a co-minister.

Chapter Nine
HOLY ORDERS

It is well known that neither in the New Testament nor in the immediate post-apostolic Church is the word *hiereus*, priest, used to designate any Christian minister. John Robinson, as always, states this fact boldly. "The unpriestly character of early Christianity must surely have been one of the things to strike an outsider, whether he were Jewish or pagan."[1] He proceeds to point out, however, another fact equally well known, namely, that "the priestly element in Judaism had not disappeared without trace: it had been transmuted."[2] It had been transmuted to express the role and the work, first of all, of Jesus, and then of the Church.

The great high priesthood of Christ is a central theme of the Letter to the Hebrews (cf. 3:1; 4:14; 6:20; 7:26; 8:1; 9:11). Though not of the priestly tribe, and therefore not a priest "according to a legal requirement regarding bodily descent" (7:16), he is a "priest forever according to the order of Melchisedech" (5:6; 7:1–25). This high priest is mediator of a new covenant in his own blood (9:15–22; 12:24), and fulfills by superseding the levitical high priesthood and cult. The levitical high priest entered annually into the holy of holies to sprinkle expiatory blood, but this only as a shadow and a type of the action of the great high priest (9:23–10:1), who now "abolishes the first order to establish the second" (10:9). There is a point, critical in the history of traditions, which is frequently ignored, but which needs to be remembered and emphasized here. It is that the presentation of Jesus as the new high priest is a presentation not of the entire New Testament corpus, but solely of the rather late Letter to the Hebrews, which grew out of troubling questions in the Jewish Christian communities after the destruction of the temple, and therefore also of the levitical priesthood, in the year 70. We shall see in a moment how those questions contributed to an extension of Jewish priestly elements even beyond Jesus.

Besides extending the notion of priesthood to Jesus, the New Testament applies priestly characteristics to the Church. But just as we must note that the priesthood assigned to Jesus is not the levitical and official Jewish priesthood of his time, but that of the order of Melchisedech of an earlier time, so also we must try to understand just what is the nature of the priestly character of the Church. For this question the contribution of the First Letter of Peter, suffused with priestly talk, is crucial. I shall concentrate on 2:4–8, for a reason which I hope will become apparent. I must quote it in full.

"Come to him, to that living stone, rejected by men but in God's sight chosen and precious; and like living stones be yourselves built into a spiritual house, to be a holy priesthood, to offer spiritual sacrifices acceptable to God through Jesus Christ. For it stands in Scripture: 'Behold, I am laying in Sion a stone, a cornerstone chosen and precious, and he who believes in him will not be put to shame.' To you, therefore, who believe, he is precious; but for those who do not believe, 'the very stone which the builders rejected has become the head of the corner,' and 'a stone that will make men stumble, a rock that will make them fall.' " The passage is full of Old Testament echoes, and it will be instructive to consider the Old Testament passages which originate the echoes. There are three of them: Is. 28:16; Ps. 118:22; Is. 8:14.

Common to all three passages is the word *lithos,* the ordinary Greek word for *stone.* In Isaiah 28:16 God is laying a *lithos* in Sion, as both a comfort to those who believe and a warning of coming doom to the scoffers (vv. 17ff). Though the wording in 1 Peter 2:6 differs from the wording in the Septuagint, they agree on one thing over the Hebrew text. The latter provides no object for "those who believe"; the former does, "those who believe in/on it (*ep' auto*)." So it is also in Romans 9:33. In Psalm 118:22, *lithos* occurs within a paean of praise for the assurance of salvation. There is a great reversal of fortune, which is "the Lord's doing . . . [and] marvelous in your eyes," and which is imaged in "the stone which the builders rejected" and which "has become the cornerstone." In the exaltation of the rejected stone is presented the fate of Israel. 1 Peter 2:8 quotes the Hebrew text of Isaiah 8:14 rather than the Septuagint, for the latter denies that the *lithos* will be a stumbling stone and the former affirms it. And whereas in Isaiah 28:16 the Lord is placing a *lithos,* here the Lord himself is the *lithos,* a stone of offense and a rock of stumbling to both houses of Israel.

Other than the *lithos* itself there seems to be no common theme in the three passages. But John Elliott draws attention to some Qumran, targumic, and rabbinic literature which seems to indicate "a pre-Christian, Jewish tradition of interpretation which figured formatively in the eventual combination of these passages."[3] In this tradition, the *lithos* texts are applied to the Messiah and to the messianic age. In the New Testament they are used with the same messianic connotation. "The image had already been prepared; the Church simply had to make the application."[4] Peter, of course, is not the only Christian author to allude to these texts, nor is his selection from and combination of them uniquely his. There is a complex of New Testament passages in which the *lithos* image is applied to Jesus as Messiah. A glance at this complex will illumine the Peter text which is our prime concern here.

In Mark 12:10–11, and in its parallels in Matthew 21:42–44 and Luke 20:17, Psalm 118:22 is placed at the conclusion of the parable of the wicked husbandman, and is attributed as a saying of Jesus. The sense of the parable is glimpsed in the rejection of the beloved son by the tenants and his subsequent exaltation, events presented in the image of the *lithos* rejected by the builders and made the cornerstone by God. Matthew 21:43 makes it clear polemically to the hearers that they are the builders, by pronouncing *their* rejection by God.[5] "The kingdom of God will be taken from *you,* and given to a nation producing the fruits of it." He adds, with Luke 20:18, the judgment that "he who falls on that stone will be broken to pieces."[6] In his speech in Acts 4 before the Jewish rulers and elders, Luke puts in Peter's mouth, via a free citation of Psalm 118:22, the same judgment on "you the builders" who rejected the *lithos,* which is identified explicitly as Jesus (vv. 10–11). In Romans 9:33, in a combined citation of Isaiah 28:16 and Isaiah 8:14, Paul implicitly identifies Jesus as "the stone that will make men stumble," and over which Israel has in fact stumbled. But, as in 1 Peter 2:6, he who believes *ep' auto* will not be put to shame. In Ephesians 2:20 the interpretation is again explicitly Christological, "Christ Jesus himself being the cornerstone." And so also in 1 Peter 2:4–8, which combines all three Old Testament texts into a frankly messianic and Christological interpretation, Jesus is identified as the living stone.

It is clear that there is in late Jewish and early Christian documents a tradition presented in the image of a *lithos* and interpreted in messianic terms. In specifically Christian circles that tradition is applied to Jesus, an application which attains its fullest expression in 1 Peter 2:4–8. Following this traditional designation of Jesus as Messiah, there is highlighted in vv. 9–10 the traditional characteristics of the messianic community, the Church. It is in this context that the priestly character of the Church is introduced.

The opening phrase of v. 9, "you are a chosen race, a royal priest-hood (*basileion hierateuma*), a holy nation," derives from the great covenant formula of Exodus 19:6. Despite a relatively wide variation in both the textual transmission and theological interpretation of this formula, Elliott's general conclusion remains convincing: it expresses the great theme of Israel's *election.* "Despite all variations and particular nuances, a fundamental significance of the expression of Exodus 19:6 can be found underlying and relating all references to this verse: God's true people, Israel, is his elect, holy and private community. . . . Its basic interpretation of Israel's election and holiness, though occasionally only implicit, remains constant."[7] It is employed in 1 Peter 2:4–10 to describe the election, the characteristics and the task of witness of the new elect community, the Church, living stones, in parallel to the elect Messiah, the living stone. For the purposes of this analysis only one characteristic of the Church needs reflection, namely, its being a holy priesthood (*hierateuma hagion*) and a royal priesthood (*basileion hierateuma*).

In the Hebrew text of Exodus 19:6 there is a parallelism between *mamleket kohanim* and *goy-quados.* In the normal reading of Hebrew parallels the emphasis falls on the second member, in this case the holy people, and the first member acts as a kind of adjectival clause modifying the second one. And so a *kingdom of priests* describes the holy people; the people is to be holy as priests are holy. Selwyn points out that *holy* describes primarily the relation of belonging to Yahweh, "for which purpose the holy person or thing is separated from the world and from secular uses and consecrated to him."[8] As a consequence of his separation from the world and his attachment to Yahweh, a priest has a special, intimate closeness to him, and therefore is holy. As a consequence of its election Israel is also a kingdom, in the dynamic sense of being called into being by a king's covenant, a *konigsbund* as Martin Buber called it.[9] It is thus a holy kingdom, holy as priests are holy; it is a kingdom of priests.

Absolutely central in this covenant text is the notion of the elect people. It is this elect people, not individuals within it, that is both holy and a kingdom of priests. There is no contrast here to the levitical priesthood, no polemic against it. "An interpretation which would find in these words an intentional contrast over against a special priesthood and office of mediation is anachronistic and unsupported by the text. . . . The contrast is not over against a levitical priesthood but over against the Gentiles, as is clear in v. 5b, 'from among the peoples.' "[10]

The writer of 1 Peter cites the Septuagint form of Exodus 19:6, not the Hebrew form; he cites the abstract *royal priesthood,* not the concrete *kingdom of priests*. But the intended meaning is still a corporate one, as v. 9 makes clear. There we encounter a succession of corporate designations: "a chosen race, a kingdom of priests, a holy nation, God's own people." That those to whom the letter is addressed are that race and kingdom and nation and people is clear from the phrase, "you are a chosen race. . . . " Those who are called to believe in the *lithos*-Messiah are a messianic Church, a kingdom called into being by the great King to be holy as priests are holy. It is precisely because they are such a Church, such a Spirit-filled household (*oikos pneumatikos*), that they are to offer spiritual sacrifices. It is the elect and holy-as-priests character of the Church that is in center stage here, not any sort of priestly, cultic function. It is the Church that is a priestly people, not its individual members who are "priests."[11] It is only as members of this priestly people that baptized Christians are priests. Even as late as the end of the eleventh century we find this notion of the priestly people underscored in the discussion of Eucharistic concelebration. Abbott Guerricus of Igny teaches that "the priest does not sacrifice by himself, he does not consecrate by himself, but the whole assembly of believers consecrates and sacrifices along with him."[12]

The notion of the Church as a priestly people continues in the forefront of the writings of the Fathers of the Church. There, however, it is linked to baptism, which itself is presented as a messianic anointing in image of the anointing of Jesus as the *Christos*. The *Apostolic Constitutions* declares that those who are baptized "are made Christians by Christ, a royal priesthood (*basileion hierateuma*), a holy nation, an Ekklesia of God, who were once not a people, but now are beloved and elected."[13] As in 1 Peter, there is the emphasis on election and on the demand for the holiness as of priests which flows from it. At the end of the second century Theophilus, bishop of Antioch, derives the name *Christian* from our anointing with the oil of God.[14] In his *De Vita Christiana*, Augustine teaches that both *Christ* and *Christian* derive from anointing, and that the anointing is to be prophet, to be priest and to be king.[15] Hesychius, a fifth century presbyter of Jerusalem, states unequivocally that "the baptized are anointed with a priestly anointing."[16] Jerome is careful to make precise that the anointing is not so much with oil as it is with the Holy Spirit.[17] But we are getting chronologically ahead of ourselves and must return to the New Testament. There we shall find that although Jewish priestly terminology is not employed to model either Christian ministers or ministries, other Jewish models are.

In the Torah tradition elders (*zeqenim*) provide colleges of leaders. These are everywhere presupposed, though nowhere is their establishment dealt with.[18] It is assumed that the colleges of elders had their origin in the earliest tribal period, prior to the amphictyony. The account in Numbers 11:16–17 where Moses, at God's command, appoints seventy elders "to bear the burden of the people with you," an account which is repeated in a more generalized way in Deuteronomy 1:9–18 in Moses' parting discourse, formalizes the tradition and validates the elders as bearers of the spirit of Moses and, therefore, of an official authority. This account became also the model for the Jewish Sanhedrin and the number of its elders. It was invoked also, as we shall see in *The Apostolic Tradition,* at the institution of Christian *presbyteroi.*

That there were presbyter-elders in the first Jerusalem Church is clear from Acts. They are mentioned for the first time, as something not requiring explanation, as something taken entirely for granted, in 11:30, where they are the recipients of the collection brought from Antioch by Saul and Barnabas. In Acts 15 Paul and Barnabas are "appointed to go up to Jerusalem to the apostles and elders" (v. 2) about the question of circumcision, and are welcomed in Jerusalem by "the apostles and elders" (v. 4), who gather to consider the matter and deliver judgment on it. They appear again in Acts 21:18 where they gather with James, who clearly presides, to hear Paul's account of his ministry. The *presbyteroi* function as an official authority in the Jerusalem congregation.

In contrast to this Jewish presbyteral organization in the Jerusalem community, the Hellenistic churches established by Paul offer quite a different picture. In the genuinely Pauline letters there is no reference whatever to *presbyteroi.* In the First Letter to the Corinthians (12:28), he declares that "God has appointed in the Church first apostles, second prophets, third teachers, then workers of power, then the charisms of healers, helpers, administrators, and speakers of tongues." In Romans (12:6–8), he speaks of the different charisms of prophet, server, teacher, almoner and almsgiver. He writes also "to all the saints in Christ Jesus who are at Philippi with their overseers (*episkopoi*) and deacons" (Phil 1:1). When talking of ministry Paul seems to mingle offices and charisms. Indeed, he seems to look upon offices precisely as charisms, and tends to give precedence to the charismatic apostles, prophets and teachers.

It is toward the end of the New Testament era that we begin to detect the development of presbyteral colleges in the Gentile churches, under the influence of Hellenistic Judaism.[19] We read about it in the Deutero-Pauline letters. In 1 Timothy 5:1 *presbyteros* is clearly an elder in age, opposed to *neoteros,* but this is not the sole meaning of these terms in the letter. In 4:14 the *presbyteroi* are a *presbyterion* (college) which laid hands on Timothy. In 5:17 *presbyteroi* rule, and in 5:19 they enjoy special disciplinary privilege. Titus was charged with appointing *presbyterous* in every town to "correct what was defective" (1:5). It seems clear from this evidence that a presbyter is not just an elder in age, but also an elder who has received institutional office in the Church. Similarly, neither is *neoteros* simply a younger in age but also someone with authority, subordinate though to the presbyters. Brown believes that *neoteros* is interchangeable with *diakonos*, as demonstrated by Luke 22:16: "Let the greatest among you become as the youngest (*neoteros*), and the leader as one who serves (*diakonos*)."[20]

The same Jewish-Christian procedure, namely, the granting of institutional office to chronological elders, can be detected in the Jewish-Christian letter of James 5:14. In case of sickness, believers are to summon "the elders (*tous presbyterous*) of the Church" to pray over the sick person and to anoint him with oil "in the name of the Lord." The summons is not for chronological elders, nor for charismatics with healing gifts. Rather is it for institutional elders, elders who hold official authority in the Church, a fact which appears from the use of the article *tous*. An essentially similar picture appears from the First Letter of Peter. Here *presbyteroi* appears in a context of exhortation from the writer, who is *sympresbyteros* (5:1). As in Acts 20:28, *presbyteroi* are to shepherd the flock, not for personal gain or for personal power, but as "examples to the flock" (v. 3). The fact that in v. 5a the *neoteroi* are instructed to be subject to the *presbyteroi* indicates not merely the dyad of chronological elder-younger, but also the patriarchal character of the institutional *presbyterion*.

In Acts 20:28 the college of presbyters is composed of *episkopoi*, whose task is described in the classical Old Testament image of pasturing the flock. In 1 Peter 5:2, in a passage addressed as we have seen to *presbyteroi*, the presbyteral task is again imaged as pasturing the flock, and as *episkopountes*. After the recollection that Titus was charged with appointing *presbyteroi*, there follows immediately the qualities to be sought in an *episkopos* (1:6–9), qualities which are listed again essentially in 1 Timothy 3:1–7. The Letter to the Philippians is addressed to "all the saints in Christ Jesus who are at Philippi *sun episkopois*" (1:1). This interplay between the words *presbyteros* and *episkopos* raises two questions. First, what is the relation between *presbyteros* and *episkopos*? Second, at what time does *episkopos* become an institutional title distinct from *presbyteros*? We must confront these questions briefly.

The approach to answering these questions should be governed by Spicq's caution, which remains true. "It is impossible to pass clear and firm judgment on *episkopos* in the letters of the New Testament, on its nature, its functions, its relations with *presbyteros;* first of all because it is mentioned rarely; then because this fluid word, borrowed from profane usage,[21] had not in the beginning a technical meaning; then because 'letters' do not define ideas and refer implicitly to facts known by their readers."[22] That caution granted, however, a general answer can still be given to the first question. "The *episkopos* of the pastorals should be considered as a *presbyteros* enjoying here or there a supreme authority, or better a more particularly defined ministry."[23] This is the common opinion.[24] *Presbyteroi* and *episkopoi* are synonymous terms, and those who are so described belong to the same presbyteral college. The homogeneity of the New Testament evidence indicates this. But by the time of the pastoral letters,[25] where *episkopos* occurs always only in the singular, the episcopal presbyter is emerging from the presbyteral college as a *primus inter pares*,[26] functioning as president, overseer, guardian, pastor and all-round vice-regent of the one president, overseer, guardian, pastor and "*episkopos* of your souls" (1 Pet 2:25), the Lord Jesus Christ.[27]

We can summarize the New Testament data relating to *presbyteros-episkopos* and Church order this way. The *un*priestly character of New Testament ministers remains evident. The New Testament communities show evidence of a variety of ministries, but priesthood is not one of them. Jesus is the sole high priest (though, to repeat, the Church situation in the Letter to the Hebrews is not to be generalized to the entire New Testament). Raymond Brown calls attention to two developments which had to occur before the idea of a specifically Christian priesthood could emerge. "First, Christians had to think of themselves as constituting a new religion distinct from Judaism." This, as is now well-accepted, was not at all a dominant view prior to the destruction of the temple in the year 70 and the excommunication of Christians from the synagogues between the years 85 and 90. Second, "Christianity had to have a sacrifice at which priesthood could preside. This second condition was fulfilled when the Eucharist was seen as an unbloody sacrifice no longer offered in the now-destroyed temple."[28] This did not happen until the end of the first century and the beginning of the second, and it is then that the cultic, priestly analogies begin to be applied to Christian ministers. Before moving on to consider these developments, however, there are other ministerial arrangements to consider in the New Testament.

We have already seen that the presbyteral form of Church order is lacking in the genuinely Pauline letters. There the ministerial emphasis is on apostles, prophets and teachers. The same can be said of the Matthean communities, as they are known to us from Matthew's Gospel. Prophets, teachers, wise men, rabbis are known (cf. Mt 5:12; 7:22; 10:41; 11:25; 13:52; 23:8–10, 34). But Matthew's attitude toward them is clear: "You are not to be called rabbi, for you have one teacher, and you are all brethren. And call no man your father on earth, for you have one Father who is in heaven. Neither be called masters, for you have one Master, the Christ" (23:8–10). Leadership in the Matthean community, as indeed it is throughout the New Testament, is a leadership of *diakonia* or service, not a leadership of power. Or, as Küng puts it more precisely, it is power deriving from service. The antonyms are not power and service, as they are sometimes said to be, but rather "the use of power as domination and the use of power as service."[29] This judgment is but an echo of Origen, who teaches that "whoever is called to the episcopacy is not called to lordship but to service of the whole Church,"[30] and of Augustine, who asks for the prayers of his flock that he might be "not so much placed over you as of service to you."[31] These, in turn, are no more than echoes of Matthew's "He who is greatest among you shall be your servant" (23:11; cf. 1 Cor 16:15; 2 Cor 4:1; 5:18; 6:3; Eph 4:11–12; Col 4:1; 2 Tim 4:5, in all of which the RSV chooses to translate *diakonia*–service as *ministry*.)

Matthew's community is concerned with righteousness and the kingdom of God (cf. 6:33 and 5:20), that is, with the rule of God and a life style that derives from and reflects this rule. All the followers of Christ, not excluding the leaders of the community, stand under the critique of righteousness, and Matthew is at pains to show how they do not measure up. His parable of the king who made a wedding feast for his son and of the sower emphasize that "bad and good" were gathered in for the wedding (22:10) and that "the good seed means the sons of the kingdom" and "the weeds are the sons of the evil one" (13:38; cf. 18:7). The disciples of Jesus, in his own time, in Matthew's time, and in our time, are believers, but "of little faith" (6:30; 8:26; 14:31; 16:8; 17:20). Even the community rock, Simon-Kepha-Peter, does not measure up (14:28–31; 16:17–23; 18:21–35; 26:40,69–75), perhaps the paradigmatic prototype not only of every Christian leader, but also of every Christian believer. Matthew's community does not seem to know the deutero-Pauline presbyteral arrangement, which was to become normative in the Christian Church. It offers evidence, rather, of a freer, more charismatic approach.

The communities that we know from the letters of John (the Gospel of John says nothing whatever about ministry) do betray a presbyteral arrangement (2 John 1; 3 John 1). But their presbyters had no authority beyond that of bearing witness to and teaching the tradition handed down by the great bearer of the tradition in these communities, namely, the "beloved disciple."[32] The real teacher in these communities is, of course, the one who guides into "all the truth" (Jn 16:13; 1 Jn 2:27), the Spirit-Paraclete. Human ministers merely hand on the teaching of this Paraclete, a task which is performed initially by the beloved disciple (Jn 19:35; 21:24) and then, after his death, by his followers. The writer of 1 John is one of those followers, and so he can claim that "that which we have seen and heard we proclaim also to you" (1:3; cf. 1:1), not because he was himself an eye-witness (he writes too late to be that), but because he stands in the tradition of the beloved disciple and teaches out of it. But when there is a conflict about that tradition, as there clearly is in 2 and 3 John, the presbyter who claims to speak, and who is accepted canonically as speaking, for the tradition can do no more than try to convince his opponents that they have seceded from the tradition. He cannot do more. He cannot command with the apostolic authority of a Peter or a Paul; he cannot excommunicate with the later authority of an Ignatius of Antioch or a Pius of Rome; he can only challenge the secessionists to consider the tradition (2 Jn 9–10), to "test the spirits to see whether they are of God" (1 Jn 4:1), for all have been anointed by the Spirit and "all know" (1 Jn 2:20).

Even this brief sketch of the evidence makes quite clear that there is in the New Testament a variety of ministerial structures, from the loosely charismatic structure of prophets and teachers (with little real distinction between these two) to the more institutionalized oversight of *presbyteroi* and *episkopoi*. This variety is linked to geographical and cultural differences ranging from early Jewish-Christian communities, through the first Gentile churches, to the later churches of the pastoral letters. The presbyteral structure is the one that became dominant, already in the second century, and became sacralized into a cultic priesthood. Such a development is entirely legitimate. From the beginning, in fact, it would appear that what the Church did was to validate the ministers that it needed to ensure substantial fidelity to the apostolic—and to the Jesus—tradition (cf. Acts 6:1–6), though the Apocalypse of Peter, which is an early document in the Matthean tradition, polemicized sharply against the institutional form of Church order.

It is striking, and perhaps something to be learned in the contemporary Church, that the more charismatic type of community disappeared entirely in the second century, or persisted only at the periphery of or quite apart from the "great Church." Schillebeeckx' comment is apposite. "Ministry without charisma becomes starved and threatens to turn into a power institution; charisma without any institutionalization threatens to be volatilized into fanaticism and pure subjectivity."[33] That notwithstanding, this much is clear: that the presbyteral form of Church order, though indeed very ancient, *ab antiquo* as Vatican II judiciously says,[34] is not from the beginning, not *ab initio*. It does not enjoy the universal support of the New Testament, nor does it derive from direct institution from Jesus. In careful acknowledgment of this fact, Vatican II's Constitution on the Church introduces changes in an important teaching of the Council of Trent, changes which, though apparently trivial in themselves, are of importance for a theology of ministers and ministry.

Trent had taught this: "If anyone says that there is not, by divine ordination (*divina ordinatione*) in the Catholic Church, a hierarchy which is composed (*constet*) of bishops, priests and ministers, let him be anathema."[35] Vatican II changed that wording to be in meticulous line with the unquestionable historical evidence. It replaced *hierarchy* with *ecclesial ministry* (*ministerium ecclesiasticum*), so that it asserts not that the hierarchical form of ministry is of divine institution, but simply the ministry itself. Further it replaces *is composed of* with *is exercised by* those who *ab antiquo* have been called bishops.[36] Recognizing the historical fact that *ab initio* ministry and forms of ministry in the Church were pluriform, it loosens the necessary and exclusive connection of ministry to hierarchy and opens up avenues for a broader concept of ministry today. But we run ahead of ourselves, and must return to the track.

FROM THE NEW TESTAMENT TO THE COUNCIL OF TRENT

The *Didache*, which is closely related to the Matthean tradition and, if Audet's dating is correct, written prior to the year 70,[37] and therefore before Matthew's Gospel, speaks of apostles (11:4–6), prophets (11:7–12) and teachers (13:2), all of whom are to be supported. The apostles, of course, are not the famous twelve, but those holding office in the *Didache* communities, and who share with prophets and teachers the task of proclaiming the Gospel (*kerygma*) and of interpreting it for the present (*didache*). The *Didache* also, almost unexpectedly, speaks of *episkopoi* and *diakonoi*, urging the communities to "choose *episkopoi* and *diakonoi* worthy of the Lord . . . for they too fulfill the office of prophets and teachers among you" (15:1–2). Significantly, it describes the prophets as *archiereis*–high priests (13:13), and states that they are to be allowed to preside at Eucharist (10:7), which is described as the clean sacrifice (14:2–3). In the subsequent tradition, of course, as is well known, it is the episcopal office that will develop along cultic and priestly lines. It is this development that I must now document.

By the end of the first century and the opening of the second, there is detectable a drive toward the universal establishment of the episcopal-presbyteral church order. A first testimony is provided by the Letter of Clement to the Corinthians, where two points are of importance. The first is that Clement defends the position and the rights of the *presbyteroi* against the Corinthian congregation by appealing to the fact that, as God sent Christ and Christ sent apostles, so also apostles sent *episkopoi* and *diakonoi* to continue their tradition (c. 42). Though he cannot claim that Jesus appointed *episkopoi*, and thus cannot claim that they are directly willed by God, he does claim that in the succession God-Jesus-apostles-*episkopoi* they are indirectly willed by him. It is its derivation in the will of God, and not just in the will of the Church, that bestows on the episcopal-presbyteral office a permanent character. In Clement, *episkopoi-presbyteroi* are regarded not just as those who carry on the apostolic tradition, but also as themselves an integral element in that tradition. It is precisely because they are such an element in that tradition that they are to be accorded the highest respect and restored to their office.

The second point of note in Clement's letter is that the ministry of the *presbyteroi* is a cultic ministry. It is a *leitourgia* (cc. 40, 42), an offering of gifts (c. 44). Again, this "exclusive orientation of the presbyteral office to cultus," as Bornkamm rightly notes, "and the patent clericalizing make it possible for Clement to proclaim the inviolability of the office bearers and the lifelong nature of their office (c. 44)."[38] The only solution, therefore, to the Corinthian problem in which Clement intervenes is for the deposed *presbyteroi* to be restored to their office, and for the rebellious congregation to submit to them (c. 57).

The Shepherd of Hermas, written in Rome in the first half of the second century, some decades after Clement, provides further insight. The Church in Rome is governed by a patriarchal presbyterate (Vis. 2:4), which is honored with the first places (Vis. 3:1). These presbyters are called also *episkopoi* (Vis. 3:5; Sim. 9:27), and their task is described in the traditional Jewish image of shepherding the flock (Sim. 9:31).[39] In Hermas the presbyteral college is peacefully established as an office in the Church.

In Ignatius of Antioch (d. c. 117) we encounter for the first time a clearly delineated different picture, in which an *episkopos* is not just a member of a presbyteral college but also its head. His letters to the

224 SYMBOL AND SACRAMENT

Magnesians and to the Smyrneans indicate similar ministerial arrangements in those places, with Damas presiding as *episkopos* over the Magnesians and Polycarp over the Smyrneans.[40] The *episkopos* presides, surrounded by his *presbyteroi*, who form an apostolic council[41] to sustain him.[42] "No one is to do anything in the Church without the *episkopos*. A valid Eucharist is one which is under either his presidency or the presidency of a representative appointed by him. . . . It is not right to baptize without the *episkopos*, nor to celebrate the agape without him. Whatever he approves is approved also by God, so that everything which is done might be stable and secure."[43] The Philadelphians are urged to desire only one Eucharist, "for there is one flesh of our Lord Jesus Christ, and one cup in the unity of his blood, one altar, as there is one *episkopos* with a presbytery and deacons."[44] The college of presbyters is attuned to its *episkopos* as the strings of a lyre, and conducted by the *episkopos* the whole Church sings as a harmonious chorus to the Father through Jesus Christ.[45]

Ignatius foreshadows a development which was to become normative in the Church. Whereas in the pastorals and in Clement and in Hermas *presbyteros* and *episkopos* are used interchangeably, so that it is difficult to specify their respective offices, Ignatius reserves *episkopos* for the clearly defined and institutionalized head of the presbytery. The college of presbyters is now an equally institutionalized council of leaders in the Church of Antioch, but it can do nothing without its episcopal head. The gap between the two offices is heightened by the imagery used of them. *Episkopos* stands "in place of God," presbyter "in place of a council of apostles."[46] The differential could not be clearer. But there is still no suggestion that the *episkopos* is *hiereus*, even though it is clear that Ignatius alone now ordinarily presides at Eucharist.[47]

If in the Eastern world Ignatius of Antioch is the first to underscore the *episkopos* as more than just a first among equals, Irenaeus of Lyons is the first in the West. Irenaeus was a student of the same Polycarp to whom Ignatius wrote as *episkopos Smyrnes*. Following a period of study in Rome, he moved to Gaul and became *episkopos* of Lyons at the end of the persecution under Marcus Aurelius in 177. His time in Smyrna had initiated him into an Eastern tradition; his time in Rome had given him an insight into a different, Western tradition. In Lyons the two traditions converge.

Irenaeus tends still to use *episkopos* and *presbyteros*, now in their Latin equivalents *episcopus* and *presbyterus*, interchangeably. He urges, for instance, that in the Church it is necessary to obey the presbyters who have succession from the apostles and who have received, together with this episcopal succession, the gift of truth.[48] False presbyters, who serve their own lusts and pride and who do not serve God, are to be avoided. Those who preserve the "doctrine of the apostles" and who display blameless conduct in their presbyterate are to be heeded.[49] It is precisely because he stands in the apostolic succession and hands on the apostolic tradition that the *episcopus*, whether of Smyrna or of Rome or of Lyons, has pre-eminent claim to the title of *presbyterus*, because as *episcopus* he stands in a line of elders who knew the apostles and who received from them the tradition that is still normative in the Church.[50]

There is as yet no equivalence between *episcopi* and apostles; apostles are unique. And so the list of the *episcopi* of Rome begins, not with Peter and Paul who "founded and constituted" it, but with Linus to whom "they handed over the *episcope* of administering the Church." The *episcope* of Linus and his successors, and of Irenaeus too, is precisely an *episcope* of ensuring fidelity to the teachings established by the apostles. By thus linking *episcope* to apostolic succession, Irenaeus adds stature to the episcopal office. But we must be clear whence that stature derives. Irenaeus "is far from attributing the privileged position of bishops to certain powers which they possess, but sees it rather in the fidelity with which they have maintained the apostolic teaching, and in the fact that they have received this tradition and the charge to keep it."[51]

But if Irenaeus maintained a clear distinction between apostles and *episcopi,* Cyprian of Carthage in the middle of the third century did not. He saw the apostles as the first *episcopi* and *episcopi* of his day as their successors, holding the very same position in the Church that the apostles held. He applies to both the Lukan word: "He who hears you hears me and he who rejects you rejects me, and he who rejects me rejects him who sent me" (10:16).[52] This allows him to argue to the superiority of the episcopacy over other orders, since "the Lord elected apostles, that is *episcopi* and leaders, whereas deacons were constituted ministers by the apostles."[53]

Based on this strong foundation, Cyprian's position on the primacy of the episcopacy is not hard to understand. "You should know that the *episcopus* is in the Church and the Church is in the *episcopus,* and whoever is not with the *episcopus* is not with the Church."[54] Interpreting the Petrine text in Matthew 16:18–19 of the episcopate, he argues that the episcopacy is the very foundation on which the Church is built.[55] This is true not only in the Church universal, but also in each and every local church: "There is one God and one Christ and one Church and one chair founded on a rock by the word of the Lord."[56] The chair founded on a rock is, of course, the *episcopus*. Authority in the Church is his, and theirs,[57] and he and they are the cement by which the Church is bound and joined together.[58] For all the exalted dignity of the *episcopus*, though, he is elected by the whole Christian community, *episcopi*, presbyters and laity alike.[59]

But more important than his highlighting and legitimating the monarchical *episcopus* is Cyprian's casting of Christian ministry into priestly terminology. The one chair founded on a rock founds not only one Church but also one altar and one priesthood,[60] which is to serve that altar and its sacrifices and its prayers.[61] Because priests are to serve the altar they must be free not only from all uncleanness,[62] but also from all worldly care and, therefore, just like the Levites of old, are to be supported by the faithful.[63] In Cyprian, the casting of episcopal ministry into priestly terms had begun. For him the *episcopus* is undoubtedly *sacerdos*. Presbyters share in his priesthood,[64] and Cyprian delegates them to preside at Eucharist[65] and *exomologesis*[66] in his absence. This sharing in the priesthood of their *episcopus* will lead to presbyters also being designated as *sacerdos*-priest. And then the transition from an originally unpriestly ministry in the Church to a priestly ministry will have been accomplished.

The priestly character of the *episcopus*, whom I shall designate henceforth as bishop, is becoming clear also in Rome earlier in the third century. In his *Apostolic Tradition* Hippolytus, a Roman presbyter (d. 235), gives us a good picture of a Roman Church order. A bishop, he tells us, is chosen by all the people, who then gather on a Sunday with their presbyters and neighboring bishops to consecrate him. The consecration is done by the assembled bishops, who impose hands on the bishop-elect while one of their number prays a very priestly prayer of consecration. "Father, who knows all hearts, grant to this thy servant whom you have chosen for the episcopacy to pasture your holy flock and to exercise the high priesthood before you without reproach, serving you day and night. Grant him to propitiate you without ceasing, to offer the gifts of thy holy Church, to have in the spirit of the high priesthood the power to remit sins according to your command."[67]

The prayer for the ordination of a presbyter also betrays a very Jewish theme, the theme of Moses and the seventy elders to whom Jewish elders trace their origin. Roman presbyters, as Roman bishops, were chosen by all the people. They were ordained by all the presbyters, including the bishop, imposing hands while the bishop alone prayed. "God the Father of our Lord Jesus Christ, look upon this thy servant, and grant unto him the spirit of grace and counsel of a presbyter, that he may care for and govern thy people with a pure heart, just as you looked upon the people of thy choice and commanded

Moses to elect presbyters, whom you filled with thy spirit which you gave your servant."[68] Though called rulers in this prayer of ordination, the power of the presbyters was severely limited by that of their bishop, and decreased as his increased. There is no indication at this time that they had any liturgical function apart from the bishop, though they could place their hands with his over the offerings, break the bread, administer the cup, and speak at the *agape* if the bishop was absent.[69] Eusebius tells us that in Rome in the mid-third century there were under the bishop forty-four presbyters, seven deacons, seven subdeacons, and fifteen hundred widows, infirm and needy.[70]

The bishops of the *Apostolic Tradition*, like those of Cyprian's Carthage, were chosen by the entire ecclesial community. This election was of such importance that the one elected was expected to bow to it, even if he was personally reluctant, as happened with the great Augustine of Hippo and his mentor, Ambrose of Milan.[71] The importance of ecclesial election, though, did not derive exclusively from the Church, but from the fact that it also proclaimed, realized and celebrated election by the Spirit of God. Episcopal ordination also was experienced as a joint action of the Church and the Spirit. The election-ordination of a bishop in the Roman Church was both from above and from below, a fact which was liturgically expressed in the ritual described by Hippolytus: a laying on of hands by neighboring bishops (in 325 the Council of Nicaea decreed that there should be three of them[72]), together with an *epiklesis,* a prayer of the Church to the Holy Spirit to make this man a bishop. At a later date, John Chrysostom will put the matter beyond doubt. "The hand of a man is imposed, but it is God who accomplishes all; and it is his hand that touches the head of the one being ordained when he ought to be ordained."[73]

The decisiveness of the activity of the Spirit in the election-ordination process is well underscored by what the *Apostolic Tradition* says of confessors, those who have suffered for the cause of Christ but who have not been put to death. Because of his suffering as a witness to Christ, such a person clearly has the gift of the Spirit: "He has the honor of the priesthood because of his confession." If he is elected subsequently as either a deacon or a presbyter, he needs no imposition of hands; if he is elected a bishop, hands must be laid on him.[74]

His election by the Church and the Spirit establishes the bishop as the high priest of the community, as the one who serves it, pastures it, propitiates in and for it, offers its gifts, remits its sins and distributes its offices. The power structure we already saw in Clement is exemplified here once again. The power with which God sent Christ and with which Christ sent apostles is now passed on to this bishop who stands in the tradition of the apostles, a fact which is not assumed but is to be tested and verified by the Church.[75] Indeed, this verification of the apostolicity of both the local church and the one whom it has elected bishop is one of the functions of the three bishops who ordain this new bishop. In this ritual act they acknowledge him and his Church as unimpeachable witnesses to the apostolic tradition, and he becomes leader both of his church to the Catholic Church and of the Catholic Church to his local church. The relationship of the bishop to an apostolic community is crucial, and later became enshrined in the law of the Church. But before expanding on that, I must say something about another ancient document which presents bishops as priests.

The third century Syrian document, *Didascalia Apostolorum*, the Greek text of which is embodied in the later third century *Apostolic Constitutions*,[76] presents a picture of a Church order which is Ignatian with a heavily Jewish flavor. Bishops are "priests ministering to your people and levites ministering to the holy tabernacle, that is, the holy Church of God, and standing at the altar of the Lord our God," to whom they offer "reasonable and unbloody offerings through Jesus the High Priest."[77] They are high priests, superior to every other minister in the Church; they are guardians of wisdom; they are mediators between God and believers; they are fathers of all after God, princes and leaders and kings; they are earthly gods after God, of whom it was said "You are gods, sons of the Most High, all of you (Ps 82:6)."[78] The faithful are instructed "to venerate the Lord God in your leaders, and to look upon your bishops as the mouth of God."[79]

The bishop of the *Didascalia* is a regal, almost divine person—a far cry from not only the ministers of the Matthean and Johannine communities, but also the *presbyteros-episkopos* of the pastorals. Here there is no longer doubt, as there was in the pastorals, about the relationship of *episkopos* and *presbyteros*. The Didascalian high priest-bishop completely overshadows his presbyters in authority, and he alone, in distinction to the community election found in the *Apostolic Tradition*, elects them to their position. Indeed, presbyters are overshadowed by deacons who are the bishop's right-hand men. Ministry in the Church of the *Didascalia* is as triune as God. The bishop occupies the place of the Father, the deacon that of the Christ, the presbyter that of the apostle who teaches "all things that I have commanded you (Mt 28:19)."[80] But for all the quasi-godliness of the bishop, his ordination depends upon the testing and verification by the Church of his apostolicity, that is, his faithfulness to the tradition of the apostles.[81] Strangely, for such an exalted office, the other characteristics required of him are the simple family-man characteristics enunciated already in the pastorals.

That the Ekklesia-community played a central role not only in the testing, election and ordination of its priest-bishop, but also in his functioning, is demonstrated by the consideration of two important facts. First, no bishop could be ordained apart from some community which elected him as its overseer. Cyprian insists, against Pope Stephen, that this is of divine origin.[82] Later, Pope Celestine decrees that "no bishop is to be imposed on people who do not want him. The consent and the wish of clerics and people is required."[83] Leo the Great, two hundred years later, is equally emphatic: "He who is to preside over all must be chosen by all. There is required the vote of the clergy, the testimony of honored witnesses, the consent of order and of the people."[84] Ministry in the Church is a public matter, in the sense that it is a matter, not for private individuals to take upon themselves or to be given apart from the Church, but for the Church as a whole to be concerned with and to call to. "Ministry is defined in essentially ecclesial terms, and not as an ontological qualification of the person of the minister apart from the determinative context of the Church."[85]

So accepted was this view that it was enshrined as the law of the Church in the Council of Chalcedon (451), which taught that the absolute ordination of a minister, that is, his ordination without appointment to a function in a particular church, was invalid. "No one may be ordained in an absolute manner (*apolelumenos* = without lien), neither a presbyter nor a deacon nor any cleric of any rank whatever in the ecclesiastical order, unless there has been assigned to him in a precise manner either an urban church, or a rural church, or a confession or a monastery. This holy council declares that the ordination of whoever is ordained absolutely is invalid and that he may not exercise the functions of ordination."[86] So strong was this feeling of the need for a minister to be linked to a community that Paulinus of Nola would later complain piously that, because he was ordained absolutely, he was "a priest only to the Lord and not also in some church."[87] The Councils of Pavia (850)[88] and Piacenza (1095)[89] declare themselves in full agreement with Chalcedon, and Isidore of Seville calls those ordained absolutely (which means, of course, that some were so ordained, contrary to the law) headless clerics, neither laity nor clerics.[90] The Decree of Gratian (ca. 1140) repeats without comment both canon 6 of Chalcedon and its invalidation of absolute ordination.[91] The Third Council of Lateran (1179) would reinterpret this practice radically, but that cannot gainsay the fact that it was the practice of the Church for many centuries.

The second fact enlightening the place of the community in the functioning of bishop-priests is one to which I have alluded briefly already. It is that the whole Church concelebrated the Eucharist under the leadership of its bishop-overseer. Guerricus of Igny, as we have already seen, asserts at the end of the eleventh century that the priest "does not sacrifice by himself, he does not consecrate by himself, but the whole assembly of believers consecrates and sacrifices along with him."[92] It is but an echo of an earlier *Liber Pontificalis* which teaches that "every age concelebrates,"[93] young and old alike. Congar has shown beyond dispute how in the early Church it was the community itself, and not just its *sacerdos*, which offered the bread and the wine.[94] The bishop presided, prayed, blessed, not with the exclusive power assigned to him by a much later theology, but simply as the leader of this church, presiding, praying and blessing in its name. Concelebration did not mean, as it came later to mean and still means today, the common celebration of Eucharist by priests who have the "power" and who recite in common the great *anaphora* of the canon. Liturgical ministry, as all ministry in the Church, was a matter for the entire Church, not just for a special caste with a special power derived from special ordination. That I have to insist on this, of course, is a sure sign that things have changed—and to that change I must now turn.

As is not uncommon in Church history, and there is valuable information here for those who ask how change can occur in the Catholic Church, the decree of Chalcedon invalidating absolute ordination was not infrequently ignored and violated. We have already heard Paulinus of Nola's complaint that he was a priest only to the Lord and not to some church, and Isidore's teaching that those who were absolutely ordained were headless clerics. And in 1088 Pope Urban II, while acknowledging the invalidation of absolute ordination by the ancient canons, allowed them to take place "because of the present necessity of the Church."[95] In 1179 the illegal practice of ordaining absolutely in contravention of the Chalcedonian law was raised to the status of Church law by the Third Lateran Council, through the simple expedient of reinterpreting the Chalcedonian statement. What was originally a prohibition of ordination without a function in some church was interpreted to be a prohibition of ordination "without prior assurance of a proper living."[96] *Titulus ecclesiae*, which originally meant having a function in a church, after Lateran III meant being assured of support.

What happened to the law of absolute ordination is just one specific example of how changes occur frequently in the Church. It is only one example, but it can be said truthfully that things have always been that way. So much, indeed, have things always been that way that the early Scholastics elevated the practice of ignoring a Church law to the level of a universal theory, the theory of the *non-acceptatio legis*. A law, whatever be its value or non-value, is simply ignored by such a majority in the Church that it becomes irrelevant, and the illegality deriving from its non-observance becomes the dominant practice of and is sanctioned ultimately by the Church. This theory fits perfectly the case of the Chalcedonian decree invalidating absolute ordinations, and the subsequent Lateran decree making legal what was originally illegal. This Lateran decree marks a momentous moment in the history of the theology of ministry in the Catholic Church. Allied to a later decree of Lateran IV in 1215, which established that "no one can accomplish (*conficere*) this sacrament (Eucharist) except a priest who has been validly and legitimately (*rite*) ordained,"[97] it changed the face of the theology of orders. Relying on Henri de Lubac's classic *Corpus Mysticum*,[98] Schillebeeckx describes this change.

In the ancient Church, the Church was known as the body of Christ, indeed as the true body of Christ (*corpus Christi verum*). To be ordained validly and legitimately to oversee this true body of Christ, a man needed to be appointed to a function in and by this body. In the medieval Church, the focus of attention switched from the Church–true body of Christ to another body of Christ, the Eucharist, called the mystical body of Christ (*corpus Christi mysticum*). To be ordained validly and legitimately to oversee this body of Christ, a man needed to be given power over this body.[99] We can see this shift of relationship from ministry-Church to power-Eucharist illustrated in the teaching of Lateran IV. Eucharistic ministry requires not only someone appointed by the Church to oversee it, but also someone with the power to accomplish it. Medieval theology responded to this new focus on Eucharist-power with a new distinction of power. There was power over a church, *potestas iurisdictionis,* and power over Eucharist, *potestas ordinis.* A man could have the latter without the former; he could accomplish Eucharist without having an ecclesial community to preside over. That, of course, used to be called absolute ordination, and prior to Lateran III was invalid. When such ordination was judged to be valid, a judgment legitimated by the distinction between *potestas ordinis* and *potestas iurisdictionis,* it was but a short step to consecrating Eucharist without a community present. That came to be known as the private Mass.

I do not wish in any way to denigrate private Masses. But I do wish to point out again the call of Vatican II: "Liturgical services are not private functions, but are celebrations of the Church. . . . It is to be stressed that whenever rites . . . make provision for communal celebration involving the presence and active participation of the faithful, this way of celebrating them is to be preferred, as far as possible, to a celebration that is individual and quasi-private. This rule applies with special force to the celebration of Mass and administration of the sacraments, even though every Mass has of itself a public and social nature."[100] Private Masses, clearly, are quite deficient in respect of communal celebration. Why they are deficient should be clear from everything I have said in this book about symbol and sacrament as community action. It is one thing to say that "every Mass has of itself a public and social character." It is quite something else to try to manifest ritually that public character without the presence of an ecclesial community. Presbyters in the Church celebrate the Church's memorial best *with*, not merely *for*, some community.

So thoroughly was presbyteral, now long established as priestly, ministry divorced from its original root in the Church during the medieval period that the high Scholastics, such as Thomas Aquinas, could pass directly from a treatment of Christ to a treatment of sacraments, including the sacrament of orders. Sacraments were judged, correctly, to have a central Christological dimension; they were judged, incorrectly, to have no central ecclesial dimension. When Thomas says, therefore, "It is manifest that the sacrament of orders is ordained to the consecration of Eucharist,"[101] when he says that "orders is a sign in the Church by which a spiritual power is handed over to the man who is ordained,"[102] when he says that "this sacrament consists principally in a power that is handed over,"[103] he is simply echoing the whole of Scholasticism to which it was, indeed, manifest beyond all doubt that the sacrament of orders was about handing over power to consecrate Eucharist. So thoroughly had the ancient discipline and theology of the Church been forgotten, and so thoroughly had the new discipline and theology of sacred power supplanted it, that any other conclusion would have been unthinkable.

But was the ancient discipline truly *forgotten?* Gratian, as we saw, had reported faithfully and happily Chalcedon's canon 6. But when the *Correctores Romani*, as they were called, reviewed it for an official edition of the Canon Law, which appeared in 1582 as the *Editio Romana*, they "changed seriously in two places the Chalcedon text to accommodate it to the theory and praxis of the sixteenth century."[104] On the one hand, they downgraded the relationship to an ecclesial community required by Chalcedon for valid and legitimate ordination, to the Lateran III meaning of benefice. On the other hand, they reduced Chalcedon's decree of the invalidity of absolute ordination to the weak sense that those absolutely, but now validly, ordained could not exercise any presbyteral function. Was the ancient discipline truly *forgotten*, or was it quite consciously *altered*? Vogel comments ironically, maybe sadly: "Perfect in Greek and Latin as they were, the *Correctores* did not commit these mistakes involuntarily."[105]

By the sixteenth century, the theology and practice of ministry in the Western Church had solidified in the direction of a priesthood empowered to preside and consecrate at Eucharist. That theology and practice, which was not supported in all respects by the theology and practice of the New Testament and the ancient Church, both Eastern and Western, was further solidified and validated by the crucially important Council of Trent in the sixteenth century.

Like all historical gatherings, the Council of Trent met in a specific historical setting, and two factors in this setting are important for an understanding of the teachings of the Council. The first is well known: the Council wished to highlight only those Catholic truths which had been denied by the Reformers. Its doctrine, therefore, as the fathers of the Council proclaimed at the beginning of their final document on the sacrament of orders, is "the true and Catholic doctrine of the sacrament of orders *to condemn the errors of our time.*"[106] The doctrine of Trent about orders, then, is to be understood only in this context. It is not a complete setting forth of a Roman Catholic position, and still less a complete setting forth of a Catholic position, but a setting forth only of those facets denied by the Reformers. And so the chapter on orders concludes with the statement that "these are the things which it has seemed good to this sacred Council to teach the faithful *generally* about the sacrament of orders."[107] *Generally*, not *specifically;* a partial teaching, not all that could be said. And there is more that could be, and needs to be, said. For the very polemical circumstances of the time led the Council to respond generally in a very one-sided, cultic way, which ignored the valid, and New Testament-based, non-cultic aspects of ministry in the Christian church.

A second historical factor in the setting of the Council of Trent is as well known as the first, but is more frequently forgotten and/or ignored. It is that there was a complete absence of any representation or influence from the Eastern churches, an influence which would have provided a balance to what Trent was willing to teach about ministry and ordination in the *Catholic* Church. To all intents and purposes Trent was a synod of the *Western*, or Roman Catholic, Church, not an ecumenical, *Catholic* synod. It is probably this fact that leads Küng to raise the question: "Is Trent, considered historically (and not merely juridically and canonically), truly representative of the whole Church? What does that entail for the effective authority of the Council?"[108]

Whatever be the answer to that question, the narrow[109] teachings of the Council of Trent dominated the theory and the practice of priestly ministry in the Roman Church down to, and indeed well beyond, Vatican II.

Four propositions drawn from the teachings of the Reformers on ministry and priesthood were presented to the Council at its Bologna session in 1547. The first stated that orders is not a sacrament, but only an office; the second that it is a power to preach, not to offer; the third that all Christians are equally priest; the fourth that bishops do not have the right to ordain and that ordinations which they perform are invalid. At its session in Trent in 1551–52, six more propositions, drawn it was claimed from the writings of Luther and Calvin, added these among other things: that there was no such thing in the New Testament as a visible, external priesthood; that there was no such power as the power to consecrate the body and blood of the Lord or the power to forgive sins; that there was only the office and the ministry to preach the Gospel and that those who did not preach the Gospel were not priests; that there was no such thing as hierarchy. To grasp the import of the teachings of Trent, we must always keep in focus that it was specifically in opposition to these propositions that it set out its teaching on the sacrament of orders, especially as it is set out in the canons. A glance at those canons will be enough to show that all Trent did was defend the order of ministry that had developed in the Western tradition and present it as Church order.

Canon 1 leaves no doubt about the position of the Western Church with respect to orders and ministry in the sixteenth century. There is a visible, external priesthood in the New Testament; there is a power to consecrate the body and blood of the Lord and to forgive sins; there is a power to do more than simply preach.[110] The canon does not say, but the corresponding chapter does, that these powers are located in the priesthood, and it was this teaching as understood in subsequent history that hardened the Western Church's conception of ministry into a one-sided view that perceived it as priestly and cultic. I say one-sided because against the evidence of the historical Catholic Church it does appear as a one-sided view, not only broadly of ministry, but also more narrowly of priesthood. I do not agree, however, that it was the Council of Trent that fabricated such a view, for there is abundant evidence, to which I have but hinted, to show that long prior to Trent such a view was already well established in the Western Church.

The one-sidedness of the Tridentine response, though, did tend to obscure the fact that the Reformers were not wrong in everything they claimed. They were not wrong, for instance, in advancing preaching as a central New Testament office and ministry.[111] They were wrong only in claiming that preaching was the exclusive ministry blessed in the New Testament. But in the polemical situation of both Protestant Reformation and Catholic Counter-Reformation, so much emphasis was laid on the cultic duties of priests that the impression was generated that cult was all there was for a priest to do. The medieval *potestas ordinis* emerged more and more as a *potestas cultus*, a fact which is easy to discern and verify from even a cursory reading of Roman statements about priesthood from Trent to the present.[112] Canon 6 added the doctrine that there was a legitimate hierarchy in the Church, drawing back in the final version from stating that this was of *divine institution,* and contenting itself with claiming that it was of divine ordination (*divina ordinatione*), by which was intended that God allowed the historical development of ministry in the Church to take this direction.[113] Canon 7 canonized the shift from Chalcedon introduced by Lateran III, teaching that bishops not only ordain validly, but also ordain validly those who are neither called by nor agreed to by the people.[114] That, of course, might entail absolute ordination, which used to be invalid. But here is a case where we must pay careful attention to the historical circumstance. The sixteenth century was a time when the "people," in the form of the secular princes, claimed the right over against the Church of appointing bishops and priests. This canon sought to assert, and so protect, the Church's right in this matter. Now that that situation of claim and counter-claim no longer exists, perhaps we could consider returning to the people its ancient right to call its ministers. We know from history that that must be a valid way both to elect and to ordain ministers, else we would be obliged to admit the unthinkable, namely, that the Catholic Church had sanctioned an invalid and illegitimate practice for close on a thousand years.

The Council of Trent, in Ganoczy's words, was "a more or less valid and effective reply to Lutheran and Calvinist questions and challenges. But [history] has also recognized that in the course of the following four centuries a too rigid desire to stick to the letter of the Council has sometimes blocked the progress which ought to have taken place within the structures of the Church, in response to new challenges and questions."[115] In the sixteenth century, there was no clear and systematic theology of the Church. The insistence of Trent, though, on the essentially hierarchical nature of ministry yielded in the following centuries a theology of Church which was equally hierarchical. Church was imaged in the model of an institutional pyramid, at whose apex ruled the Pope assisted by the hierarchy, and whose broad base was constituted by the lay faithful.[116] That model dominated the Western theology and practice of Church until Vatican II, which supplanted it with a communitarian model more in tune with the New Testament and the early history of the great Catholic, as distinct from the narrowly Western, Church. The Tridentine model of ministry was based on a model of sacred power. The Tridentine model of Church, Tridentine not in the sense that Trent taught it, but in the sense that in the post-Tridentine climate it derived inevitably from Tridentine principles, was constructed also on this notion of sacred power. Vatican II extended both the concept of ministry and the concept of Church onto a broader canvas.

We have seen that the Reformers proposed that orders was only an office and a power to preach in the Church, not a power to offer gifts. They did not invent this opinion; it was quite common at the time. Already in 1536, a local Council of Cologne had decreed that every sacramental ritual should be accompanied by some preaching, so that the faithful might understand what was being done.[117] In 1541 John Calvin required the same thing in his *Ordonnances ecclesiastiques*.[118] In 1546 the Council of Trent prepared a disciplinary decree *Super Lectione et Praedicatione,* which taught that the principal task (*praecipuum munus*) of a bishop was to preach the Gospel, a task he was to carry out every time he had the opportunity.[119] Unfortunately, the Council did not develop this idea; in fact it retreated from it in its subsequent doctrinal deliberations. By the time it reached its dogmatic decree on the priesthood it chose to ignore this principal task, for fear of appearing too "Protestant," and contented itself with condemning the claim that orders in the Church was merely an office of preaching.

With the polemical contexts of the Reformation well behind it, Vatican II had no such qualms, and explicitly taught that "among the principal duties of bishops, the preaching of the Gospel occupies an eminent place."[120] It taught of priests that "by the power of the sacrament of orders, and in the image of Christ the eternal high priest, they are consecrated to preach the Gospel, shepherd the faithful, and celebrate divine worship."[121] Priests are said to have "as their primary duty the proclamation of the Gospel of God to all."[122] The power of the priest over Eucharist is still to the fore,[123] but Trent's original desire to declare the preaching of the word a primary task is finally, four hundred years and endless polemics later, brought to fruition.[124]

ORDERS AS SACRAMENT

We can now pose the question, which is the central question of this chapter but which could not have been answered with full knowledge without the foregoing. What does it mean that orders in the Church is a sacrament? We know from Chapter One that what qualifies as a sacrament depends on how we define sacrament, and that at various historical times various realities have been designated as sacraments on the basis of various definitions. Orders was not listed as a sacrament by John Calvin, for instance, because his definition of sacrament was of a sign instituted by Christ for the whole of the faithful and, in common with the other Reformers, he judged only baptism and Eucharist to have been so instituted to be for all.[125] My treatment of institution by Christ in Chapter Two makes clear that it cannot be so easily claimed now as it was then, even for baptism and Eucharist, a fact which is widely admitted by Protestant and Catholic scholars alike. Calvin did allow of orders that he had "no objection at all to its being accepted as a sacrament. It is a ceremony taken from Scripture . . . which is by no means empty . . . but is a sign of God's spiritual grace."[126] Augustine would appear to have been the first to speak of a "sacrament of ordination,"[127] and it is included in all lists of sacraments from the great schoolmen onward. The teaching of the Catholic Church is crystallized by Trent: orders is a true and proper sacrament.[128]

The notion of sacrament that has been developed throughout this book is one of a ritual action which proclaims, realizes and celebrates realities beyond itself, not only signifying those realities, but also causing them. The question at issue now is: What is it that is signified and caused in and by the sacrament of orders? An initial answer to the question can be teased out of a traditional way of referring to initially a bishop and, later, a presbyter. Each is said to be *vicarius Christi*, a vicar of Christ, even an other Christ.

Tertullian seems to have been the first to use the term, *vicarius Christi*, though he applied it to the Holy Spirit.[129] A little later in the third century, Cyprian applies the image, if not the exact phrase, to the bishop, who acts *vice Christi*, in place of Christ.[130] There is evidence that presbyters were spoken of in the same way as early as the end of the fourth century,[131] and thenceforward that it became the common way of speaking and thinking about both bishop and priest in the Catholic churches. In modern papal pronouncements, this view of the priest's role is dominant and, as we might expect after our review of the history of orders, is presented particularly in a Eucharistic context and in function of the *potestas ordinis*. The priest is the "Redeemer's legate"; he takes the place of God (*Dei vices gerit*); he takes the place of Christ (*personam gerit Domini nostri Jesu Christi*).[132] Vatican II echoes this view, teaching that in the celebration of the Eucharist the priest acts in the name of Christ, "brings about the Eucharistic sacrifice, and offers it to God in the name of all the people." For their part, the people "join in the offering of the Eucharist by virtue of their royal priesthood."[133]

It is one thing, though, to assert that the priest is *vicarius Christi*, and quite another to ground that assertion theologically. The traditional grounding, itself grounded on the direct linkage of sacraments to Christ without any linkage to Church, has tended to deal with *vicarius Christi* as a function of the *potestas ordinis*. The representative function of the priest derives in this view from purely institutional sources. Just because he has been ordained to apostolic office in a sacramental rite administered by one who himself holds apostolic office, and who stands in a line of succession going back to the apostles and, indeed, to Christ himself, the priest is *vicarius Christi*. This traditional insistence on an almost physical succession of ordination going back to the apostles and to Jesus himself, a succession which is itself historically doubtful, has served to institutionalize and objectify the representative function of the priest. It is open to the same objection that I have made before in this book, namely, that the presence of Christ in sacrament is not just an objective presence but also, and more properly, a personal presence.

When dealing with both Eucharist and marriage, I argued that objective presence and objective representation are drawn into personal presence and personal representation only by personal and actual faith. Kilmartin agrees with this position in general, and with what I said about Eucharist in particular, when he states: "Without the exercise of the faith no sacramental presence of Christ or the *passio Christi* is possible." He is utterly correct when he goes on to insist that considerations of the role and central importance of faith "are germane to the question of the representative role of apostolic office. They point to the conclusion that office directly represents the faith of the Church and only to this extent can represent Christ."[134] In what sense is orders sacramental and what does it sacramentalize? It is sacramental in the sense that it proclaims, realizes and celebrates the Church as faithful and God in Christ as the source and guarantor of that faith. The *and* can be and has been misleading, however, especially when it is read disjunctively, and so I hasten to rephrase. Orders is a sacrament in the Church in which believers (I do not say only *male* believers) are designated as representatives of God in Christ precisely insofar as, and to the extent that, they are faith-full representatives of the faith-full Church. This assertion I must now explain.

Vatican II speaks of several modes of Christ's presence in the Church: presence "especially in its liturgical celebrations"; presence in Eucharist, "not only in the person of his minister . . . but especially under the Eucharistic species"; presence in the sacraments "by his power"; presence in the proclaimed word; presence in the praying Church.[135] The preparatory schema for this document was much stronger theologically. It sought to establish an order in those presences, from Christ's abiding presence in the ecclesial community to his presence in word, prayer, sacraments and Eucharist. That ordering effort, however, could not win enough votes in the assembly to be passed, and a theologically weaker text, the one quoted above, was agreed upon. The stumbling block to the ordering effort was the desire of the majority of bishops to give precedence to Christ's presence in the Eucharistic minister (*vicarius Christi*) and in the Eucharistic species (*corpus Christi.*)

As we have seen several times, the core kerygma of the New Testament is that God raised Jesus from the dead. It was this act of God that established for all time the objective presence of Jesus in and for the world. But that objective presence, to be personally real and fruitful for believers, needed to be drawn into personal presence. And so it was drawn into personal presence by the faith of the first believers, who believed in the mighty works of God, namely, his raising of Jesus from the dead and his showing of this resurrection to selected witnesses. It was this faith which became the faith of the Church, the apostolic faith preserved in the great Catholic Church and shared with each local church. Apostolic ministry and apostolic office is a ministry and an office to officially witness to that apostolic faith in the name of the Church, and thereby to shepherd the Church to faith too. Priestly ordination establishes believers directly in a ministry and an office of service to the faith of the Church; it establishes them as representative vicars of the Church, *vicarii Ecclesiae*. It is only to the extent that they are ordained as *vicarii Ecclesiae* that they are also ordained as *vicarii Christi*, vicars of Christ, who is at once the source and the object of the Church's faith. Ordination establishes believers as ministers of the Church, that is, as believers who act in its name, and only as a function of that ministry as ministers also of Christ, as believers who act in his name.

We recall the decree of nullity brought by the Council of Chalcedon against absolute ordinations, those in which there was no appointment to function in an ecclesial community. That decree manifests the belief of the early Church that ministry and ordination to ministry are essentially ecclesial realities, a judgment which is matched by the universal Catholic judgment that a person who did not share the faith of the Church could never be validly ordained a minister of the Church. The introduction into the Western Church of the distinction between *potestas ordinis* and *potestas iurisdictionis,* and of the view that saw them disjunctively, introduced a novel perspective. It appeared that a believer could be given and receive *potestas ordinis* without *potestas iurisdictionis,* a personal power to minister cultically unmatched by a pastoral power to minister in and to some specific church. Vatican II attempted to make clear that that is not possible and to restore the ecclesial dimension of both ministry and priesthood in the Church. There is no priestly office which is not also a pastoral office.[136]

Ordination established believers as ministers in and representative sacraments of the Church united in apostolic faith; in its turn, this Church is minister and sacrament of the Christ who is the origin and the object of its faith; and in his turn, this Christ is confessed in the Church as the minister and sacrament of the great God-Father who raised him from the dead and showed him to Peter and to the Twelve and to James and to Paul (cf. 1 Cor 15:5–8). Ordination, like every sacrament in the Church, is a sacramental act because it symbolizes and causes sacred reality far beyond the literal meanings of the words and actions which comprise it. In it, ordinary words and actions proclaim, realize and celebrate in a faithful believer the faith of the apostolic Church, which in those words and actions ordains that believer to be its representative and, because its representative, representative also of the Christ and God. We recall here what I said earlier of the election-ordination of bishops in the primitive Church, namely, that election-ordination is not merely the work of the Church, but also the work of the Holy Spirit of God. The rites and prayers of the ordination ritual seek to make that fact plain.

What is it, then, that happens in the sacrament of orders? The ordaining bishop, the representative leader of the local church to the Catholic Church and of the Catholic Church to the local church, lays his hands on each individual to be ordained and then prays over these individuals the prayer of consecration. For priests he prays: "Almighty Father, grant to these servants of yours the dignity of the priesthood. Renew within them the Spirit of holiness. As co-workers with the order of bishops may they be faithful to the ministry that they receive from you, Lord God, and be to others a model of right conduct." For bishops he prays: "Pour out upon this thine elect thy power, the Spirit which you gave to your beloved Son, Jesus Christ, which he granted to the holy apostles, who established your Church in every place as your sanctuary and for the endless glory and praise of your name."[137]

This gesture and these words, and the other words and gestures of the ordination ritual, are meaningful on several levels. They symbolize: (1) the election of this believer from the apostolic Church as one who shares its apostolic faith (absence of this faith nullifies the sacrament); (2) the public verification of the faith of this believer by the one who has the charism and function of guaranteeing the faith of the local church, its bishop-overseer; (3) the ordination of this believer to pastoral office in the Church,[138] an office which establishes him/her as a co-worker with the bishop in the Church and as a *vicarius ecclesiae,* that is, as a designated representative of the faith of the Church, both local and Catholic (all believers, of course, have the task of representing this faith, but the ordained minister is appointed to it in an official and authoritative way); (4) the ordination of this minister, therefore, as also a *vicarius Christi,* an other Christ, so that when he/she proclaims the Gospel, forgives sins, or blesses bread and wine, it is the Church and Christ which proclaim the Gospel, forgive sins and bless bread and wine; (5) the authoritative proclamation and verification of the presence of the Spirit of God in this believer, and the realization-celebration of this Spirit to strengthen him/her for the pastoral task of proclaiming the Gospel of this Spirit to others; (6) the separation of this believer from the Church to stand over against it, both to represent and to animate its faith, a separation, however, which is to be understood as maintaining rather than severing connection, much as Christ as head is both separated from and connected to the Church which is his body.[139] This election of believers, the verification of their faith, their ordination, the proclamation of the Spirit in them, their separation from the Church, all are to be understood as permanent and need not be, and therefore cannot be, repeated. It is the permanence of all these elements which constitutes the *character* which Catholic theology assigns to the reception of this sacrament.

For many, probably, the only surprising element in the foregoing will be the reference to the ordained minister as he/she, for it is well known that the Roman Catholic tradition has never had an ordained, female, presbyteral ministry, and has reiterated in recent years its opposition to such a ministry.[140] I am, of course, well aware of those facts and I acknowledge them with respect. But as a believer and as a theologian, I am constrained to acknowledge also that, if the priest directly represents the believing Church and only indirectly the Christ, as I believe and have attempted to show to be the case, then the argument offered against the ordination of women that, since the priest represents Christ the priest must be male, is quite unsound and untenable. If the priest does, indeed, represent the Church and if the Church is notoriously male and female, then it would appear symbolically and logically sound that the priesthood would be a mixed male and female priesthood. The presbyteral office directly represents the Church, which itself directly represents Christ. But it is the whole Christ, head and ecclesial members, that the Church directly and the priest indirectly represents. It is Christ as the new *adam* (cf. 1 Cor 15:21–22; Rom 5:12–21), male and female as was the first *adam* (cf. Gen 1:27 and 5:2). It would seem that if the priest is to be a *vicarius Christi* of *this* mystical Christ, the priesthood should be male and female. In Christ, indeed, as Paul stated so simply and forcefully to a New Testament Church, "there is neither Jew nor Greek, there is neither slave nor free, there is neither male nor female; for you are all one person in Christ" (Gal 3:28).

It is not part of my purpose here to debate the issue of ordination of women to the priesthood. That I intend to do in a subsequent monograph. But having taken a position which is at variance with a well-known teaching of the Roman Catholic Church, a teaching which I acknowledge to be an authentic, magisterial teaching, I owe it to the reader to offer an explanation of how such disagreement is possible and legitimate. Schillebeeckx makes an initial point. The "Declaration on the Question of the Admission of Women to the Ministerial Priesthood" was issued by the Congregation for the Doctrine of the Faith, and not directly by the Pope *motu proprio*. "This is the Roman way of keeping a matter open, though provisionally a kind of 'magisterial statement' on the issue has been made."[141] Karl Rahner agrees that the question remains open. Though the Declaration is an authentic teaching, he argues, it does not have the requirements to be a definitive, infallible teaching, and therefore could be (which is not at all the same thing as saying it is) erroneous and reformable.[142] The discussion, therefore, must go on to discover the truth of the matter. The present position is not final and absolute.

A central point of the Declaration's "none too lucid argument"[143] is the transition it makes from the concept of undoubtedly male apostle chosen by Jesus to the concept of bishop-priest. That transition is, as we know from even our brief survey of the development of the concept and the terminology of priesthood in the Christian Church, much too simplistic. Rahner goes so far as to accuse the Declaration of ignoring "all the difficult questions about the concrete emergence of the

Church and its origin from Jesus, although they are of the greatest importance for its theme."[144] Schillebeeckx, more sharply, points out a double hermeneutical standard applied in official teaching to the questions of male priesthood and celibacy. "Why must the fact that . . . Jesus only chose twelve men as apostles suddenly acquire a theological significance, while at the same time the similar fact that this same Jesus for the most part (perhaps even entirely) chose only married men for this task . . . is not allowed any theological significance?"[145] My interest here in the question of ordination of women to the priesthood is narrowly focused, namely, to state that, even in the Roman Catholic tradition, the question is still open on relevant theological grounds. I have argued only that a major constraint in the discussion has been to see the priest exclusively as a representative of the historical Christ, and not also as a representative of the mystical Christ complementarily composed of both males and females. It is only this ecclesial connection that I have proposed here as a contribution toward the necessary ongoing discussion of the question, and which I intend to develop at more length in a subsequent work.

Schillebeeckx complains, as we have seen, that though the Latin Church has elevated the fact that Jesus appointed only male apostles to the status of a not-to-be-departed-from theological precedent, it has not accorded the same status to the fact that he appointed, for the most part, married men as apostles. That double standard raises the much discussed question of presbyteral celibacy. Here, again, it is not my intention to deal with that question *in toto,* because I need not and cannot in terms of space available. In this chapter on presbyteral ordination, I need to raise only a very specific question: Is celibacy an *essential* requirement for such ordination, so that it would be impossible for a married person to be ordained a presbyter of the Church? The answer to that question is a very clear and indisputable *no.*

That answer is clear from two facts. The first is the unbroken practice of the Eastern Catholic churches which ordain married men to the priesthood, a practice which the Western Catholic Church acknowledges as perfectly valid. The second is that from the beginning presbyters in the Catholic Church were married. Not since the ill-fated effort of Bickell to demonstrate the apostolic origin of the law of celibacy, comprehensively refuted by Funk, has any Catholic author sought to claim apostolicity for the law of celibacy.[146] In the beginning, presbyters and *episkopoi* were married. Both 1 Timothy 3:1–5 and Titus 1:6 make it, indeed, a requirement for the office of presbyter and overseer that a man be the husband of one wife. That practice continued in both East and West for many centuries, and continues still today in the East. These indisputable facts led Vatican II to teach unequivocally that neither continence, nor *a fortiori* celibacy, is "demanded by the very nature of the priesthood."[147]

The Western, Latin Church, however, introduced a change. It was a change motivated, it is generally agreed, by the demands of ritual purity. "Only those who are pure can have access to the sphere of the sacred. Now sexual intercourse is impure. One must abstain from it, therefore, before a religious action."[148] Christians did not discover such an argument in the Gospel of Christ, but in both Old Testament and pagan sources—a fact which raises a serious question, especially since the Gospel portrays Jesus as abolishing Old Testament precepts of ritual purity.[149]

The search for ritual purity in connection with the celebration of Eucharist, especially when it began to be celebrated daily toward the end of the fourth century, led Western synods to demand sexual abstinence, not yet celibacy, of its priests. A Synod of Rome (386) decreed that priests are not to live with their wives;[150] a Synod of Turin (397) and of Toledo (400) that priests who have begotten children are not to be advanced to any higher order;[151] a Synod of Carthage (401) that bishops and priests who are not continent are to be removed from office.[152] This movement reached a kind of high point with the instruction of Pope Leo the Great (445) that bishops and priests are neither to have sexual intercourse with their wives nor to send them away.[153] This care for the wives of married clergy was not in evidence at the Second Council of the Lateran (1139), when the demand for abstinence gave way to the demand for celibacy. The Council decreed, "so that the law of continence and the purity which is well pleasing to God may extend among the clergy," not only that clergy should abstain from intercourse with their wives, but also that they should send them away. It further decreed that any attempted marriage by a bishop, priest, deacon or subdeacon is invalid.[154]

The introduction of the law of celibacy was to ensure ritual purity, and ecclesiastical documents which laud it do so in terms of this purity—at least up to the Second Vatican Council. There, for the first time in ecclesiastical documents, Schillebeeckx claims, the Gospel motive for it is offered, namely, "for the sake of the kingdom of heaven" (Mt 19:12).[155] That motive is a quite different, much more positive and Christian, motive than the motive of ritual purity founded on a very pessimistic and negative view of human sexuality. The Gospel motive of celibacy for the sake of the kingdom is a far cry from Jerome's infamous dictum: "Every act of sexual intercourse is impure."[156] If one were to construct an argument for or against presbyteral celibacy, the argument would be necessarily quite different in the cases of these two motives. But, again, I neither need nor wish here to construct such arguments. I need only to complete my treatment of the sacramentality of orders by raising the question of the relationship between presbyteral ordination and celibacy. The relationship is a purely extrinsic one, in no way demanded by the nature of priesthood. That judgment completes this chapter.

ENDNOTES

ABBREVIATIONS[1]

AAS   = *Acta Apostolicae Sedis: Commentarium Officiale* (Roma: Typis Polyglottis Vaticanis)

CT   = *Concilium Tridentinum Diariorum, Actorum, Epistolarum, Tractatuum*, ed. Societas Goerresiana (Freiburg: Herder: 1901–1961)

DS   = *Enchiridion Symbolorum Definitionum et Declarationum de Rebus Fidei et Morum*, ed. H. Denzinger et A. Schoenmetzer (Editio 33 emendata et aucta; Freiburg: Herder, 1965)

DV   = *The Documents of Vatican II*, ed. Walter M. Abbott (London: Chapman, 1966)

MANSI = *Sacrorum Conciliorum Nova et Amplissima Collectio* ed. J.D. Mansi (Paris: Hubert Welter, 1903–1927)

MD   = *La Maison Dieu (Paris: Editions du Cerf)*

NRT   = *Nouvelle Revue Theologique* (Tournai: Casterman)

PG   = *Patrologiae Cursus Completus: Series Graeca*, ed. J.P. Migne

PL   = *Patrologiae Cursus Completus: Series Latina*, ed. J.P. Migne

ST   = *Summa Theologiae Sancti Thomae de Aquino* (Roma: Editiones Paulinae, 1962)

TS   = *Theological Studies* (Georgetown University)

WOR   = *Worship*

[1]All abbreviations in the endnotes are listed without any underlined emphasis. All translations from languages other than English are the author's.

CHAPTER ONE. SYMBOL

1. See Joachim Jeremias, *The Eucharistic Words of Jesus* (New York: Scribner's, 1966), pp. 15–88.

2. J. Dupont, "Ceci est mon corps, Ceci est mon sang," NRT 80 (1958): 1034.

3. Cf. X. Leon-Dufour, "Prenez! Ceci est mon corps pour vous," NRT 104 (1982): 231, n. 14.

4. B. Cooke, "Synoptic Presentation of the Eucharist as Covenant Sacrifice," TS 21 (1960): 25, 26, 27; cf. Leon-Dufour, "Prenez! Ceci est mon corps pour vous," NRT 104 (1982): 225–227.

5. *Infant Baptism in the First Four Centuries* (Philadelphia: Westminster, 1972), p. 25.

6. Arnold Van Gennep, *The Rites of Passage* (London: Routledge and Kegan Paul, 1960).

7. Victor Turner, *The Forest of Symbols: Aspects of Ndembu Ritual* (Ithaca: Cornell University Press, 1967), p. 95.

8. Audrey R. Richards, *Chisungu* (London: Faber, 1956), p. 121.

9. *Forest of Symbols*, p. 102.

10. Dupont, "Ceci est mon corps," p. 1034.

11. Ernst Cassirer, *An Essay on Man: An Introduction to a Philosophy of Human Culture* (New Haven: Yale University Press, 1944), p. 26.

12. Alfred North Whitehead, *Symbolism: Its Meaning and Effect* (New York: Putnam's, 1959), pp. 2–3.

13. Ibid., p. 8.

14. Ibid., pp. 8–9.

15. Norwood R. Hanson, *Patterns of Discovery: An Inquiry into the Conceptual Foundations of Science* (Cambridge: Harvard University Press, 1958), p. 7.

16. Susanne K. Langer, *Philosophy in a New Key: A Study in the Symbolism of Reason, Rite and Art*, 3rd. ed. (Cambridge: Harvard University Press, 1967), p. 42.

17. Whitehead, *Symbolism*, pp. 74 and 66.

18. Charles S. Peirce, "How To Make Our Ideas Clear," in Justus Buchler, ed., *The Philosophy of Peirce: Selected Writings* (London: Routledge and Kegan Paul, 1940), p. 38.

19. Whitehead, *Symbolism*, pp. 73–74.

20. Ibid., p. 74.

21. Cassirer, *Essay on Man*, p. 24. Emphasis in original.

22. Ibid., p. 25.

23. Ernst Cassirer, *The Philosophy of Symbolic Forms*, trans. Ralph Manheim (New Haven: Yale University Press, 1953–57), III:93.

24. Ernst Cassirer, *Language and Myth*, trans, Susanne K. Langer (New York: Harper and Row, 1946), p. 8. Emphasis in original.

25. Cassirer, *Essay on Man*, p. 32.

26. Ibid., p. 36.

27. Paul Ricoeur, *The Symbolism of Evil*, trans. Emerson Buchanan (New York: Harper and Row, 1967), pp. 14–18.

28. Ibid., p. 15.

29. Victor Turner, "Symbolic Studies," *Annual Review of Anthropology* (1975): 151. For an extensive treatment of Turner's symbolic theory, see any of the following: *The Drums of Affliction: A Study of Religious Processes among the Ndembu of Zambia* (Oxford: Clarendon Press, 1968); *The Forest of Symbols: Aspects of Ndembu Ritual* (Ithaca: Cornell University Press, 1967); *The Ritual Process: Structure and Anti-Structure* (Chicago: Adline Publishing, 1969).

30. *Forest of Symbols*, p. 19.

31. See J. S. La Fontaine, ed., *The Interpretation of Ritual: Essays in Honor of A.I. Richards* (London: Tavistock, 1972), pp. 3 and 160–161; Susanne Langer, *Philosophy in a New Key*, p. 45 and passim; Victor Turner, *Forest of Symbols*, passim.

32. Cf. Karl Rahner, "The Hermeneutics of Eschatological Assertions," in *Theological Investigations*, Vol. IV (London: Darton, Longman and Todd, 1966), p. 340, note 16.

33. Cassirer, *An Essay on Man*, p. 36.

34. *Forest of Symbols*, p. 28.

35. Carl Jung, *Psychological Types* (London: Routledge and Kegan Paul, 1949), p. 601.

36. Edward F. Edinger, *Ego and Archetype* (New York: Putnam's, 1972), p. 109.

37. Theodore Roszak, *Where the Wasteland Ends: Politics and Transcendence in Postindustrial Society* (New York: Doubleday, 1972), p. 139. Emphasis in original.

38. Cassirer, *Essay on Man*, p. 36.

39. The characteristics of religious symbol listed here are borrowed from Paul Tillich, though my treatment of them is different from his. See his "The Meaning and Justification of Religious Symbols," in *Religious Experience and Truth*, ed. Sidney Hook (New York: New York University Press, 1961), pp. 3–11; "Theology and Symbolism," in *Religious Symbolism*, ed. F. Ernest Johnson (New York: Kennikat Press, 1969), pp. 107–116; "The Religious Symbol," in *Symbolism in Religion and Literature*, ed. Rollo May (New York: Braziller, 1960), pp. 75–98.

40. DS 1529.

41. DS 1677.

42. Karl Rahner and Angelus Haussling, *The Celebration of the Eucharist* (New York: Herder and Herder, 1968), p. 32. See Karl Rahner, "The Theology of the Symbol," *Theological Investigations*, Vol. IV (Baltimore: Helicon Press, 1966), pp. 221–252. Cf. Paul Anciaux, *The Sacrament of Penance* (New York: Sheed and Ward, 1962), pp. 149–159.

43. Anselm, *Proslogion*, c. 2. Cited in Gordon D. Kaufman, *God the Problem* (Cambridge: Harvard University Press, 1972), p. 90.

44. Theodore Roszak, *Where the Wasteland Ends*, p. 257.

45. Ibid., p. 139. Emphasis in original.

46. Cf. Tad Guzie, *Jesus and the Eucharist* (Paramus: Paulist Press, 1974), pp. 24–41.

47. Ibid., p. 29.

48. Susanne Langer, *Philosophy in a New Key*, pp. 266–294.

CHAPTER TWO.   SACRAMENT

1. Cf. M. Jugie, *Theologiae Dogmaticae Greco-Russorum Expositio de Sacramentis* (Paris: Latouzey, 1930), pp. 8–32.

2. For detailed information on the meanings of *mysterion*, see G. Bornkamm, "mysterion," TDNT IV: 802–828. In relation to Bornkamm's article, see S. Lyonnet, "Hellenisme et christianisme: a propos du Theologisches Woerterbuch," *Biblica* 26 (1945): 115–132.

3. Dan 2:18–19, 27–30, 44–47.

4. 1 Cor 2:7–10; Rom 16:25–26; Col 1:26–27; 2:3; 4:3; Eph 1:9–10; 3:3–12; 1 Tim 3:16.

5. Cf. 1 Cor 2:6.

6. Cf. 1 Cor 3:1.

7. W. Van Roo, *De Sacramentis in Genere* (Rome: Gregorian University Press, 1957), p. 11.

8. See, for example, *The Stromata or Miscellanies*, in A. Roberts and J. Donaldson (eds.), *The Ante-Nicene Fathers* (Grand Rapids: Eerdmans, 1956), p. 454.

9. Ibid., pp. 242, 322, 439. See also H.G. Marsh, "The Use of *mysterion* in the Writings of Clement of Alexandria with Special Reference to His Sacramental Doctrine," *Journal of Theological Studies* 37 (1936): 64–80.

10. Hans Urs von Balthasar, "Le mysterion d'Origene," *Recherches de Science Religieuse* 26 (1936): 513–562; 27 (1937): 38–64.

11. *Comment. in Epist. ad Rom*, 4, PG 14, 968 and 1038; *Contra Celsum*, 8, PG 14, 1603.

12. See texts in Van Roo, *De Sacramentis,* pp. 13–17.

13. Cf. A. Kolping, *Sacramentum Tertullianeum* (Regensburg, 1948), pp. 21–43.

14. Cf. C. Mohrmann, "Sacramentum dans les plus anciens textes chretiens," *Harvard Theological Review* 47 (1954): 141–152.

15. See Tacitus, *Annales* 1, 8; Pliny the Younger, *Epist. ad Traianum* 96, 7; Horace, *Odes* 2, 17, 10.

16. See Emile de Backer, "Tertullian," in *Pour l'histoire du mot sacramentum,* ed. J. de Ghellinck (Louvain: Spicilegium Sacrum Lovaniensis, 1924), pp. 145–146.

17. See, for example, *De Spectaculis* 24, PL 1, 655–656; *De Baptismo* 1, PL 1, 1197; *De Idolatria* 6, PL 1, 668; *De Corona* 11, PL 2, 91; *De Jejuniis* 10, PL 2, 966–968. *De Praescriptionibus* 40, PL 2, 54–55; *Adv. Marcionem* 1, 14, PL 2, 262.

18. *Adv. Marcionem* 4, 34, PL 2, 442; *De Pudicitia* 10, PL 2, 1000; *De Corona* 3, PL 2, 79.

19. See, for example, *Lib. ad Demetrianum* 24, PL 4, 564; *Epist* 75 12, in *Ante-Nicene Fathers,* V, 400–401; *Epist.* 72 22, ibid., 385; *Epist.* 71 1, ibid. 378. See also J.B. Poukens, "Cyprien et ses contemporains," in *Pour l'histoire du mot sacramentum,* pp. 205–212.

20. C. Coutourier, "Sacramentum et Mysterium dans l'oeuvre de Saint Augustin," in *Etudes Augustiniennes,* ed. H. Rondet (Paris, 1953); E. Hocedez, "La conception augustinienne du sacrement dans le Tractatus 80 in Joannem," *Recherches de Science Religieuse* 9 (1919): 1–29; F. Van Der Meer, "Sacramentum chez Saint Augustin," MD 13 (1948): 50–64.

21. This threefold division is accepted from Coutourier, "Sacramentum et Mysterium."

22. Cf. Van Roo, *De Sacramentis,* pp. 21–35, where all the pertinent texts are gathered.

23. *De Civ. Dei* 10, 5, PL 41, 282; *Contra Faustum* 19, 11, PL 42, 355A; *In Epist. Joannis ad Parthos* 6, 3, 11, PL 35, 2026C;

24. *Contra Litteras Petiliani* 3, 49, 59, PL 43, 378–379.

25. Cf. *Etymologiae,* lib. 6, cap. 19, nn. 39–42.

26. For a detailed treatment of Berengar's place in the development of a definition of sacrament, see D. Van den Eynde, *Les definitions des sacrements pendant la premiere periode de la theologie scholastique (1050–1240)* (Rome: Antonianum, 1950); also N.M. Haring, "Berengar's Definitions of Sacrament and Their Influence on Medieval Sacramentology," *Medieval Studies* 10 (1948): 109–146.

27. Cf. Van den Eynde, *Les definitions des sacrements,* pp. 18–26; 41; 63–68; 69–76.

28. Cf. ibid., pp. 27–31; 37–38; 40; 77–91; 105–106; 117–127.

29. *Dialogus de Sacramentis Legis Naturalis et Scriptae,* 33D–34A; 34D–35A.

30. *Liber Sententiarum* 4, dist. 1, cap. 4. Cf. Van den Eynde, pp. 40–46; 49–52; 103–110.

31. ST III, 60, 1 corp.

32. Ibid., III, 60, 2 corp.

33. Ibid., III, 60, 3 corp.

34. Ibid., III, 60, 1 corp.

35. Ibid., III, 62, 3; cp. III, 62, 1 ad 1.

36. Ibid., III, 1, 1 corp.

37. Juan Alfaro, "Faith," in *Sacramentum Mundi: An Encyclopedia of Theology* (New York: Herder, 1968), II: 315.

38. DS 1532.

39. DS 1529.

40. "Huius iustificationis causae sunt . . . instrumentalis item sacramentum baptismi, quod est 'sacramentum fidei' *sine qua* nulli umquam contigit iustificatio." Emphasis added.

41. Piet Fransen, "Sacraments: Signs of Faith," in *Readings in Sacramental Theology,* ed. C. Stephen Sullivan, p. 62. Emphasis in original.

42. DS 1606.

43. DS 1608.

44. Fransen, "Sacraments: Signs of Faith," p. 63.

45. Schillebeeckx, *Christ the Sacrament,* p. 83.

46. *In IV Sent.,* d. 15, q. 1, a. 3, sol. 3 ad 2; ibid., d. 6, q. 1, a. 3, sol. 2; ibid., d. 4, q. 3, a. 3, qc. 4, obj. 1.

47. Ibid., d. 2, q. 1, a. 4, pc. 4, sol. 4 ad 2.

48. Ibid., d. 143, q. 1, a. 1, qc. 5, sol. 5.

49. Cf. Schillebeeckx, *Christ the Sacrament,* pp. 87–88.

50. Fransen, "Sacraments: Signs of Faith," p. 63.

51. Cf. Colman O'Neill, "The Role of the Recipient and Sacramental Signification," *The Thomist* 21 (1958): 257–301; 508–540. Many of the ideas which follow are dependent on O'Neill.

52. Cf. ST III, 64, 8 ad 1; III, 64, 9 ad 1; III, 67, 5 ad 2.

53. O'Neill, "The Role of the Recipient," pp. 275–276. Emphasis in original.

54. There are, of course, difficulties with such an approach in the case of the baptism of infants. But the baptism of adults, not the baptism of infants, is the paradigm for sacramental baptism. The baptism of infants is an exception to the rule. For one solution to such difficulties, see O'Neill, ibid., pp. 276–296.

55. Schillebeeckx, *Christ the Sacrament,* pp. 133–134.

56. ST III, 49, 3 ad 1.

57. DS 1310. "Haec [sacramenta] nostra et continent gratiam et *ipsam digne suscipientibus conferunt.*" Emphasis added.

58. *Constitution on the Sacred Liturgy,* n. 59, DV, p. 158.

59. CT, V, 927, 41–42.

60. Ibid., 962, 12–21.

61. DS 1606; DS 1608.

62. Confession of Augsburg, art. XIII, quoted from S.S. Schmucker, *Elements of Popular Theology with Special Reference to the Doctrines of the Revelation as Avowed before the Diet of Augsburg* (Andover: Gould and Newman, 1834).

63. *Corpus Reformatorum,* Vol. 27, ed. H. Bindseil (Brunwig: Schwetschke, 1859), c. 571.

64. Louis Villette, *Foi et sacrement,* 2 vols. (Paris: Bloud et Gay, 1959), II: 367.

65. Ibid., p. 374.

66. *Constitution on the Church,* n. 9, DV, p. 26.

67. Villette, *Foi et sacrement,* II: 373.

68. *Constitution on the Sacred Liturgy,* n. 59, DV, p. 158.

69. A.M. Roguet, *Christ Acts through the Sacraments* (Collegeville: Liturgical Press, 1957), p. 11. See also: Bernard Cooke, "The Sacraments as the Continuing Acts of Christ," in *Readings in Sacramental Theology,* ed. C. Stephen Sullivan (Englewood Cliffs: Prentice-Hall, 1964), pp. 31–62; Karl Rahner, *The Church and the Sacraments* (New York: Herder, 1963), passim; John P. Schanz, *The Sacraments of Life and Worship* (Milwaukee: Bruce, 1966), pp. 35–52; Edward Schillebeeckx, *Christ the Sacrament of Encounter with God,* passim.

70. *Constitution on Divine Revelation,* n. 2, DV, p. 112.

71. Karl Rahner argues the same position in *The Church and the Sacraments,* pp. 11–24.

72. Cf. Schillebeeckx, *Christ the Sacrament.*

73. *Constitution on the Church,* n. 1, DV, p. 15.

74. *Constitution on the Sacred Liturgy,* n. 26, DV, p. 147.

75. *Constitution on the Church in the Modern World,* n. 45, DV, p. 247.

76. Contemporary Roman Catholic theology has specified the sacrament of holy orders into three separate sacraments, deaconate, priesthood and episcopacy. That means that there are now *nine* officially recognized paradigms of sacramentality.

77. Christopher Kiesling, "Paradigms of Sacramentality," WOR 44 (1970): 427. See his "How Many Sacraments," ibid., 268–276.

78. DS 1601; DS 1728.

79. *The New Baltimore Catechism* (New York: Benziger, 1953), q. 304, p. 137.

80. Rahner, *The Church and the Sacraments*, p. 41. Cf. Schillebeeckx, *Christ the Sacrament*, p. 115.

81. The reader who wishes to pursue the other directions may consult one of the following. Bernard Leeming, *Principles of Sacramental Theology*, rev. ed. (Westminster: Newman Press, 1960), pp. 393–431; Karl Rahner, *The Church and the Sacraments*, pp. 41–74; E. Schillebeeckx, *Christ the Sacrament*, pp. 112–132.

82. Christopher Kiesling, *Confirmation and Full Life in the Spirit* (Cincinnati: St. Anthony Messenger Press, 1973), p. 46.

83. Cf. Mt 28:19; Mk 16:15–16; Lk 22:19; 1 Cor 11:24–25.

84. Kiesling, *Confirmation*, p. 47. Emphasis in original.

85. Schillebeeckx, *Christ the Sacrament*, p. 120. See the very nuanced solution Karl Rahner offers to the problem of the sacramentality of confirmation in *The Church and the Sacraments*, pp. 51–58.

86. Cf. Van Roo, *De Sacramentis*, p. 121.

87. See above, note 46.

88. See above, note 57.

89. Piet Fransen, *The New Life of Grace* (Tournai: Desclee, 1969), p. 15.

90. Rahner calls this notion of grace the primary one. Cf. K. Rahner and H. Vorgrimler, "Grace," in *Concise Theological Dictionary* (London: Burns and Oates, 1965), p. 194.

91. Fransen, *The New Life of Grace*, p. 87. See pp. 87–96 for a brief sketch of how created grace came to be the dominant reality of grace in the Western Church.

92. Cf. M. de la Taille, "Actuation cree par acte incree," *Revue des Sciences Religieuses* 18 (1928): 252–268; Karl Rahner, "Some Implications of the Scholastic Concept of Uncreated Grace," in *Theological Investigations* I: 319–346; Robert W. Gleason, *Grace* (New York: Sheed and Ward, 1962), cc. 9 and 10. For a critique see C. Kiesling, "The Divine Indwelling in R.W. Gleason's *Grace*," *The American Ecclesiastical Review* 150 (1964): 263–284.

93. Rahner and Vorgrimler, *Theological Dictionary*, p. 161.

94. K. Rahner, "History of the World and Salvation History," in *Theological Investigations* V: 98.

95. K. Rahner, "Concerning the Relationship between Nature and Grace," *Theological Investigations* I: 316.

96. Though I believe my approach is different, the theory presented here is the same as that presented by K. Rahner, *The Church and*

the Sacraments, pp. 34–40, by E. Schillebeeckx, *Christ the Sacrament,* pp. 73–79, and by Piet Fransen, "Sacraments: Signs of Grace," in *Readings in Sacramental Theology,* ed. C. Stephen Sullivan, pp. 67–73.

97. Rahner, *The Church and the Sacraments,* p. 34.
98. DS 1606.
99. Schillebeeckx, *Christ the Sacrament,* p. 134.
100. Whitehead, *Symbolism,* p. 66.
101. *The Rite of Baptism* (Collegeville: Liturgical Press, 1970), p. 8.
102. *Rite of Marriage* (New York: Catholic Book Publishing, 1970), p. 19.
103. *The Ordination of Deacons, Priests and Bishops* (Washington: NCCB, 1969), p. 29.
104. *The Rite of Anointing and Pastoral Care of the Sick* (Collegeville: Liturgical Press, 1974), p. 49.
105. *The Rite of Baptism,* p. 9.
106. *The Ordination of Deacons, Priests and Bishops,* pp. 27, 28, 25.
107. *The Rite of Anointing,* p. 50.
108. *The Rite of Baptism,* p. 6.

CHAPTER THREE.   BAPTISM

1. See Audrey R. Richards, *Chisungu* (London: Faber, 1956), p. 121.
2. I am suggesting here not that Christian baptism grew slavishly out of proselyte baptism, but that they both grew out of common water-mythology with its life-death meanings.
3. PG 33, 1079, emphasis added; see also John Chysostom, *In Joannem Hom. XXV,* 2, PG 32, 151.
4. *De Bap.,* 2, PL 1, 1202 and 1201.
5. *Oratio XL in Sanctum Baptisma,* PG 20, 908 and 926.
6. *In Joannem Hom. XXV,* PG 32, 149–150.
7. *In Bap. Christi,* PG 25, 393 and 395; see also Chrysostom, *In Joannem Hom. XXV,* PG 32, 149; *In Joannem Hom. XXVI,* ibid., 153.
8. Gregory Nazianzen, *Oratio XL in Sanct. Bap.,* 4, PG 20, 906; cf. Chrysostom, *Ad Illum. Cat. I,* 2, PG 27, 225.
9. Gregory of Nyssa, *In Bap. Christi,* PG 25, 400–401; John Chrysostom, *Ad Illum. Cat. I,* 4, PG 27, 228; *Sermo ad Neophytos* in *Huit catecheses baptismales, Sources Chretiennes* n. 50 (Paris: Cerf, 1957), 171–72; see texts in *Baptism: Ancient Liturgies and Patristic Texts,* ed. A. Hamman (New York: Alba House, 1967).
10. The important work in liturgical history of J.M. Hanssens, *La*

liturgie d'Hippolyte. Orientalia Christiana Analecta, n. 155 (Rome, 1959), argues that the reconstructed *Apostolic Tradition* belongs to Alexandria rather than to Rome, but his argument has not been found convincing. Here I retain the *Apostolic Tradition* as evidence of Roman practice.

11. *De Bap.* 9, PL 1, 1222.

12. *Epist. 26*, PL 54, 695–700; see also Basil the Great, *Hom. in Sanct. Bap.*, 1, PG 18, 275; Augustine, *In Joannis Evang.*, Tract. XII, PL 35, 1484–88.

13. See, for example, Basil the Great, *Hom. in Sanct. Bap.*, 3, PG 18, 277–278; Gregory Nazianzen, *Oratio XL in Sanct. Bap.*, 11–28, PG 20, 910–923; John Chrysostom, *Ad Illum. Cat. I*, 1, PG 27, 223–224.

14. Desclee de Brouwer, 1959, p. 9.

15. L. Kohler, *Theologie des Alten Testaments* (Tübingen: Mohr, 1953), points out that of the 510 uses of the word *adam* in the Old Testament very few refer to an individual man.

16. Cited in F.R. Tennant, *The Sources of the Doctrines of the Fall and Original Sin* (Cambridge: University Press, 1903), p. 167.

17. Cf. Jacques Guillet, *Themes bibliques: etudes sur l'expression et le developpement de la revelation* (Paris: Aubier, 1951), p. 102.

18. See, for example, *Apoc. of Baruch*, 17:3; 23:4; 48:42–43; *IV Esdras* 3:7; 3:21.

19. A.M. Dubarle, *Le peche originel dans l'ecriture*, rev. ed. (Paris: Cerf, 1967), p. 147.

20. C.H. Dodd, *The Epistle of Paul to the Romans* (London: Fontana, 1959), p. 101.

21. Later Latin theology would distinguish the original sin of Adam and original sin in his descendants as *originating* (*peccatum originale originans*) and *originated* (*peccatum originale originatum*).

22. *De Peccatorum Meritis et Remissione*, III, 70, PL 44, 194.

23. *De Nuptiis et Concup.*, II, 5, PL 44, 244.

24. *De Pecc. Orig.*, 29, PL 44, 402 and passim.

25. *In Joannem Hom. XXVI*, PG 32, 153; cf. Cyril of Jerusalem, cited in note 9.

26. Cf. Joachim Jeremias, *Infant Baptism in the First Four Centuries;* G.R. Beasley-Murray, *Baptism in the New Testament;* J.C. Didier, *Faut-il baptiser les enfants? Reponse de la tradition* (Paris: Cerf, 1967); for a counter-view, which I do not find convincing, see Kurt Aland, *Did the Early Church Baptize Infants?* (London: SCM, 1963).

27. See, for example, *De Pecc. Originali*, 5, PL 44, 388 and passim.

28. *Epist. XCVIII*, 9, PL 33, 364.

29. ST, IIa IIae, 4, 5.

30. ST, Ia IIae, 55, 1.

31. ST, III, 68, 9.

32. ST, III, 69, 6. Emphasis added.

33. ST, IIa IIae, 10, 12; III, 68, 10.

34. IIa IIae, 10, 12.

35. IIa IIae, 10, 12 ad 2; III, 69, 10 ad 1; also IIa IIae, 10, 11 ad 4.

36. III, 69, 11 ad 1.

37. J. Lecuyer, "L'enfant est baptise dans la foi de l'eglise," MD 89 (1967): 21–37.

38. Constitution on the Church, n. 11, DV, 29.

39. See "Propositions on the Doctrine of Christian Marriage," in Origins, September 28, 1978, p. 237.

40. See P.M. Gy, "Un document de la Congregation pour la Doctrine de la Foi sur le bapteme de petits enfants," MD 104 (1970): 41–45.

41. III, 66, 1 ad 1.

42. See Chapter Two.

43. Juan Alfaro, "Faith," in Sacramentum Mundi: An Encyclopedia of Theology (New York: Herder, 1968), II: 315.

44. N. 10, DV, p. 689.

45. Ibid., n. 12, pp. 692–93.

46. N. 13, ibid., p. 600.

47. Codex Iuris Canonici, can. 1351.

48. Cf. Lactantius, Divinarum Institutionum, V, 20, PL 6, 614; Ambrose, Epist. XXVI, PL 16, 1005; Augustine, In Joannem Evang., 26, 2, PL 35, 1607; Epist. XXIII, PL 33, 98; Epist. XXXIV, PL 33, 132; Epist. XXXV, PL 33, 135; Contra Litt. Petiliani, II, 83, PL 43, 315; Gregory the Great, Epist. 47, PL 77, 510–511; Epist. 53, PL 77, 649; Council of Toledo IV, canon 57, in Mansi 10, 633; Pius XII, Mystici Corporis, AAS (1943), p. 243; Allocutio, Oct. 6, 1946, AAS (1946), p. 394.

49. Hans Urs von Balthasar, La Gloire et la Croix (Paris: Aubier, 1965), p. 490.

CHAPTER FOUR.   CONFIRMATION

1. Katechetik (Freiburg: Herder, 1955), p. 259.

2. De Institutione Laicali, 1, 7, PL 106, 133.

3. De sacramento Confirmationis, Mansi 24, 407–408.

4. See Mansi 24, 861.

5. Catechismus Concilii Tridentini, Part 2, c. 3, n. 1 (Roma: Propaganda Fidei, 1871), p. 179.

6. See Adolf Adam, *Confirmation et pastorale* (Bruxelles: Lumen Vitae, 1963), pp. 13–16.

7. Westminster: Dacre Press, 1946.

8. Ibid., pp. 31–32.

9. Ibid., p. 15.

10. *Confirmation Today: An Address* (Westminster: Dacre Press, 1946).

11. 2nd ed. (London: Longman's, 1951), pp. 317–318.

12. Controversy was by no means limited to the Anglican Church. See, for example, Louis Bouyer, "Que signifie la confirmation?" *Paroisse et Liturgie* 34 (1952): 3–12; "La signification de la confirmation," *Supplement de la Vie Spirituelle* 29 (1954): 162–179. *La Maison Dieu* 54 (1958) devoted an entire issue to the meaning of confirmation and to its relationship with baptism. Interestingly, the essays by several eminent Catholic scholars do not come to the same conclusions, though they are based on the same sources.

13. See texts in Lampe, *The Seal of the Spirit*, pp. 149–190; J. Lecuyer, "La confirmation chez les Peres," MD 54 (1958): 23–52.

14. Lecuyer, 'La confirmation," p. 39; see also his *Le sacerdoce dans le mystere du Christ* (Paris: Cerf, 1957), pp. 100f.

15. *Epist. 73, 9*, in *Saint Cyprien: Correspondence*, ed. Canon Bayard (Paris: Belles Lettres, 1961), pp. 267–268.

16. PL 3, 1187.

17. *De Resurrectione Carnis*, 8, PL 2, 806.

18. *De Baptismo*, 6–8, PL 1, 1206–1208.

19. *Epist. 25, 3*, PL 20, 554–555.

20. The use of the word *confirmation* for the ritual which confers the gift of the Spirit begins in Gaul, first in the Council of Riez in 439 (Mansi 5, 1092–1093) and then in the Council of Orange in 444 (Mansi 6, 435).

21. *Rite of Confirmation* (Washington: NCCB, 1977), pp. 25, 27, 28.

22. *Epist. 63, 8*, *Saint Cyprien: Correspondence*, p. 204.

23. *Epist. 64, 3*, ibid., 214–215.

24. See "Confirmation chez les Peres," pp. 25–26.

25. *Epist. 75, 12*, *Saint Cyprien*, pp. 298–299.

26. *Adv. Marcionem*, 1, 28, PL 2, 280.

27. *De Pud.*, 9, PL 2, 997; cf. Asterius of Amasea, *In Parabolam de Filio Prodigo*, PG 104, 214: "As both the stole and the confirmation of the gift of the Spirit are given in the regeneration of baptism, so also in the regeneration of penance."

28. *De Anima*, 1, PL 2, 647.

29. *De Baptismo*, 7, PL 1, 1207.

30. *De Baptismo*, 5, PL 1, 1206.

31. *De Baptismo*, 6, PL 1, 1206.

32. R.F. Refoule (ed.), *Tertullien: Traite de Bapteme. Sources Chretiennes* (Paris: Cerf, 1952), p. 75, note 1. See also Lampe, *The Seal of the Spirit*, pp. 157–162.

33. G.R. Beasley-Murray, *Baptism in the New Testament* (London: Macmillan, 1963), p. 276.

34. Ibid.

35. See Lampe, *The Seal of the Spirit*, pp. 97–127.

36. *The Apostolic Tradition*, 22, in B. Botte, *La Tradition Apostolique. Sources Chretiennes* 11 (Paris: Cerf, 1948), p. 52.

37. *Theology of Confirmation in Relation to Baptism*, p. 11.

38. *The Treatise on the Apostolic Tradition of St. Hippolytus of Rome* (London: SPCK, 1937), p. 38, note 1.

39. Ibid., p. lii. Emphasis in original.

40. *La Tradition Apostolique*, pp. 12–13. Emphasis added.

41. H.A. Wilson, *The Gelasian Sacramentary* (Oxford: Clarendon, 1894), pp. 87 and 117.

42. For a varied collection of sources of such an opinion and various ways of articulating it, see H. Weisweiler, "Das Sakrament der Firmung in den systematischen Werken der ersten Fruehscholastik," *Scholastik* 8 (1933): 481–523.

43. See Origen, *Comment. in Joannem* VI, PG 11, 111D; Methodius, *Convivium Decem Virginum* 8, 8, PG 12, 83; Eusebius, *De Eccles. Theologia* 3, 15, PG 15, 515; Macarii Aeg., *Hom. XLIII*, 1, PG 19, 1327; Tertullian, *De Bap.* 6, PL 1, 1207.

44. See Jean Latreille, "L'adulte chretienne, ou l'effet du sacrement de confirmation chez Saint Thomas d'Aquin," *Revue Thomiste* LVIII (1957): 5–28. What follows in the text depends on Latreille.

45. ST, III, 72, 7 ad 2.

46. ST, III, 84, 4 ad 2: "etiam in baptismo accipit homo Spiritum Sanctum."

47. *In IV Sent.*, d. 7, q. 1, a. 1, quaesta 2, sol.

48. Ibid., d. 7, q. 1, a. 1, quaesta. 2 ad 1.

49. Ibid., d. 7, q. 7, a. 2, quaesta. 2.

50. Ibid., ad 2.

51. Latreille, "L'adulte chretienne," p. 20.

52. DS 1601.

53. Rites, p. 290; AAS 63 (1971): 657; cf. Tertullian, *De Resurr. Carnis* 8, PL 2, 806.

54. *Constitution on the Liturgy*, n. 21, DV, 146.

55. Rites, p. 295; AAS 63 (1971): 663.

56. Cf. Cyril of Jerusalem, *Cat. XVIII*, 33, PG 33, 1055; *Epist. Scripta Constantinopoli ad Martyrium Episcopum Antiochenum*, PG 119, 900.

57. Rites, p. 291; AAS 63 (1971): 658; cf. Rites, p. 292; AAS 63 (1971): 660.

58. Rites, p. 307.

59. Ibid., 296.

60. Ibid., 309.

61. *Constitution on the Liturgy*, n. 71, DV, 160.

62. Rites, p. 290; AAS 63 (1971): 658.

63. Ibid. My emphasis.

64. Ibid., p. 291. My emphasis.

65. Ibid., p. 301. My emphasis.

66. Ibid., pp. 301–302.

67. Ibid., p. 298.

68. Ibid., p. 308.

69. Ibid., p. 309.

70. *Constitution on the Liturgy*, n. 26, DV, 147.

71. See "Propositions on the Doctrine of Christian Marriage," in *Origins*, Sept. 28, 1978, p. 237.

72. Rites, p. 20.

73. Ibid., p. 22.

74. Ibid., p. 32.

75. Ibid., pp. 25–26.

76. It is for this reason that I would demur from the scheme proposed by J. Moingt. Here enrollment for initiation would take place in the first months of life, baptism when children begin to understand the faith (between six and twelve years of age), Eucharist when they come to grasp the social nature of the Church (between ten and fourteen), reconciliation in adolescence, and confirmation at adult age. Moingt appears to me to give too much weight to confirmation as the sacrament of definitive initiation. I would prefer to keep baptism-confirmation-Eucharist as closely related as possible, in time as in theology. See J. Moingt, "L'initiation chretienne des jeunes. Pour une renovation de la pastorale sacrementaire," *Etudes* (1972): 437–454, 599–613, 745–763; Charles Paliard, "L'initiation chretienne des jeunes," MD 112 (1972): 96–111; Daniel Boureau, *L'avenir du bapteme* (Lyon: Chalet, 1972).

CHAPTER FIVE. PENANCE-RECONCILIATION

1. Extract from "Patimokka des Moines," cited in C. Vogel, *Le pecheur et la penitence au moyen age* (Paris: Cerf, 1969), p. 226.

2. B. Poschmann, *Penance and the Anointing of the Sick* (New York: Herder, 1964), p. 9.

3. *Constitution on the Church,* n. 8, DV, 24.

4. *De Pudicitia,* 13, PL 2, 1004–1005.

5. Cf. John O'Rourke, "The Second Letter to the Corinthians," in *The Jerome Biblical Commentary,* Vol. 2, ed. Raymond E. Brown et al. (Englewood Cliffs: Prentice-Hall, 1968), p. 278, 11; C.K. Barrett, *A Commentary on the Second Epistle to the Corinthians* (New York: Harper and Row, 1973), p. 89.

6. *2 Clement,* 14, in J.B. Lightfoot, *The Apostolic Fathers* (Grand Rapids: Baker, 1974), p. 49.

7. Ibid., p. 47; cf. *1 Clement,* 56, ibid., p. 36.

8. *2 Clement,* 16, ibid., p. 50; cf. *Didache,* 4, ibid., p. 124; *Epist. of Barnabas,* 19, ibid., p. 154.

9. *Didache,* 4, ibid., p. 125.

10. Ibid., p. 128.

11. E. Amman, "La penitence primitive," in DTC 12, c. 757; see also Poschmann, *Penance and the Anointing,* p. 23.

12. *Epist. to the Philippians,* 6, in *Apostolic Fathers,* p. 97.

13. *Epist. to the Philadelphians,* ibid., p. 79.

14. *1 Clement,* 57, ibid., p. 37.

15. *De Poenitentia,* 4, PL 1, 1233.

16. *De Poenitentia,* 9, PL 1, 1243.

17. Ibid., 1244.

18. Ibid., 1241; see also *De Pudicitia,* 3, 7, 13, PL 2, 986, 993–4, 1005.

19. *De Poenitentia,* PL 1, 1245.

20. *De Pudicitia* 18, PL 2, 1017.

21. Henceforth I shall adhere to the convention suggested by Vogel and use the term *ancient penance* instead of the more common, and misleading, *public penance.* See *Le pecheur et la penitence,* p. 10.

22. *De Pudicitia,* 7, PL 2, 1241.

23. *The Shepherd of Hermas,* Man. 4, 3, in *Apostolic Fathers,* p. 185.

24. See B. Poschmann, *Poenitentia Secunda* (Bonn: 1940).

25. *Sermo 64,* in *The Fathers of the Church,* 31, trans. Mary M. Mueller (New York: Fathers of the Church, Inc., 1956), p. 308. See also *Sermo 179,* ibid., 47, pp. 449–456.

26. *De Poenitentia,* 10, PL 1, 1245.

27. *Sermo 392*, 3, PL 39, 1711.

28. Epist. 167, ad Rusticum, inqu. 2, PL 54, 1203.

29. *Epist. 168*, 2, PL 54, 1211.

30. *Sermo 67*, 1, *Fathers of the Church*, 31, p. 319.

31. For a full treatment see James Dallen, "The Imposition of Hands in Penance: A Study in Liturgical History," WOR 51 (1977): 224–247.

32. *In Leviticum Hom.*, 2, 4, PG 12, 418–419.

33. *Epist. 16*, 2, *Fathers of the Church*, 51, p. 48; *De Lapsis*, 28, PL 4, 488–489.

34. Cf. Augustine, *De Baptismo*, 2, 7, 11; 3, 16, 21; in PL 43, 133 and 149.

35. Poschmann, *Penance and Anointing*, p. 97.

36. Cf. Augustine, *Sermo 232*, 7, 8, PL 38, 111; Jerome, *Epist. 77*, 4, PL 22, 692; Sozomen, *Hist. Eccles.*, PG 67, 1459; First Synod of Orange, can. 3.

37. *Enarratio in Pss.*, 61, 23, PL 36, 746.

38. Can. 19, Mansi, 2, 567.

39. *Sermo 232*, 7, 8, PL 38, 111.

40. *Epist. 167*, inqu. 19, PL 54, 1209.

41. Can. 15 and 44, Mansi, 8, 321 and 332.

42. The phrase is *supplicatio sacerdotum*. Its translation as "the supplication of priests" risks anachronism. For in this period, as I pointed out in the text, the title *sacerdos* was reserved to bishops.

43. *Epist. 108 ad Theodorum*, 2, PL 54, 1011.

44. *Epist. 159 ad Nicetum*, 6, PL 54, 1138.

45. *Contra Luciferianos*, 5, PL 23, 159.

46. *Sermo 45* and *Sermo 49*, 3, PL 54, 288f., 303.

47. *Epist. 25 ad Decentium*, 7, PL 20, 559.

48. Epist. 20, 26, PL 16, 1002; *Hexaemeron*, 5, 25, 91–92, PL 14, 242.

49. The critical evidence is found in Ludwig Bieler, *The Irish Penitential* (Dublin: Institute for Advanced Studies, 1963). A convenient summary is found in Thomas P. Murphy and Michael Rankin, "The Practice of Celtic Penance," in *Resonance* 2 (1966): 35–47.

50. This, at least, is the agreed on practice of the Celtic church. There is evidence that some Irish saints employed non-priests, including women, as confessors. See John McNeil and Helena Gamer, *Medieval Handbook of Penance* (New York: Columbia, 1938), pp. 28–29.

51. Again, this was the *normal* course of events. Anciaux is correct, though, when he states that "the custom developed of allowing the penitent to take part in the Eucharist before his work of satisfaction

was finished." See his *The Sacrament of Penance* (New York: Sheed and Ward, 1962), p. 62. Evidence may be seen in the eighth century, Anglo Saxon *Penitential of Theodore* (1,12,4): "Penitentes secundum canones non debent communicare ante consummationem penitentiae, nos autem pro misericordia post annum vel menses sex licentiam damus."

52. Arnold Van Gennep, *The Rites of Passage* (London: Routledge and Kegan Paul, 1960).

53. "Christian Rituals," in *Horizons* 7 (1980): 7–35.

54. PL 87, 1018.

55. Charles Curran, "The Sacrament of Penance Today," WOR 43 (1969): 510.

56. PL 16, 278; cf. *Constitution on the Church*, n. 11, DV 28.

57. Rites, 144.

58. E. Schillebeeckx, *Christ the Sacrament of Encounter with God* (New York: Sheed and Ward, 1963), p. 68. My emphasis.

59. I choose this double terminology in imitation of the new ritual which, though it is presented as a rite of penance (*Ordo Penitentiae*), offers more talk of reconciliation than of penance. Though both terms are entirely traditional, I agree with Mannion that the failure to distinguish them adequately is at the root of the malaise which presently affects the ritual of penance-reconciliation in the Church. See M. Francis Mannion, "Penance and Reconciliation: A Systemic Analysis," in WOR 60 (1986): 98–118.

60. *Constitution on the Liturgy*, n. 72, DV, p. 161.

61. Ibid., nn. 26–27, pp. 147–148.

62. Introduction to the new rite of reconciliation, n. 31. My emphasis.

63. Ibid., n. 8.

64. See AAS 64 (1972): 510–514.

65. DS 1707.

66. Cf. Ex 33:19; Rom 9:15.

67. Cf. J.M.R. Tillard, "Penitence et eucharistie," MD 90 (1967): 103–131; L. Ligier, "Penitence et eucharistie en Orient: theologie sur une interference de prieres et de rites," *Orientalia Christiana Periodica* 29 (1963): 5–78.

68. During Lent of 1976, Bishop Eric Grasar of Shrewsbury, England announced in a pastoral letter that he and his auxiliary, Bishop John Brewer, would be attending station Masses in the various deaneries of his diocese and that "all who are present will be invited to accept the forgiveness of all their past sins." He reminded all who would participate in this general confession and absolution that they were required to have the proper dispositions. In a covering note to

his clergy he explained that "in this way, many who are conscious of grave sin would find their way back to the sacraments through general absolution. Having been absolved and having received Holy Communion, they would find confession no longer the insuperable difficulty it was before absolution. (Cf. *The Tablet*, March 6, 1976, pp. 243–244.) On the first Sunday of Advent, 1976, Bishop Carroll Dozier of Memphis gave general absolution at a reconciliation service held in the Mid-South Coliseum. It is of interest to note that the very effect Bishop Grasar hoped for was reported in Memphis. Priests surveyed in the Memphis diocese reported an increase in the number of confessions during Holy Week of 1977. They attributed the increase, in some cases more than double, to the reconciliation and general absolution of the previous fall. Cf. WOR 51 (1977): 260.

69. Rites, p. 362.

70. Ibid., p. 351.

71. See the excellent summary of contemporary answers to this question in D. Dease, "General Confession and Absolution," WOR 51 (1977): 536–545.

72. See its declaration *Mysterium Ecclesiae* in AAS 65 (1973), esp. pp. 402–404.

73. Hubert Jedin, "La necessite de la confession privee selon le Concile de Trente," MD 104 (1970): 114; also A. Duval, "Le 'droit divin' de l'integrite de la confession selon le canon 7 *De Paenitentia* du Concile de Trente," *Revue des sciences phil. et theologiques* 63 (1979): 549–560; "Le Concile de Trente et la confession," MD 118 (1974): 131–180; J. Lecuyer, "La confession sacramentelle au Concile de Trente," MD 134 (1978): 74–84.

74. J. Lecuyer, "La confession sacramentelle," p. 82; see also Brian Gogan, "Penance Rites of the West Syrian Liturgy," *Irish Theological Quarterly* XLII (1975): 182–196, esp. 193–194.

75. See Zoltan Alzeghy, "Problemi Dogmatici della Celebrazione Penitenziale Communitaria," *Gregorianum* XLVIII (1967): 577–587.

76. *Rite of Penance*, nn. 12–13, Rites, p. 349. My emphasis.

77. Ibid., pp. 349–350.

78. Cf. *Constitution on the Church, n. 11, DV, 28.*

79. Rites, p. 364.

CHAPTER SIX.   EUCHARIST

1. See Joachim Jeremias, *The Eucharistic Words of Jesus* (New York: Scribner's, 1966), pp. 15–88.

2. *Ancient Israel. Its Life and Institutions* (New York: McGraw-Hill, 1961), p. 489.

3. Nahum H. Glatzer (ed.), *The Passover Haggadah* (New York: Schocken, 1969), p. 9.

4. Ibid., p. 27.

5. Cf. Harald Riesenfeld, "Sabbat et jour du Seigneur," *New Testament Essays: Studies in Memory of T. W. Manson* (Manchester: University Press, 1959), pp. 161–172; Willy Rordorf, *Der Sontag* (Zurich: Zwingli Verlag, 1969); S.C. Mosna, *Storia della domenica dalle origini agli inizi del V secolo* (Roma: Gregorian University Press, 1969); Samuele Bacchiocchi, *From Sabbath to Sunday* (Roma: Gregorian University Press, 1977); P. Grelot, "Du sabbat Juif au dimanche Chretienne," MD 123 (1975): 14–54.

6. Cf. *The Epistle of Barnabas*, 15, in J.B. Lightfoot, *The Apostolic Fathers* (Grand Rapids: Baker, 1974); Justin, *Apologia I*, 67, PG 6, 430.

7. Bacchiocchi, *From Sabbath to Sunday*, p. 301.

8. *Essays on the Lord's Supper* (Richmond: John Knox, 1959), p. 12.

9. Cf. Gustave Martelet, *Resurrection, eucharistie, et genese de l'homme* (Paris: Desclee, 1972), p. 115; Edward Schillebeeckx, *The Eucharist* (London: Sheed and Ward, 1968), p. 108.

10. Joseph de Baciochhi, *L'eucharistie. Sa signification, difficultes, celebrations actuelles* (Paris: Desclee, 1975), p. 18. Emphasis in original. Cp. J.M.R. Tillard, "Le memorial dans la vie de l'eglise," MD 106 (1971): 24.

11. *In Matt. Hom.*, 25, 3, PG 31, 331. For further texts from the Fathers, see Joannes Betz, *Die Eucharistie in der Zeit der Griechischen Vater* (Freiburg, 1955), pp. 159f.

12. DS 846.

13. DS 1740–41.

14. *Constitution on the Liturgy*, n. 47, DV, 154; cf. *Decree on the Missionary Activity of the Church*, n. 14, DV, 601.

15. AAS 59 (1967): 559–573. See esp. nn. 3 and 12.

16. J.P. Audet, "Literary Forms and Contents of a Normal Eucharistia in the First Century," in *Studia Evangelica: Papers Presented to the International Congress on the Four Gospels in 1957* (Berlin, 1959), pp. 643–644. This essay appeared also, "considerably amplified and modified," in *Revue Biblique* 65 (1958): 371–391. Cp. H. Beyer, "Eulogein," TDNT, 2, pp. 754–765; H. Conzelmann, "Eucharistein," TDNT, 9, pp. 407–415.

17. "Literary Forms," p. 646. See also his *La Didache: Instruction des apotres* (Paris: Gabalda, 1958), pp. 372–433.

18. The Greek words in the Gospels for his *blessing* are both *eu-*

charistesas and *eulogesas*. Because of the cluster we can understand also *exomologeomai*.

19. Heb 13:16; see also Roman Canon, Eucharistic Prayer I, and Charles Perrot, "Le repas du Seigneur," MD 123 (1975): 29–46.

20. See Joannes Metz, "Sacrifice et action de graces," MD 87 (1966): 78–96.

21. Francis Clark, *Eucharistic Sacrifice and the Reformation* (London: Darton, Longman, Todd, 1960), pp. 96–97. Emphases in original.

22. DS 1751–1754.

23. For the theological opinions at the time of Trent and since, see Clark, *Eucharistic Sacrifice.*

24. G. Van Der Leeuw, *La religion dans son essence et ses manifestations* (Paris, 1948), pp. 342–352.

25. See H. Haag, "Paque," in *Dictionnaire de la Bible, Supplement,* VI (Paris: Letouzey, 1960), cc. 1125–1130.

26. See Louis Bouyer, *Rite and Man* (London: Burns Oates, 1963), esp. Chap. 6, "Sacrificial Rites."

27. B. Cooke, "Synoptic Presentation of the Eucharist as Covenant Sacrifice," TS 21 (1960): 25, 26, 27; cf. X. Leon-Dufour, "Prenez! Ceci est mon corps pour vous," NRT 104 (1982): 225–227.

28. J.M.R. Tillard, *L'eucharistie, Paque de l'eglise* (Paris: Cerf, 1964), pp. 102–103.

29. See Anthony A. Stephenson, "Two Views of the Mass: Medieval Linguistic Ambiguities," TS 22 (1961): 588–609.

30. ST, III, 22, 3 ad 2. Emphasis added.

31. ST, III, 73, 4. Emphasis added.

32. ST, III, 83, 1 ad 2. Emphasis added.

33. Stephenson, "Two Views," p. 593.

34. *Mediator Dei,* AAS 39 (1947): 548.

35. *Eucharisticum Mysterium,* AAS 49 (1967): 541.

36. *Sacrosanctum Concilium,* AAS 56 (1964): 113.

37. *Euch. Mysterium,* ibid.

38. *Mysterium Fidei,* AAS 57 (1965): 762.

39. *Euch. Mysterium,* nn. 12 and 31, AAS 59 (1967): 548–49, 557. See also nn. 33 and 35.

40. "Commentaire de l'instruction sur le culte eucharistique," MD 91 (1967): 47.

41. DS 1643: "ut sumatur institutum." DS 1740: " . . . corpus et sanguinem suum sub speciebus panis et vini Deo Patri obtulit ac sub earumdem rerum symbolis apostolis . . . ut sumerent tradidit."

42. *Euch. Mysterium*, n. 12, AAS 59 (1967): 549. Cf. ST, III, 79, 7 ad 2.

43. "Nec est articulus fidei credere quod sic vel sic fiat illa conversio, sed tantummodo credere quod corpus Christi ad prolationem illorum verborum sit in altari." Cited in Hans Jorissen, *Die Entfaltung der Transsubstantiationslehre Bis Zum Beginn der Hochscholastik* (Münster: Aschendorff, 1965), p. 24.

44. *L'Eucharistie. Memorial du Seigneur. Sacrifice d'action de grace et d'intercession* (Neuchatel: Delachaux, 1959), p. 256.

45. DS 1642.

46. DS 1652.

47. AAS 57 (1965): 766. Emphasis in original.

48. *Consubstantiel et Transsubstantiation* (Bordeaux: Taffard, 1974). I have been informed that this book has been reissued recently in a much enlarged edition, but I have been unable to consult this enlarged edition.

49. See *Modern Eucharistic Agreement* (London: SPCK, 1973).

50. See *Vers une meme foi eucharistique* (Taize: Presse de Taize, 1972).

51. Cf. *Consubstantiel*, pp. 89–95.

52. Ibid., p. 12.

53. See above, note 42.

54. "Teologia, Filosofia et Fisica nella Dottrina della Transsubstanziazione," *La Scuola Cattolica* 83 (1955): 115–116. Emphasis in original. The entire article is a good account of the history of the term *transubstantiation*.

55. E. Schillebeeckx, *The Eucharist*, pp. 89–151; see also E. Kilmartin, "The Eucharist in Recent Literature," TS 32 (1971): 233–277.

56. See Chapters One and Two.

57. "Sacramentum ponitur in genere signi." ST, III, 60, 1. See also arts. 2 and 3.

58. "Transubstantiation: How Far Is this Doctrine Historically Conditioned?" CON, 4, 3, (1967): 45–46. Emphasis in original.

59. Ibid., p. 46.

60. See *Mysterium Fidei*, AAS 57 (1965): 762–766.

61. Ibid., 764.

62. Ibid., 765.

63. See note 47 above.

64. P. Schoonenberg, "Transsubstantiation," p. 47. See also A. Gerken, *Teologia dell'eucharistia* (Alba: Edizione Paoline, 1977), pp. 204–205.

65. *Catechesis XXIII*, 21, PG 33, 1124–1125.

66. *De Fide Orthodoxa,* 4, 13, PG 94, 1149.

67. DS 700. Emphasis added.

68. DS 1651. Emphasis added.

69. Cf. X. Leon-Dufour, "Prenez! Ceci est mon corps pour vous," NRT 104 (1982): 231, n. 14.

70. J. Dupont, "Ceci est mon corps, ceci est mong sang," NRT 80 (1958): 1034.

71. J. Jeremias, *Jesus' Promise to the Nations* (London: SCM, 1958), p. 60.

72. The Greek verbs which have been translated historically as *hallowed be, be done* and *come* are all in the imperative form. They are commands to God to bless his name, to do his will and to establish his kingdom. So I have translated them. More troublesome is the translation of *artos epiousios.* Traditional versions vary. Jerome has *supersubstantial.* Itala has *daily,* which Martin Luther and all subsequent translations followed. However, for a number of reasons, many modern scholars translate *epiousios* as *pertaining to tomorrow,* and hence *artos epiousios* as *tomorrow's bread.* The RSV offers "our bread for the morrow" as an alternative reading in both the Matthean (6:9–13) and Lukan (11:2–4) versions. See also J. Jeremias, *The Prayers of Jesus* (London: SCM, 1967), pp. 82–107, and Anton Vogtle, "The Lord's Prayer: A Prayer for Jews and Christians," in *The Lord's Prayer and Jewish Liturgy,* ed. Jakob Petuchowski and Michael Brocke (New York: Seabury, 1978), pp. 93–117. What, then, is "tomorrow's bread"? It is an image of the fulfillment of the end times. It is, in other words, another way of speaking of the kingdom or the rule of God, which is so often described in banquet (bread) terms.

CHAPTER SEVEN. ANOINTING OF THE SICK

1. Jgs 9, 8; 1 Sam 9:16; 10:1; 15:1, 17; 16:3, 12; 2 Sam 2:4; 3:39; 5:3, 17; 12:7; 19:10; 1 Kgs 1:34, 39, 45; 5:1; 19:15; 2 Kgs 9:3, 6; Ps 23:5; 45:7; 89;20.

2. Ex 28:41; 29:7,29; 30:30–33; 40:13; Lev 4:3; 7:36; 8:12; Num 3:3; 35:25.

3. 1 Kgs 19:16; Is. 61:1; cf. Lk 4:18.

4. Gen 28:18; 31:13; Ex 29:36; 30:23–29; 37:29; 40:9–12; Lev 8:10; Num 7:1, 10.

5. Is 1:6; Lk 10:34. The law prescribed an anointing with oil also for the purification of lepers: Lev 14:15–18, 26–29.

6. See Mishna, Shabbat 14:4. "Whoever has lumbago shall not

rub himself on the sabbath with wine or vinegar, but with oil." Jerusalem Talmud, Berachot 1:2. "For a sick person one can make a compress of old wine and oil, perfumed and mixed with water." See also Josephus, *Bellum*, 1, 33, 5; *Antiquities*, 17, 6, 5.

7. See Mishna, Shabbat 23,5. See also Mk 14:3–8; 16:1.

8. DS 1695; cf. DS 1716.

9. Martin Dibelius, *James: A Commentary on the Epistle of James*, rev. H. Greeven (Philadelphia: Fortress, 1976), p. 254.

10. Charles Gusmer, "Liturgical Traditions of Christian Illness: Rites of the Sick," WOR 46 (1972): 531.

11. For a discussion see Jean Paul Audet, *La Didache: instruction des apotres* (Paris: Gabalda, 1958). *Constitutiones Apostolicae*, 7, 27, PG 1, 1019.

12. See F. Nau, "Constitutions apostoliques," in DTC III, 2, c. 1523: "This *Didache* corresponds to the first part of Book 7 of the *Apostolic Constitutions* and reveals to us its source." Also J. Quasten, "Apostolic Constitutions," in *New Catholic Encyclopedia*, I, 690: "Book 7, 1–32, is based on the *Didache*."

13. Gregory Dix, *The Treatise on the Apostolic Tradition of St. Hippolytus of Rome* (London: SPCK, 1968), p. 10.

14. Gen. Rabba, 33, 20c, 30.

15. *Epist. ad Decentium 8*, PL 20, 560.

16. Antoine Chavasse, *Etude sur l'onction des infirmes dans l'eglise latine du IIIe au XIe siecle. I: Du IIIe siecle a la reforme Carolingienne* (Lyons: Faculte de Theologie, 1942). Unfortunately, this first volume is all that appeared.

17. PL 39, 2273.

18. PL 93, 39.

19. Ibid., 39–40.

20. PL 92, 188.

21. Can. 10, PL 97, 124.

22. Can. 17, PL 97, 326.

23. Can. 5, PL 89, 821.

24. Cf. Hincmar of Rheims, *Capitula Presbyteris Data* (852), can. 10, PL 125, 779; Rather of Verona, *Synodica* (966), cap. 7, PL 136, 559.

25. PL 106, 260–261.

26. See, for instance, C. Ruch, "Extreme onction du Ier au IXe siecle," DTC V, 2, cc. 1970–1978.

27. B. Poschmann, *Penance and Anointing*, p. 244.

28. Ibid., p. 246.

29. Jean-Charles Didier, "L'onction des malades dans la theologie contemporaine," MD 113 (1973): 61.

30. For texts see Paul Palmer, *Sacraments and Forgiveness* (Westminster: Newman, 1959), pp. 299–303.

31. ST, Suppl., 30, 2 ad 3.

32. See Palmer, *Sacraments and Forgiveness*, p. 310. Also DS 1698.

33. DS 1696.

34. DV 161.

35. *Acta Synodalia Sacrosancti Concilii Oecumenici Vaticani II*, Vol. II, Pars VI (Roma: Typis Polyglottis Vaticanis, 1973), p. 425, n. 73.

36. AAS 65 (1973): 5.

37. *Constitution on the Church*, n. 11, DV, 28.

38. RSV reads "*has done* all things *well.*" But *poiein* may mean either to do or to make and *kalos* may be translated either good or well.

39. See Otto Betz and Werner Grimm, *Wesen und Wirklichkeit Der Wunder Jesu: Heilungen-Retungen-Zeichen-Aufleuchteungen* (Frankfurt: Lang, 1977), pp. 30–53.

40. PL 78, 234. My emphasis.

41. PL 74, 1223.

42. DS 1696. My emphasis.

43. *Constitution on the Church*, n. 11, DV, 28.

44. *Constitution on the Liturgy*, nn. 26–27, DV, 147–48.

45. Rites, p. 590.

46. Cf. p. 16.

47. Rites, p. 584.

48. See *In IV Sent.*, d. 1, q. 1, a. 4, quaest. 3.

49. Rites, p. 603.

50. Cf. P.M. Gy, "Le nouveau rituel romain des malades," MD 113 (1973): 40–42.

51. Rites, p. 600.

52. See my "Christian Rituals: An Essay in Sacramental Symbolisms," Horizons 7 (1980): 13–23.

53. Cf. John A.T. Robinson, "The Man for Others," in *Honest to God* (London: SCM, 1963), pp. 64–83.

54. Rites, p. 590.

55. AAS 59 (1967): 562, n. 39.

56. Mansi, II, 674.

57. See CIC, can. 684 and can. 867, 2.

58. Rites, p. 587.

59. AAS 59 (1967): 558, n. 32.

CHAPTER EIGHT. MARRIAGE

1. Cf. Herbert W. Richardson, *Nun, Witch, Playmate: The Americanization of Sex* (New York: Harper and Row, 1971).

2. For more detailed information see M. Eliade, *Patterns in Comparative Religion* (London: Sheed and Ward, 1979); E.O. James, *The Cult of the Mother Goddess* (London: Thames and Hudson, 1959).

3. E. Schillebeeckx, *Marriage: Secular Reality and Saving Mystery* Vol. 1 (London: Sheed and Ward, 1965), p. 39.

4. F. R. Barry, *A Philosophy from Prison* (London: SCM, 1926), p. 151. Cf. Schillebeeckx, *Marriage*, p. 43; Markus Barth, *Ephesians: Translation and Commentary on Chapters 4–6* (New York: Doubleday, 1974), pp. 734–738; X. Léon-Dufour (ed.), *Vocabulaire de Theologie Biblique*, 2nd. ed. rev. (Paris: Cerf, 1970), cc. 146–152; Michael G. Lawler, *Secular Marriage, Christian Sacrament* (Mystic, CT: Twenty-Third Publications, 1985).

5. See Richard Batey, "The *mia sarx* Union of Christ and the Church," *New Testament Studies* 13 (1966–67): 272.

6. For a discussion of whether the term *myth* should be applied to any biblical passage, and for a suggestion of alternative language, see John McKenzie, "Myth and the Old Testament," *Catholic Biblical Quarterly* XXI (1959): 265–282.

7. It is of no interest to any thesis in this book whether the apostle Paul was or was not the author of the Letter to the Ephesians, and so I do not deal with that disputed question, preferring to refer only to *the author*. Those who require information on the question may consult any of the modern commentaries.

8. Martin Dibelius, *An Die Kolosser Epheser an Philemon* (Tübingen: J.C.B. Mohr, 1953), pp. 48–50.

9. Markus Barth, *Ephesians*, p. 607.

10. *The Jerusalem Bible* (London: Darton, Longman and Todd, 1966).

11. *The Holy Bible: Revised Standard Version* (London: Nelson, 1959).

12. Markus Barth, *Ephesians*, p. 609.

13. Heinrich Schlier, *Der Brief an die Epheser* (Dusseldorf: Patmos, 1962), p. 252.

14. J. Paul Sampley, *'And the Two Shall Become One Flesh': A Study of Traditions in Ephesians 5:21–33* (Cambridge: University Press, 1971), pp. 119–121.

15. Markus Barth, *Ephesians*, p. 607.

16. Ibid., p. 618. For a full development of the notion of service

in the Christian Church, see Patrick McCaslin and Michael G. Lawler, *Sacrament of Service* (New York: Paulist Press, 1986).

17. Cf. Sampley, *The Two Shall Become One Flesh*, p. 33.

18. Cf. ibid., p. 30. See pp. 30–34; cf. Barth, *Ephesians*, pp. 704–708.

19. Cf. Schlier, *Der Brief*, p. 262; Dibelius, *An Die Kolosser*, p. 95.

20. C. Taylor, *The Shepherd of Hermas*, Vol. 1 (London: SPCK, 1903), pp. 119–120.

21. Can. 17, Mansi, IV, 331.

22. Cf. H. Conzelmann, *A Commentary on the First Epistle to the Corinthians* (Philadelphia: Fortress, 1975), p. 120.

23. I wish only to state, but not develop, here that the evidence in the Fathers of the Church appears to me, in spite of some difficulty with vocabulary, to be solidly in favor of indissolubility and against divorce and remarriage. For excellent surveys of their positions, see R. Souarn, "L'adultere et le lien du mariage d'apres les peres de l'eglise," DTC, I, cc. 475–484; P. Adnes, *Le Mariage*, pp. 61–68. For the varied theories and practices of the Christian churches, see Lawler, *Secular Marriage, Christian Sacrament*, pp. 81–116.

24. Those who wish to see the opinions may consult with fruit A. Myre, "Dix ans d'exegese sur le divorce dans le Nouveau Testament," *Le Divorce: l'eglise catholique ne devrait-elle pas modifier son attitude seculaire a l'egard de l'indissolubilite du mariage* (Montreal: Fides, 1973), pp. 139–163; also J. Fitzmyer, "The Matthean Divorce Texts and Some New Palestinian Evidence," TS 37 (1976): 197–226; Bruce Malina, "Does *porneia* Mean Fornication," *Novum Testamentum* XIV (1972): 10–17.

25. *In Epist. ad Ephes. Cap. V*, PG, 62, 146–150.

26. *Epist. ad Diognetum*, 5, PG 2, 1173.

27. *Legatio pro Christianis*, 33, PG 6, 965.

28. *Adv. Haer.*, 1, 28, 1, PG 7, 690.

29. *Stromatum*, 3, 12, PG 8, 1186.

30. Ibid., 3, 17, PG 8, 1206.

31. Ibid., 2, 23, PG 8, 1086; see also *Paed.*, 2, 10, PG 8, 498: "For those who are joined in marriage, its scope and purpose is the reception of children."

32. Ibid., 2, 23, PG 8, 1090.

33. Ibid., 3, 9, PG 8, 1170.

34. Ibid., 3, 12, PG 8, 1184.

35. Ibid., 2, 23, PG 8, 1090–91.

36. Ibid., 4, 19, PG 8, 1333.

37. *In Genesim Hom. VI*, 4, PG 12, 192.

38. *Comment. in Epist. ad Rom. X*, 1, PG 14, 1249.

39. *In Cant. Cant. II*, 1, PG 13, 47.

40. See *In Jer. Hom. XI*, 5, PG 13, 374; *In Lev. Hom. VIII*, 2, PG 12, 493; *In Lev. Hom. XII*, 4, PG 12, 539; Origen's belief that genital activity was quite incompatible with prayer and the search for God led him to castrate himself so that he might totally engage himself in that search.

41. *Ad Uxorem I*, 2–3, PL 1, 1277–9.

42. *Ad Uxorem II*, 9, PL 1, 1302–3.

43. *De Pud.*, 16, PL 2, 2, 1012.

44. *De Exhort. Castitatis*, 9, PL 2, 2, 924.

45. For a summary treatment of other Fathers on marriage, see P. Adnes, *Le Mariage*, pp. 50–55 and bibliography.

46. *De Haeresibus*, 46, PL 42, 37.

47. *De Nuptiis et Concup.*, 2, 32, 54, PL 44, 468–9. See also *De Bono Coniugali*, passim, PL 40, 374–396.

48. *De Genesi ad Litt.*, 9, 7, 12, PL 34, 397; see also *De Bono Coniugali*, 24, 32, PL 40, 394; *De Pecc. Orig.*, 34, 39, PL 44, 404; *De Nuptiis et Concup.*, 1, 17, 19, PL 44, 424; *Contra Julianum Pelag.*, 5, 12, 46, PL 44, 810. For an extended analysis and bibliography see A. Reuter, *Sancti Aurelii Augustini Doctrina de Bonis Matrimonii. Analecta Gregoriana*, Vol. 27 (Rome: Gregorian University, 1942).

49. *De Bono Coniugali*, 9, 9, PL 40, 380; see ibid., PL 40, 378; *De Coniugiis Adulterinis*, 2, 12, PL 40, 479; *Contra Faustum Manich.*, 19, 26, PL 42, 365.

50. *De Genesi ad Litt.*, 9, 7, 12, PL 34, 397; *De Bono Coniug.*, 15, 17, PL 40, 385; ibid., 24, 32, PL 40, 394; *De Nupt. et Concup.*, 1, 10, 11, PL 44, 420.

51. *Contra Julianum Pelag.*, 3, 23, 53, PL 44, 730.

52. *De Bono Coniug.*, 6, 6, PL 40, 377–8; ibid., 10, 11, PL 40, 381; *De Coniug. Adulterinis*, 2, 12, PL 40, 479; *Contra Jul. Pelagianum*, 2, 7, 20, PL 44, 687.

53. *Epistolarum Liber IX*, Epist. 64, PL 77, 1196.

54. ST, III (Suppl.), 65, 1, corp.

55. Ibid., 1, 98, 2 ad 3.

56. Ibid., III (Suppl.), 41, 3 ad 6.

57. Ibid., corp.; cf. *Contra Gentiles*, 3, 126; IIa IIae, 153, 2.

58. Ibid., ad 1.

59. Ibid., III (Suppl.), 41, 4; ibid., 49, 5.

60. IIa IIae, 142, 1.

61. E.C. Messenger, *Two in One Flesh. Part 2: The Mystery of Sex in Marriage* (London: Sands, 1948), pp. 178–79.

62. *Sententiae*, 4, d. 1, c. 4.

63. Ibid., 4, d. 2, c. 1.

64. Ibid., 4, d. 26, c. 6.
65. Ibid., d. 26, a. 14, q. 2 ad 1.
66. Ibid., d. 26, q. 2, a. 3; repeated in *Suppl.*, 42, 3c.
67. *Contra Gentiles*, 4, 78.
68. DS 718.
69. DS 761.
70. DS 860.
71. DS 1310.
72. DS 1327.
73. Cf. DS 1601, 1606, 1801, 1802, 1807.
74. Cf. *Sermo 51*, 13, 21, PL 38, 344–345; *Contra Faustum Manich.*, 23, 8, PL 42, 470–471; *Contra Jul. Pelag.*, 5, 12, 46–47, PL 44, 810–811.
75. Cf. *De Perpetua Virginitate B. Mariae*, 4 and 19, PL 23, 186 and 203.
76. CIC, Can. 1015, 1.
77. DS 1813–1816.
78. Cf. pp. 78–84.
79. J. Dominian, *Christian Marriage* (London: Darton, Longman and Todd, 1968), p. ix and p. viii.
80. CIC, Can. 108, 1 and Can. 1012, 1 and 2. Emphasis added.
81. Cf. pp. 36–41.
82. Cf. p. 16.
83. Cf. pp. 57–59.
84. *Constitution on the Sacred Liturgy*, n. 59, DV, p. 158.
85. *Constitution on the Church*, n. 11, DV, p. 29.
86. Those who wish to survey the opinions may consult with profit *Foi et sacrement de mariage* (Paris: Chalet, 1974). It is noteworthy that French theologians and canon lawyers, confronted by a mass of *baptized non-believers* (see "Propositions on the Doctrine of Christian Marriage," in *Origins*, Sept. 28, 1978, p. 237), have made sustained efforts to elaborate theological and canonical theories to ground a concerted pastoral practice. The English-speaking churches, undoubtedly faced with the same problem on an ever-expanding scale, would do well similarly to confront their problems from within their own cultural situations.
87. DS 1801. Emphasis added.
88. CIC (1917) 1012, 2. Emphasis added. See also CIC (1983) 1055.
89. A. Duval, "Contrat et sacrement de mariage au Concile de Trente," MD 127 (1976): 50.
90. Ibid., p. 63.
91. This chapter was written in Rome in December 1981, while

the new Code of Canon Law was in its final stages of approbation. The new Code has since been published. It speaks in the same terms, only substituting "covenant" for "contract."

92. See pp. 76–77.

93. See above, note 86.

94. I use the words *sacrament* and *sacramental* here in their technical Roman Catholic senses. I have no problem, however, with the extended, analogical meanings given to the words by J. de Baciocchi when he argues that even the marriages of pagans, non-believers and divorced and remarried Catholics are "sacramental." See his "Propositions au sujet du mariage des baptises non-croyants," in *Foi et sacrement de mariage,* pp. 110–116. See also the comments of the International Theological Commission in "Propositions on the Doctrine of Christian Marriage," in *Origins,* Sept. 28, 1978, pp. 237–38.

95. The well-known judgment of the *Letter to Diognetus* that Christians "marry like everyone else" shows that Christians did not abandon their ancestral ways of marrying. See above, note 26. See also CIC, Can. 1098. The Code's granting of a dispensation from the presence of a designated priest in the case in which a couple would have to wait a month for him to be present seriously weakens the claim that his presence is required for validity.

96. See *La Documentation Catholique,* Dec. 7, 1969, pp. 1075–77; see also James A. Schmeiser, "Marriage: New Alternatives," WOR 55 (1981): 23–34.

97. AAS 59 (1967): 166.

98. *Constitution on the Church in the Modern World,* n. 36, DV, p. 233.

99. Ibid., n. 76, p. 288.

100. *Declaration on Religious Freedom,* n. 10, DV, pp. 689–690.

101. Much like the meaning assigned to it, for instance, by Michael Novak in *Ascent of the Mountain, Flight of the Dove: An Invitation to Religious Studies* (New York: Harper and Row, 1978).

102. See John Giles Milhaven, "Conjugal Sexual Love and Contemporary Moral Theology," in TS 35 (1974): 704–05.

103. "On Taking Sex Seriously," in *Moral Issues and Christian Response,* ed. P. Jersild and D. Johnson (New York: Holt, Rinehart, Winston, 1971), pp. 102–104.

104. John Giles Milhaven, "Conjugal Sexual Love," n. 15, p. 700.

105. Ibid., p. 705.

106. This part of my definition is adapted from J. Dominian, *Christian Marriage,* pp. 243–44.

CHAPTER NINE.   HOLY ORDERS

1. John A.T. Robinson, "Christianity's 'No' to Priesthood," in *The Christian Priesthood,* eds. N. Lash and J. Rhymer (London: Darton, Longman and Todd, 1970), p. 4. See also Raymond E. Brown, *Priest and Bishop: Biblical Reflections* (London: Chapman, 1971); E. Schillebeeckx, *Ministry: A Case for Change* (New York: Crossroad, 1981).

2. Robinson, "Christianity's 'No,' " p. 4.

3. John H. Elliott, *The Elect and the Holy* (Leiden: Brill, 1966), p. 26.

4. Ibid., p. 28.

5. "Will be taken from you" and "will be given" are examples of what Jeremias has called "the divine passive," that is, the use of the passive voice as a circumlocution for the name of God. See J. Jeremias, *New Testament Theology: The Proclamation of Jesus* (New York: Scribner's, 1971), pp. 9–14.

6. Again the pious passive-God will break them to pieces.

7. *The Elect,* p. 124.

8. E.G. Selwyn, *The First Epistle of St. Peter,* 2nd. ed. (New York: Macmillan, 1969), p. 291.

9. *Konigtum Gottes* (Heidelberg, 1956), pp. 99f.

10. Elliott, *The Elect,* p. 57.

11. See Schillebeeckx, *Ministry,* p. 51; also Elliott, *The Elect,* passim.

12. *De Purificatione B. Mariae Sermo 5,* PL 185, 87.

13. *Constitutiones Apostolicae,* III, 15, PG 1, 798.

14. *Theophile d'Antioche: Trois Livres a Autolychus,* trans. J. Sender (Paris: Cerf, 1948), 1, 12, p. 85. Cf. Rufinus, *Comment. in Symb. Apost.,* PL 21, 345.

15. PL 40, 1033. Cf. *Enarr. in Ps. XXVI,* PL 36, 200.

16. Cited in J. Lecuyer, *Le Sacerdoce dans le Mystere du Christ.* (Paris: Cerf, 1957), p. 201, n. 1.

17. *Comment. in Ps. 104,* in *Corpus Christianorum, Series Latina,* LXXII, p. 230; *Tract. de Ps. 104,* ibid., LXXVIII.

18. G. Bornkamm, "Presbyteros," TDNT, VI: 655.

19. R. Bultmann, *Theol.,* 448.

20. Raymond E. Brown, "Episkope and Episkopos: The New Testament Evidence," TS 41 (1980): 333. For an extended discussion of the dyad *presbyteros-neoteros* see J. Elliott, "Ministry and Church Order in the New Testament: A Traditio-Historical Analysis," *Cath. Biblical Quarterly* 32 (1970): 367–391.

21. For the pre-New Testament meanings of *episkopos* see C. Spicq, *Les Epitres Pastorales*, I (Paris: Gabalda, 1969), pp. 71–72, 440–450; H. Beyer, "Episkopos", TDNT, II: 608–615.

22. Spicq, *Les Epitres Pastorales*, p. 439.

23. Ibid., p. 73.

24. Jerome Crowe, in *The Acts* (Wilmington: Glazier, 1979), p. 156, takes this opinion so much as a given that he declares without any hesitation that "elders" and "overseers" or "guardians" (*episkopoi*) are synonymous terms. See also Schillebeeckx, *Ministry*, p. 18 and p. 146; Hans Küng, *Why Priests?* (London: Fount Paperback, 1977), p. 34.

25. The Pauline authorship, and therefore the dating, of the pastorals is still a vexed question. A survey of pertinent discussions can be found in *Introduction to the New Testament*, eds. P. Feine, J. Behm and W. Kummel (Nashville: Abingdon, 1966). My own judgment about both the authorship and the dating is well stated by Robert J. Karris, *The Pastoral Epistles* (Wilmington: Glazier, 1979). "The pastorals are not written by Paul, but by someone else in his name" (p. xi). "These letters of transition were all written at the same time, namely, around 110" (p. xiii). Raymond Brown claims to see "little reason for dating them later than the 80s" ("Episkope and Episkopos," p. 331, n. 20).

26. Spicq, *Epitres Pastorales*, p. 71.

27. Much has been written about the causal link from the Qumran *mebaqqer* to the *episkopos* of the pastorals. But I find the causal connection ill-established, and I am willing to concede only a parallel development in both communities of an office of singular, quasi-monarchical authority. See Bo Reicke, "The Constitution of the Church," in *The Scrolls and the New Testament*, ed. K. Stendahl, p. 154.

28. R. Brown, *Priest and Bishop*, pp. 17–19.

29. H. Küng, *Why Priests?* p. 28.

30. *In Isaiam Hom. VI*, 1, PG 13, 239.

31. *Sermo 340*, 1, PL 38, 1484.

32. See Raymond Brown, *The Community of the Beloved Disciple* (New York: Paulist, 1979); K. Donfried, "Ecclesiastical Authority in 2 and 3 John," in *L'Evangile de Jean*, ed. M. de Jonge (Gembloux, 1977), pp. 325–333.

33. Schillebeeckx, *Ministry*, p. 24.

34. *Dogmatic Constitution on the Church*, n. 28, DV, p. 53.

35. DS 1776.

36. *Constitution on the Church*, n. 28, DV, p. 53. "The divinely established ecclesiastical ministry is exercised on different levels by those who *ab antiquo* have been called bishops, priests and deacons."

37. J.P. Audet, *La Didache: Instruction des Apotres* (Paris: Gabalda,

1958), p. 192. See also W. Rordorf and A. Tuilier, *La Doctrine des Douze Apotres* (*Didache*) (Paris: Cerf, 1978), which dates the composition to the end of the first century, while acknowledging the presence of much older data.

38. Bornkamm, "Presbyteros," TDNT, VI: 673.

39. J.B. Lightfoot, *The Apostolic Fathers* (Grand Rapids: Baker, 1956), pp. 169, 170, 173, 237, 240.

40. *Epist. ad Magnesios*, 2, PG 5, 758; *Epist. ad Smyrneos*, 8–9, PG 5, 714; *Epist. ad Polycarpum*, PG 5, 718.

41. PG 5, 763; *Epist. ad Trall.*, 3, PG 5, 678.

42. *Epist. ad Trall.*, 12, PG 5, 683.

43. *Epist. ad Smyrneos*, 8, PG 5, 714.

44. *Epist. ad Philadelph.*, 4, PG 5, 699.

45. *Epist. ad Ephes.*, 4, PG 5, 647.

46. *Epist. ad Magnes.*, 6, PG 5, 763.

47. See Raymond Brown, *Priest and Bishop*, pp. 40–43.

48. *Adv. Haer.*, IV, 26, 3–4, PG 7, 1053.

49. Ibid., 1054–55.

50. Cf. ibid., III, 3, PG 7, 848–854.

51. David Power, *Ministers of Christ and his Church* (London: Chapman, 1969), p. 45.

52. *Epist. LXIX*, 4, PL 4, 403; see also *Epist. LXV*, 3, PL 4, 396.

53. *Epist. LXV*, 3, PL 4, 396.

54. *Epist. LXIX*, 8, PL 4, 406.

55. *Epist. XXVII*, 1, PL 4, 298.

56. *Epist. XL*, 5, PL 4, 336.

57. *Epist. XL*, 1, PL 4, 334–335.

58. *Epist. LXIX*, 8, PL 4, 406.

59. *Epist. LXVII*, 4–5, in *Saint Cyprien: Correspondence*, ed. Louis Bayard (Paris: Belles Lettres, 1925), pp. 229–231; see also P. Granfield, "Episcopal Election in Cyprian: Clerical and Lay Participation," TS 37 (1976): 41–52.

60. *Epist. LXIX*, 5, PL 4, 336.

61. *Epist. LXVI*, 1, PL 4, 398; also *Epist. LXVII*, 1, in *Saint Cyprien*, p. 228.

62. *Epist. LXVII*, 1, in *Saint Cyprien*, p. 228.

63. *Epist. I*, 1, in ibid., p. 2.

64. *Epist. LXI*, 3, in ibid., p. 195.

65. *Epist. XII*, 1, in ibid., p. 33; *Epist. V*, 2, in ibid., p. 13.

66. *Epist. XVIII*, 2, in ibid., p. 51.

67. *Hippolyte de Rome: La Tradition Apostolique*, ed. B. Botte (Paris: Cerf, 1968), pp. 44–46.

68. Ibid., p. 56.

69. Ibid., pp. 47, 96, 92, 108.

70. *Historia Ecclesiastica*, 6, 43, PG 20, 622.

71. Cf. Yves Congar, "Ordinations 'invitus', 'coactus', de l'eglise antique au Canon 214," RSPT 50 (1956): 169–197.

72. Can. 4, Mansi 2, 670.

73. *In Acta Apost. Hom. XIV*, PG 60, 116.

74. B. Botte, *La Tradition Apostolique de Saint Hippolyte* (Münster: Aschendorffsche, 1963), p. 29.

75. *Constitutiones Apostolicae* 8, PG 1.

76. J. Quasten, "Didascalia Apostolorum," in *New Catholic Encyclopedia* (New York: McGraw-Hill, 1967), IV: 662.

77. *Constitutiones Apostolicae* II, 25, PG 1, 662.

78. Ibid., II, 26, PG 1, 667.

79. Ibid., II, 18, PG 1, 675.

80. Ibid., II, 26, PG 1, 667.

81. Ibid., VIII, 4, PG 1, 1070–71.

82. *Epist. LXVII*, 4, in *Saint Cyprien*, pp. 229–230.

83. *Epist. 4*, 5, PL 50, 434.

84. *Ad Anas.*, PL 54, 634.

85. Schillebeeckx, *Ministry*, p. 40.

86. Mansi 7, 394–395. Cf. Cyrille Vogel, "Titre d'ordination et lien du presbytre a la communaute locale dans l'eglise ancienne," MD 115 (1973): 70–85, and "Vacua Manus Impositio: l'inconsistence de la chirotonie en Occident," in *Melanges Liturgiques offerts a Dom B. Botte* (Louvain: 1972), pp. 511–524.

87. *Epist. Ia ad Severum*, 10, *Corpus Scriptorum Ecclesiasticorum Latinorum*, 29, 9.

88. Can. 18, Mansi 14, 936.

89. Can. 15, Mansi 20, 806.

90. *De Eccles. Officiis*, 2, 3, PL 83, 779.

91. *Decretum Gratiani*, Dist. LXX, PL 187, 355.

92. *De Purificatione B. Mariae Sermo 5*, PL 185, 87.

93. See *Vita Zephyrini*, ed. L. Duchesne, I: 139; cited in Schillebeeckx, *Ministry*, p. 152, note 44.

94. "L'ecclesia ou communaute chretienne sujet integrale de l'action liturgique," in *La liturgie d'apres Vatican II* (Paris, 1967), pp. 241–282; see also B. Botte, "Note historique sur la concelebration dans l'eglise ancienne," MD 35 (1953): 9–23; R. Raes, "La concelebration eucharistique dans les rites orientaux," ibid., pp. 24–47.

95. Mansi 20, 970.

96. Mansi 22, 220.

97. Ibid., 982.

98. Henri de Lubac, *Corpus Mysticum: l'eucharistie et l'eglise au moyen age*, 2nd. ed. (Paris: Aubier, 1949).

99. *Ministry*, p. 57.

100. *Constitution on the Sacred Liturgy*, nn. 26–27, DV, pp. 147–148.

101. ST, III, 63, 3.

102. ST, III, Suppl., 34, 2.

103. Ibid., 34, 4.

104. C. Vogel, "Titre d'ordination," p. 74.

105. Ibid., p. 75.

106. DS 1763.

107. DS 1770. My emphasis.

108. *Why Priests?* p. 42.

109. I say *narrow* for two reasons. First, because nothing was said about those aspects of ministry and priesthood on which the Reformers and the Latin Church agreed—for example, the priestly character of the people of God. Second, because many more and richer things were said about ministry and priesthood in the three sessions at which the Council discussed them than were set forth summarily in its final document. The bishop of Avignon complained: "The proposed doctrine is in no way pleasing to me because it does not embrace the whole reality of this sacrament, as it promised in its preface and as it ought to do to confirm the truth of the Catholic faith and to stamp out the heresies which have arisen in our times about this sacrament." See CT, 9, 83.

110. DS 1771.

111. Fr. Jean de Corregio, one of the theologians at the Bologna session, wrote in response to the second proposition noted in our text: "The first part of the second proposition is not simply false. It is even true, for the priest has the power to preach." Cited in E. Boularand, "Le sacerdoce de la loi nouvelle d'apres le decret du Concile de Trente sur le sacrement de l'ordre," in *Bulletin de Litterature Ecclesiastique*, IV (1955): 195.

112. See, e.g., A. Rohrbasser (ed.), *Sacerdotis Imago: Papstliche Dokumente uber des Priestertum von Pius X bis Joannes XXIII* (Fribourg, 1962).

113. DS 1776.

114. DS 1777.

115. Alexandre Ganoczy, "'Splendors and Miseries' of the Tridentine Doctrine of Ministries," CON, Vol. 10, n. 8 (1972): 75.

116. Cf. Avery Dulles, *Models of the Church* (New York: Doubleday, 1974).

117. See Ganoczy, "Splendors and Miseries," p. 81.

118. Ibid., n. 23; also *Opera Calvini*, 10, pp. 103f.

119. See Ganoczy, "Splendors and Miseries," n. 25; and CT, 5, pp. 105–108.

120. *Constitution on the Church*, n. 25, DV, p. 47.

121. Ibid., n. 28, p. 53.

122. *Decree on the Life and the Ministry of Priests*, n. 4, DV, 538.

123. Ibid., nn. 2 and 5, DV, 534 and 542; see also *Constitution on the Church*, nn. 26 and 28, DV, pp. 50 and 53.

124. See "Ratio Fundamentalis Institutionis Sacerdotalis," AAS 62 (1970): 321–384, esp. 327–331.

125. J.J. von Allmen, "Ordination—A Sacrament? A Protestant Reply," CON, Vol. 4, n. 8 (1972): 40.

126. *Institutes*, IV, 19, 28.

127. *De Bono Coniugali*, 24, 32, PL 40, 394; cf. *De Bap.*, 1, 1, 2, PL 43, 109.

128. DS 1773.

129. *Adv. Valentinianos*, 16, PL 2, 569; *De Praescript. Adv. Haeret.*, 13, PL 2, 26; ibid., 28, PL 2, 40; *De Virginibus Velandis*, 1, PL 2, 889.

130. *Epist. 63*, 14, in *Saint Cyprien*, p. 209; cf. *Epist. 59*, 5, ibid., p. 174. For the contributions here of both Tertullian and Cyprian, see Michele Maccarone, *Vicarius Christi: Storia del Titolo Papale* (Roma: Lateranum, 1952), pp. 26–35.

131. Cf. Edward J. Kilmartim, "Apostolic Office: Sacrament of Christ," TS 36 (1975): 246.

132. Pius XII, *Mediator Dei*, AAS 39 (1947): 538–39, 553–56; cf. his *Mystici Corporis*, AAS 35 (1943): 232–233; and Paul VI, *Mysterium Fidei*, AAS 57 (1965): 761–763.

133. N. 10, DV, p. 27. Cf. ibid., nn. 21, 28 and 37, DV, pp. 40–41, 53–54, 64–65; *Decree on the Ministry and the Life of Priests*, nn. 2 and 13, DV, pp. 533–536 and 559–562.

134. E. Kilmartin, "Apostolic Office," p. 255. I believe it is important to state that the theological conclusions I present here, though identical to some which Kilmartin presents in his essay, were reached quite independently before my attention was directed to his essay. That fact documents another, namely, the growing consensus on these matters among Roman Catholic theologians who reflect on sacraments in general and/or on orders in particular.

135. *Constitution on the Sacred Liturgy*, n. 7, DV, p. 141. See "Schema Constitutionis de Sacra Liturgia," 1, 3, in *Acta Synodalia Sac-*

rosancti Concilii Oecumenici Vaticani Secundi, Vol. 1, pars 1 (Rome: Vatican Press, 1970), p. 265.

136. Cf. *Decree on the Bishop's Pastoral Office in the Church*, passim, DV, pp. 396–429. Cf. *Decree on Priestly Formation*, nn. 4 and 19, DV, pp. 442 and 454.

137. Apostolic Constitution *Pontificalis Romani*, AAS 60 (1968): 373.

138. See Edward Kilmartin, "Ministere et ordination dans l'eglise chretienne primitive," MD 138 (1979): 49–92.

139. Cf. the statement in *Ratio Fundamentalis Sacerdotalis.* "Every priest is taken from the people of God and constituted for this same people. But although priests, in virtue of the sacrament of orders, carry out the task of both father and teacher, nevertheless with all the Christian faithful they are disciples of the Lord. . . . They are brothers among brothers, as members of one and the same body of Christ." See AAS 62 (1970): 329. See also Yves Congar, "Ministeres et structuration de l'eglise," MD 102 (1970): 7–20, and "La hierarchie comme service selon le Nouveau Testament et les documents de la tradition," in *L'episcopat et l'eglise universelle* (Paris: Cerf, 1962), pp. 67–100.

140. "Declaration on the Question of the Admission of Women to the Ministerial Priesthood," AAS 69 (1977): 98–116.

141. Schillebeeckx, *Ministry*, p. 96.

142. K. Rahner, "Women and the Priesthood," in *Concern for the Church* (New York: Crossroad, 1981), pp. 35–47.

143. Ibid., p. 36.

144. Ibid., p. 40.

145. Schillebeeckx, *Ministry*, p. 97.

146. Roger Gryson, *Les origines du celibat ecclesiastique: du premier au septieme siecle* (Gembloux: Duculot, 1970), p. vii.

147. *Decree on the Ministry and the Life of Priests*, n. 16, DV, p. 565.

148. Gryson, *Les origines du celibat*, p. 203. Cf. Gerard Sloyan, "Biblical and Patristic Motives for Celibacy of Church Ministers," CON, Vol. 8, n. 8 (1972): 12–29; Robert L. Stern, "How Priests Came To Be Celibate," ibid., pp. 76–83.

149. Schillebeeckx, *Ministry*, p. 87.

150. Can. 9, Mansi 3, 670; see ibid., 678.

151. Can. 8, ibid., 872; cap. 1, ibid., 998.

152. Can. 3, ibid., 969.

153. *Epist. 167*, PL 54, 1204.

154. Can. 7, Mansi 21, 527–528. It is of some interest to note that as early as the middle of the fifth century Lupus of Troyes and Euphronius of Autun, in a letter to their colleague, Talasius of Augers,

had made a similar recommendation. "If you do not want clerics to have children, then do not admit married men to the altar." See *Corpus Christianorum. Series Latina,* 148, 140.

155. *Ministry,* p. 89.

156. *Adv. Jovinianum,* 1, 20, PL 23, 238. Cf. ibid., 1, 34, PL 23, 256–258; Ambrose, *De Officiis Ministrorum,* 1, 50, PL 16, 98; Augustine, *De Coniugiis Adulterinis,* 2, 20, PL 40, 486; Innocent I, *Epist. ad Victricium,* 10, PL 56, 523–524; Siricius, *Epist. ad episcopos Africae,* PL 56, 728.

GENERAL INDEX

INDEX OF BIBLICAL PASSAGES